middle eastern

cookery

middle eastern
cookery

arto der haroutunian

GRUB STREET | LONDON

Published in 2008 by
Grub Street
4 Rainham Close
London
SW11 6SS
Email: food@grubstreet.co.uk
Web: www.grubstreet.co.uk

Text copyright © Arto der Haroutunian 1982, 2008
Copyright this edition © Grub Street 2008
Design by Lizzie B Design

First published in Great Britain in 1982 by Century Publishing Co. Ltd

A CIP record for this title is available from the British Library

ISBN 978-1-904010-81-4

Printed and bound in Great Britain by MPG, Bodmin, Cornwall

This book is printed on FSC (Forest Stewardship Council) paper

contents

preface

One of the most heartening memories of my childhood is Sunday lunch, when all the members of our family, as well as guests (mostly young students from the Middle East), sat around our large table and consumed in delight and with gasps of rapture the product of my mother's work. For not only was my mother a remarkable cook but also, being thousands of miles away from home, we were in a vast culinary desert devoid of such familiar vegetables as aubergines and okra; spices such as cumin, sumac and allspice; the honey-soaked, rosewater-scented desserts of our childhood.

We ate. We argued loudly and vociferously. We drank our thick black coffee and nibbled a piece of *rahat-lokum*, a box of which someone or other had just received from home. Then, thanking the Lord for his bounteous generosity we settled comfortably into our large, Victorian armchairs and, almost in whispers, talked of home, of the sun-drenched streets of Aleppo or Baghdad, the rich souks of Alexandria or the fragrance-inflamed bazaars of Tehran. Someone would then sing 'The song of the immigrant' far away from his village and loved one. Someone else would hungrily describe how to peel and eat a watermelon — 'You know, with white goat's cheese, some warm *lavash* bread with a sprig of fresh tarragon tucked nicely in the centre and all washed down with a glass of cool *sous*' — all of us lolled in nostalgic euphoria and dreamt of home.

'Home' to us all was the Middle East, not the political entity of today with its strong regional, national and social differences. In those days (the late forties) we were, regardless of our ethnic origins, still Orientals or Levantines, a people who were just waking from centuries of slumber and ignorance, a people who had been mistreated by foreigners, be they Turks, French or English, for their own selfish interests.

In our new environments, temporary for most, permanent for few, we tried hard to emulate the past. Customs were kept, rudiments of our mother tongue were inculcated into our minds and traditions punctiliously adhered to. Lent was strictly kept and for forty days no meats, poultry or fish passed our lips — at least at home. For us children school meals (however tasteless they were) were our salvation. I remember how I relished the school pork chops and steak and kidney pies — especially during Lent.

Over the years changes did take place not only in our domestic lives but up and down the land. More immigrants arrived from India, Pakistan, South East Asia, Cyprus and the West Indies. They too soon settled down, opened their ethnic restaurants, shops and emporiums thus enriching the country with their diverse cultures and adding spice to the eating habits of the natives — particularly important for one such as I who likes his food!

My early childhood was spent in Aleppo, Syria. My father's family originated from Cilicia (Southern Turkey) and my mother's from Armenia. The Aleppo of my childhood was a medium-sized cosmopolitan city soaked in history, rich in commerce and perhaps the most enlightened region of the Levant. In our street lived Armenians, Assyrians, Greeks, Christian Arabs, a well off Turkish family with vast cotton fields and indisputably ugly slanted eyes and not forgetting Jacob the Jew, a carpet dealer and close friend of my father. We all spoke our ethnic tongues, with a little spattering of Arabic. We ate, prayed and lived our lives as had our ancestors for centuries.

This is how my preface should have started: 'The search and collection of authentic recipes from the Middle East by Your's Truly, an exile approaching middle age and in search of his roots.' Well, my roots were my family to whom I turned in earnest, but with some difficulty. For although my family originated in Armenia and Turkey we had, over the years, like the 'sands of desert', scattered all over the east and beyond. So I got in touch with my aunt in Baghdad, my cousins in Kuwait, my sister in Tehran, with other cousins in Egypt, friends of cousins in Cyprus and Ankara, material cousins in Yerevan and Tiblisi and numerous other friends of friends ad infinitum. Finally all those kind people I encountered who had inadvertently 'dropped in' to have a meal in one of our restaurants and who, throughout their meal (and often well after), were subjected to a culinary inquisition of the fiercest kind. My thanks to all those people, with special thanks to the young Saudi Arabian doctor who literally fell into my clutches and had to spend an extra day in a wet and windy Manchester one December until I was satisfied that I had squeezed the last drop of 'culinary blood' from him. But most of all thanks to my mother who was a source of inspiration and infinite information.

The result then is this book, a collection of recipes from all over the Middle East regardless of political and geographical boundaries. By which statement I mean the food of the people of the Middle East:[1] Arabs, Armenians, Assyrians, Azerbaijanians, Copts, Georgians, Kurds, Jews, Lazes, Palestinians, Persians, Turkomans, Turks and all the other minorities who, far too often, are forgotten or ignored by the cataloguers and generalizers of human achievements. For it is my opinion that the true sources of most cultures are best found amongst the indigenous minorities; e.g. the true Egyptian is the Copt, he is not only directly descended from the Ancient Egyptians, but also still retains much of his forefather's culture undiluted by later arrived, desert-oriented Muslim Arabs.

I have also included proverbs, anecdotes, songs and stories of the famous Nasrudin Hodja and Boloz-Mugoush all of which, directly or indirectly, relate to food and all emanating from the rich and varied cultures of the peoples of the Middle East, to whose glorious past and brighter future this book is dedicated.

All the recipes give the right amount of ingredients to feed four people unless I have stated otherwise.

Arto der Haroutunian

---

1 The prevailing concept of the Middle East, whether as a geographical, cultural or political entity, includes the following countries: United Arab Republic, Israel, Syria, Lebanon, Iraq, Turkey, the Caucasian republics of Armenia, Georgia and Azerbaijan, the Arab states of South West Asia and finally Iran.

introduction

geography, history and the people

Ours is the world and all who dwell upon it,
and when we assault, we assault with power.
When kings deal with their peoples unjustly
we refuse to allow injustice among us.
We are called oppressors; we never oppressed yet,
but shortly we shall be starting oppression!
When any body of ours reaches his weaning,
the tyrants fall down before him prostrating.
We have filled the land till it's too strait for us
and we are filling the seas back with our vessels.
So let no man act foolishly against us,
or we shall exceed the folly of the foolhardiest.

Amr ibnel Kulthum — pre-Islamic poet of the sixth century

The greatest single unifying factor in the Middle East is the climate which, throughout the millennia, has imposed a special way of life and has been the mainspring of all social, economic and cultural diversifications. Within the Middle East are the great rivers Nile, Tigris, Euphrates, Arax and Kura. The Nile is fed by the Blue Nile (rising in the Ethiopian Highlands) and the White Nile (rising in the Central African Highlands). The waters of the rivers Tigris and Euphrates mingle some sixty miles before reaching the Persian Gulf. Their junction creates the Shatt-al-Arab waterway which forms the boundary between Iraq and Iran and has been a bone of contention over the centuries. Both rivers rise in the Armenian Highlands and zig-zag their way to the desert lands of Syria and Iraq. The Tigris (the Arrow), so named because of the swiftness of its waters, also receives several tributaries from the Zagros mountains of Iran. The plain here is threaded by numerous tributaries fed from one river to the other creating naturally formed irrigation schemes.

The Arax and Kura rivers rise in the Caucasian Highlands and flow into the Caspian Sea. The Arax borders the Armenian SSR and Turkey, whilst the Kura passes through the Georgian and Azerbaijanian SSR. The waters of the Arax irrigate the rich Ararat plateau.

Other important rivers are the Kizel Irmak (Turkey), Sefid and Kashka (Iran) and the Karun which waters south west Iran. Whilst the smaller rivers Orontes, Litani and the Jordan irrigate Syria, Lebanon, Israel and Trans-Jordan.

With the exception of the Caspian Littoral of Iran and Azerbaijan, 'Pontic' Turkey, and the Caucasian coastline of the Black Sea, rainfall is not only inadequate, but limited to spring and winter. The entire Mediterranean, therefore, stretching from Libya and Egypt, up the Levant to Turkey receives rainfall similar to California and south western Australia.

In the summer, drought is the general rule. Ninety per cent of the entire region is arid desert or semi-desert and whatever forests it once contained have long since vanished. Only five to six per cent of the Middle East is cultivated today and one-fifth of that needs water desperately.

Water is the most important human factor throughout the region. It has been deified throughout the ages and myths have been created around it. To preserve this scant and precious commodity the Ancient Sumerians, Assyrians, Babylonians, Hittites, Urartians and Romans built cisterns and viaducts, the remains of which can still be traced throughout Iraq, Syria and Turkey.

The Persians built *qanats* — underground conduits — to bring water for hundreds of miles from the mountains to the plains. In parts of Arabia water is so scarce that, rather than waste it, Bedouin women wash their hair in camel urine. The pious Muslim substitutes sand for water as he ritually 'cleanses' himself during prayer time. In ancient Armenia and Iran there existed (and still does) the Water Festival of 'Vartavar' — Burning of Roses. On this day people drench each other with water and the ecclesiastical procession throws rosewater at the congregation. The aim is to invoke the Gods for rain.

Today extensive work is being done to 'green' the land. Huge irrigation schemes such as the building of the Aswan Dam in Egypt, the Euphrates Dam in Syria and Ataturk Dam in Turkey have been established and already the effects of intensive agricultural techniques are seen in a number of highly productive farming areas such as western Lebanon, the Aleppo region of Syria, the Ararat valley in Armenia, the oasis of Damascus and, perhaps the most spectacular of all, the Jewish settlements of Israel, particularly in the Negev.

The position that the Middle East occupies in history is unique for it was here that man first began to cultivate food-plants and to domesticate wild animals. Wheat was cultivated in Jarmo (Kurdistan) 9000 years ago. Gradually peas, lentils and other crops were added to the 'original cuisine' of the inhabitants. With the full adoption of crop and stock raising man gave up nomadism and settlements grew into villages and then towns. As the population increased in the mountain regions people moved down to the plateaux and plains of the Tigris and Euphrates. There they were confronted with hot, semi-arid earth which they had to irrigate with the abundant waters of the two great rivers. The same process undoubtedly occurred around the Nile delta and further afield in the Ganges Basin of India. Towns produced social order, city states, nations and empires with which came literature, law and order.

By about 5000 BC the Egyptians were making wine and bread, rearing animals and cultivating crops. The produce grown at this time was extensive: wheat, barley, spelt, millet, legumes, root crops, melons, olives, grapes, figs and dates and, at a slightly later date, apples, peaches, pomegranates and apricots.

Around 3000 BC the Sumerians built their irrigation canals and city states and evolved a society divided into technological–social classes — nobility, priests, traders, farmers and artisans — divisions that still hold good for most Middle Eastern people today. The Sumerians, a non-Semitic people, were soon joined in Mesopotamia by Semitic tribes coming from Arabia and, in time, a new, mixed people were formed. Further north along the middle of the Euphrates several Semitic races intermingled and created city states. In 2350 BC the entire region was united under the leadership of Sargon, and his empire, in time, was replaced by that of the Amorites (1688 BC) whose most distinguished member was Hammurabi the law giver. The Amorites fell under the rising power of the Indo-European Hittites and Hurrians from the north — the ancestors of the Armenians and most modern Turks. By 1350 BC the Hittites had occupied Syria and wrested Palestine from Egypt and had become the mightiest power in western Asia.

Meanwhile, Egypt had developed its dynastic and political institutions and created one of the seven wonders of the ancient world — the pyramids of Gizeh. The Old Kingdom was followed by the Middle Kingdom (2200 BC) ushered in by the brilliant Twelfth Dynasty when peace, prosperity and overall economic success had made her the most civilized land on earth. Then the Hyksos — the shepherd kings, initially a branch of the Hurrian races — came down from Armenia and on their march, mixing with the Semitic elements, they overran the peaceful empire of the Pharoahs. They introduced the horse, the war chariot became the dominant power until the Pharoah Ahmos succeeded in throwing them out of Egypt and launching her into an imperial stage in history, all of which culminated with Rameses II (1301–1234 BC). He agreed to end all wars and signed a pact with the Hittites which maintained a balance of power and temporary stability. This earliest of international pacts was meant to bring 'Peace and good brotherhood between the contending parties for ever.'

A new Semitic people from the city state of Ashur (Assyrians) were largely responsible for the destruction of the Hittite empire. They were followed by Babylonians whose last king, Balshazzar, was also the last Semitic ruler of the East; henceforth it was the Iranian–Aryan tribes who dominated the canvas of history. Cyrus the Great (550–529 BC) introduced not only a new language, but also a new religion — Zoroastrianism,[2] and the Persian rulers were tolerant of their subjects attempting no imposition of language or religion.

In the spring of 334 BC a twenty-one-year-old Macedonian, at the head of 35,000 fighters, crossed the Hellespont and launched his victorious campaigns all the way to India. Great as those military exploits of Alexander were in themselves 'greater they loom in their cultural consequences. They opened the way to the confrontation, harmonization and final fusion of Greek and Near Eastern ideas and institutions, thereby effecting a pioneering revolution in the world's outlook.'[3]

Alexander died young aged thirty-two and his kingdom was quickly divided between his four ablest generals[4] who henceforth began to quarrel amongst themselves. They all, particularly Seleucus, continued Alexander's policy of planting numerous Greek cities all over his kingdom. In time old soldiers, traders and craftsmen, as well as adventures, followed into the Middle East mixing with the Semitic people and giving birth to a new Hellenistic civilization which, for over a thousand years, remained a dominant feature in the Middle East and was only overtaken by that of Islam in the tenth century AD.

---

2 Zoroaster, a Median reformer, flourished about 60 BC. He preached duality in man, personifying the two opposing principles of good and evil, light and darkness. His teaching became the state religion of Persia and spread beyond. Today there are several hundred thousand Zoroastrians still living in Iran, with 2–3 million more in India (Parsis).

3 *A short history of the Near East*, Philip K. Hitti.

4 Seleucus took Syria, most of Asia Minor and Northern Iran; Antigonus the remainder of Asia Minor, barring Armenia; Antipater Macedonia; Ptolemy Egypt.

Indeed it is safe to say that in the last 2000 years of Middle Eastern history the two most powerful cultural forces have been those of Hellenism and Islam. Yet Hellenism was primarily an urban feature. The rest of the populace continued to speak their native tongues, whether Egyptian, Persian or Aramaic, and to worship their own deities. Hellenism created an economic uniformity. Transport was improved; the highways were guarded by chains of colonies; inns, resting places and market towns were created and along these routes passed cereals, oil, wine, fruits, minerals, pepper and cinnamon. Saffron came from India via Persia; frankincense and myrrh from Yemen, wheat from Egypt and gold and silver from Armenia. Great cities were founded — Antioch, Iaodicea and, perhaps greatest and most magnificent of them all, Alexandria in Egypt — for generations the cultural capital of the world. 'And then came the Roman wolf.'

In the year 66 BC, with the fall of the mighty Armenian Empire of Tigran II, the Roman general Pompeius took over the command of all the forces in the East and the Roman conquests commenced. The rule of the Romans was a continuation and development of the Hellenistic. The subject races lived in greater security and comparative affluence than their predecessors. Yet in spite of that there were still millions of people who were unhappy with their lot and many of these became ardent followers of the new ideas emanating from Bethlehem. These were swiftly synthesized into religious forms, and arrived in auspicious time in the heart of Rome.

The first nation to be converted to this new religion was Armenia, under Dirtad III in AD 301, and twenty-five years later Constantine raised it to an official state religion in his newly-founded capital Constantinople (Istanbul), strategically situated between Europe and Asia Minor on the Bosphoros. For the next 1100 years Constantinople was to be the focal centre of the entire Middle East militarily, economically and especially spiritually. The temporal triumph of Christianity did not bring the majority of men spiritual freedom or alter their economic lives and this, coupled with ethnic differences and the general resentment of the corrupt bureaucracy ruling from Constantinople, found expression in the dogmatic disputes which in time caused the eventual disintegration of the empire, and paved the way for the rapid ascendancy of Islam.

The Prophet Muhammad was born in AD 570 in Mecca. He began to undergo his religious experience about AD 610. He was vehemently opposed by the merchant-tribes of Mecca, among whom he was born, so that in the year 622, with a band of seventy converts, he fled to Medina. There he rapidly made more converts and in a short space of time almost all the tribes of Arabia submitted to his authority. After Muhammad's death (in 632) Abu Bakr became the first Caliph ('successor') and decided to employ the warlike energies of the tribes by invading Syria and Palestine. Within less than a century after the Prophet's death the Arabs had reached the Atlantic in Morocco and the river Oxus in modern Turkistan. In every country the Arabs conquered the great majority of the population, Jewish, Zoroastrian, Pagan or Christian, embraced Islam. One of the most remarkable features of the Arab conquests was the small number of warriors involved. However, Muhammad had authorized the use of women captured in war as concubines: 'The amazing extent of the Arab conquests had enabled them to acquire great numbers of such foreign concubines; Greeks, Persians, Armenians, Egyptians and North African Berbers. Thus a few generations after the conquests the "Arabs" of Syria were ethnologically a different race from the conquerors who had emerged from Arabia after the death of the Prophet.'[5]

Syria became the first seat of the empire, but in the year 750 power was transferred to Baghdad (Iraq). The Arabs reached the height of their glory in the reign of Harun el Rashid (786–809) and his son Al-Mamun (813–833), a period in history which is vividly described in the pages of the *Arabian Nights* and similar literary works. This was a time of elaborate extravagances enacted at festivals, ceremonial occasions and weddings, and artists, poets and scientists from all corners of the empire were attracted to Baghdad.

Yet slowly a cancer was settling in the heart of the empire which was gradually destroying the very fabric and goals on which it had been created. For the warlike instincts of the nomadic Arab had gradually disappeared. He surrounded himself with luxury which his ancestors could not have dreamt of in the desert and, in the words of Gertrude Bell[6]: 'The ancient ghosts of Babylonian and Assyrian palace intrigue rose from their muddy graves, mighty in evil, to overthrow the soldier Khalif, to strip him of his armour and to tie him hand and foot with silk and gold.'

In the first half of the eleventh century 'a new scourge appeared'; wild Turkish-speaking nomads (the Ghuzz) entered Persia and, under their chiefs (Seljugs), they swept across Persia to Armenia 'massacring, looting and raping as they went.' The Seljugs occupied Baghdad, Syria, Palestine and Egypt and then moved on to Asia Minor where they created the first 'Turkish' empire until its demise some 150 years later under Mongol attacks.

Only Byzantium remained as the bastion of Christianity, but she too was weakened by the loss of Armenia in 1071 at the battle of Manzazkert when Alp Arslan shattered the Byzantine-Armenian forces under the leadership of Emperor Romanus Diogenes. The new emperor, Alexius Comenus, appealed for help to the western Christian powers and the Pope, Urban II, preached his crusade in 1095. Not surprisingly, however, the crusades were a failure, and today only dim reflections of romantic troubadours, chivalric heraldry, sculptured tombstones in old cathedrals and a few Arab words, much maligned and distorted, remain of the 300 years of western Christian presence in the Levant.

Then came the Mongols, burning, pillaging and levelling cities to the ground, only to be followed by far more savage tribes from Central Asia — the Turks. From their countless tribes, in time, the 'Ottoman'[7] branch gradually expanded from their adopted homeland of north western Asia Minor and succeeded, in 1453, in capturing Constantinople. Under Suleyman 'the Magnificent' (1520–68) the Ottoman empire reached its peak and it was now a major naval power. The people of the Ottoman empire that came to rule the Middle East for nearly 400 years formed a heterogeneous complex of religious, linguistic and ethnic groups — Greeks, Slavs, Armenians, Kurds, Arabs, Christians, Muslims, Jews — all artificially held together by the Ottomans.

---

5 *Syria, Lebanon and Jordan*, J. B. Glubb.

6 From *Syria, the Desert and the Dawn*.

7 Founded by Osman, 1299–1328. A Turkish tribe, one of many originating from Central Asia. They were first Islamised in Persia then settled in western Anatolia where they absorbed their Seljug kinsmen. In time the house of Osman — Ottomans — became the masters of the entire Near East.

Throughout the life-history of the empire the Turkish element remained a minority, but one that was constantly expanding by deportation, mass murder and forced conversions of other groups. Yet the period of imperial glory did not survive for long, for the sultans, far too often, were interested in matters of the flesh. Dissipation and corruption were rife throughout the court. The seeds of weakness embedded in the Ottoman state and society began to fruit in the late sixteenth century because a government primarily created for warfare rather than welfare and peace lacked the capacity to adapt to change. The subject races had no love for their rulers.

While the Ottoman empire decayed from within the pressures upon it from outside increased. In the seventeenth century the problem was further aggravated by the emergence of two powers, Russia and Austria-Hungary; the opening of a new trade route to Asia via the Cape; the establishment of Dutch and British power in Asia and finally, the constant warfare with neighbouring Persia.

The Russians, ever covetous of 'warm waters', began a long term plan of destroying Ottoman power which began with Peter the Great (1689-1725) and culminated with the Russo-Turkish wars of 1828–9, as a result of which certain Ottoman provinces were surrendered to Imperial Russia. After the Crimean war (1854–1856) more concessions were made to Russia. The sultans tried in vain to reform, or by warfare to subdue, their subjects. Turkey was the 'sick man of Europe' soon to die and disintegrate and no imperial decree could halt that eventuality. The remnants of the empire finally gained their independence after the end of the First World War.

Throughout the centuries the people of the Middle East have remained faithful to their source — the land. Though empires have come and gone they have maintained their deep attachment to their traditions, customs, food and aspirations.

Come with old Khayam, and leave the lot
Of Kaikobad and Kaihostu forget
Let Rustum layabout his as he will,
Or Hattim Tai cry supper — heed them not.
And let us then
along some strips of Herbage strown
That just divides the desert from the sown,
sit to rest
with a loaf of bread beneath the Bough
A flask of wine, a book of verse — and thou
Beside me singing in the wilderness —
And wilderness is Paradise now.

O. Khayyam — *Rubaiyat*. Trans. E. Fitzgerald from *Oriental Caravan*.

food in history

After Anu — had created heaven,
Heaven had created — the earth.
The earth had created the rivers,
The rivers had created the canals,
The canals had created the marsh,
And the marsh had created the worm —
The worm went, weeping, before Shamash.
His tears flowing before Eai,
'What will thou give me for my food?
What will thou give me for my sucking?'
'I shall give thee the ripe fig,
And the apricot.'
'Of what use are they to me, the ripe fig
And the apricot?
Lift me up among the teeth
And in the gum cause me to dwell!
The blood of the tooth I will suck,
And of the gum I will gnaw its roots!'

Toothache Incantation from the Ancient Near East.

The raw materials of the earliest civilizations of the Middle East, those of Sumer and Babylon, consisted of barley bread and barley paste accompanied by onions — still highly popular with Iranians and Arabs. Indeed the Prophet Muhammad is reported to have had a great fondness for raw onion, to which the Arab and Persian historians of the Middle Ages attributed aphrodisiac and almost mystical qualities. Also popular were several types of beans, lentils, chickpeas and fish from the nearby rivers and all were washed down with water or, if one could afford it, beer. It was in Sumer that beer — barley beer — was first developed; indeed it is estimated that forty per cent of the barley grown then was used in its manufacture. The Egyptians, who have left us several recipes for beer fermentation, had a famed beverage called *hag* which was made from 'the red barley of the Nile'[8]. Veal, beef and game were known. However, mutton was the most popular meat — as it still is — and it was either grilled, what are nowadays called 'kebabs', or cooked in large cauldrons with cucumbers, onions and herbs like the guvedge or firin kebabs of today.

Goat and pig meat were also popular, the latter had not yet been rejected by the people of the region. It was, indeed, the Indo-Aryan tribes who (about 2000 BC when they had penetrated the Middle East proper) began a systematic anti-pig campaign since they — cattle rearing people — had a deep-rooted dislike of the pig, an animal that could not be herded, was regarded as filthy due to its eating and living habits and whose meat did not survive long in the hot climate and was therefore dangerous. This aversion towards the pig was later enshrined in the Judeo-Islamic, hence Semitic, ethics.

In the desert regions — and a large portion of the Middle East was and still is desert

8 *Oldest Book in the World*, Isaac Myes.

— the date palm had soon acquired a great importance and was incorporated into the diet of the people. The fruit could be eaten fresh or dried, its juice was made into a syrup for desserts and puddings and into intoxicating drinks such as wine or *arak*. The Parthians (of the Parni-Aryan tribe), who, from 250 BC until AD 216, were the dominant force in the region, were very fond of the date and date wines, although they were equally partial to the grape wines of Armenia. Hence the Sassanian-Persian expression 'Drunk like a Parthian, stubborn like an Armenian and arrogant as a Roman.'

The first 'raised bread' was most probably discovered in Egypt where, by the twelfth century BC it was commercially produced and sold in specialist bakeries. There were many types of bread, the cheapest and commonest one was called *ta* — a small, flat bread, the progenitor of the modern pita which is still, appropriately enough, also called *khubz Arabi* (Arab or Syrian bread). The Egyptians had undoubtedly the most sophisticated and advanced culinary art of their time. In numerous tombs dish after dish of fish, stews, beef ribs, fruits, porridges of some sort or other, as well as figs, dates, cheese, wine and beer in large casks have been found.

Herodotus (484–409 BC) in his *Histories* attributed the good health of the Egyptians to their custom of purging themselves for three days every month with emetics and clysters, which they did in the belief that all diseases originated from the food a person ate. He was impressed with the wide and rich selection of food available to the public. He notes the date wine, various beers and the numerous fish found in great abundance in the waters of the Nile — some were eaten raw after being dried in the sun or salted, a custom that still prevails in Egypt and the adjacent lands, particularly Lebanon. He noted that the wildlife was rich in small birds such as quails, magpies and swallows which were either stuffed with wheat and roasted, similar to *djejij mushwi* or *amij*, or raw after being pickled in brine — a practice still popular in Egypt, Cyprus and Lebanon.

The Greek influence on Middle Eastern eating habits is not hard to see, Alfred Zimmern's caustic remark that the Greeks ate for breakfast 'a kind of porridge' and then for lunch 'another kind of porridge'[9] is not too far from the truth, at least as far as the poor were concerned. These 'porridge' dishes (*maza* in Greek, *puls* in Latin) can perhaps better be termed 'dips' and they are still found in such classic Middle Eastern recipes as *toureto*, *fatoush*, *taramasalata*, *hummus-bi-tahina* and the many vegetable and olive oil-based dips. Incidentally the Arab word for hors d'oeuvre, *mezzeh*, is undoubtedly derived from the Greek *maza*. A typical 'porridge' of the time *kykeon* was made from barley meal and water with aromatic flavours like thyme and mint and it strongly resembles the *tarhana* or *tarkana* soup popular in the Balkans and Turkey.

Life under Rome was not much better for the poor, for their basic diet consisted of millet-porridge, coarse bread, olives, figs, beans, cheese and milk. However, the food of the rich was very different, rich and varied. Pickles were imported from Spain, cucumbers from Cappadocia, pomegranates from Libya, wheat — the granary of the empire — from Egypt, wine from Jura, spices from far flung Parthia, India and even China (Chinese cinnamon).

---

9 Pliny the Elder in his *Natural History* described this type of porridge thus 'Soak, leave it for a night to dry. Next day dry it by the fire and then grind it in a mill . . . they (then) mix three pounds of flax seed, half a pound of coriander seeds and eighth of a pint of salt, previously roasting them all. *A Natural History* – trans. H. Rackman, 1950.

When the Barbarians began to encroach and eventually overran Europe in the fifth century AD the once accessible markets were gone for good. Gaul, which supplied wine and oil; Spain, wheat, fish and pickles; the Black Sea coast, wheat and North Africa, olives and fruits, were all in enemy hands. Then, with the division of the empire into West and East, the glory that was Rome was no more.

It was the turn of Byzantium, straddling Europe and Asia Minor, to rise into prominence; a new Rome, but of Greek origin and oriental in scope and spirit. As the centuries passed the rather complex and often (to us today) obnoxious dishes with their exotic flavours disappeared, to be replaced by a much simpler cuisine primarily made from local ingredients like olive oil, sesame paste, citrus fruits, vegetables and meat — most of which are still retained in the Greek, Turkish and Armenian cuisines. The golden age of the Byzantine cuisine was perhaps the sixth century in the reign of Justinian and Theodore, when many chefs were brought to serve in the court of Constantinople from Persia, Syria, Armenia and even as far away as India.

Until the eighth century Constantinople received, via Alexandria, the rich produce of the Nile valley, Arabia Felix, Ethiopia, India and China. Luxury items such as spices, perfumes, precious stones and raw materials were then exported to Italy, the Byzantine ports of Tripoli, Antioch, Tarsus, Smyrna, Trebizond and Thessalonica did a roaring trade bringing honey and wheat from Bulgaria; fish and salt from Russia; wheat and fruits from North Africa and wine, precious metals and spices from Armenia and Persia.

The Byzantines ate three times a day — breakfast, midday and evening. Hors d'oeuvres were served first and these would have consisted of cheese, olives, cold ham, pork sausages, pickles, fish roe (*tarama*), artichokes and beans in oil — always olive oil — similar to the *plaki* dishes of today.

Soup courses would have included vegetable soups, *tarhana*, i.e. dough- or barley-based, soups, the ever popular tripe soup, a fish or meatball soup with egg and lemon sauce, similar to the *avgolemono* type soups of today, and the classic *kakkavia*, a thick fish soup, favoured by the ancient seafarers, which consisted of any small fish — eel, whiting, red or grey mullet, lobster, prawns — olive oil, onions, thyme, parsley, garlic and saffron and sometimes with wine and bay leaves as well. The main course would have consisted of grilled pig's trotters, grilled fish with white sauce. There would be ham, duck, biscuits and various cheeses — particularly the famed Vlach version. Special, often religious, occasions were always celebrated with special meals, the forty days of Lent were broken at midnight on Holy Saturday with a soup made from lamb's innards that was similar to the modern *margeritsa*. A whole lamb or a suckling pig was spit roasted on Easter Day having been first stuffed with fruits, nuts (pistachios and pine kernels), wheat and raisins all soaked in wine. It is, however, important to remember that the Byzantines — the religious and Greek element at least — were basically vegetarians and 'compelled the people to diets of interminable fish as, for that matter, did the Latin Rite'.[10] Thus the 'true' Byzantine contribution to the cuisine of the Middle East comprised olive oil-based vegetarian dishes and fish dishes — soups, appetizers and stews.

After the death of Muhammad in AD 632 the Arabs poured out of their desert confines into Syria, Egypt and Persia. Very little is known of the economic life of the

10 *The World on the Last Day*, D. Stacton.

Umayyad Caliphate. The great part of the Arabs who left Arabia remained Bedouins (nomads). Their presence wrought havoc on the agricultural activities of the settled population, for the overgrazing of goats and camels had a devastating effect on the natural vegetation. The Bedouin knew next to nothing of husbandry and agriculture. Their needs were little, their cuisine very poor. Milk and milk products from their flocks and herds formed (and still does) the mainstay of their diet. Milk was drunk warm straight after milking or thickened in a goat's skin — yoghurt was not introduced until after the conquest of Persia. Sometimes unleavened bread was made by grinding the grain in a stone quern, kneading it with a little water and then throwing it from hand to hand until it became round and thin. It was then baked on a convex metal dish (*saj*) heated on dried camel dung or, when available, dead tree branches (see *khubz saj*). Very little meat was eaten — maybe only a few times a year on festive occasions such as a wedding celebration, the birth of a son, the arrival of important guests or during the Holy weeks of Ramadan. There was no rice initially. This was introduced at a later date via Persia. There were some fruits and a great deal was made with dates. The Arabians had a penchant for locusts either roasted, ground up and stored to add flavour to future meals or grilled on twigs — like kebabs. To the Bedouin, whatever the desert offered was good fare such as large monitor lizards, gazelles, bustards and dead camels as well as his goats and sheep. Yet in a short period of time the conquering Arabs were themselves living the luxurious life of the inhabitants of the newly acquired territories.

From the late eighth to the tenth centuries 'Arab' civilization was at its peak. The empire was rich in wheat — the granaries of Syria and Egypt produced crops which so far exceeded their wants that considerable quantities were exported to other regions. The Persians introduced rice, since the 'Mawali' from Huzistan and the Caspian regions had long been accustomed to rice and there was a growing demand for it in the cities.

Dates were grown all over Iraq and southern Persia, while Syria and Upper Mesopotamia produced various fruits and nuts — walnuts, hazelnuts, and pistachios. The finest apples came from Lebanon and Palestine, figs and grapes from Syria, plums from Transjordan, apricots and melons from Armenia and oranges and lemons from Oman, Syria and Egypt.

Under the Abbasid rule there was created an enormous economic market where the supply and transport of materials, goods and foodstuffs from quite distant regions was centred. Saffron from Isfahan and Hamadhan, red wine from Armenia, olive oil from Syria and Tunisia, sugar from the Yemen — all could be found in the bazaars of Baghdad. Tradesmen, bankers and adventurers from all the corners of the empire converged on the capital which, according to Benjamin of Tudelo, the fourteenth-century traveller-historian, was, next to Constantinople, the other great city: 'Merchants came to it from every land and save for Baghdad there is no city in the world to compare with it.'[11] A vast metropolis was created out of a once small oasis where different nationalities lived in their quarters, Jews, Armenians, Christians, Persians, etc. The splendour and sensual gratifications competing to satisfy the appetites of the rich are well illustrated in the *Tales of 1001 Nights*. Food was abundant — at least to those privileged few who could retire to their inner sanctums (*kaah*), sit

---

11   *The Itinerary of Benjamin of Tudelo*, M. N. Adler, Oxford 1907.

on richly decorated mattresses and cushions, listen to the finest singers, musicians and poets and dine off gold plates. Several manuals on the art of cooking were written, three of which have survived. The historian Al-Mesudi in his *Muruj-al-dhahab* (Meadows of Gold) portrays a typical symposium at the court of Caliph Al-Mustakfi who proclaimed to his friends, 'It is my desire that we should assemble on such and such a day and converse together about the different varieties of food, and the poetry which has been composed on the subject.'[12] On the prescribed day one of the members of the circle said, 'Commander of the faithful, I have some verse by Ibn-al-Mu'tazz in which the poet describes a tray containing bowls of *kamakh*,' and he proceeded to recite. Others followed, each in turn praising dishes such as *tardina*, *medira*, *sanbusaj*, *buran* sauce and *gateif*. A rice pudding called *aruzza* was described by the poet Muhammad ibn-al-Wazir of Damascus in the following words:

O glorious aruzza! what a boon,
Thou cook as lovely as high heaven's noon!
Purer than snow thou hath been furrowed twice
By handiwork of wind and frosted ice . . .
Whilst sugar sprinkled upon every side
Flashes and gleams, like light personified.

One culinary influence on Baghdad was the Sasanian. The Sasanians received most of their culinary tradition from the Parthians, and the duality of Good and Evil, the internecine warfare between light and dark, was strongly reflected in Parthian–Persian food. The *khoresht* dishes of Iran are the product of this philosophy. Fruits — apples, plums, damsons, apricots and cherries — are cooked with chillis, nuts, vinegar, sour grapes and meats. Bitter limes or sumac powder are added to vegetables, chicken and ducks, e.g. *khoreshte-hoo* (lamb with peas and prunes), *khoresht eghooreh* (meat with sour grapes, sugar and spices) etc. This use of fruits, nuts, wine, honey, vinegar, as an ensemble was, of course, also popular with the Romans, but in the centuries that followed it virtually disappeared from the European-Byzantine cuisine. Today it only appears in the *tajin* (stew) dishes of North Africa — once part of the Greco-Roman world, in the *khoreshts* of Iran and the stews of the Caucasus.

There were other influences that infiltrated Baghdad. Kebab-type meats from Armenia, cakes from Egypt, cous-cous (semolina rice) dishes from North Africa, 'Armenian' fat bread topped with nuts, olive bread from Antioch, 'Frankish' roast lamb — similar to the *rostos* of Cyprus and Greece, *meghmuma* from India — a dish of aubergines, mutton, onions and spices — the ancestor of *mussaka*, meat or chicken pieces cooked in milk or yoghurt from the Caucasus, Persia and India. A typical example of the latter was *medira* — meat, cut into small pieces including the sheep's tail, and cooked with curd. The meat — mutton or chicken — was placed in a saucepan, a little salt was added as well as water and it was brought to the boil. When cooked a large peeled onion and leeks were added as well as coriander, cumin, mastic and ground cinnamon. All this was transferred to a bowl to which curdled milk or yoghurt was added with a little lemon juice and fresh mint. Such was the fame of this dish that

---

12 *Aspects of Islamic Civilization*, A. J. Arbemy.

the poet wrote:

Medira on the festive tray
Is like the moon in full array;
Upon the board it gleams in light
Like sunshine banishing the night . . .
Upon a platter it is brought
Of onyx, in Tehama wrought . . .
Medira cannot rivalled be
To heal the sick man's malady . . .
'Tis as delicious as 'tis good –
A very miracle of food.[13]

All this lavishness bewildered and quenched the gastronomic desires of the once 'hungry' Arabs of Baghdad and they set about systematically developing this mêleé of cuisines which, by the grace of Allah! was bequeathed to them. With the spread of Islam the food of the Caliphs penetrated all corners of the empire and beyond into Europe via Spain, Armenian Cilicia and Sicily.

There has been little change in the basic diet of the people of the Middle East since the days of the Caliphs, except for the addition of new spices and vegetables which arrived after the discovery of the New World, potato, tomato, maize, red pepper, green pepper, hot chillis, French beans, peanuts, vanilla and others, the incorporation of which has given Middle Eastern cooking its uniqueness.

The advent of the Mongols and the numerous Turkish speaking tribes from Central Asia (eleventh to fourteenth centuries) added very little to the existing repertoire. The nomadic cuisine was unique for its poverty. They ate no bread, rice or grains, fruit and very few vegetables except the occasional bulbs of the red tulip, some wild carrots and onions, etc. From March until October they depended exclusively on their flocks and herds. They lived off mutton and horse meat. 'Kazy'-type sausages made of horse flesh, or roast hump of camel, stewed feet or braised paunch were great delicacies. In leather sacks they carried a little rice flour with which they prepared dumplings which were then boiled in water with a little salt mantu.[14] These nomads who conquered Asia Minor, Persia and, for a period, most of the Middle East, depended on two basic items — blood and milk. According to Marco Polo[15] when on the move each Mongol had a string of eighteen horses and mares and they travelled 'without provisions and without making a fire, living only on the blood of their horses; for every rider pierces a vein of his horse and drinks the blood.' About half a pint a day of blood could be drunk from each horse without damaging the health of the animals. Milk and milk derivatives — curds, soured milk, cheese and a fermented drink made from mare's milk called *kumiss* (mare's milk contains four times as much vitamin C as ordinary cow's milk) — was drunk fresh or dried under the sun. This is how Marco Polo describes this drying process. 'First they bring the milk to the boil . . . they skim off the cream that floats on the surface . . . then

---

13 ibid.
14 *Manti* in Turkish; *mant'ou* in Chinese, Korean and Mongolian; *dyushbara* in Azerbaijanian; *pelmeny* in Russian; *vareniky* in Ukranian.
15 *Travels*, Marco Polo.

they stand the milk in the sun and leave it to dry. When they are going on an expedition they take about 10 lbs of this milk and every morning they take out about half a pound of it and put it in a small leather jacket shaped like a gourd, with as much water as they please then, while they ride, the milk in the flask dissolves into a fluid which they drink. And this is their breakfast.'[16] *Kumiss*, which has been described as a kind of desert champagne, has aquired a certain mystique. It was brewed in early spring — with the birth of the first foal which was a time of celebration. It was served at weddings, funerals and religious festivals. The beverage was prepared by adding a 'starter' — the process is similar to making yoghurt — of old *kumiss* to fresh mare's milk, then churning steadily for an hour or more until the liquid had reached the exact peak of alcoholic acidity. A bag of this brew always hung outside the nomad's tent — *yurt* — and a charming custom existed whereby anyone who passed within arms length would agitate the bag just to keep the *kumiss* fresh! *Kumiss* today is still prepared in parts of Turkey, but it is far more popular in the Northern Caucasus and the Central Asian republics.

When the Ottomans took over the leadership of the moribund Arab Caliphate the pendulum once again swung towards the West. The Arab-Persian cuisine was relegated to a secondary position and the Byzantine-Armenian cuisine came to the fore. A quick glance at 'Turkish' food will immediately verify this fact. The persistent use of olive oil — still almost unknown in Central Asia — the many varied fish dishes, all bearing Greek names, the numerous Anatolian–Caucasian kebabs — still unknown in the original homelands of the Turks where everything grilled, and that means mutton, is called *shashlyk* — a Russian terminology. Finally the sweet pastries such as *baklava* (from the Armenian *baki-halva*, meaning Lent sweet) or *kataif* (from the Arabic *ataif*) are completely unknown in Central Asia even today.

Yet as it was with the Arabs in Baghdad so it became with the Ottomans in Constantinople, in a short period of time the conquering races were themselves living the luxurious life of the inhabitants of the newly acquired territories!

When Suleiman I came to the throne in 1520 Constantinople had once again become 'the world's most beautiful city' and, on the occasion of his marriage to Roxelana (a Russian slave captured by raiders in Galicia), free breakfast was served to all, i.e. bread and olives for the poor, cheese, bread, fruit and rose petal jam for the better off: 'the streets of Constantinople were jammed for the celebration . . . mounds of fruit — Mardin plums, Azerbaijan pears, Smyrna grapes, Temesvir prunes . . . *hadgis* cooked on portable stoves . . . . the sherbert sellers did a roaring trade pouring the sherbert through a lump of snow stuck on the end of the vessel's spout; sherberts of lemon juice and snow flavoured with honey, amber and musk; others of water lilies, together with sherbert made of violets and honey, there were squares of rice-jelly sprinkled with rosewater or fruit soup with ice floating in it.'[17] All this a mere seventy years after the conquest!

The poor, as ever, continued to hack a miserable living as the rich wallowed in luxuries 'beyond belief', and it befell to Kaygusuz Abdel the fifteenth century mystic poet to petition the Lord concerning this injustice on behalf of the starving masses — whose lot has not improved much since the day he penned these immortal words.

16 ibid.
17 *Under the Turk in Constantinople*, G. E. Abbott.

Lord I humbly beg of You, hear my reverend request,
These are words straight from the heart, they are not spoken in jest.
First, a hundred thousand loaves, also fifty thousand pies,
One hundred sixty thousand buns, profusely buttered on both sides.
A thousand piglets should suffice, if added to a thousand sows,
With sixty of their young, some fifty thousand water buffaloes.
Ten thousand cows, a thousand oxen for a mustard stew,
The trotters separately served in vinegar, with garlic too.
A thousand sheep in casserole, an equal sum of goats at most,
But fifty thousand lambs and kids to grill upon the spit, or roast.
Innumerable chickens, ducks, and in the same proportion, geese,
Some to make succulent kebabs, and others to be fried in grease.
Pray let there be dish after dish of pigeons and of tender quail,
Partridge and pheasant caught in nets, arriving in an endless file.
Fifty thousand pots of rice, and saffron puddings are inferred,
A thousand pots of porridge, the butter with a drumstick stirred.
Soups with pleasant flavouring, meatballs gently made, I beg,
Ducklings, and on trays of brass, sweetmeats made of starch and egg.
Fifty thousand pasties and the same amount of baklava,
Honey and almond cakes galore, and countless plates of fresh okra.
Helva fit for conquerors, served on trays and heaped in bowls,
For eager fingers to scoop up, making quite enormous holes.
Forty thousand, fifty thousand pecks of apricot and cherry,
Apple, pear and vintage grape, will be enough to make us merry.

social and religious influences

The ways of life of the people of the Middle East vary from the completely westernized to the traditional peasant — Bedouin, unchanged for generations. The most European regions are Israel, the Caucasus and Lebanon where the majority of people live under completely westernized conditions and, not surprisingly, they are mostly non-Muslim.

Israel, a new nation, was created from the remnants of the second great genocide of our century. Its people have mostly come from Russia, Germany, USA and other western countries. These Askhanazim (Western Jews) are all, bar religion, Europeans; while the Sephardim (Oriental Jews) are, bar religion, indistinguishable from their neighbours — the Arabs, amongst whom they lived (prior to the birth of the State of Israel in 1948) in peace and harmony for centuries. Israel is, in essence, a western state on the periphery of the Muslim-Arab world and intrinsically so too is Lebanon, a small country that has been a haven for generations for minorities (Christian or heretic Muslims) but which, since 1975, has been undergoing serious political surgery. The majority of the Lebanese are 'Christian' of one denomination or another!

The people of the Caucasian Republics of Armenia and Georgia are Christians — belonging to the Eastern Orthodox branch. The republic of Armenia today is only a tenth of historic Armenia which stretched from the Mediterranean to the Caspian Sea.

Like the Jews the Armenians have suffered throughout the ages. A large portion of the population was forcibly converted to Islam or deported. The climax of these misdeeds culminated with the first genocide of our century (1915–20) when some two million people, out of a population of four million, were slaughtered and the survivors scattered all over the Middle East and beyond. The Georgians, an intelligent and highly gifted people, are mostly Christian. Muslim Georgians — Lazes — emigrated to the Ottoman empire in the seventeenth century.

Azerbaijanians are Muslims and are related to the Turks, particularly to those living in Iran.

Cypriots are Christians with a Muslim Turkish minority.

All these lands are on the borders of the heartland of Islam, for Islam is the dominant religion with 150 million followers throughout the Middle East, and since it is not merely a religion but more a way of life there is a strong social homogeneity throughout the region; and centuries of Muslim domination have influenced socially and culturally such non-Muslim people as Greeks, Armenians, Copts, Jews and Zoroastrians.

Outside the highly industrialized and westernized regions of the Middle East there lie, for want of a better word, the semi-westernized regions. These, in essence, are the large cities such as Cairo, Tehran, Damascus, Ankara, Istanbul, etc. where the official and professional classes and the rich merchants live under semi-European conditions. Most of these people live in houses or apartment blocks. They wear European clothing, drive cars and their homes are furnished with tables, chairs, beds, dressing tables, modern kitchens, refrigerators, radios and often televisions and cassette players. In a typical house the front door usually leads to the reception room which is commonly used by men. To get to the domestic quarters, i.e. kitchen and bedrooms, one has to use a separate door leading from the hall and this is usually barred to men. When guests arrive they will sit down first in the men's room, but after a short time the ladies are expected to 'visit' domestic quarters where the females of the house sojourn. This segregation of the sexes has almost been eradicated amongst the westernized classes where the women not only do not cover their faces, but are seen in public wearing the 'latest' styles of clothing. Female emancipation, although not yet as advanced as in Europe, has certainly arrived in the Middle East.

A generation ago the streets of Alexandria, Baghdad or Damascus were filled with women clad in black, today this phenomenon is a rarity and is only practised among the elderly, or women living in small towns or villages.

There have been attempts at social and cultural reforms — Ataturk in Turkey, Reza Shah in Iran and Nasser in Egypt — but the slow, traditional and extremely conservative mind of the average devout Muslim has built barriers which only time — a lot of it — and education will dismantle.

In the villages,[18] or in the tents of the nomads, there will often be no furniture. The guest room, *mandarah*, is spread with coloured rugs or carpets and with quilts, mattresses and cushions laid around the walls for people to sit on. Usually no chambers are furnished as bedrooms. The bed, during the day, is rolled up and placed

18   The majority of the people of Egypt, Turkey, Iran, as well as Syria and Iraq, still live in small villages. On average 80 per cent of the Middle Easterners are peasants with a significant minority of nomads.

to one side or, when one is available, in a small adjoining room called a *khazneh* which is used as a bedroom in winter. During the summer many people in the towns and villages sleep on the flat roof tops. The centre of the men's room, which is usually regarded as a reception room, is kept empty. The guests sit around with their backs to the walls.

All Middle Easterners are very hospitable. The unwritten rule is to please one's family, acquaintances, guests or hosts. It is a great honour to be a guest, but a greater honour to be host. When an unexpected guest arrives a space is immediately created for him at the head of the table and coffee or sherbet is offered. He must never refuse, to do so is taken as an offence.

When food is served it is brought either on a large dish or in numerous small dishes and placed on the ground in the centre of the room. The guest is then invited to join the family. He must refuse — at least three times — but give in upon a great deal of cajolling and entreating. Even when he has previously dined he is not expected to refuse, but to make a gesture by tasting a little of this and that. Before he sits down at the table the guest will wash his hands with soap and water in a copper basin called a *tisht* or, at least, have some water poured over his right hand. He is then offered a napkin. He must never refuse dishes that have been sampled by others present at dinner, to do so will give great offence. He must comment on the delicacy of the aroma emanating from the meal, pay little compliments such as on the tenderness of the meat or the thinness of the housewife's *kibbeh* or the sweetness of the *baklava*, etc.

Each person bares his right arm to the elbow — before he begins to eat, he says Bismillah — in the name of God. This is generally said in a low, but audible voice; and by the master of the house first. It is considered both as a grace and as an invitation to any person to partake of the meal. . . The master of the house first begins to eat, the guests or others immediately follow his example. Neither knives nor forks are used; the thumb and two fingers of the right hand serve instead of those instruments; but spoons are used for soups, or rice or other things that cannot easily be taken without . . . to pick out a delicate morsel and hand it to a friend is esteemed polite. . . Each person breaks off a small piece of bread, dips it in the dish, and then conveys it to his mouth, together with a small portion of the meat or other contents of the dish.[19] The piece of bread is generally doubled together, so as to enclose the morsel of meat.

The above lines from Edward William Lane's brilliant book *Manners and Customs of the Modern Egyptians* are as true today as when they first appeared in 1836. In the intervening 170 years very little has changed in the social and cultural attitudes of the average Middle Easterner. Perhaps he does not sit on the floor, but uses a table and chairs. He may even use knives and forks, have table napkins, several plates instead of one, but the traditional Middle Eastern manners and rules of etiquette still remain.

At the end of a meal one must lick one's fingers as a sign of great satisfaction and say 'el hamdullah' — praised be the Lord, and get up to wash one's hands and mouth. This brief description of the table manners of the Muslims also applies to the other nationalities, whether Christians or Jews. A Christian will say a few words of thanks to

---

19 Both the Bible and the Koran have numerous examples of such social and domestic customs illustrated, e.g. 'Jesus answered, He it is, to whom I shall give a sop, when I have dipped it. And when he had dipped the sop, he gave to Judas Iscariot, the son of Simon.' (St. John 13/26)

the Lord before dinner and will end by thanking the Lord for what he has just received. He will then, in turn, thank his host and the lady of the house 'May your hand remain young and fresh,' or 'May God be bounteous and generous, and increase one to a thousand,' or 'May your table always be plentiful.'

During the meal people will converse in pleasantries, but avoid discussing politics or business. The meal is a family affair even where there are several guests and the focus of attention will inevitably be on them.

There is always found an air of solemnity and dignity at a Muslim table. However, up in the Caucasus amongst the lush hills and valleys, there is a much lighter and more boistrous ambiance. When Armenians or Georgians are dining they show a liveliness and geniality not common amongst Arabs, Turks and Persians. Immediately the guests and hosts are seated a *tamada* — chairman — is democratically elected and he cannot refuse! It is his function to keep order and act as an arbiter between the diners. To be elected as a *tamada* is a great honour for it signifies a person of respect, wit and erudition. He will thank all for their presence and, one by one, introduce each guest in a light-hearted manner, reciting certain anecdotes from their past, often lavishing them with praise and, after each introduction, a toast will be drunk in honour of that particular guest. The atmosphere during dinner is always happy and gay. The *tamada* may ask someone to recite a poem, or plead with someone else to sing an old folk song — he cannot be refused — for during the dinner the *tamada* is king. A great deal of wine is consumed during such dinners for Armenians and Georgians, being of the Christian faith are, unlike the Muslims, under no religious censure. The meal will end with a few words from the *tamada* thanking the lady of the house for all her work, her wonderful cooking, expressing the appreciation of it by all and, turning to the assembled diners he will conclude:

It is time gentlemen we departed
For we have wined and dined in content;
the landlady's task for tomorrow
Has increased similarly in content.

A few words must be said about the dietary laws of the Middle Easterners. The three major religions Judaism, Christianity and Islam were the product of the desert where they were first seeded and nurtured. Today the predominant influence is that of Islam, often called a 'Christian heresy' and indeed, one can go further back and regard Christianity as a 'Judaic heresy'. These religions have a common source — the nomadic people of the Middle East, their way of life, their culture, beliefs, superstitions, fears and dreams shaped in metamorphical and surrealist colours and forms. With the development of a religion comes the 'commandments' — the law and order, the 'do' and 'don't' acts. And from amongst these social and ethical codes emerges the accepted norms of good conduct in life and the hereafter.

The dietary laws of the Semitic races — Arabs and Jews — are virtually the same. The slight differences, which have arisen over the centuries, are due more to the political and economic situation of the people at any one given time than to any purely religious uplifting or development.

Since religion has been the dominant factor in keeping the Jewish people together, this very old religion has evolved codes of behaviour that touch every aspect of a person's social life. The third book of Moses — Leviticus — is mostly devoted to health, cleanliness and social niceties as well as the permitted or forbidden diets of a devout Jew.

Whatsoever parteth the hoof, and is cloven footed, and cheweth the cud,
among the beasts, that shall ye eat. Nevertheless shall ye not eat of them that chew
the cud, or of them that divide the hoof: as the camel, because he cheweth the cud,
but divideth not the hoof; he is unclean unto you. . . . And whatsoever hath no fins
and scales ye may not eat. (Leviticus 11, 3–12)
Moreover ye shall eat no manner of blood, whether it be of fowl or of beast in any of
your dwellings. (Leviticus 7, 26–27)

In short, a practising Jew is not permitted to eat pork, shellfish and, according to some authorities, turbot.

The prophet Muhammad deals lengthily in the Koran with food:

Believers, be true to your obligations. It is lawful for you to eat
the flesh of all beasts other than that which hereby announced to you.
Game is forbidden while you are on a pilgrimage.
You are forbidden carrion, blood, and the flesh of swine.
You are forbidden the flesh of slaughtered animals, and of those beaten
or gored to death. . .
You are forbidden the flesh dedicated to any other than Allah; also of animals
sacrificed to idols. (Koran. Al-Maida 53–54)

Also permitted are 'the game of the sea' — which includes shellfish. All fruits and vegetables are permitted, as well as dairy produce. There are slight differences between Jewish and Muslim dietary laws and the more significant are:
a) Muslims do eat camel meat as well as shellfish;
b) 'Thou shalt not seethe a kid in its mother's milk' (Deuteronomy 14–21) does not generally apply to the Muslims;
c) Muslims are forbidden to drink alcoholic or fermented drinks. This does not really apply to Jews.

As for the Christians — Greeks, Copts, Armenians, Georgians, Maronites, Assyrians, Nestorians, etc. — they are permitted to eat and drink whatever they like — except during Lent. All the eastern Christians partook the forty days of Lent in earnest. The Greeks, Armenians, Georgians and Copts — the majority of Christians — fasted most rigorously as Paul Ricaut observed as far back as 1679.[20]

For as the eastern people have always been more abstemious in their diet, and less addicted to excess in their tables and ordinary banquets than the western or northern nations, so by this custom of living they support more easily the severe institution of their Lents; who in the time of their feasts are not so free in their eating and dancing,

---

20 *State of Greek and Armenian Churches*, Paul Ricaut, 1679.

as we are in our time of abstinence and fasting; for that which we call a collation, or lenten-table, will serve an Armenian for an Easter dinner.

The Christians observe 'the great Lent' before Easter, when they do not eat any fish, meat, butter, eggs, etc, but live on olive oil-based dishes, or tahina-based dishes 'the smell of which is sufficient to overcome a tender stomach'.[21] The other fasts were on the Feast of our Lady's Assumption (early August), Feast of Pentecost and Epiphany (late December).

As for the Muslims they are forbidden to eat, drink or smoke from first dawn to sunset during the month of Ramadan, i.e. in the month in which the Koran was revealed to Muhammed. (The great feast falls on the 10th of the month of *Dhuel Hijja* — the day of pilgrimage outside Mecca.) The lesser Muslim feasts come at the end of Ramadan.[22]

For Jews the Sabbath is a day of rest when all work is forbidden, which means all food must be prepared the day before. The most important feast is the Passover, when bread is banished from the home to be replaced by *matzo* — unleavened bread. The passover meals vary from the rest of the year when most vegetables — save peas and beans — are used. The 'uniqueness' of the Jewish cuisine comes to itself in the Passover period for the housewives were obliged to create different and tasty dishes to break the *matzo* monotony.

Today these dietary laws, as well as the fasts and feasts, are observed in varying degrees of laxity by the Middle Easterners, but generally pork is most uncommon, except in the Caucasus, Greece, Cyprus and parts of Lebanon. Wine is also uncommon, as are all alcoholic beverages, except with the Christians who, incidentally, produce all the wines available locally.

The long lasting influence of Islam has affected the social and, indirectly, the religious attitudes of non-Muslims who have unwittingly adopted many of the latters' customs and integrated them into their Christian beliefs.

To all those who followed the path of righteousness the Prophet promised that they:

shall recline on jewelled couches face to face,
and there shall wait on them immortal youths
with bowls and ewers and a cup of purest wine
that will neither pain their heads nor take away
their reasons,
with fruits of their own choice
And flesh of fowls that they relish,
And theirs shall be the dark-eyed houris,
Chaste as hidden pearls; a querdon
For their deeds.

(Koran. Al-wagia 56–15)

---

21 ibid.

22 The exact day and month of any festival varies because the Muslim calender (*Hagira*) is based on a lunar month cycle which also means that the exact day of a given festival will differ from country to country.

general features of the cuisine

Good wholesome food makes a good and healthy man.

Kurdish saying.

A major characteristic of the Middle Eastern cuisine is its overall simplicity; simple to prepare and simple to digest. Yet behind this apparent simplicity there lies thousands of years of experimentation with raw materials, utensils, cooking techniques and a subtle and intuitive understanding of climatic requirements.

The Middle East is rich in vegetables and fruits of exceptional quality — mainly due to the mineral rich soil and abundance of sunshine — and when these gifts of nature are better utilized with the aid of modern agricultural skills, as in the Caucasus and Israel; the produce is on a par with the finest available in the world. There is hardly any vegetable or fruit that does not grow in the region and the few exceptions are mainly those that prefer a tropical habitat such as pineapple, guava, breadfruit, calalu, soursop, etc.

Present on any Iranian table will be a large bowl of fresh vegetables which are eaten raw, 'Cucumbers are so good that Iranians eat them like fruit; once when I was working in a library, a young woman kindly peeled one and gave it to me as though it were an apple or orange.'[23]

Vegetables and fruits are often dried for winter use, e.g. okra, aubergines, peppers, tomatoes, grapes, apricots, plums, peaches, etc. For instance, aubergines of a medium size are washed, their stems removed, their flesh scooped out, washed again thoroughly and finally threaded on strings and hung to dry under the sun. Vegetables dried in this manner make excellent *dolmas* in winter and indeed some people prefer a dried vegetable to a fresh one for their *dolma*.

As a rule vegetables are never boiled, except in Israel and parts of the Caucasus where European influences, e.g. Polish and Russian are at their strongest. The people of Asia, in general fry their vegetables in oils, fats or butter.

Olive oil is used for dishes which are to be eaten cold and, since a substantial portion of all Middle Eastern food comprises cold dishes — mezzehs, salads, fried vegetables and some fish and meat dishes — olive oil is the most popular cooking ingredient, second only to *samna*.

Samna is usually made from buffalo's milk, which has been melted over boiling water and clarified. *Samna* is similar to *ghee* (see Glossary), so popular in Indian cooking, whence it most probably originated. It appeared with the advent of the Indo-Iranian tribes into the Middle East for, even today, the Iranians, Kurds, Afghans and the Caucasians use very little olive oil in their cooking, but prefer *samna* which has a strong individual flavour and a little of it will go a long way. The *samna* produced in Hama (Syria) and Isfahan (Iran) are perhaps the most famous in the region. In recent years increasing use is made of European-type butters and margarines, whilst olive oil is often substituted by corn oil, groundnut oil and particularly by sunflower seed oil.

During the Middle Ages people made much use of *alya*; the rendered fat from a sheep's tail; and sesame seed oil — tahini. There exists in the Middle East a remarkable

23 *Fall of the Peacock Throne*, W. H. Forbis.

breed of sheep with a lean body, but a tail of pure fat which can sometimes weigh up to 20–30 lbs and has to be carried on specially constructed crutches! The thrifty nomad naturally made use of this fat *alya*,[24] and almost all the Turkish, Syrian, Iraqi and Bedouin dishes, even just a generation or two ago, were fried or cooked with it. Almost every ancient manuscript suggested the use of this fat, 'dissolve tail and remove unwanted sediment, add meat into this oil and fry. . .' They also highly recommended tahini, which is still very popular in Egypt, particularly amongst the Copts; as well as throughout the Mediterranean coastline, and with the Armenians. In recent years Israelis, who seem to have developed a great liking for this oil, have incorporated it into many interesting new dishes.

If to the Chinese meat means pork, then to the Middle Easterner it implies lamb, although in recent years other animal flesh such as beef and veal are increasingly being eaten. Lamb is still the main meal of the region. The little pork that is used, mainly by Christians and 'liberated' Israelis who call the meat 'white beef', is usually grilled.

As a general rule people fry their meat and vegetables before adding water and spices when preparing soups and stews. This method of cooking gives a richer flavour and helps the meat retain its own juices by sealing the pores. This method of cooking is not restricted solely to the Middle East. It appears in Indo-Pakistani cuisine as well as that of North Africa and the Balkans.

Meat dishes have always been the food of the rich and even today the greatest honour a Bedouin can bestow on his guests will be the slaughter of a lamb — a tradition that precedes the story of Abraham and Isaac.

A great deal is made of minced meat. It is fried and used in soups and stews, mixed with chopped vegetables for kebabs and turned into sausages that can be stored for use in winter.

Middle Eastern food is spicy, but not hot. The exceptions are some dishes from the Yemen, Anatolia and those of North African origin. The finest exponents in the art of using herbs and spices are the Caucasians and Iranians. The latters' cuisine has much in common with those of the Indian subcontinent. Yet to the uninformed most Iranian food appears bland. In fact it is subtle and the Iranians have created a refined cuisine where spices and herbs — usually fresh — are used in just the right quantities and combinations to create the required flavours. They make great use of saffron — once so highly prized by the Greeks and Romans — and turmeric, also known as 'oriental saffron'. The people of the Gulf States, Iraq and Iran make the most use of turmeric, while Afghans, Iranians and, to a lesser extent the Turks and Caucasians, prefer saffron.

If it is the criterion in the West for a 'town' to have a 'Woolworth'-type store, a post office, a social security centre and a Chinese restaurant — or a take-away at least, then an equivalent 'town' in the Middle East should have a public bath, a mosque or two (or a church or synagogue, depending on the country, naturally), and a *souk* (covered market) with at least one *attarine* (spice street) where scores of small shops are filled to the brim with boxes, sacks and jars of every spice and herb imaginable.

In Turkey the most popular spices and herbs are sweet basil, dill and marjoram. In Armenia they are mint, tarragon and sumac. The Syrians love coriander, cinnamon,

---

24 *Alya* in Arabic; *tumag* in Armenian; *kuyruk yag* in Turkish.

caraway and allspice; while Egyptians go for sesame, cumin, tamarind and thyme. The Gulf States prefer cloves, cumin, chillis, coriander and cress. The Kurds have a liking for fenugreek and garlic chives as do the Iranians who also make much use of nutmeg and cardamom.

Nuts and fruits — fresh and dried — are also used to create some very unusual flavours. The habit of mixing them with vegetables and animal flesh is an old one, but it still continues in the Caucasian and Iranian cuisines.

Nuts are used in sauces, soups, *pilavs*, stuffings and meat dishes as well as desserts and pastries. Turks and Iranians make a great deal of almonds; Armenians and Georgians prefer walnuts, Syrians and Lebanese prefer pine kernels and pistachios while the Lazes of Turkey and the Iraqis have a penchant for hazelnuts.

A Middle Eastern ingredient that has in recent years been popularized in the West, is yoghurt.

Bread, cheese and yoghurt is still probably the basic diet of the majority of the people of Turkey, Iran and Kurdistan. Yoghurt on its own, or as an integral part of a meal, is at its best in the Iranian, Armenian and Turkish cuisines which between them have hundreds of such dishes.

Another staple ingredient is rice, with which *pilav* dishes are prepared — see Glossary. Before the introduction into the region of rice there was burghul — cracked wheat — which is used in soups, *pilavs*, as a stuffing and for the *kibbeh* dishes. The past masters of this ingredient are the Armenians, although it is also popular in Syria and Lebanon.

Kebabs, perhaps the most original (and in some respects the oldest) method of cooking, also began in the Middle East. It was on the mountain ranges of the Caucasus that the art of cutting meat into small portions and marinating it in oil flavoured with spices and herbs was first developed.

The finest kebab dishes are found in Anatolia, Armenia and the Caucasus where people in the villages still cook their meals in the charcoal burning clay ovens which are sunk into the ground and called *tonir* or *tandir* — similar to the *tandoori* ovens of Northern India. In the rest of the Middle East people in the past, and still today, take their food to be cooked by the *furunji* (professional bakers). These *furuns* are an integral part of the Middle Eastern scene.[25] All races and creeds intermingle and the women spend hours gossiping while the children devour freshly baked breads and cakes. A typical *furun* is on two levels. At the higher street end a salesman sits selling the freshly baked breads, cakes and savouries. A side entrance leads to the lower level and here the baker and his assistants are busy cooking both the shop's and the customer's food. He does this by placing the casserole dishes on a long wooden paddle which he carefully pushes into the centre of the oven — traditionally heated with wood, but more often today with gas. The entire oven is covered with stone so that the food is equally cooked all over. This method of cooking is slow. Several times the baker retrieves the dishes to check their progress and when done the casseroles, or breads, are counted, paid for and hurriedly taken home to be consumed.

All this smacks of the Middle Ages, not surprisingly, for there is much in the psyche of the Middle Easterner that impels him to keep in touch with his origins. Perhaps it is

---

25 From Sanskrit *pur*, *phour* in Greek, *pour* in Armenian, *firm* in Turkish.

because of the unchanging desert, or the rigid religious doctrines that still prevail; the strong family ties with the strict code of honour, dignity, respect, virtue and tradition.

This deep deference to the past is perhaps one of the prime reasons for the unwavering attachment to the ancestral dishes, and the almost reverential treatment of their continuity into the future. 'I am what I am for I eat what I eat' said Boloz Mugush one day when confronted by an arrogant and ill-tempered Turkoman. 'My great grandmother passed it to my grandmother who in turn passed it to my mother, who passed it on to her daughters, the secret of enjoyment, happiness and satisfaction, that is why I am what I am. You are what you are for you do not know how to eat.'

mezzeh

Mezzeh is the food of the traveller, whether on a picnic, pilgrimage or long journey. *Mezzeh* is a large selection of little things and the ideal places to acquaint oneself with this 'way of life' are — or rather were before civil war intervened — the mountain resorts of Zahleh, Bikfayah, and Jounieh in Lebanon. In small open-air restaurants literally hundreds of dishes were arranged on tables containing, amongst others, most of the recipes in this chapter and many such as salads, *kibbehs*, kebabs and pickles from other chapters; for strictly speaking there is no such thing as a *mezzeh* and yet everything can be called *mezzeh*.

Mezzeh is a way of life for everyone from the Bedouins in a desert oasis sharing their tit-bits to the large family sitting around the table sharing a little of this, a little of that, something cold, something warm, a plate of chopped fried liver left from yesterday, a few olives, cubed cheese, hot or cold minced meat balls, etc. Everything available in the kitchen can be part of the *mezzeh* — and herein lies its beauty, for a little of this and that usually mounts up to create a rich and sumptuous table with a variety of dazzling colours and contrasting textures and flavours.

Mezzeh makes an ideal buffet table and is particularly suitable to the Western way of life as it has been for centuries in the East.

Once the proprietor of a well-known restaurant in Zahleh, Lebanon boasted that he could, in a matter of a few hours, lay a *mezzeh* table containing over 200 items. His challenge was accepted. Three hours later, when our party arrived, the proprietor apologized that due to unforseen circumstances he had lost his bet. The *mezzeh* table — a magnificent sight stretching from one end of the open-air balcony to the other (over fifteen metres) contained 'only 175 items'.

He had proved his point.

muhammarah pomegranate and walnut dip

A Syrian speciality also popular with Armenians who call it *garmeroug*. This is a hot, piquant dip which makes an excellent appetizer and this Aleppan saying vouches for its 'acridity': 'Only the devil can cope with our Aysha's *muhammarah*, and he only comes this way once a lifetime — thank the Lord.'

It is a must on any *mezzeh* table, but is also a good accompaniment for all kinds of cooked meats and kebabs.

2 tablespoons red chilli pepper
150 ml/¼ pint olive oil
25 g/1 oz stale, dry breadcrumbs
1 tablespoon pomegranate juice
   (if available) or 2 tablespoons
   lemon juice

175 g/6 oz walnuts, ground
1 teaspoon ground cumin
1 teaspoon allspice
salt to taste

Garnish chopped parsley

Moisten the chilli pepper with 2 tablespoons of water in a bowl. Add all the remaining ingredients and mix thoroughly until well blended. Spoon into a small bowl and garnish with a little chopped parsley. Chill until ready to serve.

hab-el-jose walnut balls

Easy to make, attractive and very tasty they are one of the specialities of Antioch of Crusader fame. Once it was the capital of a Christian kingdom, a seat of learning and one of the great cities of antiquity. Today it is a shabby little town in southern Turkey — such is the destiny of men and mice!

Antioch was built in the year 300 BC by Seleucus the Great who:

... consulted with the priest Amphion for the choice of a site for the new capital that he wished to give to his immense Empire ... an eagle flew rapidly to the summit of Mount Silpius and let fall there the viscera of victims slain on the altar. The divine will was made manifest ... and yet no city in the world has suffered more or oftener from the cataclysms of nature, famine, floods, earthquakes and plague; or from the lust and cruelty of man who has betrayed, burnt, pillaged and utterly destroyed it.

(*Syria As It Is*)

150 g/5 oz walnuts, ground
50 g/2 oz breadcrumbs
½ teaspoon cumin
tahina cream

½ teaspoon cayenne pepper
salt to taste
olive oil to grease fingers
50 g/2 oz sesame seeds

Garnish pinch paprika

In a bowl mix together the walnuts, breadcrumbs and cumin. Add sufficient tahina to form a soft paste. Add the cayenne pepper and salt to taste. Now grease your fingers with the oil and break the paste into small pieces. Shape into walnut-sized balls. Pour the sesame seeds on to a plate and roll each walnut ball in them. Arrange on a large plate and stick a cocktail stick in each. Sprinkle with the paprika.

avocado im egozim avocado with walnuts

Here is a new recipe from a new land — Israel — and yet see how Middle Eastern it really is! Avocados were first introduced by Jewish settlers early this century in Palestine and over the years many exciting dishes have been created — or so the creators thought. In reality they are nearly all variations on age-old recipes, all tried and tested by time.

A refreshing and delightful first course. Serve it with pita bread.

1 large, ripe avocado, stoned and
  peeled
2 tablespoons lemon juice
1 small onion, finely chopped
3 pickled cucumbers, thinly sliced

1 stick celery, chopped
75 g/3 oz walnuts, quartered
1 teaspoon salt
$1/2$ teaspoon black pepper
$1/2$ teaspoon ground cumin

Garnish
$1/2$ small red pepper, thinly sliced

25 g/1 oz black olives, stoned

Cube the avocado flesh, place in a bowl and sprinkle with the lemon juice. Add the onion, cucumbers, celery and walnuts. Season with the salt, pepper and cumin, toss and chill for 30 minutes. Before serving garnish with the strips of red pepper and the black olives.

sumpoogi aghtsan aubergine and pepper salad

An Armenian speciality, this is a cold, spicy salad of cooked aubergines, with onion, peppers, garlic and spices.

There are several variations of this salad not only in the Middle East, but in Greece, Bulgaria and even in Romania where aubergines are not all that popular. This particular recipe is from Tarsus — the birthplace of St. Paul.

For some years Hoca Nasrettin was the *Cadi* (judge) of a large agricultural region in Anatolia and one day he was called upon to settle a quarrel between two neighbouring farmers who had fought in the court of the Mosque. One had prayed for rain to help grow his aubergines, the other wished Allah to keep the weather fine for the threshing. Hoca Nasrettin listened to one first and said 'But my dear man, you were perfectly right.' Then he listened to the other and replied 'But my dear man, you were perfectly right.' His wife heard him pronounce judgement, flushed red with anger and shouted 'How can a just *Cadi* agree with both parties to a suit? Are you crazy?' The Hoca smiled and said 'You also, dear wife, are perfectly right.'

4 medium aubergines
1 green pepper, seeded and
   thinly sliced
1 small onion, thinly sliced
4 tomatoes, thinly sliced
2 cloves garlic, crushed

1 teaspoon salt
$1/2$ teaspoon chilli pepper
2 teaspoons ground cumin
4–6 tablespoons olive oil
juice 2 lemons
2 tablespoons parsley, chopped

Pierce each aubergine 2 or 3 times with a sharp knife. Place them whole in a hot oven and bake until they are soft when poked with a finger (about 20–30 minutes). Remove from the oven and leave until cool enough to handle. Peel off the skin, scraping off and retaining any flesh which may come away with it. Chop the flesh and put in a large bowl. Add the green pepper, onion, tomatoes and garlic. In a small bowl mix the spices with the olive oil and lemon juice. Pour the dressing over the vegetables and mix thoroughly. Stir in the parsley, taste and adjust seasoning if necessary.

Serves 4-6 people.

hunkar beyendi aubergine with cheese

A classic aubergine dip from Turkey. This version is with grated cheese. There is one from Istanbul which excludes the cheese, but has very finely chopped green pepper, parsley and onion. Serve on its own as a *mezzeh* or as an accompaniment to kebab and lamb dishes. 'The king likes it' is the literal meaning of this dish.

2 aubergines
1 tablespoon lemon juice
25 g/1 oz butter
2 level tablespoons flour
6 tablespoons hot milk

3 tablespoons grated cheese,
    Cheddar, feta or mozzarella
1 teaspoon salt
1/2 teaspoon chilli pepper

Make 2 or 3 slits in each aubergine and cook them over charcoal, under the grill or in a hot oven until the skins are black and the flesh soft when poked with a finger. Remove from the heat and, when cool enough to handle, peel off the skins reserving any flesh that gets stripped off with the skin. Put the flesh in a saucepan and mash with a fork. Add the lemon juice and simmer over a low heat for five minutes, stirring frequently. Meanwhile, in another saucepan melt the butter, add the flour and cook until it turns golden brown, stirring constantly. Stir this into the aubergines and then gradually stir in the milk until the mixture is creamy. Add the cheese, salt and chilli pepper and cook for 2 more minutes until the mixture forms a thick purée.

mutabbal aubergine dip with tahina

A Syrian-Lebanese classic. The aubergine flesh is grilled then finely chopped and mixed with tahina and spices. It is served with pita bread or, more traditionally, *khubuz-saj*. Of all aubergine hors d'oeuvres this is the one most regularly served in hotels and restaurants throughout the Arab world.

I have also included two other aubergine dips. One, *salat chatzilim*, is from Israel and substitutes mayonnaise for the tahina. The other is Armenian *khentzorov sumpoog* and combines aubergine with apple. This combination of fruit and vegetable is typical of Caucasian cooking.

3 large aubergines
3 cloves garlic, crushed
1 teaspoon salt
50–75 ml/2–3 fl oz tahina paste

juice 2 lemons
1 teaspoon chilli pepper
1 teaspoon ground cumin
1 tablespoon olive oil

Garnish
2 tablespoons parsley, chopped

a few black olives

Make 2 or 3 slits in each aubergine then cook over charcoal, under a hot grill or in a hot oven until the skins are black and the flesh feels soft when poked with a finger. When cool enough to handle peel off the skin, scraping off and reserving any flesh which comes away with it. Put the flesh into a large bowl and mash with a fork. Add the garlic and salt and continue to mash or pound the mixture until it is reduced to a pulp. Add the tahina, lemon juice and chilli pepper and stir thoroughly. Spoon the mixture on to a large plate, smooth it over and sprinkle with the cumin. Pour the olive oil over the top and garnish with the parsley and black olives.

salat chatzilim

2 aubergines
50 ml/2 fl oz mayonnaise
2 hard-boiled eggs, finely chopped
1 tablespoon parsley, finely chopped
2 tablespoons onion, finely chopped

1 large clove garlic, crushed
2 tablespoons olive oil
2 tablespoons lemon juice
1 teaspoon salt
1/2 teaspoon black pepper

Garnish
1 green pepper, thinly sliced
1 lemon, cut into wedges

3 tomatoes, quartered
2 spring onions, sliced

Make 2 or 3 slits in each aubergine and cook over charcoal, under a hot grill or in a hot oven until the skins are black and flesh soft when poked with a finger. When cool enough to handle peel off the skin, scraping and reserving any flesh which comes away with it. Chop the flesh and then mash until smooth. Place the aubergine purée in a salad bowl, add the remaining ingredients except the garnish and mix thoroughly. Chill the mixture for 2–3 hours.

To serve arrange the salad over the centre of a large plate. Form a pattern over it with the strips of green pepper and arrange the lemon wedges, tomato pieces and spring onions decoratively around the edge of the plate.

khentzorov sumpoog

450 g/1 lb aubergines
3 tablespoons vegetable oil
2 medium onions
1 tablespoon lemon juice
1 teaspoon sugar

1 teaspoon salt
1/2 teaspoon black pepper
1/2 teaspoon dillweed
2 eating apples
1 tablespoon sumac powder (optional)

Make 2 or 3 slits in each aubergine and cook over charcoal, under a hot grill or in a hot oven until the skins are black and the flesh soft when poked with a finger. When cool enough to handle peel off the skin, scraping off and reserving any flesh which comes away with it. Chop the flesh. Heat 2 tablespoons of the oil in a large frying pan, add the aubergine flesh and sauté for 2–3 minutes, stirring constantly.

Remove the flesh with a slotted spoon and drain on kitchen paper, then place in a large bowl.

Meanwhile, slice 1 onion and finely chop the other and set both aside. Add the remaining oil to the frying pan, add the sliced onion and sauté until soft and golden. Add the fried onion to the aubergine flesh together with the lemon juice, sugar, salt, black pepper and dillweed. Peel, core and finely chop the apples and add to the bowl together with the chopped onion. Mix thoroughly, sprinkle with the sumac powder, and chill before serving.

imam bayildi

aubergines stuffed with peppers, tomatoes and onions

You might as well expect tears from the dead as a decent meal from an Imam.
Turkish proverb.

One of the great classics of the 'Ottoman' cuisine — I have quoted the name Ottoman as I know there exists a great deal of controversy about the origin of this dish. The Greeks vehemently claim it to be theirs while any self-respecting Kurd or Armenian will be offended if it is called anything but theirs. There are very few dishes in the Middle East that have stirred up as much controversy as the dish that made the Imam faint. Why did this poor man collapse on to his patterned divan? Some say that he lost consciousness because his wife had used too much expensive olive oil in its preparation, others, more cynical, innuendoed to the effect that the Imam ate so much of the dish (free, naturally) that he just made it home before passing out on the now famed patterned couch.

There was a rumour circulating in Akflenir (where Hoca Nasrettin lived) that he was once invited to the house of the local *Papaz* (Christian priest) and that the latter's wife prepared this magnificent aubergine dish stuffed with peppers, onions, tomatoes and spices all cooked in the finest grade of olive oil. There was apparently nothing else but this dish — since it was the Christian Lent and no meat, poultry or fish could be consumed. Well, the Hoca ate and ate and ate and went home and complained that Allah was unfair since he gave opportunity for the *Gavours* (Christians) to be able to prepare such magnificent dishes, due to their religious laws.

'Hoca effendi, do you want to change your religion for a mere dish?' asked his wife. 'Allah forbid,' said the Hoca, 'but the mere thought of that dish would make many a faint heart succumb to the temptation. However, wife, I have cajoled from the *Papaz* the recipe. Here it is. Make some for supper.'

Here is the selfsame recipe, with not quite so much olive oil!

4 medium aubergines, washed and
   dried, leave the stalks on
6 tablespoons olive oil
2 onions, thinly sliced
2 green peppers, seeded and
   thinly sliced
2 fat cloves garlic, coarsely
   chopped
2 ripe tomatoes, sliced

3 tablespoons tomato purée
2 teaspoons salt
1/2 teaspoon cayenne pepper
1 teaspoon allspice
2 tablespoons parsley, chopped
12 tablespoons cooking oil
450 ml/3/4 pint water

Garnish **parsley, chopped**

Make a slit about 5 cm/2 in long down each aubergine. Salt the insides and leave for 15 minutes.

Meanwhile, heat the olive oil in a large saucepan. Add the onions, green peppers and garlic and fry gently until the onion is soft but not brown. Add the sliced tomatoes, tomato purée, salt, cayenne pepper and allspice and cook for 5 more minutes, stirring occasionally. Stir in the chopped parsley, remove from the heat and set aside.

Rinse out the aubergines under cold running water and then pat dry.

Heat the cooking oil in a frying pan, add the aubergines and fry gently, turning several times, until the flesh begins to soften. Take care not to spoil the shape. Remove the aubergines from the pan with a slotted spoon and place, side by side, in an ovenproof dish, slits uppermost. Carefully prise open the slits and spoon some of the onion mixture into each aubergine. Add the water to any remaining onion mixture, stir and pour over the aubergines. Bake in an oven preheated to 190°C, 375°F, gas mark 5 for about 1 hour.

Remove and set aside to cool. Transfer to a serving dish and chill until ready to serve. Garnish with some chopped parsley.

hummus-bi-tahini chickpeas with tahina

A classic of the Syrian-Lebanese cuisine which is also very popular in Israel, and Jordan. This purée of chickpeas, tahina, garlic and cumin is served in all the hotels and restaurants. There are several slight variations. The recipe below is the one my mother brought over with her from Syria.

I suggest you reserve a tablespoon of the unpuréed chickpeas and when the dish is to be served use them to decorate the surface. A must on the *mezzeh* table, serve with pita, *lavash* or *kubuz saj*.

450 g/1 lb chickpeas, soaked overnight in cold water	1 teaspoon chilli pepper
	3 teaspoons salt
3 cloves garlic, peeled	2 teaspoons ground cumin
300 ml/1/2 pint tahina	juice 2 lemons

Garnish a little red pepper, cumin, olive oil, lemon juice and chopped parsley

Rinse the chickpeas under cold running water and place in a large saucepan 3/4 filled with cold water. Bring to the boil then lower the heat and simmer until the chickpeas are tender. Remove any scum which appears on the surface and add more water if necessary. Drain the chickpeas into a sieve and wash thoroughly under cold running water. Retain a few of the chickpeas to use as a garnish. Using a liquidizer reduce the rest to a thick paste or purée. You will need to add a little water to facilitate the blending, but take care not to add too much or the purée will become too thin. While liquidizing the chickpeas add the cloves of garlic — this will ensure they are properly ground and distributed.

Empty the purée into a large bowl, add the tahina, chilli pepper, salt, cumin and lemon juice and mix very thoroughly. Taste and adjust seasoning to your own liking.

To serve — use either individual bowls or a large serving dish. Smooth the hummus with the back of a soup spoon from the centre out so that there is a slight hollow in the centre. Decorate in a star pattern with alternating dribbles of red pepper and cumin. Pour a little olive oil and lemon juice into the centre and then garnish with a little chopped parsley and the whole chickpeas. Serves 8–10 people.

nvig chickpeas with spinach

An Armenian dish served during the forty days of Lent when traditionally no meat, poultry or fish dishes were permitted.

Makes an excellent appetizer or a side dish with roasts and kebabs or an excellent light lunch or supper dish with pickles, salads, breads and yoghurt.

100 g/4 oz chickpeas, soaked overnight in cold water. You can use a 425 g/15 oz tin of cooked chickpeas
450 g/1 lb fresh spinach, washed thoroughly and chopped. If you use frozen spinach buy leaf spinach and chop it. The ready chopped variety is too fine

300 ml/1/2 pint water
4 tablespoons tomato purée
50 g/2 oz butter
1 teaspoon salt
1 teaspoon sugar
1/2 teaspoon black pepper
1 tablespoon cumin

If you are using tinned chickpeas drain them and follow the recipe from the next paragraph. Wash the chickpeas and place in a saucepan half filled with water. Bring to the boil then lower heat and simmer for 45 minutes to 1 hour or until the chickpeas are tender. Remove any scum and add more water if necessary. Strain and leave until cool enough to handle. Remove the skins from the chickpeas. The easiest way to do this is to hold a pea between thumb and forefinger and squeeze the pea from the skin.

Put the spinach and chickpeas into a saucepan, add the water, tomato purée, butter, salt, sugar, black pepper and cumin. Stir the mixture, bring to the boil then simmer for 30–40 minutes or until the spinach is tender and the water has evaporated.

Chill before serving.

falafel chickpea rissoles

One of Egypt's classic dishes inherited from the days of the Pharaohs. *Falafel* is the equivalent of fish and chips in Britain or hamburgers in the New World and, like the latter, it has spread beyond its native land and is today equally popular in Syria, Lebanon and Israel where it is sold in small take-aways as a sandwich with chopped salad, pickles and a little tahina sauce all enclosed inside a hot pita bread.

The recipe below is an Egyptian one using chickpeas only, however there are slight variations. In Lebanon dried broad beans are popular and are often used in 50/50 proportions with chickpeas. The breadcrumbs are eliminated. *Falafel* is better known as *tameya* amongst the Copts of Egypt (who are the direct descendants of the Pharaohs). They prepare this dish during Lent and distribute it to non-Coptic friends as an act of penance.

Sometimes the chickpeas are substituted altogether with *ful nabed* — dried white broad beans. If you would like to try *tameya* with broad beans buy them ready-skinned and soak for twenty-four hours (see Glossary for further instructions) and then use the following recipe.

A dry *falafel* 'ready-mix' is now sold in many Middle Eastern shops. There are many brands, but I have found that one from Alexandria called 'St George' makes the most successful rissoles. However, it does need 'spicing up' a little and I suggest you add 1/2 teaspoon cumin, 1 tablespoon finely chopped parsley, 1 clove garlic crushed and 1 teaspoon coriander with the water when you mix it.

450 g/1 lb chickpeas soaked
   overnight in cold water and
   then cooked in 75 ml/3 fl oz water
1 egg, lightly beaten
1 teaspoon salt
1/2 teaspoon black pepper
1/2 teaspoon turmeric
2 tablespoons coriander leaves
   or parsley, finely chopped

1/2 teaspoon ground coriander
1/2 teaspoon cayenne pepper
1 clove garlic, crushed
1 tablespoon tahina paste or olive oil
50 g/2 oz fresh white breadcrumbs
50 g/2 oz flour
sufficient oil for deep frying

Pass the chickpeas twice through a mincer and place in a large bowl. Add all the remaining ingredients except the flour and frying oil. Knead the ingredients until the mixture is soft but firm. Form into 2.5 cm/1 in balls and then flatten slightly between the palms of your hands. Coat with the flour.

Heat the oil and when hot add the rissoles, a few at a time, and fry for about 3 minutes or until they are evenly browned. Remove with a slotted spoon, drain on kitchen paper and serve hot with pita bread and salad.

Serves 8–10 people.

tahinov tzaghgagaghamp

cauliflower with tahina

A speciality from Antioch (Turkey). This dish appears in both the Syrian and Turkish cuisines. It is simple and appetizing and makes a clever use of cauliflower and tahina. Cauliflowers are widely used in the Middle East. They are often fried in oil or, as in Egypt, boiled, drained, dipped in beaten eggs and breadcrumbs and then fried in olive oil (see section on Salads, page 83).

1 head of cauliflower, about
   700 g/1 1/2 lbs
150 ml/1/4 pint tahina paste
2 cloves garlic, crushed

150 ml/1/4 pint cold water
1 teaspoon salt
2 tablespoons parsley, finely chopped
juice of 1 lemon

Break the cauliflower into florets and rinse.

Half fill a large saucepan with lightly salted water and bring to the boil. Add the cauliflower and simmer until just tender.

Meanwhile, pour the tahina into a bowl. Add the garlic, lemon juice and half the water. Using a fork mix thoroughly adding more water, a little at a time, until the mixture has the consistency of thick mayonnaise. Taste and adjust the seasoning if necessary.

Drain the cauliflower, pat dry and chop into smaller pieces. Place in a serving dish, pour the tahina mixture over and mix thoroughly. Sprinkle with the parsley and serve hot or cold.

tahiniyeh garlic and tahina dip

This dip is also known as *tarator-bi-tahina*. It is usually served with hot bread, pickles and olives.

150 ml/1/4 pint tahina paste
juice 2 lemons
300 ml/1/2 pint milk
2 cloves garlic, crushed

1 tablespoon parsley, finely chopped
1 teaspoon salt
1/2 teaspoon chilli pepper
50 g/2 oz white breadcrumbs

Garnish 1 tablespoon parsley, finely chopped, 1/2 teaspoon cumin

Pour the tahina into a bowl and stir in the lemon juice. The mixture will become very thick. Slowly add the milk, stirring until you have a mixture of a thick creamy consistency. Add the garlic, parsley, salt and chilli pepper. Taste and adjust the seasoning if necessary. Add the breadcrumbs and mix thoroughly. Pour the mixture into a serving bowl and sprinkle with the parsley and cumin.

This dip will keep for several days in a refrigerator if covered. If you find it thickens then stir in a little more milk.

kadoo pish gaza courgette dip

A simple recipe from Iran which is traditionally served at breakfast time, or as a starter, with thin, flat bread.

3 medium courgettes
1 tablespoon vinegar
2 teaspoons salt
3 tablespoons vegetable oil
1 onion, grated

225 g/8 oz tomatoes, blanched,
  skinned and chopped
juice 1/2 lemon
1/2 teaspoon black pepper
1/2 teaspoon paprika

Garnish 2 tablespoons parsley or fresh tarragon leaves, finely chopped

Cut 0.6cm/1/4 in from the head and tail of each courgette and then cut into 0.6cm/1/4 in rounds. Place the slices into a bowl of cold water, add the vinegar and 1 teaspoon of the salt and set aside for 30 minutes.

Meanwhile, heat the oil in a saucepan and fry the onion for a few minutes until soft and golden brown. Drain the courgettes and add to the onion. Add the tomatoes, remaining salt, lemon juice, pepper and paprika and about 225 ml/8 fl oz of water. Cover and simmer for about 30 minutes or until the courgettes are tender. Reduce this mixture to a purée either through using a liquidizer or a potato masher. Pour the dip into a shallow bowl and sprinkle with the garnish.

el-ful egyptian brown beans

What do you expect from the children of El-Ful?
Arab insult about Egyptians.

One of the national dishes of Egypt, but also popular in adjacent territories. It is often eaten for breakfast — and I well remember my childhood when for a halfpenny I used to get a bowl of *ful* and a crust of flat bread at the *'Ful* shop' near my school. Naturally one had to queue, sometimes up to fifteen minutes, then gobble the food and depart quickly.

If a host is to honour a guest he orders a bowl of *el-ful* from the nearest shop and to refuse to eat would be tantamount to an insult.

Adored and worshipped by the Egyptians (rich and poor) *el-ful* is brown broad beans cooked slowly in a special pot that tapers to a narrow neck (*idra*) which helps to stop over-evaporation by permitting the steam to condense on the sloping sides and drop back into the pot.

You can buy tinned Egyptian and Cypriot *el-ful* — also known as *ful-medames* from most continental and Middle Eastern stores. Or you can buy the dry beans and follow the simple recipe below.

The Egyptians and Sudanese like to add hard-boiled eggs (*hamine*) to the dish to give it substance. While the Alexandrians like to smother their *ful* in a sauce of tomatoes flavoured with garlic (see section on sauces, page 279). Always serve *el-ful* with pita bread.

700 g/1 1/2 lbs Egyptian broad beans, soaked overnight and then drained
3 cloves garlic, crushed
2 tablespoons olive oil
juice 2 lemons

1 teaspoon salt
1/2 teaspoon black pepper
4 hard-boiled eggs, shelled
2 tablespoons parsley, finely chopped

Put the beans into an ovenproof casserole and cover with water. Bring to the boil, then place in an oven preheated to 120°C, 250°F, gas mark 1/2 and bake for 4–7 hours, depending on the quality of the beans. At the end of the cooking time the beans should be soft but not broken up. Drain the cooking liquid from the beans and discard it. Stir the garlic, olive oil, lemon juice, salt and pepper into the beans. Spoon the mixture into 4 soup bowls, place a hard-boiled egg in the centre of each one. Sprinkle the parsley thickly over the top and serve immediately.

engouyzov lupia green beans in a walnut sauce

The Caucasians have a great penchant for walnuts. The famed *cerkez tavugu* and the various *satsivi* sauces are all made with the large and flavoursome walnuts of the region.

This is an Armenian recipe, but it is equally popular with the Abkhazians and particularly with the Georgians — famed for their nimble folk dancers and that tyrant of a leader, Joseph Stalin.

The dish can be served hot or cold, but I prefer the latter.

450 g/1 lb french beans, fresh or frozen, trimmed and cut into 5 cm/2 in pieces
75 g/3 oz walnuts
2 cloves garlic, chopped
1 small onion, finely chopped
3 tablespoons chopped coriander leaves, if available

1 teaspoon ground coriander
2 tablespoons olive oil
2 tablespoons wine vinegar
1 tablespoon lemon juice
2 teaspoons paprika
1–2 teaspoons salt to taste
a little chicken stock
1 tablespoon parsley, finely chopped

Garnish **pinch cayenne pepper**

Half fill a large saucepan with lightly salted water and bring to the boil. Add the beans and cook briskly for 8–10 minutes by which time the beans should be cooked but still crisp. Drain and leave to cool.

In a blender or mortar crush the walnuts and garlic to a paste. Empty the paste into a large bowl and add the onion, coriander, oil, vinegar, lemon juice, paprika and salt and mix well. The mixture needs to have a thick, creamy consistency and so if you think it is too dry then stir in a little chicken stock. Taste and adjust seasoning if necessary. Add the beans and stir until they are coated with the sauce. Lightly mix in the parsley and then pile into a serving bowl. Sprinkle with a little cayenne pepper.

hulba fenugreek dip

A speciality of Yemen, this is a hot, spicy dip made from fenugreek, chillies, onion, garlic, lentils and rice. Sometimes lamb or chicken meat is finely chopped and added to the dip to make it more substantial. If you prefer you can eliminate the rice and make up the quantities with lentils, or vice versa.

Please note this is a hot dish — no exaggeration — particularly if you can find the hot chillies that a Yemeni would appreciate.

4 tablespoons ground fenugreek
225 ml/8 fl oz water
4 hot chillies
1 teaspoon salt
1 large tomato, peeled and finely
    chopped
2 spring onions, finely chopped,
    including heads
2 cloves garlic, crushed

1/2 teaspoon black pepper
1/4 teaspoon ground cardamom
1/4 teaspoon turmeric
75 g/3 oz boiled lentils
75 g/3 oz boiled rice
1 teaspoon coriander leaves, chopped
2 tablespoons ghee (clarified butter)
about 150 ml/1/4 pint stock
Garnish 1/2 teaspoon powdered saffron

Place the fenugreek in a bowl, add the water and leave to soak for 5–6 hours. Carefully pour off the water then beat the fenugreek with a fork until frothy.

Cut the chillies in half, remove and discard seeds and stalks then chop the flesh very finely. Add the chillies to the fenugreek together with the salt, tomato, spring onions, garlic, black pepper, cardamom and turmeric and mix well. Now add the cooked lentils and rice and mix thoroughly with a wooden spoon. Transfer the mixture to a saucepan and stir in the coriander leaves, *ghee* and stock. Cook over a low heat, stirring occasionally, until the mixture is thick. Add a little more water if necessary. Pour the *hulba* into a large bowl, decorate with 1/2 teaspoon saffron and serve with flat bread as a *mezzeh* dip.

fasoulya piyazi turkish bean salad

There are several variations of this bean salad. The recipe below makes use of green peppers, onion and olives, but in Syria the olives are omitted and a finely chopped tomato is added. In western Turkey two hard-boiled eggs (each cut into eight lengthways) are added with the tomato.

You can serve this dish as an appetizer, as a meal on its own with warm bread, or as a side dish with kebabs.

225 g/8 oz haricot beans,
    soaked in cold water overnight
1 clove garlic, crushed
2 tablespoons olive oil
1 small onion, thinly sliced

1 small green pepper, thinly sliced
salt and pepper
1 tablespoon parsley, chopped
25 g/1 oz black olives, stoned and halved
juice 1 lemon

Drain the beans and put them into a large saucepan. Cover with water, add 1/2 teaspoon salt and bring to the boil. Lower the heat and simmer until the beans are tender. Add more water if necessary. Strain the beans and place in a bowl. Add the garlic, olive oil, onion, green pepper and salt and pepper to taste. Stir well and set aside to cool. Taste and adjust the seasoning if necessary. Sprinkle with the parsley and olives and squeeze the lemon juice over the top.

besarah broad bean dip

This recipe is from Egypt and is similar to other vegetable dips of the region. It makes use of dried broad beans (*ful nabed*) which are available from most Middle Eastern shops. However, normally these beans still have their skins on. To remove these soak the beans in cold water for forty-eight hours, changing the water two or three times. Remove the skins.

Egyptians often add one to two teaspoons of melokhia to this dish to give it a green tint, but Libyans do not do this. Also in Egypt this dish is always served with a garnish of an onion sauce called *taleyeh* (see below).

Serve hot in individual bowls with bread of your choice.

350 g/12 oz dried broad beans soaked and skinned	1/2 teaspoon black pepper
900 ml/1 1/2 pints water	2 teaspoons dried mint
1 1/2 teaspoons salt	1 teaspoon melokhia (optional)

Garnish	Taleyeh
Olive oil, chopped onion, spring onions, radishes and lemon wedges	1 large onion
	4–5 tablespoons olive oil
	1 clove garlic, finely chopped

First prepare the *taleyeh* by halving the onion lengthways and then slicing thinly to give the pieces a semi-circular shape.

Heat the oil in a small saucepan, add the onion and fry until golden. Add the chopped garlic and fry for a further 1–2 minutes. Remove from the heat and set aside.

Place the soaked and skinned beans in a saucepan, cover with the water, bring to the boil then lower the heat and simmer for 1 1/2 hours by which time the beans should be soft. Add a little more water if the beans are likely to boil dry. Blend the beans in a liquidizer or pass through a sieve and return the purée to the saucepan. Add the salt, pepper, mint and melokhia if available and cook over a low heat until the mixture is thick and bubbling. Transfer to bowls and garnish each with a little of the *taleyeh*.

Serve the other garnishes separately so that people can help themselves according to their taste.

tabouleh burghul and vegetable salad

Made with cracked wheat *tabouleh* is a mixture of burghul and vegetables, and has an 'earthy' flavour. Popular in Syria and Jordan it is perhaps at its best in Lebanon where it almost reaches a sublime stage when prepared by a Maronite housewife whose skills in mixing the ingredients of this dish cannot really be surpassed. She piles the *tabouleh* on to a large plate like a pyramid and decorates it with tomatoes, black olives, small pickling-type cucumbers, sprigs of parsley, strips of red and green pepper and pomegranate seeds. Always part of the *mezzeh* table, *tabouleh* has several variations. The recipe below is a standard one from Lebanon.

75 g/3 oz fine burghul
1 cucumber, peeled and finely chopped
4 tomatoes, finely chopped
1 green pepper, seeded and finely
    chopped
1/2 onion, finely chopped

4 tablespoons parsley, finely chopped
2 tablespoons dried mint or fresh mint,
    finely chopped
1 teaspoon salt
juice 2–3 lemons
4 tablespoons olive oil

To serve 1 lettuce, preferably Cos, washed

Rinse the burghul in a large bowl several times until the water you pour away is clean. Squeeze out any excess water. Put the chopped vegetables, parsley and mint into the bowl and mix thoroughly with the burghul. Stir in the salt, lemon juice and olive oil. Mix well together, leave for 15 minutes and then taste and adjust seasoning if necessary. Arrange lettuce leaves around the edge of a plate and pile the salad into the centre.

The ideal way to eat this is to make a parcel of *tabouleh* by folding a little of it up in a lettuce leaf or a pita bread.

each armenian burghul salad

If *tabouleh* is the pride of the Maronite Christian Lebanese, *each* is the pride of the Cilician Armenians. This is a speciality from the region of Gavour Daglari (Christian Mountains) once the stronghold of crusading nobles and their marauding armies.

Each is an appetizer made with burghul and vegetables incorporating pomegranate juice (the Armenian touch) and cumin. It can be eaten with pita bread or, like *tabouleh*, with lettuce leaves. I regard this as superior to *tabouleh*.

150 g/5 oz burghul
6 tablespoons parsley, finely chopped
1 onion, finely chopped
2 spring onions, finely chopped
2 tomatoes, finely chopped
1 teaspoon salt

1/2 teaspoon cumin
1/2 teaspoon cayenne pepper
1 tablespoon tomato purée
11/2 tablespoons pomegranate juice
    or about 3 tablespoons lemon juice
4 tablespoons olive oil

Garnish **Cos lettuce leaves**

Rinse the burghul in a large bowl and squeeze out any excess water. Add all the remaining ingredients and mix well. Set aside for 15 minutes then taste and adjust seasoning if necessary. Arrange the lettuce leaves around the edge of a serving plate and pile the salad into the centre.

To eat make a parcel of the each by folding a little of it up in a lettuce leaf or in pita bread.

bazerghen burghul and walnut salad

Some years back an Assyrian friend of mine was incensed when I described *bazerghen* as a Syrian dish. 'It's ours,' he protested indignantly. 'It's been enough to lose one's lands, but it is the ultimate in "massacres" to steal and monopolize even our food. *Bazerghen* is ours!'

So, the recipe below is most definitely of ancient origin — Assyrian in fact. Although it is also very popular with the Kurds of Syria and Iraq and the Syrian peasants in general.

Serve it as an appetizer with pita, lavash or any other flat bread and lettuce leaves and home-made pickles.

100 g/4 oz fine burghul
4 tablespoons olive oil
1/2 onion, finely chopped
1/2 teaspoon oregano
1/2 teaspoon coriander
1/2 teaspoon allspice
1 teaspoon salt

1/2 teaspoon black pepper
3 tablespoons parsley, finely chopped
2 tablespoons walnuts, finely chopped
1/2 teaspoon cumin
1/2 teaspoon cayenne pepper
50 g/2 oz tomato purée diluted in
    2–3 tablespoons water

Garnish
black olives
lettuce leaves

3–4 radishes, thinly sliced

Place the burghul in a bowl and rinse several times with cold water until the water you pour off is clean. Soak the burghul in water for 5 minutes and then drain and squeeze out excess water.

Meanwhile, heat the oil in a small saucepan and fry the onion for a few minutes until soft and transparent.

Place the burghul in a bowl and add the onion and oil. Add all the remaining ingredients and mix very thoroughly. Place in the refrigerator to chill. Before serving spoon the salad on to a bed of lettuce leaves and garnish with the olives and radishes.

houm miss raw meat with burghul

There are two versions of this classic appetizer made with raw meat and cracked wheat. One is popular amongst Armenians, the other amongst the Lebanese. In *houm miss* the meat/burghul proportions are about equal and the mixture is divided into small patties and eaten dipped into a hot, cooked meat and nuts mixture. The Lebanese version *kibbeh naya* has twice as much meat as burghul and is usually eaten with olive oil and bread or lettuce leaves.

Like many Middle Eastern dishes the origin of this one is lost in the mists of time. On the one hand it has certain resemblances to the famed steak tartare which Marco Polo first encountered on his travels in China. On the other hand it resembles a great many Assyrian raw fish and meat dishes still popular in scattered regions of the Middle East. What, however, is certain is that it cannot be of Arab origin since raw meat or fish is forbidden to pious Muslims as the meat still retains blood. It is strictly a Levantine speciality and particularly popular with the Christian Lebanese and Syrians who are of Greek, Armenian and Crusader origin. It is best made just before you are ready to eat it as it will dry fairly quickly.

100 g/4 oz fine burghul
100 g/4 oz raw very lean lamb,
   minced twice
1/2 tablespoon onion, very finely chopped

1 teaspoon salt
1/2 teaspoon black pepper
1/2 teaspoon chilli pepper

Accompaniment
50 g/2 oz minced lamb
1/2 tablespoon onion, chopped
3–4 walnuts, chopped

1/2 teaspoon salt
pinch black pepper
1/2 tablespoon parsley, finely chopped

Garnish pine kernels or split almonds   1/2 tablespoon parsley, finely chopped

First prepare the accompaniment by placing the minced lamb and onion in a small pan and frying over a low heat, stirring frequently for 10 minutes. Add the walnuts, salt and pepper and continue to fry until the meat is cooked. Stir in the parsley, remove from the heat and set aside.

Wash the burghul in a bowl until the water you pour off is clear. Empty the burghul on to a baking sheet and knead for 5 minutes, dampening your hands with warm water occasionally. Add the lean lamb, onion, salt and peppers and knead into the burghul for 5–10 minutes, dampening your hands occasionally.

Get your serving dish ready and fill a small bowl with water. Wet your hands, take a piece of the burghul mixture about the size of a walnut and squeeze it in the palm of your hand to make a boat shape. Use up all the mixture in this way and arrange the patties around the edge of the plate. Stick one pine kernel or split almond into the top of each piece. Heat the cooked meat through and empty it into the middle of the plate and sprinkle with the parsley. To eat dip one end of each patty into the hot meat.

kibbeh naya

50 g/2 oz fine burghul
1 level teaspoon salt
1/2 teaspoon black pepper
100 g/4 oz very lean lamb, minced twice

1 tablespoon onion, very finely chopped
1 tablespoon olive oil
pinch chilli pepper
1 teaspoon pine kernels

Accompaniment
bowlful of Cos lettuce leaves

1 onion, quartered

Wash the burghul in a large bowl until the water you pour off is clean. Empty the burghul on to a large plate or baking sheet, season with the salt and black pepper and knead for 5 minutes, wetting your hands if the mixture sticks to them. Add the minced lamb and chopped onion and knead for a further 5–10 minutes until the mixture is smooth. Keep wetting your hands if it makes the kneading easier. Spread the *kibbeh* mixture over a large plate and press until smooth forming a slight depression in the middle. Pour the olive oil into the centre and sprinkle a little chilli pepper all over the surface. Sprinkle the pine kernels over the top and serve immediately accompanied by the lettuce and onion.

banri aghtsan cheese and tomato salad with spices

This is a family recipe which is superb in its simplicity. It is ideal as an appetizer with warm bread.

It is traditionally made with feta cheese. You can make your own for real authenticity. However this salad is equally successful made with white Stilton or even cottage cheese.

225 g/8 oz feta cheese, or white
  Stilton or cottage cheese
2 tablespoons onion, finely chopped
2 large tomatoes, finely chopped
2 tablespoons olive oil

1 tablespoon lemon juice
1 tablespoon ground allspice
1 tablespoon dried thyme
  or 2 tablespoons fresh thyme
1/2 tablespoon black pepper

Garnish
1 tablespoon parsley, finely chopped

lettuce leaves

Rinse the feta under cold water and cut the cheese in 0.6 cm/1/4 in cubes and place in a large bowl. Add all the remaining ingredients and mix well with a fork. At this stage taste the salad. Feta cheese is often quite salty and it may not be necessary to add any salt, but if you are using another kind of white cheese you may need it.

Decorate a serving dish with a few lettuce leaves and pile the cheese salad into the centre. Sprinkle with the parsley and serve.

mortadella sausages with eggs cooked in wine

The only thing this sausage has in common with the Genoese version is its name — a relic of bygone ages of profitable commerce when shiploads of Venetian and Genoese merchants traversed the Middle East, sealing commercial deals with Christian, Muslim, enemy and friend, and carrying to Europe the gold, silver, silks and spices of the east.

Very little has remained in the Middle East of these glorious days: a few ruined castles scattered along the Mediterranean coastline; some words in the native languages; and a few dishes. Mortadella is one of them. However, through the ages it has changed and localized — in this case 'Armenianized', for mortadella (sometimes called *gololig*) is considered a 'classic' Armenian appetizer. It consists of boiled eggs wrapped in spiced lean meat, shaped into sausages and cooked in wine.

This recipe makes three fair-sized sausages each of which serves four people, and which will keep in the refrigerator for a week. If you wish to freeze the sausages then simply prepare the recipe without the hard-boiled egg filling.

1.35 kg/3 lb lean lamb
50 g/2 oz fresh breadcrumbs
2 eggs, beaten
3 teaspoons salt
2 teaspoons black pepper

2 teaspoons cinnamon
2 teaspoons allspice
6 cloves garlic, crushed
6 boiled eggs, shelled
300 ml/1/2 pint red wine

Remove all the fat and gristle from the meat and mince twice.

Put the meat on to a large, clean surface. Make a well in the centre, add the breadcrumbs, beaten eggs, spices and garlic, and mix until well blended. Knead the mixture until the texture is smooth. Divide the mixture into 3 balls and shape each one into a rectangle 15 x 7.5 cm/6 x 3 in. Hollow out the middle slightly and build up the sides of each rectangle. Place 2 hard-boiled eggs, end to end, down the middle of each rectangle. Ease the meat up over the eggs and seal so that the eggs are completely enclosed. Roll them gently between your palms until they have a smooth sausage shape and then tie each one up like a parcel with string.

Empty the wine into a saucepan, then add sufficient water to cover the parcels. Bring to the boil then simmer for 3/4–1 hour. Remove sausages and leave to cool, then serve cut into thin slices arranged on a bed of lettuce leaves and garnished with olives, radishes and spring onions.

yershig string sausage with garlic and spices

An Armenian speciality which is also popular in Turkey where it is called *soujuk*.

Yershig is a spicy sausage that is fried or grilled and eaten on its own as an appetizer or part of a *mezzeh* table. It is also often fried with mushrooms, tomatoes and eggs to form an omelette.

In the old days the villagers made *yershig* towards the end of the summer and kept them for the harsh winter days ahead when it was difficult to get out and when fresh milk, meat and vegetables were impossible to find. It is laborious to make, but you can prepare enough to last for months as it will freeze well.

There are all kinds of superstitions based on the qualities of this dish as well as several folk songs.

2.75 kg/6 lb minced lamb
4 teaspoons crushed garlic
4–5 teaspoons salt
2 teaspoons each black and chilli pepper

2 teaspoons ground cumin
4 teaspoons ground allspice
4 teaspoons nutmeg

Put all the ingredients into a very large bowl and knead until everything is well blended. Taste and adjust seasoning to your own liking. Cover the mixture and leave in the refrigerator overnight.

Bags

If you are going to store the mixture in bags then

a   Cut 12 oblongs, 10 x 15 cm/4 x 6 in, out of a light cotton material e.g. muslin. Make the oblongs up into 6 bags by sewing up 3 sides of each bag.
b   Divide the mixture into 6 portions and spoon one into each bag.
c   Pass a rolling pin over each bag so that the mixture is distributed evenly and is about 2.5 cm/1 in thick.
d   Leave about 5 cm/2 in empty at the open end, fold this over and fasten with a few stitches in a thick thread.
e   Leave about 30 cm/1 ft of thread so that the bags can be hung up to dry.
f   Hang the bags up in a cool place, e.g. larder for 2–3 weeks.
g   Store in a refrigerator if you are going to use them fairly quickly or else store in a deep freeze.

Skins

This is the ideal way to make *yershig*. The prepared meat is put into intestines and divided into the required size. Intestines can be purchased from most butchers if you order them in advance and they are usually already cleaned and prepared. Put them into water for about three hours before you need them. This softens them and makes them easier to handle. To put the mixture in the intestines you need a large plastic funnel with a nozzle width of about 2.5 cm/1 in.

a   Fit one end of an intestine over the nozzle and gently work the whole of the intestine on to the nozzle.

b   Force the meat down through the funnel into the intestine. As the intestine fills up it will slip off the nozzle.

c   When the whole intestine is full run it lightly through one hand to distribute the meat evenly. Set aside.

d   Continue in this way until you have used up all the meat mixture.

e   To make into sausages — fold one intestine in half and then tie or knot at certain intervals to give you sausages of the length you require.

f   Hang up to dry and store in same way as *yershig* in bags.

To serve

Peel off the cotton material or intestine and cut the *yershig* into 2.5 cm/1 in pieces. Heat some butter, *ghee* or cooking oil in a frying pan, add the pieces of *yershig* and fry for 5–10 minutes, turning occasionally. Remove with a slotted spoon.

Serve sprinkled with a little chopped parsley and garnish with lemon wedges.

aboukht/basturma dried beef in fenugreek

A classic of the Armenian cuisine, this is a speciality of the regions of Van and Kaissery. *Aboukht* is salted beef, dried under the sun and cured with a hot fenugreek paste (*chaimen*). Unfortunately good *aboukht* is not easily available outside an Armenian home although pale imitations can sometimes be purchased from a few Middle Eastern or Greek stores. Therefore I suggest you try making your own. It makes an excellent appetizer when sliced thinly and eaten with bread, olives and pickles. It also makes a tasty omelette, *aboukhty tzoo*.

1 rib of beef with bones removed

Paste

3 tablespoons ground fenugreek	**1/2 tablespoon cumin**
3 tablespoons paprika	**1/2 tablespoon allspice**
1/2 tablespoon salt	**1/4 tablespoon cayenne pepper**
1/2 tablespoon ground black pepper	**3 cloves garlic, crushed**

Cut the meat into slices 2.5 cm/1 in thick, 7.5 cm/3 in wide and any length you like. Put a thick piece of string through one end of each piece of meat and tie into loops. Immerse the pieces of meat in a large pan of brine and leave for a week at least.

Remove the meat, wash under cold running water and then leave in a pan of cold water for about 1 hour and then hang by the loops over the pan to drain for 1–2 hours. Lay a piece of muslin on a flat surface and arrange the pieces of meat on it side by side. Put another piece of muslin over the top. Place a board across the meat and lay a heavy weight on top to squeeze the juices from the meat. Change the cloths when they become saturated. Most of the moisture will have been extracted at the end of 3 days.

Hang up the meat again in a cool dry place where there is a good movement of air for 1–2 weeks until the meat is quite dry.

Put all the ingredients for the paste in a bowl and, adding a little water at a time, mix to a thick, smooth paste. Put the paste in a large bowl, add the pieces of meat, turn to coat with the paste and leave for 1–2 weeks. When removed each piece of meat should have a thick coating of paste. Hang for another week. It is then ready to use.

It will keep for several months in a cool dry place if you wrap it well. It will also freeze, but you must wrap it several times or else its strong flavour will permeate other food. If it becomes too dry then soak it in the *chaimen* (paste) until it softens enough to slice without breaking.

To serve slice the *aboukht* very thinly. It is generally eaten as part of a larger hors d'oeuvre selection, or in bread as a sandwich.

herissah chicken with wheat

On the feast of St Mary people go to church, slaughter a lamb or chicken, cook *herissah* and feed 'the multitude' — relations, friends and passers-by as well as strangers who are on a pilgrimage.

Although now part of the Christian Church's festive rituals, *herissah* predates Christianity by millenia and was connected with the sacrificial slaughtering festivities of Zoroaster and perhaps even older to the times of Abraham and Isaac.

It is traditionally made with whole-grain *gorghod* which is soaked overnight in water and then drained. Skinless grain is virtually unobtainable outside Armenia and Turkey therefore I suggest you substitute pearl barley or a coarse burghul. Lamb or chicken meat is used. The recipe below is for chicken. There are, of course, several variations of *herissah* in other Middle Eastern countries. In Turkey it is known as *keskek* and in Syria and Lebanon as *herisa*, but they all descend from the same origin — the high mountains of Anatolia where Urartians sacrificed animals to their Gods and were wise enough not to throw them to the vultures, but cooked them mixed with wheat and spices.

175 g/6 oz whole grain, skinless wheat
    which you might be able to find in
    a Middle Eastern store
    or 175 g/6 oz pearl barley
    or 350 g/12 oz coarse burghul
900–1350 g/2–3 lb chicken, cut
    into serving pieces

salt and black pepper to paste
1 teaspoon cinnamon
50 g/2 oz butter
1 teaspoon paprika
2 teaspoons ground cumin

Put the chicken pieces in a large saucepan, cover with water, season with salt and pepper and simmer until the flesh is tender. Remove the chicken from the stock and leave to cool, remove the flesh and discard the bones. Shred the meat as finely as possible and return to the stock.

Add the wheat, pearl barley or burghul and cinnamon to the stock and simmer for about 30 minutes or until the grain is tender. While it is cooking beat constantly with a wooden spoon until the mixture has the consistency of smooth porridge.

Melt the butter in a small pan and stir in the paprika.

Spoon the *herissah* into individual soup bowls. Before serving spoon a tablespoon of the butter mixture into the centre of each bowl. Sprinkle a little of the cumin powder over each portion and serve immediately. Serve with *lavash* or *pita* bread and some home-made pickles, fresh tarragon leaves and spring onions.

çerkez tavugu circassian chicken

A great Georgian speciality — almost everything with a walnut sauce hails from the Caucasus including most of the so-called Turkish *tarator* sauces. This dish was probably introduced into Turkey by the beautiful Circassian girls who were bought for the whiteness of their skin, their fair hair and nimble fingers and who, for centuries, adorned the harems of the sultans and the rich.

This dish can be served cold as an appetizer (as here) or warm as a main course.

1.35 kg/3 lb chicken, cut into 4 pieces
1 onion, coarsely, chopped
1 carrot, peeled and cut into rings
175 g/6 oz walnuts

2 thick slices of white bread
1 teaspoon salt
1/2 teaspoon black pepper

Garnish
1 tablespoon olive oil
1 teaspoon paprika

1 tablespoon parsley and/or tarragon, finely chopped

Place the chicken pieces in a large saucepan, cover with water, add the onion, carrot and a pinch of salt and bring to the boil. Lower the heat and simmer for about 45 minutes or until the chicken is tender. Transfer the chicken pieces to a plate and when cool enough to handle strip the flesh from the bones.

Return the bones to the stock and boil until the stock is reduced.

Cut the chicken flesh into strips about 5 cm/2 in long and 1.2 cm/1/2 in thick.

Grind the walnuts and bread in an electric blender and empty into a saucepan. Slowly stir in some of the stock until you have a smooth paste. Season with the salt and pepper. If you find the sauce is too thin then simmer over a low heat until it thickens.

Put the paprika and oil in a small bowl and set aside.

Pile the shredded chicken into the centre of a serving plate and spoon the sauce over the top. Set aside to cool. Just before serving dribble the oil-paprika mixture over the chicken and sprinkle with the parsley and/or tarragon.

arnavut çigeri albanian fried liver

The Ottoman empire comprised many races and nationalities. It included Albanians who played a major part in her success. They were reputed to be honest — a rare distinction in any time — brave and fair. They produced some of the best known soldiers and administrators of the empire thus originating the expression: 'Live in a *vilayet* (district) where the *vali* (governor) is an Albanian and you may live to see old age.'

This is one of the best hors d'oeuvres from the time of the Ottomans and was introduced by the mountain people of Albania.

It is simple and tasty.

1 small onion, thinly sliced	2 tablespoons flour
or 5 spring onions, chopped	2 tablespoons paprika
450 g/1 lb lamb's liver,	50 ml/2 fl oz olive oil
you can use calf's liver instead	1 clove garlic, crushed

Garnish **2 tablespoons parsley, finely chopped**

Arrange the onion on a serving plate.

Wash the liver, pat dry and cut into small pieces about 2.5 cm/1 in square, removing skin or tough pieces.

Place the flour in a small bowl, add 1 teaspoon of the paprika and mix. Add the liver pieces to the flour and toss until well coated. Heat the oil in a frying pan, add the liver pieces and fry for 2–3 minutes, turning once or twice. Do not overcook. The pieces of meat should still be pink and juicy inside. Remove with a slotted spoon and arrange on the onion.

Pour off all but about 3 tablespoons of the oil from the pan. Add the remaining paprika and the garlic and cook for 1 minute, stirring all the time. Pour this paprika-oil mixture over the liver and set aside to cool. Garnish with parsley and serve.

lsannat mtabbili lamb's tongue salad

A speciality from Syria, Lebanon and Palestine. It has, in recent years, become very popular in seaside restaurants always accompanied by a glass of *arak* and bread.

Often a lemon juice and olive oil dressing is poured over the salad, but in Lebanon and Palestine a *tahineyeh* sauce similar to the *tahineyeh* dip, but using water instead of milk to mix, is used as dressing. I prefer to sprinkle the salad with 1 teaspoon of cumin and juice of 1 lemon.

6 small lamb's tongues	1 teaspoon salt
1 onion, peeled and quartered	3–4 peppercorns, crushed
1 clove garlic	1 tablespoon lemon juice
1 stick celery, washed and cut into	2 tablespoons olive oil
12 cm/1/2 in slices	or 3–4 tablespoons of tahina dressing
1 clove	(see recipe for *tahineyeh* on page 283)
2 bay leaves	

Garnish
2 tablespoons parsley, finely chopped	1/2 teaspoon paprika
wedges of lemon	

Wash the tongues under cold running water. Place them in a large saucepan and add sufficient water to cover. Add the onion, garlic, celery, clove, bay leaves, salt and crushed peppercorns. Bring to the boil, lower the heat, cover and simmer for about 1 hour or until the tongues are tender. Leave to cool and then peel each tongue by carefully cutting one edge and removing the skin with your fingers. With a sharp knife cut the tongues into slices about 3 mm/1/8 in thick. Arrange the slices decoratively over a plate and chill for about 1 hour.

Mix the lemon juice and oil in a small bowl and pour over the slices *or* pour over 3–4 tablespoons of the tahina dressing. Garnish with the parsley, paprika and lemon wedges. Serves 4–6 people.

taramasalata fish roe dip

Taramasalata is a Greek and Cypriot speciality. It is the roe of the grey and red mullets which are found in abundance in the waters of the eastern Mediterranean.

Outside Greece, Turkey and Cyprus fresh tarama roe is not readily available, but it can be purchased in jars from most Middle Eastern shops. Tarama has a strong flavour and this is broken down with the addition of bread. Cypriots sometimes substitute the bread with mashed potato — a custom I dislike for the taste is not that of the traditional tarama. You can use carp or red caviar's roe instead.

Taramasalata is also popular on the Aegean coast of Turkey.

4 slices white bread, trimmed of crusts
100 g/4 oz tarama
4 tablespoons cold water

2 teaspoons onion, finely chopped
juice 1 1/2 lemons
100 ml/4 fl oz olive oil

Garnish
1 tablespoon parsley, finely chopped
radishes, cucumber, celery

black olives

Soak the bread in water and then squeeze dry. Place in a shallow bowl, preferably a wooden one. Gradually add the tarama and crush the eggs in with a mortar. Little by little add the cold water. Add the onion and the lemon juice and keep crushing with a mortar or transfer to a blender. Add the oil, a little at a time, until the mixture is smooth and has a light, pinkish colour. Transfer to a serving dish and refrigerate.

Garnish with the parsley and black olives and serve with radishes, etc. and warm pita bread.

barbunya bilakisi fish plaki

This dish is Greek-Turkish (Byzantine) as most *plaki* dishes are. In Turkey *barbunya* (red mullet) is usually used, but since this fish is not always easily available in this country I suggest you use halibut, cod, hake or any other firm-fleshed white fish.

This Turkish recipe incorporates potatoes which the Greeks often omit. The latter often like to add extra flavour with oregano and bay leaves.

4 small pieces white fish, e.g.
  halibut, cod, hake or mullet
4 medium carrots, peeled
  and thinly sliced
6 sticks celery, cut into 2.5 cm/
  1 in long pieces
1 small onion, thinly sliced
1 green pepper, seeded and cut
  into 8 pieces

2 large potatoes, peeled and cut into
  1.2 cm/$^1/_2$ in thick slices
6 tablespoons olive oil
3 cloves garlic, crushed
2 tablespoons tomato purée
1 teaspoon salt
$^1/_2$ teaspoon cayenne pepper
900 ml/1$^1/_2$ pints water

Garnish
1 tablespoon parsley, chopped

lemon wedges

Place all the vegetables in a large colander and wash thoroughly, then drain. Heat the olive oil in a large saucepan, add the vegetables, stir well, cover and then cook for about 30 minutes, shaking the pan occasionally.

Meanwhile, brush the base of an ovenproof dish with olive oil and arrange the washed and dried fish in it. After 30 minutes remove the vegetables from the saucepan with a slotted spoon and arrange over the fish.

Return the saucepan to the fire and heat up any oil that remains and add one more tablespoon of oil. Add the garlic and fry for 1 minute. Now add the tomato purée, salt and pepper, stir well and cook gently for 3 minutes. Stir in the water, raise the heat and bring to the boil. Pour this sauce over the vegetables, place in an oven preheated to 200°C, 400°F, gas mark 6 and cook for about 45 minutes or until the carrots are tender. Remove from the oven and set aside to cool.

Arrange the pieces of fish on a serving dish and spoon the vegetables and sauce over the top. Sprinkle with the parsley and serve with the lemon wedges.

midya litsk stuffed mussels served cold

One of the most sophisticated dishes from Armenia popularized by the nineteenth-century chef-hotelier Tokatlian of Istanbul. The mussels are cleaned and then stuffed with rice, pine kernels, currants and spices.

about 30 mussels
4–6 tablespoons olive oil
2 medium onions, finely chopped
75 g/3 oz rice, washed thoroughly
50 g/2 oz pine kernels or walnuts, coarsely chopped

50 g/2 oz currants
1 tablespoon parsley, chopped
1 heaped teaspoon salt
1 level teaspoon allspice
$1/2$ teaspoon chilli pepper

Garnish lemon wedges

Put the mussels to soak in a large saucepan filled with salted water. Discard any mussels with open or broken shells or any that float to the surface.

To prepare the filling, first heat 4–6 tablespoons of olive oil in a saucepan, add the onions and fry until soft. Add the rice and fry for about 3–5 minutes, stirring frequently to prevent sticking. Stir in all the remaining ingredients and cook for a further 5–10 minutes. Taste and adjust seasoning if necessary. Remove from the heat.

Scrub and wash each mussel shell thoroughly. Force open each mussel with a sharp knife. If you find them difficult to open put them in a very thick-bottomed saucepan, cover, put over a low heat and steam for a few minutes — they should then begin to open. Cut off the beard — the fibrous bits that keep the mussel attached to its shell — but do not remove the flesh. Leave in slightly salted water until ready to use.

To fill take one mussel at a time and put a teaspoon of the filling inside — do not pack too tightly as the rice will swell when cooked. If you loosen the joint a little the shell should stay closed, but if not tie up with cotton. Pack tightly into a saucepan, cover with an inverted plate to stop them moving while cooking and pour in enough water to cover. Bring to the boil then lower the heat and simmer for 1–$1^{1}/_{2}$ hours. Drain off the water, allow to cool and arrange on a serving dish with lemon wedges.

Serves 4–6 people.

tunig mackerel in olive oil

This dish is better known in Turkey as *uskumru pilakisi*. The Armenians' favourite fish is *ishkan* (salmon trout) found only in Lake Sevan. The Turks undoubtedly favour *barbunya* (red mullet), but both nations agree that mackerel comes a good second. It is salted, pickled (*lakerda*), used in soups, fried, grilled and prepared in the following way in olive oil and wine. This is a marvellous starter.

4 medium sized mackerel
300 ml/1/2 pint olive oil
4 onions, thinly sliced
2 carrots, peeled and thinly sliced
2 cloves garlic, halved
1/2 teaspoon chilli pepper

1 tablespoon tomato purée
1 glass white wine (or extra stock
   or water)
600 ml/1 pint fish stock or water
salt to taste

Garnish
1 tablespoon parsley, chopped

lemon wedges

Scale and clean the insides of the fish, but do not cut off heads or tails.

Heat half the oil in a large frying pan, add the onions and fry until soft. Add the carrots and garlic and fry for a further 10 minutes. Remove from the heat and stir in the rest of the ingredients. Bring to the boil, lower the heat, cover and simmer for 15 minutes. Arrange the mackerel in the sauce, cover and cook for a further 20 minutes or until the mackerel are tender. Turn off the heat and leave to cool. Place the mackerel on a serving dish, pour the sauce over them and sprinkle with the parsley. Serve with the lemon wedges.

sardalya tavasi fried sardines and other small fish

All along the Mediterranean coastline small fish restaurants serve sardines or other small fish such as sprats or whitebait. They all occur in abundance in the Black Sea and Sea of Marmara.

The fish are simply cleaned, tossed in flour and fried in oil. All they need then is a few drops of lemon juice squeezed over them and they are ready to eat.

sardalya sarmasi

This is another clever Turkish method of cooking sardines or other small fish. Each one is cleaned, wrapped in a vine leaf, brushed all over with oil and then deep fried in sizzling oil, a few at a time, for about 3 minutes until crisp on all sides.

Serve with lemon juice and pickles.

Both these methods are popular with Turks, Syrians, and Cypriots while fried small fish (*blehat samk*) are much loved by Egyptians, Libyans and the Lebanese who eat them — heads, tails and all!

nkhaat mtabbli   brain salad

A great delicacy throughout the Middle East, brains (lamb or calf) are prepared as salads, as here, in omelettes or are fried as in the following recipe. There are many regional variations. This is a typical one from Palestine-Jordan.

450 g/1 lb lamb or calf brains
2 tablespoons vinegar
3^1/2 teaspoons salt
1 clove garlic

^{1}/2 teaspoon black pepper
juice 1 lemon
4 tablespoons olive oil

Garnish 1 tablespoon parsley, finely chopped

Place the brains in a bowl, add enough cold water to cover together with the vinegar and 2 teaspoons of salt. Leave for 20–30 minutes and then drain.

Place the brains in a saucepan with enough cold water to cover and 1 teaspoon of salt and bring just to the boil. Lower the heat and simmer for 15 minutes or until the brains are tender. Drain and when cool enough to handle peel off the skin and any veins. Cut the brains into bite-sized pieces and place in a salad bowl.

In a small bowl mash the garlic with the remaining salt and the pepper. Add the lemon juice and oil and mix well. Pour the dressing over the brains covering all the pieces. Do not toss. Sprinkle with the parsley and serve.

erebouni   lamb's brain fritters

The origins of most ancient cities are lost in legends and myths and it can only be a miracle which has kept the foundation date of one of the oldest of them all — Erebouni — carved in Urartian script on stone and dated 782 BC. It was built by slaves for the mighty King Argishti I.

This Armenian recipe does not claim such longevity, it is simply named in honour of the fortress-capital which lies a few miles away from the modern capital Erevan.

about 450 g/1 lb lamb's brains
2 tablespoons vinegar
salt
2 egg yolks

1 tablespoon fresh dill, finely chopped
   or ^{1}/2 tablespoon dried dillweed
50 g/2 oz grated cheese, e.g. kasseri,
   kashkaval or Cheddar
oil for frying

Garnish lemon wedges

Place the brains in a large bowl, add enough cold water to cover together with the vinegar and 2 teaspoons of salt and leave to soak for 20–30 minutes. Drain and remove any skin and veins. Place the brains in a saucepan with enough cold water to cover, add a teaspoon of salt and bring just to the boil. Lower the heat and simmer for about 15 minutes or until tender. Drain, place the brains in a bowl and mash with a fork. When the brains are cool, add the egg yolks, dill and cheese and mix to a smooth paste. Taste the mixture and add a little salt if necessary.

Put enough oil in a large frying pan to cover the bottom by about 0.6 cm/1/4 in and heat. Take tablespoons of the mixture and place in the oil. The mixture will spread a little so do not put them too close together. When set and golden on the undersides turn and cook the other sides until golden. Remove and drain on kitchen paper. Keep warm while you cook the remaining mixture in the same way.

Serve garnished with the lemon wedges.

aloo-chap spicy potato dip

A recipe from the Abadan region of Iran for those who like hot, spicy food. Adjust the quantity of chilli pepper to suit your particular taste. This dip is usually accompanied with a glass of ice cold vodka. It can be eaten either warm or cold.

450 g/1 lb potatoes, peeled and
   boiled until tender
100 ml/4 fl oz milk
3 tablespoons onion, finely chopped

2 tablespoons parsley, finely chopped
1 teaspoon salt
1 teaspoon chilli pepper (or more)
1/2 teaspoon black pepper

Garnish
1 tablespoon parsley, finely chopped
pinch cumin

pinch paprika

Put the cooked potatoes in a large bowl with the milk and mash until completely smooth. Add the remaining ingredients and mix until they are all well blended.

To serve place in a shallow bowl, smooth over the surface and garnish attractively with the parsley, paprika and cumin.

churba — soups

There are no consommé-type soups in the Middle East for their soups are often eaten as a meal with bread.

The repertoire is rich and varied, ranging from simple vegetable soups to meat and vegetable soups. Pulses — lentils, chickpeas, beans and peas as well as fruits and nuts are incorporated. Also pomegranate seeds, tripe, yoghurt, soured cream, rice, barley, wheat and burghul.

Often dried bread — toasted or fried in a little butter — is added to give more substance. The soups are garnished with hard-boiled eggs or parsley, tarragon or basil and when unexpected guests drop in — as they often do in the East — the hostess immediately adds some more stock so that the soup will go further and honour will be preserved.

To drink 'soup from the same spoon' is the greatest honour a Kurd can bestow a guest — be he friend or stranger and to 'share a bowl of soup' to most Middle Easterners is synonymous with the American Indians 'smoking the pipe of peace'.

vartabedi chorba lentil soup

And Esau said to Jacob, Feed me, I pray thee, with that same red pottage;
for I am faint . . .
And Jacob said, Sell me this day thy birthright.
And Esau said, Behold, I am at the point to die: and what profit shall this
birthright do to me?
And Jacob said, Swear to me this day; and he sware unto him:
and he sold his birthright unto Jacob.
Then Jacob gave Esau bread and pottage of lentils; . . .
thus Easu despised his birthright. (Genesis 25, 30-34)

Lentil soup is perhaps, next to the yoghurt-based soups, the most popular soup in the Middle East. Red, green or brown lentils can be used and there are literally hundreds of recipes. To try and do them justice I have included below two of the more famed ones. The first recipe is the simplest. It is called 'the young priest's soup'. This version is with macaroni, but often it comes with rice or with a combination of the two.

175 g/6 oz brown or red lentils, rinsed
1.8 litres/3 pints stock or water
100 g/4 oz macaroni, cut into
   2.5 cm/1 in pieces

50 g/2 oz butter or oil
1 onion, finely chopped
salt and chilli pepper to taste

Place the lentils in a large saucepan, add the stock or water and bring to the boil. Lower the heat and simmer until the lentils are nearly tender. You may need to add more stock or water, especially if using brown lentils which take longer to cook. Add the pieces of macaroni and continue simmering. You may need to add a little more water again. When both the lentils and macaroni are cooked heat the butter or oil in a small saucepan, add the onion and fry until golden. Pour into the soup, season with salt and chilli pepper to taste and serve.

   Serves 4–6 people.

shreet ads majroosh lentil soup with cumin

Popular throughout the Arab lands, Israel and Turkey. Arabs often break bread into small pieces and add to the soup to give it body. You can make croutons to serve in it by cutting a thick slice of bread into 1.2 cm/^{1}/$_2$ in cubes and frying in hot oil.

450 g/1 lb *ads majroosh* — red lentils, rinsed
1.8 litres/3 pints stock or water
1 onion, quartered
1 tomato, quartered
1 stick celery with leaves, chopped

1 clove garlic, coarsely chopped
50 g/2 oz butter
1 tablespoon onion, chopped
2 teaspoons ground cumin
1 teaspoon salt
1/4 teaspoon black pepper

Garnish lemon wedges, croutons

Place the stock or water in a large saucepan and bring to the boil. Add the lentils, onion, tomato, celery and garlic and stir. Reduce the heat and simmer for 30–45 minutes or until the lentils are tender. The length of time will depend on the quality of the lentils.

Meanwhile in a small pan melt half the butter and fry the chopped onion until golden. Remove from the heat.

Purée the soup in a liquidizer or by rubbing through a sieve with the back of a wooden spoon and discarding any remaining bits of vegetables. Return the soup to the saucepan and cook for a further 5 minutes, stirring all the time. Add the cumin, salt and pepper. Just before serving stir in the remaining butter. If you like a light soup add a little more water, otherwise simmer for a few more minutes.

Serve in individual bowls topped with a few freshly fried croutons and sprinkled with the fried onion. Serve the lemon wedges separately.

bezelye çorbasi split pea soup

A Turkish recipe from Anatolia which is old, tested and tasty. It is traditionally served with a bowl of natural yoghurt. A simpler version, which is an Arab favourite, omits the spinach and replaces the carrot with a finely chopped stalk of celery.

225 g/8 oz split peas, soaked overnight in cold water
25 g/1 oz butter
1 onion, thinly sliced
1 carrot, chopped

2 bay leaves
1 teaspoon salt
1/2 teaspoon black pepper
225 g/8 oz spinach, finely chopped
a little milk

Garnish
2 tablespoons fresh mint, finely chopped or 2 teaspoons dried mint

1 tablespoon paprika

Drain the split peas. Half fill a large saucepan with water or stock, add the split peas, bring to the boil.

Melt the butter in a small saucepan, add the onion and fry until soft.

Add the onion and butter to the split peas together with the carrot, bay leaves, salt and pepper. Simmer until the split peas are almost tender. Add the chopped spinach, mix well and continue to simmer. Add a little more water or stock if necessary. When all the ingredients are tender remove the bay leaves and purée the soup in a liquidizer. Return the soup to the saucepan and thin to the required consistency with a little milk. Stir in half the paprika and bring to the boil. Taste and adjust the seasoning if necessary. Serve in individual bowls sprinkled with the remaining paprika and the mint.

ab-gusht-e-bademjan aubergine and lentil soup

Bademjaneh Bam avaf nadoreh. Nothing in heaven or earth can stop the growth of Bam's aubergines. (Bam being a town in Iran famed for its aubergines.)

There are several variations of this Iranian aubergine soup. Some incorporate chunks of meat cut into 5 cm/2 in pieces. However, the recipe below is simple fare which is served with hot bread and a bowl of natural yoghurt. Turmeric gives the soup a light golden hue.

The Armenian soup *sumpoogi abour* incorporates 250 g/9 oz chickpeas and 1/2 teaspoon each of the following: thyme, mint, marjoram and cumin, but omits the lentils, turmeric, cinnamon and tomato purée. The chickpeas are boiled until tender and then half are added to the soup and the remaining are puréed and added to the soup just before serving to thicken it. It is garnished with chopped tarragon or parsley and a sprinkling of cumin.

2 small aubergines, peeled and sliced	1/2 teaspoon black pepper
50 g/2 oz butter	1 tablespoon tomato purée
1 onion, thinly sliced	1 teaspoon turmeric
100 g/4 oz brown lentils, rinsed	1/2 teaspoon cinnamon
1 teaspoon salt	1.8 litres/3 pints water

Arrange the aubergine slices on a large plate, sprinkle with salt and set aside for 30 minutes.

Meanwhile melt half the butter in a large saucepan and sauté the onion until soft and golden. Add the remaining butter.

Rinse the aubergine slices, dry with kitchen paper and add to the saucepan. Fry for a few minutes until lightly browned all over. Add all the remaining ingredients, stir well and bring to the boil. Cover the pan, lower the heat and simmer for 30–45 minutes or until the lentils are tender. Add a little more water if the soup becomes too thick.

Serves 4–6 people.

spanak çorbasi spinach soup

A recipe from eastern Turkey from the region of Kars famous for its kebabs and brigands.

25 g/1 oz butter
1 onion, thinly sliced
2 sticks rhubarb, sliced
1 stick celery, thinly sliced
1.8 litres/3 pints water
1½ teaspoons salt

450g/1 lb fresh spinach
 or 225 g/8 oz frozen leaf spinach
2 eggs, beaten
150 ml/¼ pint *smetana* (soured cream)
juice 1 lemon
½ teaspoon black pepper

Melt the butter in a saucepan, add the onion and fry until soft. Add the rhubarb and celery and a small amount of water. Cover and cook over a low heat until tender. Add the water and the salt and bring to a quick boil. If using fresh spinach wash very thoroughly and squeeze out excess water. If using frozen spinach then thaw and squeeze out the water. Chop the spinach and add it to the soup. If the spinach is fresh cook for 15 minutes, if frozen cook for 5 minutes.

Make a sauce of the beaten eggs, *smetana* and lemon juice with a little of the hot stock. Remove the soup from the heat and stir in the sauce until well blended. Add the black pepper and a little more salt if it is needed. Serve immediately.

Serves 4-6 people.

havuç çorbasi carrot soup

A wonderful soup from Anatolia with a creamy texture and delicate flavour.

50 g/2 oz butter
450 g/1 lb carrots, peeled
  and chopped into small pieces
1 teaspoon salt
½ teaspoon black pepper
1 teaspoon sugar

½ teaspoon dillweed
1.2 litres/2 pints water
scant 1 tablespoon flour
75 ml/3 fl oz milk
2 egg yolks

Garnish **2 tablespoons walnuts, finely chopped**

Melt half the butter in a saucepan, add the carrots and sauté for a few minutes until well coated with butter. Add about 300 ml/½ pint water, together with the salt, pepper, sugar and dillweed. Bring to the boil and simmer until the carrots are very soft. Drain the carrots retaining a little of the liquid to help purée them if necessary. Place the carrots in a liquidizer and blend to a smooth purée.

Bring 1.2 litres/2 pints of water to the boil in a large saucepan, add the carrot purée, stir well and continue simmering.

Meanwhile melt the remaining butter in a small saucepan, remove from the heat and stir in the flour. Slowly add the milk and stir until smooth. Return to the heat and stir constantly until the mixture thickens. Remove from the heat, add the egg yolks and stir until well blended and smooth. Add some of the hot soup, a little at a time, and stir constantly until it is thin and well blended. Return this mixture to the soup, stir and heat through, but do not boil or it will curdle. Serve in individual bowls sprinkled with the chopped walnuts.

tarkana burghul and yoghurt soup

One of the very few ancient recipes that has come down to us virtually intact. The nomadic tribes of Asia made *tarkana* from pellet-shaped pieces of dough, made from flour, salt, eggs and water, which were left to dry in the sun. They were cooked in salted water and eaten either as thick soup, or in stews and casseroles made with meat, poultry or wild game.

Tarkana is made in this way in Hungary, Romania and the Balkans. In the Middle East however — Turkey, Armenia and Syria only — burghul and yoghurt are used to make it. This is wholesome, earthy soup which is a favourite in winter. You can buy *tarkana* ready made from Greek and Armenian shops. The Syrians and Lebanese call it *kishk*. However, as always where possible, I suggest you make your own. It is quite simple to make.

Tarkana

12.5 g/^{1}/$_2$ oz yeast	^{1}/$_2$ teaspoon salt
250 ml/8 fl oz warm water	225 g/8 oz large burghul
225 g/8 oz plain flour, sifted	300 ml/^{1}/$_2$ pint yoghurt

Dissolve the yeast in 3 tablespoons of the water in a large bowl. Mix in the rest of the water. Add the flour, salt, burghul and yoghurt and mix with a wooden spoon until well blended. Cover with a clean tea towel and leave to rest overnight.

The following day form the dough into walnut-sized pieces, then flatten between your palms to 0.3 cm/^{1}/$_8$ in thickness. Arrange on a baking sheet.

Traditionally these *tarkanas* are dried under the sun, but a warm oven will do just as well. Place in a warm oven, about 160°C, 325°F, gas mark 3, and when dried on one side turn over with a spatula and dry thoroughly.

Break into smaller pieces and store in airtight jars. This quantity will make enough *tarkana* for 6 separate meals.

Tarkana soup

about 1.2 litres/2 pints water or stock	1^1/$_2$ teaspoons dried mint
50 g/2 oz tarkana	^{1}/$_2$ teaspoon salt
25 g/1 oz butter	^{1}/$_4$ teaspoon paprika
1 large onion, finely chopped	150 ml/^{1}/$_4$ pint yoghurt

Bring the water or stock to the boil in a large saucepan. Add the *tarkana*, lower the heat and simmer for about 30 minutes or until the *tarkana* is soft.

Meanwhile, melt the butter in a small saucepan, add the onion and fry until soft and golden. Add the mint, salt and paprika and mix well. Remove and keep warm.

When the *tarkana* is done add the mint-mixture, mix well and simmer for a further 5 minutes. Remove from the heat and just before serving stir in the yoghurt little by little. Serve immediately.

churba kavkaski vegetable and rice soup

A soup from the Caucasus which is rich and wholesome with a creamy-pink colour. It is similar to many southern Russian soups, but it has a definite Middle Eastern flavour.

25 g/1 oz butter or ghee
1 onion, finely chopped
175 g/6 oz white cabbage, shredded
1 beetroot, peeled and diced
2 sticks celery, diced
2 carrots, peeled and diced
3 tomatoes, blanched, peeled and sliced

1.8 litres/3 pints water
1½ teaspoons salt
½ teaspoon black pepper
175 g/6 oz long grain rice, washed
    thoroughly under cold water
2 egg yolks
200 ml/⅓ pint milk

Melt the butter or *ghee* in a large saucepan, add the onion and fry until golden. Lower the heat, add the remaining vegetables and fry gently for 5 minutes. Add the water, salt and pepper and bring to the boil. Lower the heat and simmer for 15 minutes. Add the rice, cover and continue to simmer for about 20 minutes or until the rice and carrots are tender. Turn off the heat, remove the lid and leave to cool.

Beat the egg yolks and milk together in a small bowl and very slowly stir into the soup. Do make sure that the soup is really cool or else it will curdle. When ready to serve re-heat, but do not allow to boil. Taste, adjust seasoning if necessary and serve immediately. Serves 4–6 people.

gololig rice, tomatoes and meatballs soup

A filling Armenian soup of rice, tomatoes and meatballs flavoured with tarragon.

There are many such soups in the Caucasus, some having chunks of meat or pieces of chicken or even fishballs.

225 g/8 oz lamb, minced twice
    if possible as this will make it
    easier to knead
1 large onion, finely chopped
1 tablespoon parsley, finely chopped
1 egg, beaten

salt and pepper to taste
1.8 litres/3 pints stock or water
2 tablespoons tomato purée
1 heaped teaspoon dried tarragon
50 g/2 oz long grain rice, washed
12.5 g/½ oz butter

Put the meat into a large mixing bowl, add half the onion, the parsley, egg and ½ a teaspoon each of the salt and black pepper. Knead the mixture until well blended and smooth. It will help if you dampen your hands with cold water from time to time. Break off small pieces of the mixture and roll between your palms to make small balls about 2 cm/3/4 in in diameter.

Bring the stock or water to the boil in a large saucepan and season it with tomato purée, tarragon and salt and pepper to taste. Gently add the meatballs and simmer for 20 minutes. Stir in the rice and cook for a further 10–15 minutes or until the rice is tender.

Just before serving melt the butter in a small saucepan, add the remaining onion and fry until golden. Stir into the soup and serve immediately. Serves 4–6 people.

melokhia melokhia leaf soup

A classic Egyptian soup, pre-dating the pyramids, that was the food of the peasants — *fellehine* — but today is the pride and joy of the middle class Egyptians.

Melokhia (see Glossary) is usually eaten twice daily and each family has its 'authentic' recipe.

It is rather difficult to purchase fresh *melokhia* outside Egypt, Libya and Cyprus, but dried versions can be bought from some Middle Eastern stores.

Stock

a chicken or a rabbit or a knuckle
   of beef or veal
1 onion, quartered

2 tomatoes, blanched, peeled
   and quartered
1 clove garlic
salt and pepper to taste

Soup

50 g/2 oz dried *melokhia* leaves
   or 450 g/1 lb fresh leaves if you
   can find them
3 cloves garlic

2 tablespoons butter or oil
1 tablespoon cayenne pepper
1 tablespoon ground coriander
Salt and pepper to taste

First make the stock by placing all the ingredients in a large saucepan, covering well with water and simmering for 2–3 hours. Add more water from time to time when necessary. You will need about 1 litre/2–3 pints of stock for the soup. Remove any scum which may form and adjust the seasoning at the end of the cooking time. Strain the stock into a large saucepan.

Crush the dried *melokhia* leaves. If they are not brittle enough then dry them out in a warm oven for a few minutes. Place them in a bowl and moisten with a little hot water until they double in bulk. Add them to the stock and simmer for 20–30 minutes.

Make the garlic sauce — *taklia* — by crushing the garlic with a little salt and frying in the butter or oil. When it turns brown add the cayenne pepper and coriander and stir to a smooth paste. Add this to the soup, cover and simmer for a further 2 minutes. It is important to stir occasionally and not to overcook as the leaves will otherwise sink to the bottom.

Finally check the seasoning and adjust accordingly. Serves 4–6 people.

churba-bi-banadora tomato and onion soup

A typical Arab soup — this one is from Syria-Lebanon. There are many variations. Sometimes the soup is prepared without meat, but traditionally chunks of lamb, or goat, are added to give substance. The Syrian peasants also add pieces of dry bread to make a really hearty meal.

40 g/1¹/₂ oz butter or ghee
2 onions, thinly sliced
450 g/1 lb lamb, cut into
   3.5–5 cm/1¹/₂–2 in cubes
2 cloves garlic, finely chopped
900 g/2 lbs tomatoes, blanched
   and chopped

1 tablespoon tomato purée
1.8 litres/3 pints water
1 teaspoon salt
¹/₂ teaspoon black pepper
¹/₂ teaspoon dillweed

Garnish 2 tablespoons parsley, finely chopped

Melt the butter or *ghee* in a large, deep saucepan. Add the onions and cook for about 5 minutes or until soft, but do not overcook. Add the meat and garlic, stir well, cover the pan and leave to simmer for 15 minutes. Add the chopped tomatoes, stir well and continue cooking. Dilute the tomato purée in a little water and add to the pan. Stir well then add the remaining water, the salt, pepper and dillweed and bring to the boil. Lower the heat, cover the pan and simmer for about 1 hour or until the meat is very tender. Taste and adjust seasoning if necessary. Serve immediately with a garnish of a little chopped parsley.
   Serves 4–6 people.

marak avocado im batzal

onion and avocado soup

An Israeli soup making use of avocados which the *kibbutzim* first introduced into the region in the early years of this century. Avocados have become big business, are imported in large quantities and have inspired Israeli chefs to exploit this pear-shaped fruit with its distinctive flavour.

4 tablespoons oil
1 onion, chopped
2 spring onions, chopped
2 cloves garlic, crushed
1.2 litres/2 pints chicken stock
salt to taste

¹/₂ teaspoon black pepper
¹/₄ teaspoon nutmeg
1 ripe avocado, peeled and mashed
1 teaspoon lemon juice
grated rind 1 lemon
1 egg yolk

Garnish 1 tablespoon parsley, finely chopped

Heat the oil in a large saucepan, add the onion, spring onions and garlic and sauté for about 5 minutes, stirring frequently, until the onion is golden. Add the stock, salt, pepper and nutmeg and bring to the boil. Lower the heat and simmer for 30 minutes, stirring occasionally. Mash the lemon juice and rind into the avocado and add it to the soup. Mix it in well and simmer for a further 5 minutes.

Beat the egg yolk in a small bowl, add a few tablespoons of the soup and mix well. Add the egg mixture to the soup, stir well and simmer for a further 5 minutes. Serve garnished with the chopped parsley.

mantabour dumpling soup

One day the villagers were gathered under the old walnut tree dining on bread, cheese, fresh vegetables and some fruit. A large cauldron of *mantabour* adorned the dinner table. Boloz Mugush passed by on his donkey.

'Welcome brother Mugush,' the villagers called. 'Just the man to give an answer to an intriguing problem.'

He got off his donkey and joined the villagers.

'Problems?' he enquired. Just then his eyes caught sight of the cauldron, his nostrils inhaled the rich aroma of the soup. He felt a pang in his stomach. He had not eaten for over twelve hours.

'Life, brother,' said the village elder, 'death and immortality.'

'Life is a bowl of mantabour. Some like it, some don't, some want it cool, others warm, some with tomato, others prefer yoghurt. Life and death can be found in a bowl of wholesome mantabour. As for eternity it is mere extension. When I have finished eating a bowl of this soup, what is there left? Only the memory of a wonderful experience.'

His eyes were now fixed on the bubbling cauldron.

'Eternity, I'll tell you about eternity. The Mongols came in their hordes, burning, raping, destroying all. Where are they now? Gone to eternity. What have they left behind?'

'Nothing.' Someone shouted.

'Wrong,' he interjected, 'Manti; thank God for that.' Saying this he got up and helped himself to a bowl of hot mantabour.

'This then, my friend, is immortality.'

Manti then, is of Mongolian origin (*mantu* in Korean and Chinese), and variations of this dish exist throughout Europe and Asia under different names; *manti* in Turkish, *dyushbara* in Azerbaijanian, *mantabour* in Armenian, *vareniky* in Ukrainian and *pelmeny* in Russian. The finest *manti* dishes are prepared by the Turkomans of Anatolia and the Armenians.

There are many variations. I have chosen two; one with a tomato sauce and the other with a yoghurt sauce.

Dough

225 g/8 oz plain flour
salt

1 egg
cold water

Filling

225 g/8 oz minced lamb
1 onion, chopped
1 tablespoon parsley, chopped

1 egg
1$^{1}/_{2}$ teaspoons salt
1 teaspoon black pepper

Tomato sauce

1.8 litres/3 pints water or stock
50 g/2 oz butter
6 tomatoes, blanched, peeled
    and chopped

4 cloves garlic, crushed
1 teaspoon basil
2 tablespoons tomato purée
salt and black pepper

Sift the flour and salt into a mixing bowl, break an egg into the centre and begin to knead. Adding a little water at a time, continue kneading until you have a dough which comes away from the sides of the bowl and the fingers easily. Continue kneading for a few minutes and then set aside.

In another bowl mix together the ingredients for the filling.

Flour a large working surface. Divide the dough in two and roll out one ball until it is as thin as possible. With a circular cutter 2.5–3.5 cm/1–1$^{1}/_{2}$ in in diameter, cut out as many circles of pastry as possible. Gather up the scraps, roll them out and cut more circles. Repeat with the other ball of dough. Place a small ball of the meat mixture in the centre of each circle. Dampen the edge of the circle and then pinch the edges up to make 4 corners which trap the meat inside but do not hide it completely from view. Continue until you have used up all the ingredients. You have now made the *manti*.

In a large saucepan bring to the boil about 1.8 litres/3 pints of lightly salted water or stock. Put the *manti* in gently and simmer for 30 minutes.

Meanwhile, melt the butter in a small saucepan, add the tomatoes and cook for 2–3 minutes. Add the garlic, basil, tomato purée and salt and pepper to taste. Stir this tomato mixture into the soup and simmer for a further 10 minutes. Taste to check the seasoning and add a little more water if the sauce is too thick. Serves 4–6 people.

Yoghurt sauce

1.2 litres/2 pints stock
1 teaspoon salt
225 g/8 oz labna (drained yoghurt) — see recipe p. 376

1 clove garlic, crushed
2–3 teaspoons dried mint

Follow the instructions above up to the third paragraph, but use stock for boiling instead of water. When ready to serve bring the stock to the boil in a large saucepan. Carefully transfer the *manti* to the stock and simmer for 5 minutes. Remove from the heat, add the *labna* and garlic and stir gently for about 3 minutes. Do not boil the soup or it will curdle. Rub the mint to a powder between the palms of your hands and stir into the soup. Serve immediately.

eshkaneh onion soup

A classic of the Iranian cuisine, this soup is a speciality of the region of Shiraz. It is an unusual soup with a sweet and sour flavour, traditionally eaten with bread and a bowl of fresh herbs.

If you cannot find limes then use lemons as suggested.

60 g/2¹/₂ oz butter
3 onions, thinly sliced
2 tablespoons flour
1.8 litres/3 pints water
1¹/₂ teaspoons salt
1 teaspoon black pepper

1 teaspoon turmeric
juice 2 lemons or 1 lime
2 tablespoons sugar
1 tablespoon dried mint
¹/₂ teaspoon cinnamon
2 eggs

Melt the butter in a large saucepan, add the sliced onions and fry for several minutes until soft and golden.

Place the flour in a small bowl and dissolve in a few tablespoons of water. Stir this mixture into the fried onions. Now add the water and stir well. Add the salt, pepper and turmeric, stir and simmer for about 30 minutes. Now stir in the lemon or lime juice and the sugar and simmer for a further 10 minutes. Just before removing from the heat stir in the mint and cinnamon. When ready to serve break the eggs into a bowl, beat thoroughly, stir into the soup and serve immediately.

Serves 4-6 people.

ashe-e-joe barley soup

A staple diet of Anatolian villagers, barley soup has many variations. This recipe is from Iranian Azerbaijan and is a rather richer version. Often meat is added; about 350 g/12 oz cut into 5 cm/2 in chunks; as well as kidney beans, lentils and vegetables such as spinach, leeks, fresh coriander, etc. Yoghurt is an essential part of this soup.

100 g/4 oz pearl barley
40 g/1¹/₂ oz butter
1 large onion, finely chopped
100 g/4 oz chickpeas, soaked
    overnight in cold water
1.2 litres/2 pints stock

1 teaspoon salt
¹/₂ teaspoon black pepper
1 teaspoon turmeric
100 g/4 oz fresh dillweed or
    spinach, washed and finely chopped
300 ml/¹/₂ pint yoghurt

Garnish
1 tablespoon dried mint sautéed in 1 tablespoon butter

Place the barley in a bowl, cover with water and leave to soak for 1 hour.

Melt the butter in a small saucepan, add the onion and fry until the onion is soft and turning golden.

Drain the chickpeas and pearl barley and place in a large saucepan with the stock and bring to the boil. Remove any scum that appears on the surface. Add the salt, pepper and turmeric, stir well, lower the heat and simmer for 30 minutes. Add the dillweed or spinach and any other chopped vegetables of your choice and simmer for a further 30 minutes or until the chickpeas are tender.

Put the yoghurt in a bowl and, adding a few tablespoons of the hot soup at a time, stir until the yoghurt has been well diluted. Pour the soup into a large tureen and stir in the yoghurt mixture.

Quickly sauté the mint in the butter and then pour over the top of the soup. Serve immediately.

ashe-e-anar pomegranate soup

A locked garden is my sister, my bride
a closed spring, a sealed fountain.
Your branches are a pomegranate orchard
with all precious fruit, henna and roses
saffron and spikenard, cassia, cinnamon
with frankincense trees, myrrh and aloes,
all perfect spices. . .
Eat, my friend, drink —
lover, be drunk with love.
The Song of Songs

This soup is popular throughout the Caucasus and northern Iran. It has recently been introduced into Israel by immigrants from the USSR.

You can buy pomegranate syrup, *dibs ruman,* from good Middle Eastern stores or you can prepare your own as suggested in the Glossary section.

The people on the Caspian coastline often add small meatballs, while the Armenians prefer small *gololig* made of burghul and meat — see section on *kibbi.*

1 tablespoon butter
1 onion, chopped
4 spring onions, thinly sliced
75 g/3 oz long grain rice, washed
   thoroughly under cold running
   water
1¹/2 teaspoons salt
¹/2 teaspoon black pepper
1 teaspoon dried oregano

4 tablespoons parsley, finely chopped
100 g/4 oz fresh spinach washed
   thoroughly, squeezed dry and chopped
1.8 litres/3 pints water and
   2 tablespoons pomegranate syrup
   or 1.5 litres/2¹/2 pints water and
   about 300 ml/¹/2 pint pomegranate
   juice and 2 tablespoons sugar

Garnish
1 tablespoon dried mint
¹/2 teaspoon white pepper

¹/2 teaspoon cinnamon

Melt the butter in a large saucepan, add the onion and fry until soft and turning golden. Add the rice, salt and pepper and fry gently for a few minutes. Stir in the oregano, parsley and spinach. Add the water and pomegranate syrup or juice and bring to the boil. Lower the heat and simmer for 20–25 minutes or until the rice and spinach are tender. Remove the soup from the heat.

Mix the mint, cinnamon and white pepper together and sprinkle over the soup. Taste for seasoning. The soup should have a pungent sweet-sour flavour.

Serves 4–6 people.

avgolemono soupa egg and lemon soup

Popular throughout Turkey and the Arab speaking countries, this is a Greek speciality — hence its Greek name. In Arabic it is called *beid bi lemoun* and in Turkish *terbiyeli çorba*.

This soup does not reheat well so make just the amount you need and prepare it just before serving.

Although in Greece fish or meat stocks are used, amongst Turks and Arabs chicken stock is the norm and I prefer the latter.

1.5 litres/2¹/2 pints stock, chicken,
  meat or fish
50 g/2 oz long grain rice, washed
  thoroughly under cold running water
  or 50 g/2 oz any type of small
  soup noodles

1/2 teaspoon salt
3 eggs, separated
juice 2 lemons
1/4 teaspoon white pepper

Garnish 2 tablespoons parsley or chives, finely chopped

Bring the stock to the boil in a large saucepan. Add the rice or noodles and salt, lower the heat and simmer for 15–20 minutes or until tender.

Meanwhile, in a large bowl beat the egg whites until stiff. Add the egg yolks and continue beating until creamy. Gradually add the lemon juice, beating constantly until thick and frothy. Add a few ladlesful of the hot soup to the eggs and stir vigorously.

Remove the soup from the heat and gradually pour the egg mixture back into the saucepan making sure that you beat constantly or else the soup will curdle. Beat for 1–2 minutes, season with the pepper and serve immediately garnished with the parsley or chives.

NB Once the rice or noodles are cooked it is important that the soup is not brought to the boil again.

churba-ful-sudani peanut soup

An Egyptian soup of African origin. It has a rich earthy flavour and is popular amongst the *felehine*.

450 g/1 lb fresh, shelled peanuts	600 ml/1 pint stock
600 ml/1 pint milk	salt and pepper to taste

Garnish 4 tablespoons of double cream or 2 tablespoons melted *ghee*

Spread the peanuts over a baking tray and place in an oven preheated to 190°C, 375°F, gas mark 5. Roast for about 15 minutes or until the skins can be easily removed. The length of time will depend on the freshness of the peanuts. Leave to cool and then rub off the skins by squeezing the nuts between thumb and forefinger. Grind the nuts in a blender or pass through a mincer. Pour the powdered nuts into a large saucepan and add the milk, little by little, stirring constantly. Stir in the stock and bring to the boil. Season to taste with the salt and pepper. Simmer for about 10 minutes, stirring frequently. Add a little more water or stock if the soup is too thick for your taste.

Serve in individual bowls topped with a little cream or melted *ghee*.

madzounabour yoghurt soup

'No one will call his madzoun black.' — No one will accept his mistakes.

The Middle Eastern repertoire is particularly rich in yoghurt-based soups; and I have been reliably informed that there are more such soups than the entire range offered by Messrs Heinz! Consequently it has been difficult to choose between rivalling recipes. I have categorized my choice thus:

a) Plain yoghurt soups

b) Soups with rice, noodles, barley, etc.

c) Yoghurt with meat

Always use fresh natural yoghurt and make sure it is stabilized. (See Glossary, for the preparation of yoghurt and on how to stabilize it.)

600 ml/1 pint yoghurt	3/4 teaspoon black pepper
1 egg	50 g/2 oz butter
600 ml/1 pint water	1 small onion, finely chopped
1 teaspoon salt	2 teaspoons mint, dried and crushed

Garnish

2 thick slices bread cut into 1.2 cm/1/2 in cubes	cooking oil

Put the yoghurt into a saucepan. Add the egg to the yoghurt and mix well with a wooden spoon. Put on a low heat and stir continuously until the yoghurt is just begining to boil. Add the water, season with the salt and pepper and return to the low heat.

Meanwhile, in a small saucepan melt the butter, add the onion and mint and cook until the onion is soft, but not brown. Pour into the soup, bring to the boil and simmer very gently for a few minutes.

Heat a little cooking oil in a small saucepan and when it is very hot add the cubes of bread and fry until golden and crisp. Remove from the fat and put into a bowl.

To serve put the soup into individual bowls and add the croutons at the last moment.

tutmaj yoghurt soup with noodles

Any small pasta is suitable although, ideally, the noodles should be made at home as they still are in most villages in Turkey and Iran.

Traditionally *chortan* — dried powdered yoghurt — was used to make most yoghurt soups, but fresh natural yoghurt, preferably home-made, is perfectly suitable.

900 ml/1¹/₂ pints yoghurt
2 egg yolks
450 ml/³/₄ pint water
100–125 g/4–5 oz noodles
1 teaspoon salt

1/2 teaspoon pepper
50 g/2 oz butter
1 onion, finely chopped
2 tablespoons dried mint, crushed

Place the yoghurt and egg yolks in a large saucepan and mix well with a wooden spoon. Bring slowly to the boil over a low heat, stirring constantly. Stir in the water, noodles, salt and pepper and bring to the boil. Lower the heat and simmer for 8–10 minutes until the pasta is just cooked.

Meanwhile, melt the butter in a small saucepan, add the onion and mint, and fry until the onions are soft. Pour the onion mixture into the soup and stir well. Serve immediately.

NB Another soup — *gololigi-tutmaj* — has the same ingredients as above with the addition of 225 g/8 oz minced meat seasoned with 1 teaspoon salt, 1/2 teaspoon black pepper and 1/2 teaspoon paprika, shaped into small marble-sized balls and fried in butter, then added to the soup to give it substance.

dovga yoghurt soup with meatballs

An Azerbaijanian soup from the Caucasus which is rich and full of flavour. Wherever possible use fresh herbs.

225 g/8 oz minced meat (lamb or beef)
1 onion, finely chopped
salt and black pepper to taste
900 ml/1½ pints yoghurt
1 tablespoon flour
1.2 litres/2 pints stock or water
25 g/1 oz long grain rice, washed
   thoroughly under cold, running
   water

50 g/2 oz chickpeas, soaked
   overnight in cold water, cooked in
   water until just tender and drained
100 g/4 oz spinach, chopped
3 tablespoons parsley, finely chopped
2 spring onions, finely chopped
3 tablespoons fresh dill, chopped or
   1 tablespoon dried dillweed

In a large bowl mix the meat, onion, salt and pepper. Knead until well blended and smooth. Make small walnut-sized balls and put to one side.

Pour the yoghurt into a large saucepan.

Put the flour into a small bowl and blend to a smooth paste with a little of the stock or water. Stir this into the yoghurt and then stir in the remaining stock or water. Season with a little salt and pepper. Add the meatballs and rice and, on a low heat, simmer for 10–12 minutes, stirring gently and very frequently. Add the cooked chickpeas and the spinach and simmer for a further 10–12 minutes until the rice is tender and the meat is cooked. Add the parsley, onion and dill and cook for a further 5 minutes. Serve immediately.

NB An Armenian soup — *gololig tzavarov* — incorporates 50 g/2 oz coarse burghul and omits the rice and chickpeas.

Serves 4-6 people.

ashe-e-reshteh   vegetable and noodle soup

A thick wholesome soup from Kurdistan that is a meal in itself. You can omit the spinach and leek and incorporate potatoes cut into large cubes, or you can increase the quantity of noodles to 75 or 100 g/3 or 4 oz.

Here is a story about Nasrudin Hodja and his deep knowledge of Kurdish. Hearing that a man wanted to learn the Kurdish language, Nasrudin offered to teach him. Nasrudin's own knowledge of Kurdish was limited to a few words.

'We shall start with the word for "hot soup"' said the Mulla. 'In Kurdish, this is Aash.'
'I don't understand, Mulla. How would you say "cold soup"?
'You never say "cold soup". The Kurds like their soup hot.'

25 g/1 oz butter
1 onion, sliced
1 tablespoon chickpeas, soaked
   overnight in cold water
1 tablespoon dried haricot beans,
   soaked overnight in cold water
1 tablespoon brown lentils
1/4 teaspoon turmeric
2 1/2 litres/4 pints stock
1 tablespoon salt

few grindings black pepper
2 tablespoons parsley, chopped
100 g/4 oz leek, chopped and washed
100 g/4 oz spinach, chopped and
   washed
50 g/2 oz egg noodles
1 tablespoon flour mixed to a paste
   with 1–2 tablespoons water
300 ml/1/2 pint yoghurt

Garnish
25 g/1 oz butter

1 tablespoon chopped fresh mint
   or 1 teaspoon dried mint

Melt the butter in a large saucepan, add the onion and fry until soft and golden. Drain the chickpeas and beans and add to the pan together with the lentils, turmeric, stock, salt and pepper. Bring to the boil, lower the heat, cover and simmer for 1 hour or until the chickpeas and beans are tender. Add more water if necessary. Add the parsley, leek and spinach and simmer for 20 minutes. Stir in the noodles and cook for a further 10–12 minutes until tender.

Spoon a few tablespoons of the soup into the paste and then stir the paste slowly into the soup. Remove the soup from the heat and stir in the yoghurt. Just before serving melt the butter in a small pan and fry the mint for a few minutes. Pour it over the soup and serve.

Serves 4–6 people.

dugun çorbasi wedding soup

Soon after his return from the mosque, the bridegroom leaves his friends in a lower apartment enjoying their pipes and coffee and sherbet. If the bridegroom is a youth or young man, it is considered proper that he, as well as the bride, should exhibit some degree of bashfulness; the bride has a shawl thrown over her head; and the bridegroom must give her a present of money which is called 'the price of the uncovering of the face', before he attempts to remove this, which she does not allow him to do without some apparent reluctance, if not violent resistance, in order to show her maidenly modesty ... the bridegroom now, in most cases, sees the face of his bride for the first time. Having satisfied his curiosity respecting her personal charms, he calls to the women (who generally collect at the door, where they wait in anxious suspense) to raise their cries of joy; and the shrill sounds make known to the persons below and in the neighbourhood, and often, responded to by other women, spread still further the news, that he has acknowledged himself satisfied with his bride. (From *Modern Egyptians*.)

He then descends to join his friends and no doubt eat heartily a bowl of the wedding soup — and, who knows, more often than not he probably needed it!

50 g/2 oz butter	2–3 teaspoons salt
1 onion, thinly sliced	1/2 teaspoon black pepper
450 g/1 lb lean leg of lamb, cut into	2 eggs
2.5 cm/1 in pieces (450 g/1 lb of	1 tablespoon lemon juice
lean beef can be substituted)	2 tablespoons yoghurt
1.8 litres/3 pints water	

Melt the butter in a large saucepan; add the onion and sauté until golden. Add the meat and sauté for 5–8 minutes or until nicely browned. Add the water and simmer for half an hour or until the meat is tender — removing any scum which may appear on the surface. Add the salt and pepper and mix well.

In a small bowl beat together the eggs, lemon juice and yoghurt. Stir a few tablespoons of the stock into the yoghurt mixture, mixing well between each one. Pour the yoghurt mixture into the soup, taste and adjust seasoning if necessary. Serve immediately.

Serves 4 - 6 people.

midya çorbasi mussel soup

A classic from the days when the Ottoman rulers paraded up and down the Sea of Marmara in their gilded craft, embraced by their ageing entourage of followers, slaves, eunuchs and concubines. They no doubt stopped at one of the many small restaurants on the Bosphorous to eat a bowl of mussel soup followed by a kebab of red mullet, pike or bass.

1.5 litres /2¹/2 pints mussels
1.5 litres/2¹/2 pints water
2 cloves garlic, chopped
1 large onion, coarsely chopped

2 tablespoons flour
4 tablespoons milk
¹/2 teaspoon black pepper
¹/2 teaspoon allspice

Garnish **2 tablespoons parsley, finely chopped**

Scrape the mussels, transfer to a colander and wash thoroughly under cold running water. Place the mussels in a large saucepan with the water, garlic and onion and bring to the boil. Simmer until the mussels open up and then remove them with a slotted spoon and reserve. Strain the liquid in the pan through a fine sieve into another pan.

Now remove the mussel shells with a sharp knife and set the mussels aside.

Return the soup to the heat and bring to the boil.

Place the flour in a small bowl and mix to a smooth paste with the milk. Stir in a few tablespoons of the soup to make a thin paste and then stir into the soup. Add the mussels, stir gently and cook for 3-4 minutes. Season with the black pepper and allspice, stir and remove from the heat. Transfer to a soup tureen, garnish with the parsley and serve immediately.

kharcho chicken soup with walnuts

A soup from Georgia with a fascinating combination of chicken, walnuts and sour plums.

1-1.5 kg/2-3 lb chicken, cut into
    serving pieces
1.8 litres/3 pints water
1 teaspoon salt
1 large onion, finely chopped
3 large tomatoes, blanched, peeled,
seeded and mashed

175 g/6 oz walnuts, coarsely chopped
6-8 sour plums, thinly sliced
2 cloves garlic, crushed
    1 teaspoon cinnamon
    ¹/2 teaspoon black pepper
    2 bay leaves

Garnish **3-4 tablespoons coriander leaves, fresh dill or parsley, finely chopped**

Put the chicken pieces in a large saucepan with the water and salt. Bring to the boil and remove any scum which appears on the surface. Add the onion, lower the heat, cover and simmer for about 1 hour or until the chicken is tender. Remove the pieces of chicken and, when cool enough to handle, remove the flesh and cut into small pieces. Return the chicken to the pan and add the tomatoes, walnuts, plums, garlic, cinnamon, pepper and bay leaves. Bring to the boil and cook, uncovered, for a further 10-15 minutes. Serve garnished with the herbs of your choice.

Serves 4-6 people.

shusha gololig stuffed meatball soup

A classic of the Armenian cuisine from the region of Susha in Kharapak. Instead of each meatball being stuffed with a whole hard-boiled egg, some people like to chop the eggs and mix with 1 tablespoon chopped pistachio nuts (or walnuts), 2 tablespoons fried minced onion and 1/2 teaspoon salt. This is then formed into 4 balls which are then enclosed in the minced meat mixture. You can use large burghul (cracked wheat) instead of rice.

Meatballs

450 g/1 lb lamb or beef,
    minced twice
1 teaspoon salt
1 small onion, finely chopped
2 teaspoons plain flour
1 tablespoon milk

1 tablespoon brandy
1 small egg, beaten
1/2 teaspoon black pepper
2 tablespoons parsley, finely chopped
4 hard-boiled eggs, shelled

Soup

3 tablespoons *ghee*
1 small onion, finely chopped
1.8 litres/3 pints stock, lamb or beef
1 tablespoon salt

75 g/3 oz long grain rice, washed
    under cold running water
3 tablespoons fresh tarragon, finely
    chopped or 2 teaspoons dried tarragon

Garnish 1 tablespoon sumac powder (optional)

Place the minced meat and salt in a large bowl and knead. Add the chopped onion, flour, milk, brandy, egg, pepper and parsley and knead for 5–10 minutes until the mixture is well blended and smooth. Cover and refrigerate for 30 minutes.

Remove the bowl from the refrigerator and divide the meat into 4 equal parts. Keeping your hand damp, roll each portion of meat into a ball and then hollow out each ball. Place a hard-boiled egg in each hollow and build the meat up around them until the eggs are completely and evenly enclosed. With dampened hands smooth off the surfaces and form into slightly oval shapes. Refrigerate the meatballs while you prepare the soup.

Melt the *ghee* in a small pan, add the onion and fry until golden.

Bring the stock to the boil in a large saucepan, add the salt and rice, lower the heat and simmer for 10 minutes. Add the meatballs and cook for a further 10–12 minutes. Add the onion mixture and the tarragon to the soup and simmer for a further 5 minutes. Just before serving halve the meatballs and serve in individual bowls with a little sumac sprinkled over the top.

Serves 4–6 people.

salads

To Middle Easterners a salad ranges from *hummus-bi-tahina*, *taramasalata* and similar puréed dishes through the numerous boiled and fried vegetable salads to the fresh vegetables dressed in olive oil, lemon juice, yoghurt and other combinations. Indeed, all the dishes under the headings '*Mezzeh*' and 'Vegetables', together with those in this section, would be regarded as salads.

Colour, texture and presentation are paramount in the mind of the housewife when she prepares her salads. Unusual combinations of fruit and vegetables; nuts and vegetables; as well as cold meats such as tongue, liver and meatballs; are served prior to, or traditionally with, warm meat, poultry, kebabs or stews.

Talmudic, Koranic and the native folklore traditions recommend the use of certain vegetables for medicinal, sexual and psychological cures; 'Radishes are good for fever .... which may be caused by eating hot bread' or 'Garlic destroys parasites in the entrails' are amongst many beliefs still held by most Middle Easterners.

The four basic dressing ingredients are: olive oil — believed to possess almost supernatural healing qualities; lemon juice; wine-vinegar and yoghurt — the supposed cure for all intestinal maladies.

olive oil and lemon dressing

Although by far the most popular, this dressing of Greek origin — *latho-lemono* — is almost unknown throughout Iran, Iraq, the Gulf States and parts of the Caucasus where vegetables are eaten raw sprinkled with a little salt — *aghtsan*.

100 ml/4 fl oz olive oil
4–5 tablespoons fresh lemon juice
2 teaspoons parsley, finely chopped,
   or oregano or mint or dillweed

1 clove garlic, crushed (optional)
1 teaspoon salt
1/2 teaspoon black pepper

Mix the ingredients together in a bowl with a fork before pouring over the vegetables.
   You can keep this dressing in a screw-top bottle or jar and refrigerate for further use. Before using remember to shake well.
   You can increase or decrease the proportions according to your personal taste. It is excellent with all fresh or boiled vegetables.

oil and vinegar dressing

Popular in Cyprus, Greece, Turkey, Syria and Lebanon.
   The vinegar should be wine vinegar.

Prepare as for the oil and lemon dressing above.
   Cypriots often add 1/2 teaspoon or more of dry mustard — *lathoxitho*.
   In Turkey this dressing — *sirkeli salatasi* — is served with any raw vegetable, as well as dried beans and beetroot salads.

yoghurt dressing

Yoghurt is a must with many dishes, particularly in Turkey, Armenia and Iran. Fresh natural yoghurt is an ideal accompaniment, but it is often mixed with herbs and spices.
   One of the most popular dressings is a mixture of garlic and yoghurt — *sughtorov madzoon*.

300 ml/ 1/2 pint yoghurt
1 clove garlic, crushed
1/2 teaspoon salt

1/2 teaspoon dried mint
1 spring onion, finely chopped (optional)

Pour the yoghurt into a bowl. Mix the garlic and salt together, add to the yoghurt and mix well. Sprinkle the dried mint and onion over the top. Serve with all types of fried vegetables and fresh vegetables of your choice.

domates salatasi tomato salad

Popular throughout the Middle East this salad, in its simplest form, contains only tomatoes, onions or spring onions and chopped parsley with an olive oil-lemon juice dressing.

The recipe below is from Turkey and is richer, very attractive and appears with all roasts, kebabs and stews.

4 tomatoes, sliced
1 cucumber, thinly sliced
juice 1 lemon
2 tablespoons olive oil
1 tablespoon parsley, finely chopped

1 teaspoon mint, finely chopped or
   1/2 teaspoon dried mint
1/2 teaspoon salt
1/4 teaspoon black pepper
a few black olives

Garnish **pinch cumin**

On a large plate arrange the tomato and cucumber slices decoratively. In a cup mix the lemon juice, oil, parsley, mint, salt and pepper. Pour this dressing over the tomatoes and cucumbers and chill for 1–2 hours. Just before serving arrange some black olives on the plate. Sprinkle with the cumin and serve.

kefit aghtzan mixed salad with tahina

The literal meaning of this salad is 'of your choice or taste' — suggesting that there are no set rules — except the *tahiniyeh* dressing.

Any vegetable available is suitable, e.g. radishes, mushrooms, etc. However the recipe below is a typical one from Armenia.

1 green pepper, seeded and
   with white pith removed
2 tomatoes
1/2 cucumber
1 cooked potato, peeled
2 sticks celery

2 carrots, peeled and grated
handful of black olives, stoned
2 hard-boiled eggs
3–4 tablespoons *tahiniyeh* dressing
   (see below)

Garnish **1 tablespoon parsley, finely chopped**

Tahiniyeh dressing
150 ml/1/4 pint tahina paste
juice 2–3 lemons
approximately 300 ml/1/2 pint
   milk or water or a mixture of the two

2 cloves garlic, crushed
1 teaspoon salt
1/2 teaspoon chilli pepper
1 heaped teaspoon ground cumin

Prepare this dressing first by pouring the tahina into a mixing bowl, adding the lemon juice and stirring until the mixture thickens. Slowly stir in the milk and/or water until a thick, creamy texture is obtained. Season with the garlic, salt, pepper and cumin. This will make about 450 ml/ 3/4 pint and it will keep in the refrigerator for at least a week.

Cut the green pepper, tomatoes, cucumber, potato and celery into small pieces and put into a large mixing bowl. Add the grated carrots and black olives. Shell the eggs, chop them coarsely and stir carefully into the vegetables. Spoon in the *tahiniyeh* dressing and gently mix everything together. Pile into a serving dish and sprinkle with the chopped parsley.

garmir gaghamp cabbage salad

A Caucasian favourite where the cabbage is first pickled with beetroot, giving it a crimson colour.

As well as the recipe below this pickled cabbage can be thinly shredded and served with grated carrot with an olive oil-lemon juice dressing, and in the recipe that follows clever use is made of apples and grapes.

Delicious with all kinds of meat and poultry dishes.

Pickling

900 g/2 lb white cabbage	10 sprigs parsley
900 g/2 lb beetroot	450 ml/3/4 pint red wine vinegar
leaves of 5–6 stalks celery	2 teaspoons paprika

Wash the cabbage and remove the outer leaves. Put it into a large saucepan, cover with water, bring to the boil and simmer for about 30 minutes. Remove the cabbage from the water and set aside to drain and leave until cool enough to handle. Pull back the outer leaves gently and carefully open and separate the inner ones, but without detaching them from their base. Put the cabbage into a deep casserole.

Peel the beetroot, cut into 2.5 cm/1 in pieces and add to the cabbage. Add the celery leaves, parsley, vinegar and paprika. Add sufficient water to cover the cabbage by about 7.5 cm/3 in. Cover and leave for approximately 1 week.

At the end of the week remove the cabbage, which should now be deep red in colour and have a marvellously piquant flavour. This pickled cabbage is known as *garmir gaghamp* and it is often served as a salad by itself simply put on a plate and cut into quarters.

gaghampi aghtzan cabbage salad with chives

900 g/2 lb pickled white cabbage
(see page 86)
1 onion, peeled and thinly sliced
2 apples, peeled, thinly sliced and
tossed in 2 teaspoons lemon juice

50 g/2 oz grapes, halved and seeded
100 g/4 oz black or green olives, stoned
2 tablespoons olive oil
salt and black pepper

Garnish **pinch of basil, 1 teaspoon paprika**

Shred the cabbage and put into a large salad bowl. Add the onion, apples, grapes and olives. Stir in the olive oil and salt and pepper to taste. Place in the refrigerator for 2–4 hours. When serving arrange the vegetables in a pyramid shape and sprinkle with the basil and paprika.

Another Armenian variation is to put the shredded cabbage in a salad bowl with 50 g/2 oz finely chopped walnuts, 1 tablespoon sesame seeds, 1 clove garlic, finely chopped, 1 teaspoon salt and 1 teaspoon sumac.

Mix thoroughly and chill for at least 2 hours before serving.

salat benoosach hakibbutz kibbutz salad

This salad is a by-product of the *kibbutzim* of Israel which are an experiment in practical communism — as against theoretical waffle! — that seems still, after several decades, to attract considerable notice and adherents.

It is an array of vegetable salads that also include Cos lettuce and homegrown herbs, e.g. basil, tarragon, mint, parsley, etc.

Also included on the table would be hard-boiled eggs, pickled herrings, etc — in short anything and everything that the kibbutz produces.

The basic idea is to mix and season the vegetables according to one's own taste. Quantities are not included as this type of salad is best suited to large groups, e.g. buffets, parties and picnics.

fennel, raisins, celery seeds, lemon juice, olive oil
Grate the fennel; add the raisins and season with the celery seeds, lemon juice and olive oil.

tangerines, mayonnaise, cinnamon, chopped hazelnuts
Divide the tangerines into segments. Mix the mayonnaise with the cinnamon and hazelnuts. Dress the tangerines with this mixture.

cucumber, yogurt, dried mint
Slice the cucumber, add the yoghurt and sprinkle with the dried mint.

leeks, black olives, radishes (sliced), lime juice, olive oil, chopped tarragon
Wash and slice the leeks into a bowl, add all the remaining ingredients and mix well.

tomatoes, chopped parsley, olive oil, sumac powder
Slice the tomatoes and sprinkle with the parsley, olive oil and sumac.

Onions (sliced into rings), pimentos (chopped), olive oil and lemon juice, salt, oregano
Arrange the onion rings on a plate. Mix the remaining ingredients together and pour over the onions.

Serve each salad in a separate bowl.

Garnish them with extras, e.g. lettuce, herbs, spring onions, radishes, etc.

fattoush bread salad

The Egyptians 'shew a great respect for bread, as the staff of life — the name they give to it is *eysh* which literally signifies Life — and they on no account suffer the smallest portion of it to be wasted if they can avoid it. I have often observed an Egyptian take up a small piece of bread which had by accident fallen in the street or road and, after putting it before his lips and forehead three times, place it on one side in order that a dog might eat it, rather than let it remain to be trodden under foot.' (From *Modern Egyptians*.)

This respect for bread is general throughout the region, since for centuries people's existence chiefly depended on this 'life'. Indeed the Armenian expression *hatz oudel* — to eat bread — is most apt for it implied 'to dine' and bread was the paramount ingredient. As this Syrian salad shows, not a morsel was wasted, for when bread dried they made *fattoush* with it. This is a wonderful salad with an unusual texture. Prepare it in advance and chill, but do not stir in the bread until just before serving or it will lose its crispness.

1 large cucumber, chopped
1 lettuce heart, shredded
5 tomatoes, chopped
10 spring onions, chopped
1 small green pepper, chopped
1 tablespoon fresh coriander leaves, chopped
1 tablespoon parsley, finely chopped

1 tablespoon fresh mint, finely chopped
1 clove garlic, crushed
6 tablespoons olive oil
juice 2 lemons
$1/2$ teaspoon salt
$1/4$ teaspoon black pepper
5 thin slices bread, lightly toasted and cut into small cubes

Place all the ingredients, except the bread, in a large mixing bowl. Toss the salad so that all the vegetables are coated with the oil and lemon juice. Chill until ready to serve and then stir in the cubes of bread and serve immediately.

adas salatasi lentil salad

A popular peasant salad. This is a Kurdish recipe from Diarbekir, Turkey. The Kurdish cuisine varies from region to region since, as a nation, they are spread between Turkey, Iraq and Iran. However, their food is, in general, perhaps nearer to the Armenians with whom they seem to have had a love-hate relationship for generations.

5 tablespoons oil
1 onion, finely chopped
225 g/8 oz lentils, washed
juice 1 lemon
1 clove garlic, crushed

600 ml/1 pint water
1 teaspoon salt
1/2 teaspoon black pepper
1/2 teaspoon paprika
1/2 teaspoon cumin

Garnish 3 tablespoons parsley or tarragon, finely chopped

Heat the oil in a saucepan, add the onion and fry until soft. Add the lentils, lemon juice, garlic and water and bring to the boil. Lower the heat and simmer for about 45 minutes or until the lentils are tender. Add a little more water if necessary. Do not let the lentils get too soft. About 5 minutes before serving strain off any remaining water and add the salt, pepper, paprika and cumin and mix well. Transfer to a serving dish and garnish with the parsley or tarragon. Serve cold with all kinds of roast and grilled meats.

fasulya piyazi white bean salad

A popular salad throughout Greece, Turkey and Armenia.

There are several variations. The simpler versions may only include, apart from the beans, stoned and halved olives and a sliced tomato.

The recipe below is from Istanbul and is usually served cold, although it can also be eaten warm. If it is to be eaten cold then cook in olive oil, if warm then cook in butter.

Serve with cold meats and fish dishes.

225 g/8 oz haricot beans, soaked
   overnight in cold water
3 tablespoons oil (or butter if it
   is to be eaten warm)
1 large onion, thinly sliced
5 tomatoes, blanched, peeled and
   chopped

2 cloves garlic, crushed
1/2 teaspoon dried basil
3 tablespoons parsley, finely chopped
1 teaspoon salt
1/4 teaspoon black pepper
1/4 teaspoon allspice

Garnish
1 tablespoon parsley, finely chopped, lemon wedges, 2 hard-boiled eggs, quartered

Bring a large saucepan half-filled with lightly salted water to the boil, add the drained beans and simmer until soft. The time will depend on the quality and age of the beans and so add a little more water if necessary.

Heat the oil or butter in a large saucepan, add the onion and fry until soft and golden. Add the tomatoes, garlic, basil, parsley, salt, black pepper and allspice and mix thoroughly. Cook over a low heat for 5–10 minutes, stirring frequently.

Strain the beans and place in a serving dish. Retain a little of the cooking water. Pour the tomato mixture over the beans and mix well. If you think the mixture is too dry then you can stir in a little of the bean water. If this dish is to be eaten cold then refrigerate for 2–3 hours. Serve garnished with the parsley, eggs and lemon wedges.

salad-e-esfanaj spinach and nut salad

A Kurdish-Iranian salad, popular in the Caucasus. For this recipe only fresh spinach is suitable. Ready salted pistachios are also recommended.

450 g/1 lb fresh spinach
1/2 cucumber, peeled, quartered
   and thinly sliced
6–8 black olives, stoned and
   thinly sliced
1/2 medium onion, thinly sliced
3 spring onions, thinly sliced
3 tablespoons parsley, finely chopped

3–4 tablespoons fresh tarragon,
   finely chopped
4–5 radishes, thinly sliced
2 tablespoons pistachios, chopped
4 tablespoons olive oil
juice 1 lemon
11/2 teaspoons salt
1 teaspoon paprika
1/2 teaspoon black pepper

Garnish
1/2 teaspoon sweet basil

1/2 teaspoon marjoram

Wash the spinach thoroughly under cold running water, remove the stems and dry the leaves. Cut leaves into small pieces. In a bowl combine the spinach, cucumber, olives, onion, spring onions, parsley, tarragon and radishes. Add the pistachio nuts.

In a separate bowl mix together the oil, lemon juice, salt, paprika and black pepper. Pour this mixture over the salad and toss well. Refrigerate for 1–2 hours. Just before serving garnish with the basil and marjoram.

Azerbaijanian variation
Wash, drain and thinly shred 450 g/1 lb fresh spinach and place in a salad bowl with 150 ml/1/4 pint double cream, 1 teaspoon salt, 1/2 teaspoon black pepper, juice 11/2 lemons and 1/2 teaspoon dillweed. Shell and slice 2 hard-boiled eggs, remove the yolks, chop and sprinkle over the salad. Decorate with the rings of egg whites and sprinkle with 1 teaspoon paprika.

chirov aghtzan fruit and vegetable salad

A brilliant recipe from the Caucasus. Fresh fruits mix with vegetables to make a salad that goes well with poultry, pork and veal.

1 apple, peeled, cored and thinly sliced
1 quince, peeled, cored and thinly sliced
1 hard pear, peeled, cored and
   thinly sliced
1 ring of pineapple, chopped (optional)

1/4 cucumber, peeled and thinly sliced
2 spring onions, thinly sliced
3 tablespoons olive oil
1 tablespoon raisins, soaked for
   30 minutes in water beforehand

Garnish
5-6 lettuce leaves, washed and dried

1 tablespoon sumac

Mix all the ingredients together in a large bowl. Arrange the lettuce leaves around the edge of a large plate. Pile the salad into the middle of the plate. Sprinkle the sumac over the top and serve immediately.

asbourag aghtzan asparagus salad

He who boils asparagus and then fries them in fat, and then pours upon them the yolks of eggs with pounded condiments, and eats every day of this dish, will grow very strong — and find it a stimulant for his amorous desires. (From *The Perfumed Garden*.)
Serve with veal, poultry, pork and roast meats.

1 lb fresh asparagus
1 teaspoon salt

1 teaspoon dried dillweed
2 hard-boiled eggs, shelled and chopped

Dressing *sughtorov–madzoun* (see recipe, page 280)

Garnish **sprinkling of paprika**

Cut off the tough and coarse ends of the asparagus and discard. Wash, clean and dry with a paper towel. Cut into 2.5 cm/1 in pieces. Half-fill a large saucepan with water, bring to the boil and add the salt and the asparagus pieces. Cook for 10-20 minutes or until tender. Drain in a colander and set aside to cool. Place the pieces in a salad bowl, add the chopped eggs, dillweed and the yoghurt dressing and mix well. Serve cold, garnished with a sprinkling of paprika.

enginar artichokes in oil

*The Yahoudi [Jew] has as much in common with Jerusalem as has the artichokes —
i.e. both are foreigners to the place.* (Palestinian saying.)

This, however, is neither a Jewish nor a Palestinian recipe. It hails from Turkey and
is similar to the Greek *aginares me anitho*, although it was no doubt around before
any of the above mentioned people were even heard of. It is often served as an
appetizer, but also makes a good accompaniment to chicken, turkey, veal and game
dishes.

4 globe artichokes
juice 2 lemons
12.5 g/^{1}/$_2$ oz flour
150 ml/^{1}/$_4$ pint olive oil
1 tablespoon sugar
^{1}/$_2$ teaspoon salt

^{1}/$_4$ teaspoon black pepper
2 cardamom seeds
4 black peppercorns
1 carrot, peeled and diced
8 spring onions, chopped

Garnish
1 tablespoon parsley, finely chopped

1 tablespoon fresh dill or 1 teaspoon
dried dillweed

Wash the artichokes, place in a large saucepan of boiling water and simmer for 15
minutes. Remove from the water and, when cool enough to handle, hold each one by
the stalk and remove the coarse outer leaves.

In a large saucepan bring 1.2 litres/2 pints of water to the boil together with the
juice of 1 of the lemons.

Place the flour in a small bowl, add 4–5 tablespoons of the water and mix to a thin
paste and then stir this into the pan of water.

Slice away the top of the artichoke leaves, pull out the prickly leaves and then use
a teaspoon to scrape out the hairy choke. Place the artichokes immediately in the pan
of water, stalks uppermost. Add all the remaining ingredients including the rest of the
lemon juice. If the bases of the artichokes are not covered, add a little of the water in
which they were first boiled. Bring to the boil, cover pan, lower heat and simmer for
about 1 hour. Remove from the heat and leave to cool. Remove the artichokes and
arrange in a serving dish. Pour over half the juice in which they were cooked and
sprinkle with the parsley and dill.

salatit shawander beetroot salad

Popular in all countries beetroot is served with a variety of dressings including olive oil-lemon juice, tahina and yoghurt.

This goes well with all meat, poultry and fish dishes.

700 g/1¹/₂ lb beetroot, washed
1 tablespoon salt

water

Place the beetroot in a large saucepan, add the salt and sufficient water to cover by about 5 cm/2 in. Bring to the boil and then lower the heat and simmer for 45–60 minutes or until tender. Strain into a colander and leave until cool enough to handle. Rub off the skins and then slice or cube the beetroot into a bowl.

You can now make use of an olive oil-lemon juice dressing (see recipe page 84) or prepare a favourite Egyptian salad called *shawander tahiniyeh*, where the beetroot is tossed in a *tahiniyeh* dressing.

To prepare the *tahiniyeh* dressing see the recipe on page 85 and then make half the quantity suggested there. Put the cubed or sliced cooked beetroot in a bowl and chill. When ready to serve pour the dressing over the beetroot, toss well and serve immediately.

borani chogondar

This recipe from Iran is a yoghurt dressing. It uses *labna* (drained yoghurt), but there is no reason why you cannot use ordinary yoghurt.

300 ml/¹/₂ pint yoghurt or *labna*
¹/₂ teaspoon salt

¹/₄ teaspoon black pepper
2 tablespoons lemon juice or vinegar

Garnish 1 tablespoon fresh mint, finely chopped, or 1 teaspoon dried mint

Put the cubed or sliced cooked beetroot in a bowl and chill until ready to use. Add the yoghurt, salt, and pepper to the bowl and mix well then stir in the lemon juice. Pile into a serving dish, garnish with the reserved beetroot and the mint and serve immediately.

mshat arnabeet cauliflower cheese

In the Middle East cauliflower is usually first lightly cooked in salted water and then served with one of the following dressings:

(a) olive oil-lemon juice (see page 84)

(b) *tahiniyeh* (see page 283)

(c) *sughtorov-madzoon* (see page 280)

This recipe, however, from Palestine and Jordan, makes use of cheese and nutmeg which gives a beautiful fragrance to an otherwise rather bland vegetable.

Makes an ideal accompaniment to meat and poultry dishes.

1 cauliflower

225 g/8 oz grated cheese, Cheddar
is very suitable

2 tablespoons flour

1 egg

150 ml/¼ pint milk

1 teaspoon salt

½ teaspoon black pepper

½ teaspoon grated nutmeg

oil for frying

Garnish

2 tablespoons parsley, finely chopped   1 lemon cut into wedges

Wash the cauliflower, break into florets and dry with kitchen paper.

In a large bowl mix the cheese, flour, egg and milk together to form a thick batter. Season with the salt, pepper and nutmeg.

Heat some oil in a large frying pan. Now dip the florets, one at a time, into the cheese batter and then fry gently until soft and golden. Drain on kitchen paper. Arrange the cauliflower cheese on a serving plate, sprinkle with the parsley and garnish with the lemon wedges.

bakla broad bean salad

Give me a woman juicy as a mulberry,
Broad hipped and soft as a broad bean
And throw all those okra-shaped ones
To the devil.
Kurdish wisdom

If young broad beans can be found then they are often cooked in their pods, as in this recipe. They are delicious with an olive oil and lemon dressing. However Turks, Kurds, Assyrians and particularly the Iranians like to prepare the beans in the following manner and serve them with a yoghurt dressing.

900 g/2 lb young broad bean pods,
    washed and stringed
juice 1 lemon
1 teaspoon salt
4–5 spring onions, cut into 1.2 cm/
    1/2 in pieces
2 tablespoons fresh mint, chopped,
    or 1 tablespoon dried mint

2 tablespoons fresh dillweed, chopped,
    or 1 tablespoon dried dillweed
1/2 teaspoon allspice
350 ml/12 fl oz water
100 ml/4 fl oz oil
1 tablespoon parsley, finely chopped

Sauce *sughtorov-madzoon* dressing — see recipe page 280

Put the washed beans in a large bowl, add the lemon juice and salt, toss and leave to rest for 15 minutes.

Meanwhile, line the bottom of a saucepan with vine leaves or cabbage leaves. Cover the leaves with a layer of beans. Sprinkle the spring onions, mint and dillweed over the beans and then arrange the remaining beans over the top. Add the allspice, water and oil, cover and cook for 1–11/2 hours or until the beans are tender. Remove from the heat and leave to cool. Transfer to a serving dish and sprinkle with the parsley. To serve prepare the yoghurt sauce and pour over the beans.
Serves 4–6 people.

brass aghtzan leek with yoghurt sauce

Leek is a remedy for snake bite. — Tosefta Shabbeth.

This salad makes a fine accompaniment for fish and chicken dishes.

8 leeks
600 ml/1 pint water
juice 1 lemon
10 or more peppercorns
1 teaspoon salt

4 coriander seeds
3 spring onions, finely chopped,
  including green heads
3 sprigs parsley

Yoghurt-mustard dressing
300 ml/$1/2$ pint natural yoghurt
3 egg yolks
2 teaspoons lemon juice
1 teaspoon salt

$1/2$ teaspoon black pepper
$3/4$ teaspoon fennel seeds
1 teaspoon sumac powder
$1^1/2$ teaspoons Dijon mustard

Garnish 2 tablespoons parsley, chopped

Cut the roots and most of the green tops off the leeks and remove any coarse outer leaves. Wash carefully under cold running water to remove all the grit and sand between the layers.

Prepare a stock by bringing 600 ml/1 pint of water to the boil in a saucepan. Add the lemon juice, peppercorns, salt, coriander seeds, chopped onions and the sprigs of parsley and simmer for about 10 minutes. Arrange the leeks in a large frying pan or flameproof dish and pour the stock over the top. Cover and simmer gently for 20–30 minutes or until the leeks are tender. Switch off the heat and leave to cool.

Meanwhile prepare the yoghurt-mustard sauce. Place the yoghurt, egg yolks and lemon juice in a bowl and beat thoroughly. Place the bowl over a pan of simmering water and cook the sauce for 12–15 minutes, stirring frequently until the sauce is thick. Add the remaining ingredients, mix well and remove from the heat.

Remove the leeks and drain on kitchen paper. Arrange them on a large plate and pour the yoghurt-mustard sauce over the top. Sprinkle with the parsley and serve.

NB A variation popular amongst Arabs and Turks is to cut the leeks into 5 cm/2 in pieces and cook in lightly salted water until tender. Drain and leave to cool. Place in a serving dish, pour over an olive oil-lemon juice dressing and toss.

Sprinkle with 1 tablespoon chopped parsley or mint.

kaleh joosh date and walnut salad

Dates act as a laxative. — Gittin.

This Iranian dish can be served either as an appetizer or as a salad accompaniment to poultry and fish dishes. It has a delicate flavour and very attractive appearance, and is traditionally made with *kashk* — liquid whey, but yoghurt is an excellent substitute.

50 g/2 oz butter
1 large onion, finely chopped
1 tablespoon flour
300 ml/¹/₂ pint fresh natural yogurt
2 teaspoons dried mint
2 cloves garlic, finely chopped

¹/₂ teaspoon saffron
1 teaspoon warm water
8–10 stoned dates, thinly sliced
   lengthwise
3 tablespoons walnuts, chopped

Melt half the butter in a pan, add the onion and fry until soft, stirring frequently. Sprinkle the flour over the onions and mix well. Add the yoghurt, stir and bring the mixture almost to the boil. Do not actually boil or the mixture will curdle. Remove the pan from the heat and transfer the mixture to a shallow serving dish.

   Melt the remaining butter, add the mint and garlic and mix well. Pour this mixture over the yoghurt. Dissolve the saffron in the warm water and sprinkle over the yoghurt mixture. Now sprinkle the sliced dates and chopped walnuts over the mixture and serve.

jajig yoghurt and cucumber salad

Mint to the quantity of three eggs, one of cumin and one of sesame are good for angina pectoris. — Gittin.

A classic of the Middle Eastern cuisine, this salad, with several variations, appears everywhere from the Balkans down through to India.

   The first recipe — the standard one — hails from Armenia, the second is Turkish from the region of Manisa — the ancient Greek city of Magnesia ad Sipylum.

   These salads can be eaten with everything. They are particularly good with all roasts, kebabs, *pilavs*, *kibbeh* dishes and *dolmas*.

600 ml/1 pint yoghurt
¹/₂ teaspoon salt
1 clove garlic, crushed
1 cucumber, peeled, quartered
   lengthways and finely chopped

2 tablespoons fresh mint, finely
   chopped, or 2 teaspoons dried mint
1 little red pepper as a garnish

Place the yoghurt in a mixing bowl and stir in the salt, garlic, cucumber and mint. Place in a refrigerator to chill. Pour into 1 bowl or individual bowls, sprinkle with a little red pepper and serve.

biberli jajig

6 small, green, hot peppers
600 ml/1 pint yoghurt
1 teaspoon salt
1 clove garlic, crushed

3 tablespoons parsley, finely chopped
1 clove garlic, thinly sliced
2 tablespoons olive oil

Grill the peppers for about 4 minutes, turning once. Leave to cool then peel off the skins and remove the seeds. Cut them into small pieces about 0.6 cm/¼ in square.

Pour the yoghurt into a large bowl, add the salt and crushed garlic and stir for several minutes. Add the chopped peppers, parsley and sliced garlic and mix again. Serve in individual bowls with a little olive oil poured over the top.

In another variation the Iranians make this salad with *labna* (drained yoghurt) to which, as well as cucumber and mint, they add 1 large grated onion, 3-4 grated radishes, 50 g/2 oz chopped walnuts, 1 teaspoon dried dillweed and 50 g/2 oz seedless raisins.

The ingredients are mixed thoroughly then shaped (use an ice cream scoop if you have one) into balls and arranged on lettuce leaves.

kebabi peyvaz kebab salad

The relish with which Arabs and Iranians enjoy onions, which they often eat as though munching an apple, cannot just be explained by the fact that they, as good Muslims, wish to emulate the Prophet Muhammad who is reputed to have had a great fondness for this sad vegetable. A further reason must be their belief in the aphrodisiac qualities that this down to earth bulb of the lily family was claimed by the Ancients to possess. No wonder the children of Israel, while fleeing from Egypt, cried out bitterly when they were deprived of the famed Egyptian onions which they preferred to manna! Yet Hippocrates — that Greek hypocrite — declared them bad for the body.

I prefer the opinion of Shayhk Nefzawi who eulogizes the onion's excellent virtues in *The Perfumed Garden*:

Take one part of the juice pressed out of pounded onions and mix it with two parts of purified honey. Heat the mixture over a fire until the onion juice has disappeared and the honey only remains . . . this beverage is to be partaken of during winter and on going to bed. Only a small quantity is to be taken and only for one day. The member of him who has drunk of it will not give him much rest during the night!

Now I know why the Israelis were crying in the desert!
The recipe is a classic, simple and a must with all kinds of kebabs.

2 large onions, thinly sliced

1 bunch fresh parsley or tarragon,
   finely chopped

2–3 tablespoons sumac powder

Mix all the ingredients together in a large salad bowl. Spread this salad over a serving plate and lay the kebabs over the top. When serving the kebabs give a little of this salad with each one.

leninakani aghtzan   vegetable kebab salad

The Caucasians — like the Californians and the Australians — love to eat out and they create excuses to have picnic parties where they barbecue whole pigs and lambs as well as the kebabs for which they are famed.

   Almost always the accompaniment to these kebabs are *jajig*, *kebabi peyvaz* and this vegetable salad from Leninakan.

   It is also excellent with all kinds of roasts.

1 aubergine, cut in 1/2 lengthways
   and then into 2.5–3.5 cm /1–11/2 in
   cubes

1 green pepper, seeded and quartered

2 tomatoes

8 mushrooms

2 tablespoons onion, finely chopped

2 tablespoons fresh tarragon
   or parsley, finely chopped

2 tablespoons olive oil

2 tablespoons lemon juice

salt and black pepper

Thread the vegetables on to 1 or 2 skewers. Grill, preferably over charcoal, but an electric or gas grill will do, until the vegetables are cooked. Skin and quarter the tomatoes. Combine all the vegetables in a salad bowl and add the onion, tarragon or parsley. Stir in the olive oil, lemon juice and salt and pepper to taste. Mix well and serve either warm or cold.

eggah and kookoo — egg dishes

Egg and egg-based dishes are very popular throughout the Middle East. The Ancient Egyptians evolved special hatcheries — *maamal el-faroog*, which were operated by using artifical heat, i.e. dung, where eggs were placed in small ovens, a heat of 100–103°F, 38–9°C was raised and by the twentieth day the eggs were hatched and the chickens distributed amongst the peasants who had first supplied the eggs.

Eggs, coloured and hard-boiled, or, hard-boiled and then deep fried, are sold by street vendors or in small 'sandwich bars' with little cornets of paper filled with salt, or salt and cumin, to dip them in.

On festive occasions — Easter for the Christians and the birth of Muhammad for the Muslims — the eggs are coloured and, amongst the Greeks and Armenians, decorated in patterns and religious images, similar to the Russian Easter eggs.

Eggs are also used in stews or encased in minced meats or made into *eggah* or *kookoo* type omelettes which a traveller in Persia in 1824 described as 'a large omelette about 5 cm/2 in thick'. These dishes are not omelettes in the Western sense of the word for they are usually thick and heavy with various kinds of herbs, vegetables, meat or chicken and are almost meals in themselves — they are often eaten as such with yoghurt, bread and salads.

Eggah (Arabic) or *kookoo* (Persian) can be eaten hot or cold and they are often cut into small segments and served as appetizers or on a buffet table.

Small *eggah* are cooked in specially made copper or tin pans similar to 'rock-cake' tins while larger ones are prepared in heavy frying pans usually with lids. These dishes can be cooked either on top of the cooker or in the oven. The choice of oil varies. The Syrians and Armenians prefer olive oil, especially if they are to be eaten cold, while the Iranians make their *kookoos* in *ghee* or butter. The *kookoo* dishes of Iran form an integral part of the cuisine and they are exceptionally rich and varied in the choice of ingredients and their subtle blending. This type of omelette originated in Northern Iran from whence it spread to the Arab lands and the Caucasus.

beid hamine coloured boiled eggs

These eggs are boiled in water with onion skins to give the shells a light brown colour. My mother used to add 'Turkish' ground coffee to give the eggs a darker colour. To make them red she used to add some cut beetroot to the water. Nowadays, with the advent of food dyes, only one's artistic preferences limit the choice of colour.

On Easter Sunday Christians have a basketful of coloured eggs with which they play a game called 'Find the champion'. One person takes an egg and holds it in one hand covering as much as possible leaving only a little of one end showing between thumb and forefinger. Another person picks up an egg and, using one end of it, tries to crack the shell of the other egg. Whosoever's egg first cracks at both ends loses and the winner goes on challenging all comers until the champion is found.

The eggs are peeled and eaten dipped in salt and pepper or salt and cumin or in a mixture of salt, cumin, coriander and cinnamon, with an accompaniment of bread, salads and pickled vegetables. There are various semi-religious connotations for the colouring of eggs and they all stem from the pre-Christian rituals of re-birth and regeneration of Ancient Egypt and Mesopotamia.

12–15 eggs

water

skins of several onions — these will give a reddish-brown colour. If you want a darker colour use a little ground coffee. Or use food dyes — the quantity you use depends on the strength of colour you want

2–3 tablespoons oil

To serve salt, cumin

Half fill a large saucepan with cold water and carefully arrange the eggs in the water. Add the onion skins — and coffee if you are using it or the food dye. Add the oil. This will slow down the rate of evaporation of the water. Bring gently to the boil and then simmer over a very low heat for 5–6 hours, keeping an eye on the water level and adding more if necessary. Remove from the heat and leave to cool. Serve in their shells so that the colour can be admired.

betzaim eggs in wine

'Lady', insisted the corner grocer, 'these are the best eggs we've had for months.'
'Then keep them,' snapped the customer. 'Who needs eggs you've had for that long?'

This Israeli recipe where the eggs are poached in a wine sauce makes a tasty breakfast or snack.

200 ml/8 fl oz dry white wine
200 ml/8 fl oz water
1/2 teaspoon salt
pinch white pepper
4 teaspoons flour

6 eggs
6 slices toast
1 teaspoon dried mint
1 teaspoon mixed herbs
1/2 teaspoon paprika

Pour the wine and water into a large saucepan and season with the salt and pepper. Bring to the boil.

Put the flour into a bowl, add a few tablespoons of the stock and mix to a smooth paste. Stir this into the stock and simmer until it thickens, stirring constantly. Break the eggs carefully into the sauce and cook gently until the eggs have set. Remove with a slotted spoon and place each egg on a round of toast. Sprinkle lightly with the mint, herbs and paprika and serve. Serves 6 people.

betza sabra egg sabra

A recipe from Israel dedicated to the Sabras — Israeli-born youth who derive their names from the prickly cactus growing wild in the desert.

Sabras — incidentally this is also the Arab name for this fruit — have a very thick, greenish skin, but are juicy and sweet inside. Thus are reputed to be the youth of Israel (the Jew not the Palestinian!).

This recipe needs care as it is a little elaborate, but it is quite simple in essence and is well worth the effort. Serve as an appetizer or a savoury.

4 eggs, hard-boiled	4–5 cream cracker biscuits, crushed
2 tablespoons *tahiniyeh*	very finely
(see recipe page 283)	oil for frying
1 egg, well beaten	4 lettuce leaves
1/2 teaspoon Worcestershire sauce	

Garnish

black olives	gherkins
tomato slices	1/2 teaspoon paprika

Shell the eggs and cut each one in half lengthways. Remove the yolks. Place the yolks in a bowl with the *tahina tarator* and mash until smooth. Divide this mixture into 4 and put each part back between two of the egg whites. Reshape into 4 whole eggs.

In a small bowl mix the beaten egg with the Worcestershire sauce. Carefully dip the stuffed eggs into the egg-sauce mixture. Roll each egg in the biscuit crumbs until covered generously.

Heat some oil in a small saucepan. Place the eggs very gently in the pan, two at a time, and deep fry until golden, turning very carefully. Serve on individual plates with each egg bedded in a lettuce leaf. Garnish with the olives, tomato slices and gherkins and sprinkle with a little paprika.

çilbir eggs on toast with yoghurt

A classic dish which, in the context of the Middle Eastern cuisine, means old, traditional, of peasant origin and simple. This savoury snack fits all these requirements. It has that particular Anatolian touch — yoghurt.

40 g/1¹/₂ oz butter
6 eggs
6 large rounds of toast
300 ml/¹/₂ pint yoghurt
1 teaspoon salt

¹/₂ teaspoon black pepper
¹/₂ teaspoon cumin
25 g/1 oz melted butter
1 teaspoon paprika

Melt the butter in a large frying pan. Break the eggs gently into the pan and cook until firm.

Meanwhile, arrange the rounds of toast on a large serving plate. Place 1 egg on top of each round of toast. Beat the yoghurt with the salt, pepper and cumin and spoon over the eggs. Mix the melted butter and paprika together and dribble over the eggs. Serve immediately.

Serves 6 people.

yumurtali incir eggs with figs

An omelette of figs! — not really so unusual. The Middle East is full of such delightful recipes, particularly the Turkish-Armenian cuisine where, aside from figs, cherries, apples and quinces are treated in this way with the addition of herbs and nuts.

A particularly good omelette *tzirani tzvadzegh* makes use of dried apricots, thinly sliced and cooked with eggs, ¹/₂ teaspoon cinnamon, 1 tablespoon finely chopped pistachio nuts and 1 tablespoon seedless raisins.

For the recipe below, from Turkey, use fresh or dried figs and accompany with salads, bread and pickles.

8 eggs
4 tablespoons single cream or milk
¹/₂ teaspoon salt

60 g/2¹/₂ oz butter
175 g/6 oz fresh or dried figs, thinly
    sliced or chopped

Break the eggs into a bowl and beat lightly. Add the cream and salt and stir.

Melt the butter in a frying pan. Add the chopped or sliced figs and fry for 4-5 minutes, stirring occasionally. Pour the egg mixture over the figs and cook gently until set. Serve immediately.

tzvazegh small omelettes with mint

Traditionally served at Easter these small omelettes can be eaten hot or cold. I prefer the latter, especially when they are sandwiched in the pouch of a warm pita bread.

They make a good appetizer and look attractive on a *mezzeh* or buffet table. This is a family recipe, but there are many other fine variations. My mother had a special pan for making them, but I have used a 'rock-cake' tin and it is perfectly satisfactory.

They will keep in the refrigerator 2–3 days — if permitted to do so!

3 teacups parsley, finely chopped
1¹/₂ teacups onion, finely chopped
2 tablespoons dried crushed mint
6 eggs, beaten
1 tablespoon flour

3 cloves garlic, crushed
2 teaspoons salt
1¹/₂ teaspoons black pepper
cooking oil

Place all the ingredients, except the oil, in a large bowl and beat with a fork until well blended.

One third fill each compartment of the cake tin with oil and place over a moderate heat. When the oil is hot put one heaped soup spoonful of the mixture into each compartment and cook gently until the mixture is completely set and golden underneath. Turn each small omelette over and cook until the other side is also golden. When they are ready remove to a serving dish.

If necessary add a little more oil to each compartment and continue cooking the mixture until it is finished.

If preferred the mixture can be cooked as one large omelette in a frying pan.

mirza ghassemi eggs and aubergines

A speciality of Gilan in northern Iran on the Caspian coast. It is named after a great eighteenth century poet and philosopher, Mira Ghassemi. Serve with hot flat bread, pickles and salad.

2 medium aubergines
50 g/2 oz butter
6 cloves garlic, finely chopped
1 large onion, finely chopped
1 teaspoon turmeric

1 teaspoon salt
¹/₂ teaspoon black pepper
1 tomato, blanched, peeled and finely
  chopped
4 eggs, well beaten

Make 2 or 3 slits in each aubergine and cook in a hot oven until the skins are black and the flesh soft when poked with a finger. When cool enough to handle peel off the skin, scraping off and reserving any flesh which comes away with it. Put the flesh into a bowl and mash with a fork.

Melt the butter in a large frying pan. Add the garlic and onion and fry for a few minutes until the onion is soft. Add the turmeric and mashed aubergine and stir thoroughly. Add the salt, pepper and tomato and cook over a low heat for about 5 minutes. Pour the beaten eggs over the mixture. Stir lightly from time to time and when the eggs are just set remove from the heat and serve immediately.

eggah-bi-qarnabit cauliflower eggah

Hit the egg with a stone and it goes to the devil.
Hit the stone with the egg and again it goes to the devil.

A Syrian recipe popular throughout the Arab countries, this makes a fine quick lunch. Serve it with salad, bread, pickles and perhaps some cold meats.

40 g/1¹/₂ oz butter
1 small onion, finely chopped
about 225 g/8 oz cauliflower florets,
    broken into very small pieces
2 spring onions, finely chopped
3 tablespoons parsley, finely chopped

4 eggs
150 ml/¹/₄ pint milk
1 teaspoon salt
¹/₄ teaspoon black pepper
pinch nutmeg
Garnish ¹/₂ teaspoon paprika

Melt half the butter in a pan and add the onion, cauliflower and spring onions. Fry for a few minutes until the onion softens. Remove from the heat and stir in the parsley.

In a bowl beat the eggs and milk together and then stir in the salt, pepper and nutmeg. Stir the cauliflower mixture into the eggs.

Melt the remaining butter in an ovenproof dish and pour the mixture into the dish. Place in the centre of an oven preheated to 190°C, 375°F, gas mark 5 and bake for about 30 minutes or until nicely browned. Remove from the oven, sprinkle with the paprika and serve.

eggah-bi-djadj wa rishta

chicken and macaroni eggah

A rich and sumptious meal when served with fresh salads. You can use macaroni, spaghetti or tagliatelle, although traditionally, of course, the housewives prepared their own *rishta* (noodles) which was a long and laborious job.

350 g/12 oz macaroni, etc.
350 g/12 oz cooked chicken meat,
    cut into small pieces
2.5 litres/4 pints chicken stock
4 large eggs
3 cardamom pods, cracked or a
    pinch of ground cardamom

1 teaspoon salt
¹/₂ teaspoon black pepper
¹/₄ teaspoon allspice
2 tablespoons parsley, finely chopped
40 g/1¹/₂ oz butter
1 green or red pepper, thinly sliced

Garnish

25 g/1 oz butter   2 large eggs
1 tablespoon paprika

Bring the chicken stock to the boil in a large saucepan, add the macaroni, stir and boil briskly for 5 minutes. Pour into a colander and leave to drain.

Meanwhile, break the eggs into a large bowl and whisk with a fork. Add the chicken pieces, cardamom, macaroni, salt, pepper, allspice and parsley and mix well.

Melt the butter in a large frying pan, add the green or red pepper and fry until just soft. Add the egg mixture and move the pan from side to side to spread evenly. Cook over a low heat for about 30 minutes or until set.

Meanwhile, melt remaining butter for garnish in a small frying pan. Break the 2 eggs into a small bowl, whisk, pour into the pan and cook until set.

Slide the omelette on to the eggah, sprinkle liberally with the paprika and serve straight from the pan.

kookoo-ye-sabzi herb kookoo

This, the most famed *kookoo*, is prepared with fresh herbs and is traditionally served on New Year's Day — *Norouz*. The abundance of fresh herbs symbolizes the coming years' fruitfulness.

All kinds of herbs — some unfortunately only found in Iran — can be used so do experiment. As well as those mentioned below try chervil, tarragon, etc.

40 g/1¹/₂ oz butter
2 lettuce leaves, finely chopped
6 spring onions, finely chopped
2 leeks, washed thoroughly and finely
  chopped
6 tablespoons parsley, finely chopped
3 tablespoons coriander,
  finely chopped
6 eggs

3 tablespoons spinach, finely chopped,
  optional
¹/₂ teaspoon turmeric
¹/₄ teaspoon cinnamon
¹/₂ teaspoon dillweed
1 teaspoon salt
¹/₄ teaspoon black pepper
3 tablespoons walnuts, chopped
2 tablespoons raisins or sultanas

Melt half the butter in a large frying pan. Add the lettuce, spring onions, leeks, parsley, coriander and spinach and fry for 5 minutes, stirring regularly.

Meanwhile, break the eggs into a bowl. Add the remaining ingredients except the butter and mix well.

Use the remaining butter to grease the bottom and sides of an ovenproof casserole dish. Pour in the egg mixture, add the fried vegetables and mix well. Bake in the centre of an oven preheated to 180°C, 350°F, gas mark 4 for about 45 minutes or until set and lightly golden. Remove, cut into wedges and serve hot or cold.

kookoo-ye-loobia bean kookoo

Kookoo dishes are usually cooked in the oven, this recipe, however, is often cooked on top of the stove. Serve with rice, salad and pickles.

350 g/12 oz string beans, washed,
   drained and cut into
   1.2 cm/1/2 in pieces
50 g/2 oz butter
1 small onion, finely chopped

1/2 teaspoon saffron
6 eggs
1 teaspoon salt
1/4 teaspoon black pepper

Place the beans in a large saucepan with some lightly salted water and bring to the boil. Simmer until just tender and then drain.

Meanwhile, melt half the butter in a large frying pan, add the onion and sauté until golden. Stir in the saffron and the beans and fry for 2–3 minutes.

Break the eggs into a mixing bowl, add the salt and pepper and beat thoroughly. Add the onions and beans and mix well.

EITHER — melt the remaining butter in an ovenproof dish, add the egg mixture and bake in an oven preheated to 180°C, 350°F, gas mark 4 for 30–45 minutes until firm and golden;

OR — melt the remaining butter in a large frying pan, add the egg mixture and cook over a low heat. When the centre is almost firm, very carefully place a large plate over the pan and invert, dropping the omelette on to the plate.

Very carefully slide the omelette back into the pan and cook for another 3–4 minutes.

Cut the *kookoo* into wedges and serve.

kookoo-ye-tareh ba gerdoo

leek and walnut kookoo

This tasty *kookoo* of leeks and walnuts makes a good snack or appetizer and a substantial meal when served with yoghurt, salad and bread.

50 g/2 oz butter
350 g/3/4 lb leeks, washed carefully
   and finely chopped
5 tablespoons walnuts, finely chopped
1 tablespoon flour

1/2 tablespoon turmeric
1 teaspoon salt
1/4 teaspoon black pepper
6 eggs, well beaten
2 tablespoons parsley, finely chopped

Melt half of the butter in a frying pan. Remove from the heat and stir in the leeks, walnuts, flour, turmeric, salt and pepper. Now add the beaten eggs and parsley and stir thoroughly.

Melt the remaining butter in a baking or casserole dish and pour in the egg mixture. Spread the mixture evenly with the back of a spoon. Place in the centre of an oven preheated to 180°C, 350°F, gas mark 4 and bake for about 45 minutes or until the *kookoo* is set and golden. Remove from the oven, cut into squares and serve with yoghurt, salad, etc.

kookoo-ye-sibzamini potato kookoo

There are several variations of this popular dish where, as well as potatoes, other vegetables such as onions, tarragon and spinach are included. On the Caspian Sea coast mushrooms are incorporated. While in Iraq *eggeh-bi-batata* is prepared with thinly sliced potatoes, onions and tomatoes which are fried in *ghee* for 15 minutes and then added to an egg mixture seasoned with I teaspoon salt, 1/2 teaspoon turmeric, 1/2 teaspoon black pepper and 1/2 teaspoon caraway. The whole is then cooked in a frying pan, over a low heat, for 30–40 minutes or until well set.

This recipe is from Shiraz, Iran.

2 large potatoes
50 g/2 oz butter
6 eggs, well beaten
4 spring onions, finely chopped

2 tablespoons parsley, finely chopped
1 teaspoon dried dillweed
1 teaspoon salt
1/2 teaspoon black pepper

Garnish 1 teaspoon paprika

Peel and boil the potatoes in lightly salted water until tender. Strain and mash the potatoes. Add half of the butter, the beaten eggs, onions, parsley, dill, salt and pepper and beat until smooth.

Melt the remaining butter in a baking dish and swirl it around to coat the sides. Pour the potato mixture into the dish, smooth it over evenly, place in an oven preheated to 180°C, 350°F, gas mark 4 and bake for about 45 minutes or until a light golden colour. Sprinkle with the paprika and serve warm.

pastas, pies and boreks

There is a charmingly innocent scene in a film about the adventures of Marco Polo — the thirteenth century Venetian merchant-traveller — where he naively asks a Chinese man what the thin reeds in his hand are.

'Spagget,' answers the man, *'you eat it.'*

Marco Polo immediately takes a handful and adds it to his other 'finds' from the mysterious East which he later, we are told, introduces into Europe.

This, as usual when dealing with things Eastern, is far from the truth. For, had Marco Polo stopped at one of the many eating houses on his visits to Ajaccio (Cilician Armenia) or Constantinople or Persia, he would have been served several spagget-type dishes. Indeed pastas were known and used by the Ancients, as well as the Romans whose legions often, for days, depended on them between battles.

Pasta recipes appear in medieval Arab, Persian and Armenian recipes — usually under the name of *rishta* or *arshta* — a Persian word meaning thread.

Today in the villages of Turkey, the Greek islands, Armenia and most Arab-speaking countries, *rishta* is still home-made and I have included a few recipes using this type of pasta. However, commercially produced pastas of all kinds are becoming increasingly popular.

On page 110 is a basic recipe for *rishta*, which makes long thin threads of dough similar to flat pastas like tagliatelle.

rishta

450 g/1 lb plain flour

1 teaspoon salt

2 eggs, beaten

5–6 tablespoons water

Sift the flour and salt into a large bowl. Make a well in the centre and add the beaten eggs and 4 tablespoons of the water. Mix well and knead until the dough is firm. Add a little more water if necessary. Knead for about 10 minutes.

Lightly flour a working top and divide the dough into 3-4 portions. Roll each portion out as thinly as possible, working from the centre. When all the sheets are rolled as thinly as possible leave them to rest for 45 minutes. Carefully roll each sheet up tightly — like a Swiss roll — and then cut them into 0.6 cm/¼ in, or less, slices. Unroll the threads and spread them out on the floured surface for at least 10 minutes. To serve, bring some lightly salted water to the boil in a large saucepan, add the *rishta* and simmer for about 5-6 minutes. The exact amount of time will depend on the thickness. Drain and use as required.

baki mussaka spaghetti with aubergines

For this recipe you can make your own *rishta* or use spaghetti, marcaroni or tagliatelle.

This dish is traditionally prepared during the forty days of Lent. Sometimes it is served as an hors d'oeuvre, but it is at its best as a savoury meal with salad and pickles.

2 medium aubergines, sliced

350 g/12 oz spaghetti or marcaroni

4 tablespoons oil

1 onion, finely chopped

1 clove garlic, crushed

1 green pepper, finely chopped

2 tomatoes, blanched, peeled
    and chopped

2 tablespoons tomato purée

1 teaspoon salt

½ teaspoon cinnamon

½ teaspoon cayenne pepper

225 g/8 oz grated cheese, e.g. haloumi,
    Gruyère, Parmesan or Cheddar

butter

Arrange the aubergine slices on a large plate, sprinkle with salt and set aside for 30 minutes. Rinse under cold running water and dry with kitchen paper.

Meanwhile, bring a large saucepan half filled with lightly salted water to the boil, add the pasta and boil for a few minutes. Drain into a colander, rinse under warm water and set aside.

Heat the oil in a large saucepan, add the onion and fry until soft. Add the garlic and continue to fry until the onion is golden. Add the aubergine slices and fry for a few minutes until lightly coloured all over. Add a little more oil if necessary. Now add the green pepper, tomatoes, tomato purée, salt, cinnamon and cayenne pepper. Lower the heat and simmer until the aubergines are soft. Add just a little water if the mixture is very dry and turn gently so that the slices don't break up.

Butter a large baking dish and arrange half of the pasta over the bottom. Arrange the aubergine mixture over the pasta and then arrange the remaining pasta evenly over the aubergine filling. Sprinkle the cheese evenly over the top and place in the centre of an oven preheated to 190°C, 375°F, gas mark 5 for about 30 minutes or until the surface is golden. Remove from the oven, cut into squares and serve warm.

banirov arshda pasta with cheese

Here is a story about a niggard of Isfahan who loved cheese.

A merchant who had lately died at Isfahan and left a large sum of money, was a great niggard; that for many years he denied himself and his son, a young boy, every support except a crust of coarse bread. He was, however, one day tempted by the description a friend gave of the flavour of a cheese to buy a small piece; but before he got home he began to reproach himself with extravagance and, instead of eating the cheese, he put it into a bottle and contented himself, and obliged his son to do the same, with rubbing the crust against the bottle and enjoying the cheese in imagination. One day he returned home later than usual and found his son eating his crust and rubbing it against the door.

'What are you about, you fool?'

'It's dinner time father, you have the key so I could not open the door — I was rubbing my bread against it because I could not get to the bottle.'

'Can you not go without cheese one day, you luxurious little rascal?

You'll never be rich!'

(*Sketches of Persia*, J. Murray)

An Armenian favourite which makes a fine starter or lunch when served with salads and pickles.

1 egg	100 g/4 oz butter, melted
5 tablespoons parsley, finely chopped	350 g/12 oz grated cheese, e.g.
1/2 teaspoon salt	haloumi, kashkaval or Cheddar
1/2 teaspoon black pepper	225 g/8 oz marcaroni
1 clove garlic, crushed	

Mix the egg, parsley, salt, pepper, garlic and 2 tablespoons of the melted butter together in a bowl. Add the grated cheese, mix well and set aside.

Bring a large saucepan half filled with lightly salted water to the boil. Add the macaroni and cook for about 10 minutes or until just tender. Strain in a colander, return to the saucepan and stir in 2 tablespoons of the butter.

Lightly grease an ovenproof dish about 22.5 cm/9 in in diameter and spread half the macaroni over the bottom. Spread two thirds of the cheese mixture over the macaroni and top with the remaining macaroni. Spread the remaining cheese over the top and sprinkle with the rest of the butter. Place in the centre of an oven preheated to 200°C, 400°F, gas mark 6 and bake for 20–30 minutes. Cut into squares and serve hot.

chrod borek water pastry

A classic from Anatolia, both Turks and Armenians claim this as their speciality. However, since *borek*-type pastries are a speciality of both nations and since, for centuries, they were the backbone of the Ottoman Empire I have come to a Solomonian decision. *Chrod borek* is fifty per cent Turkish and fifty per cent Armenian — the Turkish half the 'water' and the Armenian half the 'pastry'!

The pastry is dipped in boiling water, then immediately into cold water to give it that crisp effect.

This recipe is a family one based on my great grandmother's.

Some people include meat, chicken or spinach fillings with this pastry, but I prefer it as it is.

Pastry
6 eggs
1 teaspoon salt
2 teaspoons cooking oil
450 g/1 lb plain flour
175 g/6 oz butter, melted

Filling
450 g/1 lb cooking cheese, grated
3 tablespoons parsley, chopped
salt and pepper to taste

Beat the eggs together in a large mixing bowl and stir in the salt and oil. Add the flour and mix until you have a soft dough. Knead for several minutes until the dough is smooth. Divide the dough into about 12 portions and roll each into a ball. Grease a baking tray, place the balls on it set well apart from each other, cover with a teatowel and leave to rest in a cool place overnight. Roll each ball out thinly to the shape of the baking tray. Set them aside.

In a very large saucepan boil up about 7$\frac{1}{2}$ litres/12 pints of water with 1 tablespoon salt.

Fill another large pan with cold water.

Dip each sheet of dough into the boiling water and hold for about 30 seconds. Remove and dip immediately into the cold water. Dry on a teatowel and set aside.

Make the filling by mixing together in a bowl the cheese and parsley with salt and pepper to taste.

Place 2 sheets of the dough in the baking tray. Pour 1–2 tablespoons of the melted butter over the second sheet. Continue buttering every second sheet until you have used up half of the sheets. Spread the filling over the 6th sheet. Continue adding the sheets and buttering every second one until they are all used up. Pour any remaining butter over the last sheet. Cook in an oven preheated to 200°C, 400°F, gas mark 6 for about 30 minutes. Remove from the oven and leave to rest for 5 minutes. If you like it soft then cover for 5 minutes, but if you prefer it crunchy then leave it uncovered.

Cut into 7.5 cm/3 in squares and serve warm.

kyurza meat filled pastries

A speciality from Azerbaijan similar to the numerous dumpling-type pastries which originated with the Mongols. Indeed, Azerbaijanians are part ethnically and part in culture the descendants of the Mongol and Tartar nomads who traversed this important transit area in search of pastures green.

Kyurza-type dishes are found from the Balkans (they are called *majcomboc* in Hungary, *wutzerlin* in Romania) through to Afghanistan (*aushag*) to Central Asia (*chebureki*) and finally to China (*jui pao*).

These pastries are boiled in salted water and served with yoghurt.

Dough — see recipe for *rishta*, page 110.

Filling	Garnish
4 tablespoons *ghee*	1 teaspoon cinnamon
225g/8 oz minced lamb	2 tablespoons parsley or tarragon,
1 onion, finely chopped	finely chopped
1 teaspoon salt	
1/2 teaspoon black pepper	To serve **natural yoghurt**

Prepare the *rishta* dough, divide into 2 balls, cover with a lightly dampened cloth and set aside.

Melt the *ghee* in a saucepan, add the meat and onion and fry, stirring frequently, until the onion is soft and the meat browned. Season with the salt and pepper and set aside.

Sprinkle a work top with some flour, take one of the balls of dough and roll out as thinly as possible. With a 7.5 cm/3 in pastry cutter cut out as many circles of dough as possible. Repeat with the other ball of dough.

Place about 1 1/2 teaspoons of the meat mixture in the lower half of each circle. Moisten the edges with cold water and fold the top half over to make a half-moon shape. Seal the edges with your fingertips or with the prongs of a fork. Repeat until all the ingredients have been used up.

Half fill a large saucepan with lightly salted water and bring to the boil. Drop 6–8 pastries into the water and simmer for 8–10 minutes or until the pastries rise to the surface. Remove with a slotted spoon, drain on kitchen paper, arrange on a serving dish and keep warm in the oven. Cook the remaining pastries in the same way.

If there is any meat filling left over heat it through and spoon over the pastries. Sprinkle with the cinnamon and chopped parsley or tarragon and serve with a bowl of yoghurt.

NB *Kaloyrka* is a Cypriot dish similar to *kyurza*. It has 2–3 tablespoons freshly chopped parsley added to the filling. After they have been cooked as above they are served topped by hot saltsa tomato sauce (see recipe, page 281). Grated cheese, e.g. Cheddar, haloumi or Parmesan is often served with it.

mante small, boat-shaped pastries

'What a lucky person. Throw him into the sea, he'll soon float like a mante.'

   Mante also appears in the chapter on soups — see *mantabour*, page 71, while here it features as small, meat-filled pies — versatile little pastries! This recipe is a family one and it looks very attractive.

Dough

225 g/8 oz plain flour

1/2 teaspoon salt

50 ml/2 fl oz oil

about 100 ml/4 fl oz cold water

Filling

1 tablespoon oil

1 onion, finely chopped

2 tablespoons parsley, finely chopped

1 tablespoon tarragon or mint,
   finely chopped, or 1 teaspoon
   dried tarragon or mint

a little melted *ghee*

1 teaspoon salt

1/2 teaspoon black pepper

1/2 teaspoon allspice

1/2 teaspoon cumin

450 g/1 lb minced lamb

150–200 ml/6–8 fl oz stock

Sift the flour and salt into a mixing bowl and make a well in the centre. Add the oil and gradually add the water and mix to a soft dough. Knead for 5–10 minutes until the dough is smooth then shape into a ball, cover with a damp cloth and leave to rest for 30–40 minutes.

   Meanwhile, to prepare the filling heat the oil in a saucepan, add the onion and fry until soft. Add the parsley, tarragon or mint, salt, pepper, allspice and cumin, stir well and cook for a further 2 minutes. Put this mixture into a bowl, add the minced meat and mix well.

   Lightly flour a work top and roll out the pastry as thinly as possible. Cut into 5 cm/2 in squares. Place a teaspoon of the filling in the centre of each square, fold up the 2 opposite sides and pinch at the 2 ends to seal firmly. This should leave the meat exposed at the top and the pastry shaped like a small boat.

   Grease a baking dish and pack the *mante* in tightly, meat sides uppermost. Brush all over the tops with the melted butter.

   Bake in an oven preheated to 180°C, 350°F, gas mark 4 for about 45 minutes.

   Heat the stock until boiling, pour all over the *mante* and return the dish to the oven for a further 15 minutes. Serve with yoghurt, salads and pickles.

borek

There are many large pie-type dishes in the Middle East with different fillings, e.g. *kottopitta* — chicken pie with filo pastry, *tyropitta* — with a cheese filling; *tagine min laham* — meat pie and *pirasapide* — leek pie.

Nevertheless, the housewives have lavished their attention and artistic flair on the smaller savoury pies and pastries.

They are found throughout the region, but it is in modern Turkey where the finest examples are found. This is why I have used the Turkish word *borek* as a general heading. These *borek* come in many shapes — triangles, fingers, half moons and small parcels, as well as in individual pots.

The usual doughs are the following: filo, flaky and shortcrust. Some *boreks* have their own doughs, a few of which I have included.

Shapes vary from region to region as do fillings, but generally the most popular ones are — cheese, meat, spinach and chicken.

Borek can be fried, boiled or baked. They are served as appetizers or savouries; can be eaten hot or cold and are often accompanied by salads and pickles.

There are many *borek*-type recipes in Arab, Turkish and Armenian manuscripts, one of the oldest is *sanbusak* which is found in Masudi's 'Meadows of Gold'. Another is *oughi-dobrag* — brains in a bag — which is found in an eleventh-century Armenian manuscript and the recipe for which I have given.

borek hamuru pastry for borek

This is one of the traditional doughs used for making *borek*. It does take a little time to make, but is not difficult and the *borek* will be soft and flaky.

You can, however, substitute commercial puff pastry with very satisfactory results.

450 g/1 lb plain flour, sifted
1 teaspoon salt
200 ml/8 fl oz cold water

1 teaspoon lemon juice
50 g/2 oz butter, melted and clarified
225 g/8 oz butter, chilled

Mix the flour and salt together in a large bowl. Make a well in the centre, add the water and lemon juice and, with a wooden spoon, mix thoroughly. Add the melted butter and knead with your hands for 10 minutes. Shape the dough into one large ball, cover with a damp cloth and leave for 30 minutes.

Lightly flour a work top. Roll the dough out until about 0.6 cm/¼ in thick. Now put the block of butter in the middle of the dough. Fold the pastry back over the fat so that it is completely hidden. With a rolling pin, well floured, flatten the dough to 1.2 cm/½ in thickness. Fold the dough in half and refrigerate for 10 minutes. Return to the floured work top and roll out until 0.6 cm/¼ in thick. Fold in half and refrigerate for a further 10 minutes. Keeping the working top well-floured roll the dough out once more as thinly as possible. Now cut into the desired size and shape for the *borek*.

savoury fillings — cheese

The quantity of cheese fillings below, and all other savoury fillings given, are for pastry made with 450 g/1 lb flour, etc. So increase or decrease depending on the quantity of *borek* you want.

450 g/1 lb grated cheese, e.g.
   haloumi, feta, Cheddar,
   Gruyère, or a mixture of these
2 eggs, beaten

1/2 teaspoon black pepper
salt to taste — amount will depend
   on the saltiness of the cheese

Mix together, taste and adjust seasoning if necessary.

450 g/1 lb crumbly white feta cheese
   or Stilton, Munster or even
   cottage cheese
4 tablespoons parsley, finely chopped
1/2 teaspoon black pepper

1 small clove garlic, crushed
salt to taste — feta is a salty cheese
   and if using it taste before adding

Crumble cheese into a bowl with a fork, add remaining ingredients and mix well.

herb fillings

450 g/1 lb grated cheese, e.g. feta,
   Cheddar, Gruyère, etc.
2 tablespoons parsley, finely chopped
1 tablespoon dill, chopped

1 tablespoon mint, chopped
1/2 teaspoon black pepper
1/4 teaspoon allspice
salt to taste

Mix together and taste before adding the salt.

egg and cheese

450 g/1 lb grated cheese,
   e.g. Cheddar, feta, etc.
2 eggs, beaten
10 tablespoons milk

3 tablespoons oregano
1/2 teaspoon white pepper
salt to taste

Mix all the ingredients together and taste before adding any salt.

savoury fillings — meat

a

2 tablespoons *ghee* or butter
1 onion, finely chopped
450 g/1 lb minced lamb or beef
2 tablespoons pine kernels
   or chopped walnuts

1 teaspoon salt
1/2 teaspoon black pepper
1/2 teaspoon allspice

Melt the butter in a pan, add the onion and fry until soft. Add the meat and fry until browned, stirring frequently. Add the nuts, salt, pepper and allspice, stir well and cook for 15–20 minutes or until the meat is tender. If the mixture becomes dry moisten with a few tablespoons water. Remove from the heat and leave to cool.

b

2 tablespoons *ghee* or oil
1 large onion, finely chopped
450 g/1 lb minced meat
6 tablespoons parsley, finely chopped

1 teaspoon ground cinnamon
1/2 teaspoon sugar
1 teaspoon salt
1/2 teaspoon black pepper

Heat the *ghee* or oil, add the onion and fry until soft. Add the meat and fry until browned, stirring frequently. Add the remaining ingredients, stir well and cook for 15–20 minutes or until the meat is tender. If the mixture is too dry moisten with a few tablespoons of water and continue cooking. Set aside to cool.

cerkez puf boregi circassian meat borek

The dough used here is the Middle Eastern version of puff pastry. The *borek* are deep fried. Serve with yoghurt.

Filling
25 g/1 oz butter
1 small onion, finely chopped
450 g/1 lb lamb, minced twice

3 tablespoons parsley, finely chopped
1 teaspoon salt
1/2 teaspoon black pepper

Dough
450 g/1 lb plain flour
1 teaspoon salt
2 egg yolks
1 tablespoon yoghurt
4 tablespoons olive oil

1/2 teaspoon lemon juice
100 ml/4 fl oz milk
50–75 g/2–3 oz butter, melted
oil for frying

First prepare the filling by melting the butter in a saucepan. Add the onion and fry until soft. Add the minced meat, parsley, salt and pepper, mix well and continue frying for 15–20 minutes until the meat is cooked. Remove from the heat and leave to cool while you prepare the dough.

Sift the flour and salt into a large bowl. Make a well in the centre and add the egg yolks, yoghurt, olive oil and lemon juice. Mix the ingredients with a wooden spoon. Now knead the mixture for about 10 minutes, adding a little of the milk at a time, until you have a soft, smooth dough. Shape the dough into a large round ball and dust with flour. Sprinkle a work surface with flour and, breaking off lumps of dough about the size of a walnut, roll each out as thinly as possible into a circle about 20 cm/8 in in diameter. Continue until you have used up all the dough. Brush the upper surface of one circle of dough with the melted butter, place another circle of dough on top of it and brush its upper surface with fat. Continue stacking the circles of dough in this way, brushing each upper surface with the fat until they form one pile.

Liberally sprinkle the work surface and the rolling pin with flour and roll out the pile of dough circles until you have one large sheet of dough which is very thin. Cover with a clean cloth and leave to rest for 30 minutes. Cut the pastry into 10 cm/4 in squares. Place 2 teaspoons of the filling in the centre of each square.

Either (a) fold into a triangle, pinching the edges with your thumbs or a fork or (b) spread the filling in a ridge about 1.2 cm/1/2 in from one edge then fold the edge over it and turn in the 2 sides and roll into a sausage shape.

Continue until you have used all the dough and all the filling.

Heat sufficient oil in a pan to deep fry the *borek* and fry, a few at a time, until golden. Remove with a slotted spoon, drain on kitchen paper, arrange on a serving plate and keep warm while you cook the remaining *borek*. Serve hot.

kutab caucasian meat borek

There are several variations of this dish. This recipe is from Baku on the Caspian Sea coast.

Dough **see recipe for *borek hamuru*, page 115**

Filling

450 g/1 lb minced lamb	1 teaspoon cinnamon
1 onion, finely chopped	1/2 teaspoon basil
2 tablespoons freshly squeezed	1 teaspoon salt
pomegranate juice (if available) or	1/4 teaspoon black pepper
1 tablespoon lemon juice	

Frying **8–10 tablespoons *ghee***

First prepare the dough. Then place all the filling ingredients in a large bowl and knead well. If you dampen your hands it will make it easier.

Sprinkle a work top with flour and roll out the pastry until 0.3 cm/1/8 in thick. Cut the dough into 7.5 cm/3 in circles. Put 1½ teaspoons of the filling in the centre of one half of each circle. Dampen the edges with cold water and fold over to make a half moon shape. Seal the edges with your fingers or the prongs of a fork.

Heat the fat in a large pan, add the *borek*, a few at a time, and fry gently until one side is golden. Turn with a slotted spoon and cook the other side in the same way. Do not cook too quickly or the filling will not be cooked through.

With a slotted spoon transfer to a serving dish and keep warm while you cook the remaining *borek* in the same way.

Serve warm, sprinkled with sumac and accompanied by yoghurt, salads and pickles.

savoury fillings — spinach

a

450 g/1 lb fresh spinach or
    225 g/8 oz frozen leaf spinach
8 tablespoons oil
1 small onion, finely chopped

1 teaspoon salt
½ teaspoon black pepper
juice 1 lemon

If using fresh spinach trim stems, wash thoroughly several times in cold water and drain. If using frozen spinach then allow it to thaw.

Half fill a large saucepan with lightly salted water and bring to the boil. Add the spinach and simmer for 8–10 minutes and then strain into a colander. When cool enough to handle squeeze as much moisture as possible from the spinach and then chop. Heat the oil in a large pan, add the onion and fry until soft. Add the spinach, salt and pepper and cook over a low heat for about 5 minutes, stirring occasionally. Stir in the lemon juice and set aside to cool.

b

450 g/1 lb fresh spinach or
    225 g/8 oz frozen spinach
1 tablespoon *ghee*
110 g/4 oz grated cheese,
    e.g. Cheddar, Gruyère, etc.

1 egg, beaten
½ teaspoon black pepper
salt to taste

Wash the fresh spinach thoroughly and drain or thaw the frozen spinach. Chop the leaves finely and place in a saucepan with the *ghee*. Cover and cook over a low heat until the leaves are tender, stirring occasionally. Add the cheese, egg, pepper and salt to taste, mix well and set aside to cool.

450 g/1 lb fresh spinach or
   225 g/8 oz frozen spinach
2 tablespoons oil
1 medium onion, finely chopped
2 tablespoons pine kernels or
   chopped walnuts

2 tablespoons raisins
1 teaspoon salt
$1/2$ teaspoon black pepper
$1/2$ teaspoon allspice

Prepare spinach as described under the first filling. Heat the oil in a pan, add the onion and fry until soft. Add the remaining ingredients, mix well and set aside to cool.
NB Sometimes the nuts are fried in oil before being added to the spinach.

tahinov-spanaki borek spinach and tahina borek

This is an Armenian speciality made during Lent, using tahina paste.

Dough see recipe for *borek hamuru* page 115, or use a large packet of puff pastry

Filling

350 g/12 oz fresh spinach or about
   175 g/6 oz frozen leaf spinach
3 tablespoons *ghee* or oil
2 onions, finely chopped
40 g/$1^1/2$ oz long grain rice, washed
100 ml/4 fl oz water
25 g/1 oz sesame seeds
6–7 tablespoons parsley, finely chopped

2 tablespoons walnuts, finely chopped
2 tablespoons tomato purée
175 g/6 oz tahina paste
$1/4$ teaspoon black pepper
$1/2$ teaspoon allspice
1 teaspoon cayenne pepper
2 teaspoons salt
To glaze milk or beaten egg

Prepare the dough as described. If using fresh spinach trim stems, wash thoroughly several times in cold water and drain. If using frozen spinach then allow it to thaw. Half fill a large saucepan with lightly salted water and bring to the boil. Add the spinach and simmer for 8–10 minutes and then strain into a colander. When cool enough to handle squeeze as much moisture as possible from the spinach and then chop.

Heat the *ghee* or oil in a pan, add the onion and fry until soft, remove with a slotted spoon and reserve.

Place the rice in a small pan with the water, bring to the boil, then simmer until the water has been absorbed.

Place the sesame seeds on a piece of foil and toast under a hot grill until golden.

Place all the filling ingredients in a large bowl and mix thoroughly.

Sprinkle a work top with flour and roll out the pastry to 0.3 cm/$1/8$ in thickness. Using a pastry cutter cut the pastry into 7.5 cm/3 in rounds. Put 1 teaspoon of the filling in the lower half of each circle. Moisten the edges with cold water and fold over to form a half-moon shape. Seal the edges either with your fingertips or with the prongs of a fork.

Lightly grease some large baking trays and arrange the *borek* on them, making sure they do not touch each other. Brush with a little milk or beaten egg and cook in an oven preheated to 225°C, 425°F, gas mark 7 for about 15 minutes or until risen and golden. Serve hot or cold.

NB These lenten *borek* are sometimes made larger by using 15 cm/6 in squares or circles and filling with 2 tablespoons of the filling.

savoury fillings — chicken or turkey

Chicken and turkey meat are interchangeable in the recipes below.

450 g/1 lb cooked chicken meat, cut into small pieces
2 tablespoons *ghee* or butter
2 tablespoons flour

300 ml/^{1}/$_2$ pint milk
1 teaspoon salt
^{1}/$_2$ teaspoon white pepper
1 egg, beaten

Melt the *ghee* or butter in a small pan, add the flour and stir to a smooth paste. Gradually add the milk, stirring constantly, and cook over a low heat until the sauce thickens. Season with the salt and pepper and cook very gently for a few minutes. Remove from the heat, allow to cool a little and then stir in the beaten egg and pieces of chicken. Set aside to cool.

tartar boregi

This is a speciality of the Tartars who were once the scourge of Asia until destroyed by the Russians in the eighteenth and nineteenth centuries.

This recipe from Turkey is made with a milk-based dough — *tartar hamuru* — and it is served with a tasty tomato sauce.

Dough
450 g/1 lb plain flour, sifted
2 eggs, beaten

100 ml/4 fl oz milk

Filling
25 g/1 oz butter
1 tablespoon flour
300 ml/^{1}/$_2$ pint chicken stock
350 g/12 oz cooked breast of chicken, chopped
1 teaspoon salt

^{1}/$_4$ teaspoon black pepper
^{1}/$_4$ teaspoon marjoram
50 g/2 oz white cheese, grated, e.g. feta, Stilton, Lancashire, etc.
50 g/2 oz butter, melted

Sauce
25 g/1 oz butter
6 tablespoons water

1 tablespoon tomato purée
50 g/2 oz grated cheese

Place the flour in a bowl and make a well in the centre. Add the eggs and mix in. Slowly add the milk and knead until you have a soft, smooth dough which is pliable. Cover with a cloth and leave to rest while you prepare the filling.

Melt the butter in a saucepan then remove from the heat and stir in the flour. Stir in the stock, return to the heat and cook gently until the sauce thickens, stirring constantly. Remove from the heat and stir in the chicken, salt, pepper, marjoram and cheese.

Lightly flour a work top and roll out the pastry as thinly as possible. Cut the pastry into 10 cm/4 in squares. Brush each square with some of the melted butter. Place about 2 teaspoons of the filling in the centre of each square and then roll up and seal the ends securely with a fork. Place on lightly-greased baking sheets and brush with any remaining butter. Bake in an oven preheated to 180°C, 350°F, gas mark 4 for 20–30 minutes or until golden.

Meanwhile, place all the sauce ingredients in a saucepan and cook over a moderate heat for about 2 minutes. Remove the *boreg* from the oven, place on a serving dish, pour the sauce over them and serve.

other savoury fillings

kabak boregi — courgette

450 g/1 lb courgettes, peeled and
   grated
2 eggs, beaten
150 g/5 oz grated feta cheese (or
   Cheddar, Gruyère, etc.)

1/2 teaspoon salt — taste before
   adding more as feta cheese is quite
   salty
1/4 teaspoon black pepper
1 teaspoon dried mint

Place the courgettes in a fine sieve and squeeze out as much of the water content as possible. Place the pulp in a bowl, add the remaining ingredients and mix well.

sokhi borek — onion

900 g/2 lb onions
2 tablespoons salt
3 tablespoons walnuts, chopped

1 teaspoon chilli pepper
1 teaspoon dried mint
100 ml/4 fl oz tahina paste

Slice the onions, sprinkle with the salt, squeeze tightly and set aside in a bowl for about 8–10 hours.

Drain the onions, which should now have lost much of their bitterness. Add the remaining ingredients and mix thoroughly.

oughi dobrag brains borek

One of the popular dishes of our kingdom [Vaspoorakan — the region of Lake Van — Armenia] is one called oughi dobrag *— a bag of brains . . . You take ten mutton's brains, wash and soak them in water with vinegar, then boil in salt water. After which, they are cut to small pieces and to which all kinds of greens are added. We use tarragon, onions, garlic, parsley, dill, sumac, purslane and many others.*

This then is wrapped — like a bag — in khumor *[dough] and fried in* temag *[sheep's tail fat]. The brains of calves are superior to those of mutton, for the latter, when eaten in large quantities, will make a person short-sighted and slow-witted like the animal itself.*

(From eleventh century Armenian illuminated manuscript.)

A modern version of this recipe is the following one.

450 g/1 lb sheep's brains, soaked in cold water for 5 hours with 1 tablespoon vinegar. Change the water at least twice
40 g/1¹/2 oz butter
2 tablespoons onion, finely chopped

1 tablespoon cornflour
about 175–225 ml/6–8 fl oz water
10 tablespoons grated cheese
1¹/2 teaspoons salt
³/4 teaspoon black pepper
1 hard-boiled egg, chopped

Remove the brains from the water, rinse and cut away and discard the loose outer membranes. Place the brains in a saucepan, add enough water to cover, with a tablespoon of vinegar and bring to the boil. Simmer for 5 minutes then drain the brains and, when cool enough to handle, cut into small pieces.

Melt the fat in a small pan, add the onion and sauté until soft. Stir in the flour and then gradually add the water, stirring constantly and cook over a low heat until the sauce thickens. Add the cheese, salt and pepper and cook for 1–2 minutes, stirring constantly. Remove from the heat, stir in the brains and egg and set aside to cool. Use as a filling for a pastry of your choice.

koteh dolmeh lentil borek

An Iranian recipe, also popular in the Gulf region, this makes a light, crispy savoury meal. Serve with yoghurt and pickles.

Dough
15 g/¹/2 oz yeast
225 ml/8 fl oz warm water
1 tablespoon rosewater
450 g/1 lb plain flour

1 teaspoon salt
¹/2 teaspoon ground cardamom
2 tablespoons melted *ghee*

Filling

175 g/6 oz brown lentils, washed thoroughly

1.2 litres/about 2 pints water

3 tablespoons *ghee*

oil for frying

3 medium onions, finely chopped

1¹/₂ teaspoons salt

1 tablespoon brown sugar

Dissolve the yeast in 50 ml/2 fl oz of the warm water in a bowl, put in a warm place. When it begins to froth add the rest of the water and the rosewater.

Sift the flour and salt into a large mixing bowl and add the cardamom. Make a well in the centre, add the yeast mixture and knead to a smooth dough. Add the melted *ghee* and knead for about 10 minutes or until it is soft and elastic. Cover with a cloth and leave in a warm place for about 1 hour or until the dough has doubled in size.

Meanwhile, place the lentils and water in a saucepan, bring to the boil, cover the pan, lower the heat and cook for about 1 hour or until the lentils are soft and the water absorbed. The exact time will depend on the age of the lentils, so add a little more water if necessary. With a fork, or a potato masher mash the lentils to a coarse purée and reserve.

Melt the *ghee* in a frying pan, add the onions and fry until soft. Add the lentils and fry for a further 5–6 minutes. Season with the salt and sugar, mix well and set aside to cool.

Punch down the dough and knead for a few minutes. Divide the dough into 2 equal portions and form each into a ball. Roll each ball out, on a lightly floured work surface, until about 0.3 cm/¹/₈ in thick. Cut into 7.5 cm/3 in circles. Put 1–1¹/₂ teaspoons of the filling in the lower half of each circle. Dampen the edges with cold water then fold over to make a half-moon shape. Seal the edges with your fingertips or with the prongs of a fork.

Heat some oil in a deep saucepan, add 4–5 *dolmehs* at a time and deep fry the *dolmehs* for about 3 minutes, turning once or twice, until golden and puffed. Remove with a slotted spoon, drain on kitchen paper and keep warm while you cook the remaining *dolmehs* in the same way. Serve warm with salads, yoghurt and pickles.

lahma-bi-ageen meat pizza

If you are poor, you rub garlic on bread and thank Allah!
If you are rich, you spread meat and nuts on bread and thank Allah.
If, like us, you are very poor
You sit opposite the bakery and dream of mouth-watering sfiha.

I have never much cared for things chauvinistic, but even I, who have been brought up amongst people who, next to death, regard patriotism as a taboo subject, am obliged to scream 'Stop, enough is enough! *Sfiha* is Arabic, but *miss-hatz (lahma-bi-ageen* or *lahmajoon)* isn't and that is final!'

When you compare the two recipes below perhaps you may ask what all the fuss is about because they look so much alike — but they aren't. Lahma-bi-ageen, which literally translated means meat and bread, is pastry topped with meat and vegetables similar in concept to the Italian pizza. We know pizzas were popularized in Naples (I did not say commercialized — that honour belongs to the Americans), and we also know that Neapolitans are of Greek extraction and that the Greeks of Naples came from Greece and Byzantium when that Empire disintegrated. These Byzantines were largely Greek-speaking Anatolians, and the Anatolians were the indigenous inhabitants of modern Turkey, Syria and Armenia. Finally, since even today lahma-bi-ageen is completely unknown in Greece and western Turkey, its natural habitat must be northern Syria and Cilician Armenia (southern Turkey). Therefore, lahma-bi-ageen (the original pizza) originated somewhere in the region of Aleppo, Syria. The word pizza, on the other hand, is most probably derived from the Greek and Turkish words *piaz* (onion) and *pita* (bread) since the original pizza did not contain tomatoes, but instead great use was made of onions, e.g. pissaladiere — a Provençal pizza of onions, anchovy fillets and olives on yeast pastry.

So you can see that to call this dish Arab because it has an Arabic name is ridiculous. The reason for its name was commercial — by that I mean that when a minority lives amongst a majority the fomer invariably uses the latter's language for commercial purposes. Recently, on a visit to war-torn Beirut (Lebanon) when I was seeking *lahma-bi-ageen* recipes from family and friends, I was directed to *lahma-bi-ageen* shops and all, as it turned out, were owned and operated by Armenians; for *lahma-bi-ageen*, or *miss-hatz*, is of Armenian origin. I should know because my grandfather, the baker, was the uncrowned king of this great Middle Eastern classic.

Sfiha are small (*miss-hatz* type) meat tarts popular in Syria, Lebanon and parts of Iraq where, over the centuries, my people have migrated for safety and business reasons.

sfiha

Dough
600 ml/1 pint lukewarm water
1 tablespoon dried yeast or
   12 g/1/2 oz fresh yeast

900 g/2 lb plain flour
11/2 tablespoons salt
3 tablespoons olive oil

Filling
3 tablespoons olive oil or butter
75 g/3 oz pine kernels
1 onion, finely chopped
900 g/2 lb lean minced meat
1 small green pepper, finely chopped
4 tablespoons parsley, finely chopped

1 tablespoon pomegranate syrup
   or 1 tablespoon sumac powder or
   2–3 tablespoons lemon juice
1/2 teaspoon allspice
1/2 teaspoon cayenne pepper
1 teaspoon salt
1/4 teaspoon black pepper

First prepare the dough. Measure 4 tablespoons of the water into a bowl, sprinkle or crumble the yeast over the top and leave to rest for 3 minutes. Stir to dissolve and set aside in a warm place until it begins to froth.

Sift the flour and salt into a large mixing bowl, make a well in the centre and pour in the yeast mixture. Slowly stir the flour into the liquid until they are well mixed and the dough can be gathered into a ball. If the dough is a little too stiff then add a little more water.

Sprinkle a table top with some flour. Place the dough on the table top and begin kneading. Do this by pressing the dough down, pushing it under with the heels of your hands and folding it back on itself. Knead 2 tablespoons of the olive oil into the dough. Continue until the dough is smooth and elastic. Sprinkle with a little flour now and again to prevent it sticking to the table. Shape into a ball and rub the remaining tablespoon of oil over the surface of the ball, place in a clean bowl, cover with a cloth and leave in a warm place for about 1 hour. When the dough has about doubled in size punch it down with your fists a few times and then divide into about 15 pieces. Roll each piece into a ball about 4 cm/1/1/2 in in diameter and leave to rest for 30 minutes.

Meanwhile, prepare the filling. Heat 1 tablespoon of the oil in a saucepan and fry the pine kernels for 1–2 minutes. Add the onion, meat, green pepper, parsley, pomegranate syrup (or sumac powder or lemon juice), allspice, cayenne pepper, salt and black pepper. Mix thoroughly, taste and adjust seasoning if necessary. Set aside.

Now roll each ball of dough into a circle about 10 cm/4 in in diameter and 0.6 cm/1/4 in thick. When completed take a small piece of filling about the size of an egg and place in the centre of one of the circles and either flatten it and spread it evenly over the dough to within 1.2 cm/1/2 in of the edge, bringing the edges up slightly all round, or leave the meat as a ball and bring 3 sides of the pastry up over the meat to enclose it and form a triangular pie. Pinch the top securely.

Continue until you have used up all the ingredients. Use the remaining oil or butter to grease some baking sheets and arrange the tarts on them leaving a space between each one. Place in an oven preheated to 180°C, 350°F, gas mark 4 and bake for 20–30 minutes or until the pastry is golden. Do not overcook, especially the open tarts or the meat will dry out.

NB The Sephardic Jews of Syria make a greater use of pomegranate syrup and include 4–5 tablespoons which gives the pizzas a dark brown appearance.

Today chopped tomatoes are often added to the meat mixture, but they were not a traditional ingredient.

Serve as an appetizer or as a savoury with lemon wedges, salad and yoghurt.

lahma-bi-ageen **or** miss-hatz

Dough

6 g/¹/₄ oz fresh yeast
   or 12 g/¹/₂ oz dried yeast
1 teaspoon sugar
350 g/12 oz plain flour

1 teaspoon salt
¹/₂ teaspoon allspice
180–225 ml/7–8 fl oz water, lukewarm

Filling

450 g/1 lb minced lamb
1 onion, finely chopped
1 small bunch parsley, chopped,
   about 4–6 tablespoons
1 green pepper, chopped
1 clove garlic, chopped

450 g/1 lb ripe tomatoes, blanched,
   skinned and chopped
1 tablespoon tomato purée
1 teaspoon salt
¹/₂ teaspoon cayenne pepper
¹/₄ teaspoon black pepper

Place the yeast and sugar in a small bowl and add a few tablespoons of the warm water. Stir to dissolve and leave in a warm place until it begins to froth.

Sift the flour into a large bowl, add the salt, allspice and yeast mixture together with enough of the water to make a soft dough. Place on a floured working surface and knead vigorously for about 10 minutes, by which time it should be smooth and elastic and come cleanly away from your hands. Gather the dough into a ball, place in a clean bowl, cover with a cloth and leave in a warm place for about 1 hour or until it has doubled in size.

Meanwhile, prepare the topping by placing all the ingredients in a large bowl and kneading until well blended and smooth.

When the dough is ready divide it into golf ball-sized pieces and allow to rest for 10 minutes. Roll out on a floured surface into circles 12–15 cm/5–6 in in diameter. Spread a generous layer of topping over each surface right to the edges. Place on greased baking trays as you make them, leaving a little space between them.

Bake in an oven preheated to 230°C, 450°F, gas mark 8 for 10–15 minutes. The dough should be lightly golden, but still soft enough to fold.

To eat squeeze a little lemon juice over the surface, roll up like a pancake and eat with your fingers. Accompany with a salad.

NB The classic way to serve *miss-hatz*, however, is with grilled aubergine *seorme*. Make 2 or 3 slits in each aubergine and cook over charcoal or in a hot oven until the skins are black and the flesh soft when poked with a finger. When cool enough to handle peel off the skins and slice the flesh lengthways into thin strips. Lay 1 or 2 strips down the *miss-hatz*, roll up and eat with *jajig*, pickles and fresh salads.

kibbehs and kuftas

Kibbeh is the pride and joy of the Syrians and Lebanese. It is also one of the oldest surviving legacies of the ancient Assyrian cuisine that has come down to us almost unchanged.

Kibbeh dishes prevail throughout the Mediterranean coastline and they also appear in Armenia and northern Iraq. But it is in Syria and Lebanon, particularly amongst the Christian elements, that *kibbeh* is regarded as a national dish entwined in semi-religious mystiques. Some women are supposed to have '*kibbeh* fingers'. Often women are praised more for their *kibbeh*-making abilities than, say, for their looks or intellect. To possess '*kibbeh* fingers' is a God-given gift akin to having pianist's fingers.

There are many variations of *kibbeh*. Some are established classics, e.g. *kibbeh-naye*, *kibbeh-tarablousiyeh*, *kibbeh-bi-sanieh* and *kharperti-kufta*. Others are of a more regional fame, but they all (with just a few exceptions) have the following ingredients in common: burghul (cracked wheat), minced meat, nuts, herbs and spices. *Kibbeh* can be eaten raw, fried, boiled, grilled or baked. Their preparation, sizes, shapes and methods of consumption are a binding link between the present and the distant past.

I have included as many recipes as possible as I regard *kibbeh*-type dishes as one of the most original methods of food preparation known to us. Two of the recipes — *kibbeh-naye* and *houm-miss* occur in the *mezzeh* section beginning on page 31.

basic kibbeh mixture

The recipe below is a standard one and I suggest you use it wherever possible. Variations are given in full.

Meat for *kibbeh* must be lean and it must be minced twice. Use lamb if possible as it is the ideal meat. However, if you want to use beef then add 2 tablespoons of cornflour and 1 small beaten egg — this will help the minced beef to act as a binder as beef does not possess the same elasticity as lamb.

175 g/6 oz fine burghul
225 g/8 oz lean lamb, minced twice
1 tablespoon onion, very finely
   chopped

$1/2$ teaspoon black pepper
$1/2$ teaspoon chilli pepper
1 teaspoon allspice
$11/2$ teaspoons salt

Place the burghul in a bowl, add cold water and then pour it away thus getting rid of any dirt, chaff, etc. Repeat 1 or 2 times. Spread the burghul out on a baking sheet and leave while you prepare the meat.

Place the meat in a bowl, add the onion, seasonings and 2 tablespoons cold water and knead until well blended and smooth. Add the meat mixture to the burghul and knead until all the burghul is gathered up with the meat into a ball. Keeping your hands damp, knead the mixture for at least 10 minutes or until the *kibbeh* has the texture of a soft dough. Do not skimp on the kneading time or the texture of the *kibbeh* will be coarse when cooked. When you have prepared your *kibbeh* and made the balls for some of the soups, or *tarablousieh* for deep frying you might decide that you have much more than you need for the present serving. In this case the *kibbeh*, stuffed or 'blind', will freeze very well until you wish to use them.

amram grilled kibbeh

Prepare the basic mixture. Divide it into 12 equal portions. Roll into balls between damp palms and then flatten them into rounds 7–10 cm/3–4 in in diameter and 1.2–1.8 cm/$1/2$–$3/4$ in thick. Cook over charcoal or under the grill for about 10 minutes, turning occasionally. Serve on a bed of lettuce leaves with a yoghurt dressing of your choice spooned over them.

dabgvadz kufta fried kibbeh

Ghee or oil for frying
1 recipe of basic *kibbeh* mixture —
   to which mix in the following:
$1/2$ teaspoon curry powder

$1/4$ teaspoon cinnamon
$1/2$ teaspoon paprika
1 egg

Garnish Lettuce leaves, 1 tablespoon parsley, finely chopped, lemon wedges

Shape the mixture as with *amram*.

Heat the *ghee* or oil in a large saucepan, drop in the *kibbeh*, a few at a time, and fry for about 8–10 minutes until golden brown all over. Place on a serving dish garnished with lettuce leaves and sprinkle with the parsley.

To eat, squeeze lemon juice from the wedges over the *kibbeh*. Serve with yoghurt or *jajig* and a fresh salad.

NB These can also be made into sausage shapes 10 x 2.5 cm/4 x 1 in or finger shapes 5 cm x 1.2 cm/2 x 1/2 in.

khorovadz kufta skewered kibbeh

Prepare the basic mixture. Divide the mixture into 12–16 portions and roll into balls between lightly dampened palms. Pass a skewer through one of the balls and then squeeze out the *kibbeh* to form a thin sausage shape. Continue with the remaining mixture. Cook over charcoal for about 10 minutes, turning occasionally. Serve immediately with yoghurt spooned over them and a bowl of fresh salad and some pickles.

basic kibbeh and kufta fillings

There are several fillings, but the following two are the most traditional.

Meat and onion filling

2 tablespoons oil or *ghee*

225 g/8 oz minced meat

2 onions, finely chopped

1 teaspoon salt

25 g/1 oz pine kernels or chopped walnuts

1/2 teaspoon black pepper

1/2 teaspoon allspice

1/2 teaspoon cinnamon

1 tablespoon dried rose petals (optional)

Heat the oil or *ghee* in a saucepan, add the meat and fry for 5 minutes, stirring frequently. Add the onions and salt and fry for about 30 minutes until the meat is cooked. Add the remaining ingredients, mix well and set aside to cool.

You can prepare this filling well in advance, cover and keep in the refrigerator and you can use it for any stuffed *kibbeh* including *kibbeh-bil-sanieh*.

Fatty filling

The traditional fat used for this filling is sheep's tail (*alya*), but as this is not available in the West the most suitable substitute is suet. However, you can even use butter or block margarine.

Suet
You can use lamb or beef. Blend in a mixer or knead together:

225 g/8 oz suet
25 g/1 oz chopped pine kernels
   or walnuts

1/2 teaspoon black pepper
1/2 teaspoon allspice
1 teaspoon salt

Chill for several hours before handling.

Butter
Blend 225 g/8 oz of butter with the above spices and chill for several hours before handling.

kibbeh-bil-sanieh kibbeh baked in a tray

A classic which makes a fine first course or main dish. It can be baked in advance and warmed when needed.

It is popular throughout Syria, Lebanon, Palestine and Israel. It is also known as *sineh kufta* amongst Armenians, Turks and the Kurds of southern Turkey.

Serve with a bowl of fresh salad, yoghurt and pickles.

Filling
2 tablespoons oil
25 g/1 oz pine kernels or 25 g/
   1 oz walnuts, chopped
225 g/8 oz minced lamb
1 onion, chopped

1 teaspoon salt
1 teaspoon black pepper
1/2 teaspoon allspice
1/4 teaspoon cinnamon
1 tablespoon parsley, finely chopped

Kibbeh
175 g/6 oz fine burghul
225 g/8 oz lean lamb, minced twice
1 tablespoon onion, very finely
   chopped
pinch allspice

50 g/2 oz butter
2 tablespoons oil mixed with
   4 tablespoons water
11/2 teaspoons salt
1 teaspoon black pepper

To make the filling heat the oil, fry the nuts for about 2 minutes and then remove with a slotted spoon and drain. Add the meat to the oil and cook for about 15 minutes, stirring frequently. Add the onion and seasonings and cook for a further 15–20 minutes, stirring frequently. Stir in the nuts and parsley and set aside.

Wash the burghul in a bowl and pour away excess water. Spread the burghul out on a baking sheet and leave for 5–10 minutes. Add the minced lamb, onion and seasonings and knead for at least 10–15 minutes, keeping your hands damp with cold water. Divide the mixture into 2 equal parts.

Butter a shallow circular baking dish 20–22 cm/8–9 in in diameter and sprinkle it with a pinch of allspice. With your fingers spread one half of the burghul mixture evenly over the bottom of the dish. Spread the filling evenly over this.

Arrange the remaining burghul mixture evenly over the top. The easiest way to do this is to break off large lumps of the *kibbeh*, press it flat between your palms and place on the filling. Fit the pieces together something like a jigsaw and then draw the edges together and smooth over. Wet your hands and press the mixture well down over the filling. Wet a sharp knife and run it around the edge of the dish to loosen the *kibbeh*. Cut the *kibbeh* into diamond shapes. Place a small dab of butter on each diamond and pour the oil and water over the top. Bake in an oven preheated to 190°C, 375°F, gas mark 5 until golden brown and crisp around the edges.

NB A Caucasian variation similar to this uses pork (minced twice) in the *kibbeh* mixture while lamb or beef is used in the filling.

kibbeh tarablousieh syrian 'torpedo' kibbeh

Probably the most famed dish of all — the preparation of which is an art which takes several years to perfect. I understand that in the USA they are called 'Armenian bombs', but they should more accurately be called *Tripoli kibbeh* for they are the speciality of the second largest city of Lebanon (Tarablous).

Although difficult at first I strongly recommend you persevere as they are magnificent to look at and taste equally excellent.

Basically they are oval shells filled with a meat mixture and then deep fried. Often they are made only 4 cm/1½ in long, fried and then served cold as an appetizer. Traditionally though, they are served warm, often as a main meal, with salads and yoghurt.

The smaller versions are sometimes added to stews of meat and courgettes, pumpkins or aubergines.

Filling

2 tablespoons oil	1 teaspoon salt
25 g/1 oz pine kernels or chopped walnuts	1 teaspoon black pepper
	1 teaspoon allspice
225 g/8 oz minced meat	1 tablespoon parsley, finely chopped
1 onion, finely chopped	

Kibbeh

225 g/8 oz fine burghul	oil for deep frying
450 g/1 lb lean lamb, minced twice	2 teaspoons salt
2 tablespoons onion, very finely chopped	1 teaspoon black pepper

To Serve lemon wedges

First prepare the filling by heating the oil in a pan, add the nuts and fry for a minute or two. Remove with a slotted spoon and drain.

Add the meat to the oil and cook for about 15 minutes, stirring frequently. Add the onion and seasonings and cook for a further 15–20 minutes. Stir in the nuts and parsley and set aside.

Wash the burghul in a bowl and pour away the excess water. Spread the burghul out on a baking sheet and knead for a few minutes. Add the meat, onion and seasonings and knead for at least 10–15 minutes, keeping your hands damp with cold water.

To stuff the *kibbeh*, wet your hands and break off a piece of *kibbeh* about the size of an egg. Hold the ball of *kibbeh* in the palm of one hand and, with the index finger of the other hand, make a hole in the *kibbeh*. Press the index finger down into the palm of the other hand squeezing out the *kibbeh* and making the shell a little thinner. Slowly rotate the ball of *kibbeh* so that the finger is pressing down on a new part of the *kibbeh* shell and making it thinner. Continue turning the shell round and round and pressing it up the finger until you have a long oval shape with a slightly wider mouth. The art is to get the shell as thin as possible without cracking it. It will be a little easier to do this if you keep your hands damp. Place a tablespoon of the filling into the shell and then close the opening by drawing the edges together and sealing. Wet your hands again and roll the *kibbeh* between your palms to smooth off and ensure that it is a real oval shape. Continue in this way until you have used up all the *kibbeh* mixture and meat filling.

To cook add sufficient oil to a pan to deep fry and heat until hot. Add a few *kibbeh* at a time and fry until golden brown all over. Remove and drain. Serve hot with lemon wedges. To eat cut the *kibbeh* in half and squeeze lemon juice over the filling.

anteb yogurtli kufta kibbehs in a yoghurt sauce

A classic beloved of Syrians, Armenians — who call it *madzounov kufte* and the Lebanese — who call it *kibbeh-bi-laban*.

There are several variations of these stuffed *kibbehs* in a yoghurt sauce, but by far the best is from the city of Anteb (*gazi Antab*) in southern Turkey. It is a fascinating city. It was, for centuries, part of Armenia and then was conquered by the Ottomans. The inhabitants were almost equally divided between Turks, Armenians and Arabs with a scattering of Jews, Kurds, Alouites, Nestorians, Assyrians, Maronites — the list is endless. The result was an intriguing city of rich cross currents and a justifiably famed local cuisine, of which this dish is part.

Use either of the basic fillings suggested. I very much like the suet one, but I am aware that it is rather heavy for the uninitiated.

This is a really substantial meal and should serve at least 6 people. Serve in soup bowls with bread.

Filling
Prepare either of the basic fillings (see recipes, pages 130-1) or you can cook these *kibbehs* 'blind' i.e. without a filling.

Kufta
Prepare 1½ times the basic *kibbeh* mixture (see recipe, page 129), i.e. 350 g/12 oz meat, 250 g/9 oz burghul etc.

Sauce

1–1.5 kg/2–3 lb chicken, cut into joints	1½ litres/2–2½ pints yoghurt
2 teaspoons salt	2 eggs
100 g/4 oz chickpeas, soaked	50 g/2 oz butter
overnight in cold water	1 tablespoon dried mint

Half fill a large saucepan with water, add the chicken, salt and chickpeas and bring to the boil. Remove any scum which appears on the surface and cook until the chicken and chickpeas are tender.

If using a suet filling remove it from the refrigerator and make from it small balls about the size of a pea.

If making 'blind' *kufta* simply break off pieces of the *kibbeh* mixture and roll into marble-sized balls. Keep your hand damp — it will make the work easier!

If stuffing the *kufta* break off a piece of *kibbeh* about the size of a small walnut and roll into a ball. Push your forefinger into the centre and then, holding it so that your forefinger is parallel to the palm of the other hand, press your finger down into the *kibbeh* thus making it thinner. Slowly rotate the ball in the palm of your hand all the while pressing down with your forefinger making the shell of the ball uniformly thinner. Put a ball of suet or a teaspoon of the meat and onion filling into the hole. Bring the edges of the opening together and seal. Dampen your hands and roll the ball between your palms to give it a round shape and smooth surface. Repeat until you have used all the ingredients.

Mix the yoghurt and eggs together in a small bowl, add a little of the hot chicken stock and stir well. Pour the yoghurt sauce into the large pan of stock with the chicken and chickpeas. Simmer very gently. Add the *kufta* balls and simmer, very gently, for 10–15 minutes until cooked.

Meanwhile melt the butter in a small pan, add the mint, stir and pour into the soup. Serve the dish hot by placing several *kufta* in a soup bowl with some of the chicken and chickpeas and plenty of the sauce.

Serves 6–8 people.

yougov kibbeh fried onion kibbeh

Let onions grow in his navel. A curse.

This recipe, and all its variations, is Armenian from southern Turkey. They make excellent appetizers and snacks and are also often served as meals with salads, yoghurt and pickles.

6 tablespoons oil	1/2 teaspoon chilli pepper
1 onion, finely chopped	225 g/8 oz fine or medium burghul
3–4 tomatoes, blanched, peeled and chopped	1 small green pepper, finely chopped
2 tablespoons tomato purée	2 spring onions, finely chopped
1 tablespoon salt	2–3 tablespoons parsley, finely chopped

Heat the oil in a large saucepan, add the onion and fry until soft and turning golden, stirring frequently. Add the tomatoes, tomato purée, salt and chilli pepper and mix well. Simmer this mixture for a few minutes and then transfer to a large bowl.

Place the burghul in a small bowl, add cold water, stir and pour away the water together with any husks, etc. Add the burghul to the tomato mixture, mix well, cover and leave to cool for at least 20 minutes so that the burghul becomes softened.

In a small bowl mix together the green pepper, onions and parsley.

Knead the *kufta* for about 5 minutes until well blended. Mix in the chopped vegetables and knead a little longer. Arrange the *kufta* in a dish and serve with a spoon.

NB A variation from Kilis — southern Turkey — includes sumac which gives a dark red colour and a strong tangy flavour.

Place 3 tablespoons sumac powder in a small pan with 50 ml/2 fl oz water and bring to the boil. Strain the juice through a fine sieve, add it to the *kufta* mixture and knead as described above.

kibbeh hali alouite kibbeh

A speciality from northern Syria where people of the Alouite sect are found. A mysterious and secretive people, the Alouites have incorporated much from ancient cults in the tenets of their many sects — Nosairis, Haidaris, Charbis, Chamalis and Kalazes. All of which are variants of a pantheistic worship of the sun, the sky, the air and the Syrian lunar deity. They are not Muslims, but followers of Ali to whom God was manifested, and from whom Muhammad was issued. 'An Alouite never speaks' is an apt Syrian expression and to have secured this recipe of theirs was a great achievement!

225 g/8 oz fine burghul
100 g/4 oz plain flour or fine matzo
   meal or oatmeal

1 egg

Sauce

4 tablespoons oil
1 onion, finely chopped
2 cloves garlic, finely chopped
1 tablespoon ground coriander
3 tablespoons tomato purée
   diluted in 300 ml/$^1/_2$ pint water
1$^1/_2$ teaspoons salt

2 bay leaves
$^1/_2$ teaspoon allspice
1 teaspoon cayenne pepper
$^1/_2$ teaspoon black pepper
900 ml/1$^1/_2$ pints water
juice 1 lemon

Garnish 2 tablespoons parsley, finely chopped

Wash the burghul in a bowl and pour away excess water. Spread the burghul out on a baking tray and knead for a few minutes. Add the flour, matzo meal or oatmeal and the egg. Mix everything together and then knead until you have a paste thick enough to mould. If you find the mixture a little too sticky then leave it for 15–30 minutes by which time the burghul will have absorbed much of the excess moisture. Keeping your palms damp, shape teaspoons of the mixture into small balls about the size of marbles. Set these balls aside while you prepare the sauce.

Heat the oil in a saucepan, add onion and fry until soft and lightly browned. Add the garlic and coriander and fry for a further 2 minutes, stirring frequently. Add the diluted tomato purée, salt, bay leaves, allspice, cayenne and black peppers and the water and stir well. Bring to the boil, add *kibbeh* balls and simmer for about 30 minutes or until the sauce thickens then stir in the lemon juice. Transfer to a serving dish and sprinkle with the parsley.

kharperti kufta stuffed kibbeh in tomato sauce

Kharpert (Harput) is a small town in Turkey famed for nothing else perhaps, save this *kibbeh* dish, which is excellent on a cold winter's day.

Kibbeh see basic *kibbeh* mixture (recipe, page 129)

Filling

2 tablespoons *ghee*

1 large onion, finely chopped

225 g/8 oz minced lamb

2 tablespoons green pepper, chopped

2 tablespoons parsley, chopped

$1/2$ teaspoon dried basil

1 teaspoon salt

$1/2$ teaspoon black pepper

$1/2$ teaspoon cinnamon

3 tablespoons walnuts, chopped

Sauce

1.8 litres/3 pints stock

3 tablespoons tomato purée

$11/2$ teaspoons salt

1 teaspoon dried mint

Heat the *ghee* in a saucepan, add the onion and fry until soft. Add the meat and green pepper and fry for about 30 minutes, stirring occasionally, until the meat is cooked. Add the remaining ingredients and set aside to cool. When you have prepared the *kibbeh* mixture break off lumps and form into balls about 4 cm/$11/2$ in in diameter.

To stuff the *kibbeh* take one of the balls and, keeping your hands damp, hold it in the palm of one hand and push the forefinger of the other hand into the centre. Press all around the wall while rotating the ball slowly and evenly. Continue until the walls are as thin as possible. Place a tablespoon of the filling in the opening, lightly moisten your hands, draw the edges together and seal tightly. Roll the ball between your palms to give it a round and smooth shape and then press gently between your palms to flatten slightly. Reserve and proceed until you have used up all the ingredients.

Bring the stock to the boil in a large saucepan and stir in the tomato purée, salt and dried mint. Add the *kibbehs*, a few at a time, and cook for 10–15 minutes or until they rise to the surface. Serve a few *kibbehs* in each soup bowl with some of the sauce.

vospov kufta lentil kibbeh

Kibbehs and *kuftas* — the latter is derived from old Aramaic meaning 'minced', shredded — are also made with other ingredients such as lentils, split peas and rice. The latter two are popular in areas where either burghul is unknown or difficult to find such as Iran, Caucasus, Egypt and southern Iraq.

One of the best known of these 'burghul-less' *kibbehs* is the recipe below which is popular with Armenians, Turks and the Kurds of southern Turkey. It is a traditional Lenten dish for Christian Armenians, but often it is the staple food for thousands of peasants. Serve with yoghurt salads of your choice, fresh salads, pickles, etc.

175 g/6 oz brown lentils, washed
   and drained
approximately 900 ml/1¹/₂ pints water
1¹/₂ teaspoons salt
100 g/4 oz fine burghul
200 ml/¹/₃ pint olive oil
1 onion, finely chopped

2 spring onions, including green
   tops, finely chopped
1 green pepper, seeded and finely
   chopped
2 tablespoons parsley, finely chopped
2 tablespoons fresh mint, finely chopped
   or 1 tablespoon dried mint

Garnish **paprika**

Place the lentils in a large saucepan with the water and salt. Bring to the boil, lower heat and simmer for about 30 minutes or until the lentils are tender. Add a little more water if necessary. Stir in the burghul and half of the oil. Simmer for a few minutes then turn off the heat, cover and set aside for 15 minutes — at the end of which time the water should have been absorbed.

Meanwhile, heat the remaining oil in a small pan, add the chopped onion and fry until soft and golden.

Empty the lentil and burghul mixture into a large mixing bowl and add the cooked onion with the oil. Knead the mixture well, keeping your hands damp with warm water, until smooth. Mix in half the spring onions, green pepper, parsley and mint. Taste and adjust seasoning if necessary. Keeping your hands moist shape the mixture into small patties about 2.5–4 cm/1–1¹/₂ in long and 2 cm/³/₄ in wide. Arrange on a serving dish and sprinkle with the paprika and remaining spring onion, green pepper, parsley and mint. Serve warm.

topig stuffed chickpea and wheat balls

A classic Armenian Lenten dish traditionally served by the churches and charitable organizations.

Serve cold as an appetizer or as a main dish with olive oil sprinkled over them and garnished with lemon wedges.

There are several variations. One of the traditional ingredients is skinless wheat, but if this is not available mashed potato is a suitable substitute.

Filling

3 tablespoons olive oil
1 large onion, finely chopped
2 tablespoons flour
3 tablespoons pine kernels
3 tablespoons raisins or sultanas
2 tablespoons parsley, finely chopped

1/4 teaspoon allspice
1 1/2 teaspoons salt
1/2 teaspoon black pepper
pinch cinnamon
3 tablespoons tahina paste

Kufta shell

100 g/4 oz whole-grain wheat, skinless
   — if this is not available
   peel 100 g/4 oz potatoes, boil until
   tender and mash
175 g/6 oz chickpeas, soaked
   overnight in cold water
paprika
cumin

100 g/4 oz fine burghul
3 tablespoons onion, finely chopped
1 egg
1/2 teaspoon paprika
1 teaspoon salt
1/4 teaspoon cayenne pepper
olive oil

Garnish **lemon wedges**

Prepare the filling first — preferably the day before — by heating the oil in a large saucepan. Add the onion and fry until soft. Add the flour and fry for 2–3 minutes, stirring frequently. Remove from the heat and stir in the remaining filling ingredients. Mix thoroughly, transfer to a bowl and chill in the refrigerator — preferably overnight.

To prepare the *kufta* first half fill a saucepan with water, bring to the boil, add the wheat, turn off the heat and leave the wheat to soak for 2 hours.

Drain and rinse the chickpeas and place in a large saucepan half-filled with water. Bring to the boil then lower heat and simmer until tender. Remove any scum that appears on the surface. Add more water if necessary. Drain chickpeas and, when cool enough to handle, remove and discard the skins by pressing each chickpea gently between thumb and forefinger. Pass the chickpeas (and wheat if using it) through a meat mincer or chop finely.

Place burghul in a bowl and wash with cold water until water poured off is clean. Place the burghul, chickpeas and wheat or mashed potato in a large bowl. Add the onion, egg, paprika, salt and cayenne pepper and knead for about 5 minutes or until the mixture is smooth. Add a little water if necessary, but do not make it too damp or it will be difficult to shape. To make the stuffed *kufta* break off a piece of the *kufta* and roll into a ball about 4 cm/1 1/2 in in diameter. Keeping your palms damp hold the ball in one hand and make a hole in it with the index finger of the other hand. Press the index finger down into the palm of the other hand squeezing out the *kufta* and making the shell thinner. Fill the opening with 2.5–4 cm/1–1 1/2 teaspoons of the filling and then close the opening by drawing the edges together and sealing. Roll the *kufta* between your palms to make a smooth round shape. Slowly rotate the ball of *kufta* so that the finger is pressing down on a new part of the *kufta* shell and making it thinner. Continue until all the filling and *kufta* have been used up.

Two thirds fill a large deep saucepan with water and bring to the boil. Drop in a few *kuftas* at a time and simmer for 10 minutes. Remove with a slotted spoon to a large plate. Repeat until all the *kuftas* are cooked. Sprinkle the *kuftas* generously with the cumin and paprika and refrigerate for a few hours. Sprinkle with olive oil and serve with lemon wedges.

Serves 6 people.

ttoo kufta *a sour meat and kibbeh stew*

This stew of meat, chickpeas, onions, mint and marble-sized *kibbehs* has a slightly sharp flavour from the added lemon juice. It is a regional recipe from Cilician Armenia and is usually eaten as it comes with bread. My mother often added pumpkin or aubergine to make it a very substantial meal. I strongly recommend the pumpkin version.

Sauce

3 tablespoons oil
2 medium onions, sliced
225 g/8 oz lamb, cut into
   1.2 cm/1/2 in pieces
100 g/4 oz chickpeas, soaked
   overnight

2 tablespoons tomato purée
2 teaspoons salt
1 teaspoon black pepper
2 cloves garlic, crushed
1 level tablespoon mint
2 tablespoons lemon juice

Kufta see recipe for basic *kibbeh* on page 129

Heat the oil in a large saucepan, add the onions and meat and fry for about 5 minutes, turning frequently. Drain the chickpeas and add to the pan with plenty of water. Bring to the boil and then lower the heat and simmer until the meat and chickpeas are tender. Remove any scum which appears on the surface. Stir in all the other sauce ingredients and simmer for a further 20–30 minutes. Taste and adjust seasoning if necessary.

Prepare the *kufta* as described in the basic *kibbeh* recipe.

These *kuftas* are 'blind', i.e. they have no filling. To make them keep your hands damp with cold water, break off small pieces of *kibbeh* and roll between your palms to form small marble-sized balls. Add these to the sauce and simmer gently for about 30 minutes Serve in soup bowls, accompanied by bread.

Variations

450 g/1 lb pumpkin, peeled and cut into 2.5 cm/1 in cubes
   or 450 g/1 lb aubergine, cut into 2.5 cm/1 in cubes

Add these vegetables to the sauce when you add the *kuftas*.

kabat al batatis min burkul

potato kibbeh with apricot filling

This recipe from Iraq, also popular in the Gulf States, has a fascinating and unusual meat and apricot filling associated more with Iranian-Caucasian dishes than with the more simple food of the nomad.

The *kibbehs* are fried in oil and served with fresh vegetables.

Filling

2 tablespoons *ghee* or oil
1 onion, finely chopped
350 g/12 oz minced lamb
2 tablespoons chopped almonds or
    hazlenuts
100 g/4 oz dried apricots, chopped
1/4 teaspoon ground cloves

1/4 teaspoon cumin
1/4 teaspoon nutmeg
1/2 teaspoon paprika
1 teaspoon salt
1/2 teaspoon black pepper
3 tablespoons water

Kibbeh

450 g/1 lb potatoes, boiled and mashed
100 g/4 oz fine burghul
25 g/1 oz plain flour
oil for frying

1 egg
1¹/2 teaspoons salt
1/2 teaspoon black pepper
2 tablespoons water

Garnish fresh vegetables, e.g. radishes, cucumber, tomatoes, lettuce, etc.

First prepare the filling by heating the *ghee* or oil, adding the onion and frying until soft. Add the meat and fry for 5–10 minutes until browned and the lumps have been broken down. Add the remaining filling ingredients, mix well and cook for 15–20 minutes, stirring frequently. Set aside to cool.

Place all the *kibbeh* ingredients in a large bowl and knead for about 5–10 minutes. Shape and stuff the *kibbeh* balls following the instructions for *kharperti kufta*, on page 137, keeping your hands damp with cold water.

Heat enough oil in a saucepan to deep fry, add the *kibbeh*, a few at a time and fry gently for 8–10 minutes or until golden. Remove with a slotted spoon, drain, arrange on a serving dish and keep warm while you cook the remaining *kibbeh*. Serve hot with fresh vegetables.

yoghurt dishes

One of the most important ingredients in Middle Eastern cooking, yoghurt (see Glossary for methods of preparation, *labna* and stabilized yoghurt, page 375) is not only used as an accompaniment to dishes, in salads or as a refreshing drink; it also appears in soups and stews — often as a main ingredient — as well as in cakes, breads and desserts.

I have included in this chapter a fragment of the vast repertoire of yoghurt dishes that I like — the choice is very personal indeed and the dishes included are not necessarily the most well known.

Having explained traditional methods of preparation in the Glossary, there are a few recipes following which make use of *labna*, drained yoghurt.

mast-e-kisei labna with herbs

In restaurants and at home the usual breakfast will be a plate of *labna* topped with a little olive oil and served with bread. The Iranians like to add chopped fresh dillweed, parsley, mint, chives, tarragon or other herbs that are freshly available.

Mix the *labna* and chopped herbs together, spread on a plate, garnish with a few chopped spring onions and dribble a little olive oil over the surface. Serve with hot bread for breakfast.

The choice of herbs depends on availability and the mixture is strictly personal and so there is plenty of scope to experiment.

madzna banir yoghurt cheese

A variation of the above from Armenia.

Prepare *labna* from yoghurt (see Glossary). Shape the *labna* into walnut-sized balls — a 'melon scoop' makes this an easy job. Arrange the balls in a serving dish and pour a little olive oil over them. Mix together 1 tablespoon fresh mint, 1 tablespoon fresh dillweed and 2 tablespoons chives — all finely chopped — and sprinkle over the balls.

shomin spinach and yoghurt salad

Spinach and yoghurt are like horses and carriages and love and marriage. Although I cannot vouch that all horses and carriages work harmoniously I know for sure that spinach and yoghurt always succeed. There are many such recipes throughout the Middle East. I have selected two classics, one from Armenia and the second from Iran.

450 g/1 lb fresh or
   225 g/8 oz frozen spinach
50 g/2 oz butter

1 small onion, finely chopped
salt and black pepper to taste
300 ml/$\frac{1}{2}$ pint yoghurt
2 cloves garlic, crushed

Garnish
2 tablespoons finely chopped toasted
   walnuts (optional)

paprika

Strip the leaves from the stalks of the fresh spinach and wash very thoroughly to remove all grit and sand. Thaw out frozen spinach. Half fill a large pan with water, bring to the boil and add the spinach. Simmer for about 8–10 minutes or until the spinach is just cooked. Strain into a colander and leave until cool enough to handle. Squeeze out as much of the moisture as possible and then chop the spinach.

Melt the butter in a large frying pan, add the onion and fry until soft and beginning to brown. Add the spinach and fry for a further 5 minutes, stirring frequently.

Season to taste with salt and black pepper.

Keep on a low heat while you mix the yoghurt and crushed garlic together in a small bowl. Divide the spinach into 4 portions and arrange each on a small plate in a circular shape. Spoon some of the yoghurt into the centre of each circle and then sprinkle the yoghurt with a little paprika. Garnish with a few chopped walnuts if you wish.

borani-ye-esfenjag

This is usually served with meat dishes but, as the *shomin*, it can be eaten as an appetizer or a savoury dish with bread.

225 g/8 oz fresh spinach	1/2 teaspoon salt
2 tablespoons lemon juice	pinch black pepper
1 tablespoon onion, finely chopped	300 ml/1/2 pint yoghurt

Garnish 1 tablespoon fresh mint, finely chopped, or 1 teaspoon dried mint

Wash the spinach several times in cold water until all the sand and grit has been removed. Strip the leaves from the stalks and discard the stalks.

Bring water to the boil in a large saucepan. Add the spinach, lower the heat and simmer for about 8–10 minutes. Drain the spinach into a colander and leave until cool enough to handle. Squeeze as much moisture as possible out of the spinach, chop it finely and place in a salad bowl. Add the lemon juice, onion, salt and pepper and mix. Add the yoghurt and mix thoroughly. Refrigerate for at least 1 hour. Serve garnished with the mint.

yogurtlu çop kebab braised beef with yoghurt

This recipe is from Trakya (the European part of Turkey) and, more precisely, from the region of Edirne (Greek Adrianople). It is also popular in Greece and Bulgaria. It is of course not a true kebab as the meat is neither skewered nor grilled, but rather a stew of sliced beef cooked in yoghurt.

It is an extremely tasty dish from the days of the Ottoman rule.

3 tomatoes, blanched, peeled and sliced	1 1/2 teaspoons marjoram
1 small onion, finely chopped	3 whole chillies
salt and black pepper	hot water
675 g/1 1/2 lb lean braising beef,	300 ml/1/2 pint yoghurt
cut into 1.2 cm/1/2 in pieces	2 eggs
50 g/2 oz butter, melted	2 teaspoons flour
1 teaspoon paprika	2 teaspoons malt vinegar

Garnish some parsley, finely chopped

Butter a heavy saucepan or casserole dish — the latter preferably so that you can take it straight to the table and serve from it. Arrange the tomato slices over the base and then cover with the chopped onion. Sprinkle with a little salt and black pepper. Arrange the meat over the onions, pour the melted butter over the top and then sprinkle with a little more salt and pepper, the paprika and the marjoram. Add the chillies and sufficient hot water to half fill the casserole. Bring to the boil and then simmer gently until the meat is tender and very little liquid remains. Add a little more water while cooking if necessary.

Put the yoghurt into a mixing bowl and beat in the eggs, flour and vinegar. Stir the yoghurt mixture into the casserole. Bring just to the boil, stirring gently until the sauce thickens. Remove from the heat, sprinkle with the parsley and serve immediately.

borani-ye goosht a lentil and yoghurt stew

This is a typical Middle Eastern stew of lentils, aubergines, lamb and yoghurt. Popular throughout the many lands, this particular recipe is from Iran — hence the local touch of saffron.

Borani is the Persian word for cold dishes made of yoghurt mixed with various vegetables and herbs, named after Poorandok — the daughter of King Khossow Parviz who, it is said, had a special fondness for yoghurt and yoghurt dishes. The many Indian biriani dishes have undoubtedly been influenced by their Iranian counterparts. Serve it cold with bread or hot with a rice *pilav*.

1 large aubergine
25 g/1 oz butter
1 onion, finely chopped
450 g/1 lb shoulder of lamb, cut
    into 1.2 cm/1/2 in pieces
600 ml/1 pint stock
1 teaspoon salt

1/2 teaspoon black pepper
1/2 teaspoon saffron diluted in
    1 tablespoon hot water
1/2 teaspoon oregano
75 g/3 oz whole brown lentils
600 ml/1 pint yoghurt
1 clove garlic, finely chopped

Peel the aubergine, cut in half lengthways and then cut crossways into 0.6 cm/1/4 in slices. Arrange the slices over a large plate, sprinkle with salt and set aside for 30 minutes. Then drain, rinse and dry with kitchen paper.

Melt the butter in a large saucepan and sauté the onion until soft and golden. Add the meat and cook for a few minutes, turning frequently. Add the stock, salt, pepper, saffron and oregano and bring to the boil. Cover and simmer for 1 hour. Rinse the lentils and add to the pan, cover and simmer for a further 30 minutes or until the lentils are tender. Add more water if necessary. Add the aubergine slices, cover again and simmer for a further 20–30 minutes.

At this stage it is possible to serve the stew with the yoghurt stirred through it. However, the whole stew is usually cooled slightly and then liquidized to a pulp or pounded to a paste in a large mortar. The yoghurt is then stirred into the pulp and the garlic is sprinkled over the top.

badami goosht lamb with saffron and almonds

A dish that is equally at home in North-West India, Pakistan and Afghanistan as in its original habitat of Iran. The Indian touch can be discerned in the use of a cinnamon stick, ginger and cardamom pods.

An exoitic and colourful dish. Serve with a rice *pilav*.

1/2 teaspoon saffron strands
   soaked in 2 teaspoons hot water
300 ml/1/2 pint yoghurt, stabilized
   with 1 egg or 1 tablespoon flour
2 teaspoons salt
900 g/2 lb leg of lamb, boned,
   excess fat removed, meat cut into
   2.5 cm/1 in cubes
50 g/2 oz *ghee* or butter
1 small stick cinnamon

3 whole cloves
1 onion, finely chopped
2 cloves garlic, finely chopped
1 teaspoon grated fresh ginger
1 teaspoon ground cumin
1 1/2 tablespoons ground almonds
3 cardamom pods, optional
300 ml/1/2 pint water
1 tablespoon fresh mint, chopped, or
   1 teaspoon dried mint

Squeeze the saffron strands to remove as much of the colour and fragrance as possible. Put the stabilized yoghurt into a large bowl and stir in the saffron water and salt. Add the meat cubes, turn until coated and then set aside.

In a large saucepan or casserole melt the *ghee* or butter, add the cinnamon stick and cloves and fry for a few minutes. Add the onion, garlic and ginger and fry gently for a few minutes until the onion is golden. Now add the cumin and fry for 2 more minutes. Drain the pieces of meat from the marinade, but reserve the marinade, add the meat to the pan and toss in the spices until well coated.

Stir in the yoghurt marinade, almonds, cardamom pods and 300 ml/1/2 pint water, lower the heat and simmer for about 1 hour or until the lamb is tender and the sauce is thick. Stir frequently to prevent the meat sticking to the pan. Stir in the mint and serve immediately on a bed of *pilav*.

immos assyrian meat and yoghurt stew

This very old dish, of Assyrian origin, is still popular in Syria and Lebanon. The name, literally translated, means 'cooked in its mother's image'. Before the appearance of yoghurt many such dishes were cooked in milk, a method still popular in parts of Russia and also in Central and Southern India. A rich and creamy meal which is best served with a rice or burghul *pilav*.

300 ml/½ pint water
1 tablespoon oil
2 onions, sliced
900 g/2 lb leg of lamb, cut into
  2.5 cm/1 in pieces
1 teaspoon salt
½ teaspoon black pepper

2 cloves garlic, crushed
1 teaspoon fresh parsley stalks, chopped
600 ml/1 pint yoghurt
1 tablespoon cornflour mixed to
  a paste with 1–2 tablespoons water
grated rind 1 lemon

Garnish 1 tablespoon fresh coriander or parsley, chopped

Bring the water and oil to the boil in a large saucepan. Add the onions, meat, half the salt, the pepper, garlic and parsley stalks. Cover the pan, reduce heat and simmer gently until the lamb is tender and the liquid has been reduced by two thirds.

Place the yoghurt and cornflour mixture in a saucepan with the remaining salt and bring gently to the boil, stirring constantly. Reduce heat to very low and cook for 8–10 minutes. Add the yoghurt mixture and lemon rind to the lamb mixture and simmer, uncovered, for a further 15 minutes. Pour into a large serving dish and sprinkle with the coriander or parsley.

mansaaf lamb with yoghurt

A famed Arab dish very popular in Jordan, Palestine and Saudi Arabia. Seated in their colourful tents the Bedouins prepare this festive dish (often a whole lamb) which is boiled, piled on top of a bed of pilav and served with thin Arab bread — *khubz-el-saj*.

With this dish the Bedouins honour their guests. The food is eaten in the right hand — a lump of meat is pulled off, rice is rolled around it and the mixture popped into the mouth.

Below is my slightly simplified version of how to prepare, serve and eat this traditional dish.

900 g/2 lb stewing meat, cut into
  5 cm/2 in pieces
1 onion, quartered
1½ teaspoons salt
900 ml/1½ pints water

450 ml/¾ pint yoghurt
1 egg
2 tablespoons vegetable oil
2 tablespoons pine kernels
2 tablespoons almonds

Place the meat, onion, salt and water in a large saucepan and bring to the boil. Simmer for about 45–60 minutes or until the meat is tender. Remove any scum which appears on the surface and add more water if necessary. Remove the meat from the pan and retain the stock.

Put the yoghurt in a large saucepan, add the egg and beat. Slowly bring to the boil, stirring constantly in one direction. Add about 300–450 ml/½–¾ pint of the meat stock, stir well and bring to the boil. Add the pieces of meat and heat through. Remove the pan from the heat.

Heat the oil in a small pan, add the nuts and fry gently until golden. Spread a plain rice *pilav* on a large serving dish, pile the meat in the middle and cover with half the yoghurt sauce. Sprinkle with the nuts and serve immediately with the remaining sauce in a separate jug.

dami ghalebi ba morgh

rice with chicken and dried fruit

A delicious and decorative dish from Iran.

It is usually cooked in a mould and inverted on to a serving dish showing a golden brown crust. However, it can be layered into a casserole and baked in the oven or steamed over a low heat.

Serve with salads of your choice.

4 large prunes, stoned
8 dates, stoned
8 dried apricots
8 dried peaches (optional)
2 teaspoons salt
350 g/12 oz rice, washed thoroughly under cold water and drained
900 ml/1^1/$_2$ pints water
4 chicken breasts, washed and dried

1 onion, thinly sliced
150 ml/^{1}/$_4$ pint chicken stock or water
1 teaspoon salt
^{1}/$_2$ teaspoon black pepper
100 g/4 oz butter, melted
^{1}/$_2$ teaspoon saffron
150 ml/^{1}/$_4$ pint yoghurt
50 g/2 oz walnuts, chopped
50 g/2 oz raisins

Cut the dried fruits into small pieces, place in a bowl of cold water and set aside.

Place the salt and water in a large saucepan and bring to the boil. Add the rice and simmer for about 20 minutes or until the water has been absorbed.

Meanwhile, place chicken breasts in a large saucepan with the onion, stock, salt and pepper, cover and simmer for about 30 minutes or until tender. Turn occasionally. Cool the chicken and remove and discard any bones. Reserve the stock.

In a small bowl mix together half the melted butter, the saffron, the yoghurt and 1 teacup of the cooked rice.

Drain the dried fruit. If using a mould coat its entire surface with this mixture. Over this mixture arrange first a layer of plain rice, then some dried fruit, some chicken pieces, some of the chopped walnuts and raisins and 1–2 tablespoons of the stock. Continue alternating layers until the mould is full ending with a layer of rice. Bake in an oven preheated to 190°C, 375°F, gas mark 5 for about 1 hour.

To unmould dip the mould up to the rim, in cold water for 2 minutes and invert on to a serving dish.

If using a saucepan or casserole first spread the butter-yoghurt-rice mixture over the base and then alternate the ingredients as described for the mould method. If using an ovenproof casserole bake at 190°C, 375°F or gas mark 5. Otherwise place the saucepan over low heat, wrap the lid in a tea towel and fit firmly on the pan. Steam for between 30–45 minutes.

dajaj souryani assyrian chicken with yoghurt

The Assyrians, once a mightly nation who 'came down like hungry wolves', are still found scattered throughout Turkey, Iraq, Syria and Iran. Their glorious days are over, but they continue to practice their age-old customs.

The recipe below is from Baghdad and was given to me by an Assyrian student I befriended in Britain. He asked me, in one of my books to 'include our chicken and emphasize that it is Assyrian — that is very important'. I have kept my promise and I hope you like it.

1.35 kg/3 lb roasting chicken,
   cut into 8 serving pieces
4 tablespoons butter or *ghee*
1 onion, finely chopped
1 green pepper, thinly sliced

600 ml/1 pint chicken stock
1 teaspoon salt
$1/2$ teaspoon black pepper
2 tablespoons sumac powder
2 tablespoons ground almonds
300 ml/$1/2$ pint yoghurt

Garnish
1 teaspoon cayenne pepper

1 teaspoon cumin

Melt the butter or *ghee* in a large saucepan and cook the chicken pieces until golden brown all over. Remove the chicken pieces from the pan to a large plate and keep warm. Add the onion and green pepper to the pan and sauté for a few minutes until the vegetables are soft. Add the stock, salt, pepper and sumac and bring to the boil. Return the chicken pieces to the pan, cover, lower the heat and simmer for 40–60 minutes or until the chicken is tender. Transfer the chicken pieces to a serving dish and keep warm.

Add a few tablespoons of water to the ground almonds and stir to a smooth paste. Stir into the juices in the pan and bring to the boil stirring constantly. Remove from the heat and stir in the yoghurt. Pour the sauce over the chicken and sprinkle with the cayenne pepper and cumin. Serve with a rice or burghul *pilav*.

nourov jud chicken with pomegranates

What's in your pocket?
that's what I want.
In your shirt pocket?
An apple you've found?

It's a pomegranate.
It's yours if you give
as many kisses as
the pomegranate has seeds.

Pomegranates can have
a thousand red seeds!
A thousand kisses?
How could that be?

When two love
become one love
It's easily done.
A thousand come quickly,
A thousand and one!
(Armenian folk song)

A family favourite which is simple and very attractive to look at when decorated with the sparkling seeds of the pomegranate.

1.35 kg/3 lb chicken	1 teaspoon salt
50 g/2 oz butter	1/2 teaspoon black pepper
1 onion, thinly sliced	1/2 teaspoon cumin
300 ml/1/2 pint chicken stock or water	600 ml/1 pint yoghurt, stabilized with 1 egg or 1 tablespoon plain flour

Garnish
2 pomegranates, skins removed and red seeds separated and retained in a bowl

Wash and dry the chicken and cut into 8 serving pieces. Melt the butter in a large saucepan and sauté the onion until golden. Add the chicken pieces, stock, salt, pepper and cumin and bring to the boil. Cover and simmer for about 45 minutes or until tender, turning occasionally. When ready to serve remove from the heat and spoon a few tablespoons of the hot sauce into the yoghurt. Gently stir the yoghurt into the saucepan and heat through. Arrange the chicken joints in a serving dish, pour the sauce over the top and then sprinkle the pomegranate seeds all over.

saray ordek duck in yoghurt

One of the many creations of the great nineteenth-century chef-hotelier Tokatlian of Istanbul.

There are some Middle Eastern superstitions about duck featuring in your dreams: to see one means to leave home for distant lands; to hunt one means to wish to return to a distant loved one; to eat one means to live in poverty abroad — how wrong can you be! To eat duck nowadays means to wallow in unashamed luxury — just look at the prices in the shops!

1.35–1.8 kg/3–4 lb oven ready duck
25 g/1 oz butter
5 tablespoons dry white wine
450 ml/3/4 pint yoghurt stabilized with
   1 egg or 1 tablespoon plain flour

450 ml/3/4 pint chicken stock or water
1 teaspoon salt
1/2 teaspoon black pepper
10 button onions
50 g/2 oz green olives, stuffed
50 g/2 oz black olives, stoned

Garnish
2 spring onions, finely chopped

2 tablespoons parsley, finely chopped

Wash and clean the duck, prick all over with a fork to let the fat run out during cooking. Melt the butter in a large pan, add the duck and brown it all over. Remove the duck to a plate, sprinkle with the wine and keep warm.

In a large, deep saucepan mix the yoghurt and chicken stock together, season with the salt and pepper, add the duck, cover and cook over a low heat until the duck is tender, turning it a few times during cooking.

Meanwhile, cook the onions in the butter remaining in the first pan and, when soft and golden, add the olives, stir and remove from the heat.

Arrange the duck on a large plate; either whole or cut into quarters; and surround with the onions and olives. Garnish with the spring onions and parsley. Serve the sauce separately.

ganachi — cooked vegetables

A table without vegetables is like an old man devoid of wisdom. — Arab saying.

'Never serve boiled vegetables' was one of my mother's first pieces of advice to her future daughter-in-law. 'Fry, stew, braise, pour sauces over, but never boil in water. It isn't our custom and remember, a man's heart is reached through his stomach.' How right she was!

In the Middle East vegetables are only ever boiled, drained and served when feeding the infirm and the sick.

The area is famed for its wealth of excellent, high quality vegetables, all of which can now be found in Europe and America. Some, such as courgettes, okra, aubergines, green peppers and pumpkins have been, until recently, little known and appreciated, but through the influx of people from the Mediterranean regions and the Far East they are becoming daily more available. Visit your local Greek or Indian grocer and see how the aubergines, okra, silverbeet, artichokes, flat-leaved parsley, avocados, yams, etc., are displayed there.

When served cold, vegetables should be cooked in olive oil, but when served hot they can be cooked in butter, *ghee* or a vegetable oil. They are eaten raw with a little seasoning and lemon juice, or with a yoghurt dressing; they are baked in the oven, grilled, stuffed with fruits, nuts, rice or meat mixtures. They are stewed with dried legumes, high in food values, such as lentils, chickpeas and beans, and with meats.

Whenever possible use fresh vegetables and only when not available resort to frozen or tinned versions — however good these may be they can never equal their fresh counterparts.

fried vegetables

Deep fried vegetables are very popular in the Middle East. They are either cooked plain or dipped in egg or in egg and flour.

Traditionally olive oil is used, but since this item is increasingly becoming almost a luxury other oils such as corn oil or, a Middle Eastern favourite, sunflower seed oil are good substitutes.

fried aubergines

450 g/1 lb aubergines, cut
   crossways into 0.6 cm/^{1}/4 in slices
2 tablespoons salt
150–300 ml/^{1}/4–^{1}/2 pint oil
2 eggs, beaten

1 clove garlic, crushed (optional)
1 teaspoon salt
^{1}/2 teaspoon black pepper
1 teaspoon dillweed
1 teaspoon dried mint

Arrange the aubergine slices on a plate, sprinkle with the salt and set aside for 30 minutes. Rinse under cold water and dry with kitchen paper.

Heat the oil in a large frying pan.

Mix the eggs with the garlic, salt, pepper, dill and mint.

Dip the aubergine slices, a few at a time, into the egg mixture and then fry, turning once, until golden on both sides. Remove with a slotted spoon, drain and keep warm while you fry the remaining slices in the same way. Serve warm as an accompaniment to all kinds of meat dishes.

It is also sometimes served cold as an appetizer.

fried courgettes

Courgettes are thinly sliced — to help them lose their capacity for absorbing too much oil — and then either simply fried in oil, or dipped in egg and fried or dipped into a batter made from 100 g/4 oz plain flour, 150 ml/^{1}/4 pint of water and 1 egg and then fried.

Serve with lemon wedges and garnished with chopped parsley, tarragon or mint fried in the same oil.

fried broad beans

450 g/1 lb young broad beans
900 ml/2 pints lightly salted water

flour
oil for frying

Remove the tops and tails of the broad beans and pull off the strings, but do not cut or shell. Bring the lightly salted water to the boil in a large saucepan, add the beans and cook for 4–5 minutes. Remove, drain and leave to dry on kitchen paper.

Heat enough oil in a pan to cover the bottom by about 5 cm/2 in. Roll the beans, a few at a time, in the flour and fry in the oil, turning once, until golden all over. Remove, drain and keep warm while you cook the remaining beans in the same way. Serve warm, with lemon wedges, with all kinds of meat dishes.

fried cauliflowers

1 cauliflower, washed and separated
  into florets
1.2 litres/2 pints lightly salted water
2 eggs, beaten

$1^1/_2$ teaspoons salt
1 teaspoon black pepper
oil for frying
fine breadcrumbs

Bring the lightly salted water to the boil in a large saucepan, add the florets and cook for about 10 minutes or until just tender. Drain in a colander and dry with kitchen paper.

Mix the eggs with the salt and pepper in a shallow dish.

Heat enough oil in a large saucepan to cover the base by about 5 cm/2 in. Dip the florets, a few at a time, into the eggs and then roll in the breadcrumbs to coat completely and fry in the oil until evenly browned. Remove with a slotted spoon, drain and keep hot while you cook the remaining florets in the same way. Serve as an accompaniment to all kinds of meat dishes or with natural yoghurt or with *tarator salsasi* (see recipe, page 284).

fried carrots

450 g/1 lb carrots, peeled and cut
  diagonally into 0.6 cm/$^1/_4$ in slices
1.2 litres/2 pints lightly salted water

Beer batter
100 g/4 oz plain flour, sifted
$1^1/_2$ teaspoons salt
175–200 ml/6–7 fl oz beer
oil for frying

Boil the carrots in the lightly salted water for 5 minutes. Drain and pat dry with kitchen paper.

In a bowl mix together the flour, salt and beer until you have a smooth batter — add a little more beer if necessary.

Heat enough oil in a frying pan to cover the bottom by about 5 cm/2 in. Dip the slices, a few at a time, into the batter and fry gently until tender and golden on both sides. Remove with a slotted spoon, drain and keep warm while you cook the remaining slices in the same way. Serve with all types of meat, poultry or fish dishes.

This beer-batter is popular in Turkey, the Balkans and Southern Russia where it originated.

You can fry other vegetables, e.g. sliced potatoes, pumpkin, turnips, etc. with these methods, i.e. plain, dipped in egg, or egg and flour in a batter.

They can all be served as appetizers with plain yoghurt, a garlic-yoghurt dressing or *tarator salsasi* (see recipe, page 284).

badenjam min tamar-el-hind

aubergines with tamarind

This recipe from the Gulf States is undoubtedly of Indian origin and related to *bhagar baigan* of North India. Tamarind juice can be purchased from Indian grocers, but if you cannot find it then buy tamarind pods and make the juice as directed below.

900 g/2 lb aubergines, hulled,
    trimmed and cut into quarters
100 g/4 oz *ghee*
2 large onions, sliced
1 teaspoon mustard seeds
2 teaspoons ground coriander
1 green chilli, seeds removed,
    finely chopped

2 cloves garlic, crushed
1/2 teaspoon turmeric
1/2 teaspoon cumin
3 tablespoons ground almonds
1/2 teaspoon salt
1/2 teaspoon black pepper
100 ml/4 fl oz tamarind juice

If tamarind juice is not available buy tamarind pods and put into about 125 ml/5 fl oz of hot water and leave to soak for 20 minutes.

Melt the *ghee* in a large frying pan, add the aubergine slices and fry for a few minutes until the skins become brown. Add a little more fat if necessary. Remove with a slotted spoon and reserve. Now add the onions and mustard seeds to the pan and fry for about 5 minutes or until the onions are golden, stirring frequently. Add the coriander and chilli and fry for a further minute or two. Add the garlic, turmeric, cumin, almonds, salt and pepper and mix well. Add the tamarind juice (or if it is not available squeeze out the pods and add the required amount of liquid) to the pan together with the aubergine slices. Turn carefully to mix, cover the pan and simmer for about 15 minutes or until aubergines are tender, stirring occasionally. Serve hot with meats of your choice.

nourov sumpoog

fried aubergines with pomegranate sauce

One of the many features of the Iranian and Caucasian cuisines is their clever use of fruit and nuts in food. Pomegranates, quinces, plums, apricots, cherries, etc. are mixed with meat, poultry, rice and other dishes with unusual and fascinating results.

The simple fried aubergines take on a new dimension when prepared with pomegranates and walnuts.

Ideal with kebabs of all kinds, particularly of pork and veal.

450 g/1 lb aubergines, cut crossways
    into 0.6 cm/¹/₄ in slices
2 tablespoons salt
150–300 ml/¹/₄–¹/₂ pint oil
1 green pepper, seeded and finely
    chopped
3 tablespoons pomegranate sauce
    (see below)

2 tablespoons cold water
1 clove garlic, crushed
2 tablespoons walnuts, coarsely chopped
¹/₄ teaspoon salt
¹/₂ teaspoon oregano

Garnish
1–2 tablespoons pomegranate seeds

First prepare the pomegranate sauce. The quantity given below should make about 100 ml/4 fl oz. Use what you need and then reserve the rest in a glass jar for future use. Squeeze the juice from the seeds of 6 large, ripe pomegranates and place in a saucepan with 75 g/3 oz sugar. Heat slowly, stirring until the sugar dissolves and then simmer until the mixture thickens to a syrupy consistency. Leave until cold then pour into a glass jar and seal.

Arrange the aubergine slices on a large plate, sprinkle with the salt and set aside for 30 minutes. Rinse under cold running water and pat dry with kitchen paper. Heat the oil in a large frying pan, add a few of the slices at a time and fry, turning once, until golden on each side. Remove, drain and reserve while you fry the remaining slices in the same way. Arrange the slices over a serving dish and sprinkle with the chopped green pepper.

Dilute the 3 tablespoons pomegranate syrup in the water, add the garlic, walnuts, salt and oregano and mix thoroughly. Pour this mixture over the aubergines and chill before serving. Garnish with the pomegranate seeds.

fasulyeh-bi-banadora beans with tomatoes

This is a typical vegetable dish popular throughout the Arab lands, as well as Turkey and the Caucasus.

You can prepare other vegetables such as cauliflower, carrots, peas, etc. in the same way. It can be served hot with pasta dishes, kebabs and roasts or cold with *sughtorov-madzoon* or other yoghurt dressing and bread.

450 g/1 lb fresh beans, whole
about 75 ml/3 fl oz olive
 or vegetable oil
1 large onion, finely chopped
1 teaspoon salt

1/2 teaspoon black pepper
1/2 teaspoon allspice
2 large tomatoes, coarsely chopped
450 ml/3/4 pint water

Wash the beans, snip off the ends and cut into 5 cm/2 in pieces.

Heat the oil in a large saucepan and sauté the onion until soft but not brown. Add the beans, salt, pepper and allspice. Cover and cook for 5 minutes.

Uncover, add the tomatoes and water and cook over a medium heat for about 30 minutes, stirring occasionally, until the beans are tender and much of the water evaporated. Serve hot or cold.

bamia basrani okra with tomatoes

A recipe from Iraq which is also popular throughout the Gulf States. There are several such dishes in the Middle East, all making use of okra — still a relatively unknown vegetable in the West. This recipe from the city of Basra — famed for its delicious dates — makes use of coriander, turmeric and tomatoes. Use fresh okra if possible. However, if using the tinned variety the cooking time will be considerably less.

Serve hot with meat and poultry dishes or cold with bread and fresh vegetables.

700 g/11/2 lb fresh okra
5 tablespoons olive oil
2 onions, thinly sliced
2 cloves garlic, quartered
450 g/1 lb tomatoes, blanched,
 peeled and sliced

1/2 teaspoon turmeric
1/2 teaspoon coriander
1 teaspoon salt
1/2 teaspoon black pepper
juice 1 lemon

Wash the okra thoroughly and cut off the stems taking care not to cut into the vegetable.

Heat the oil in a large saucepan and sauté the onions and garlic until soft and lightly browned. Add the okra and cook for a few minutes, stirring gently, but frequently. Now add the tomatoes and continue frying for a few more minutes. Add the turmeric, coriander, salt and pepper. Cover with water, bring quickly to the boil then lower the heat and simmer for 30–45 minutes or until the okra is tender. Stir in the lemon juice and cook for a further 10–15 minutes. Serve hot or cold.

nokhod rawandiz chickpeas, lentils and spinach

The Kurds and Assyrians of Rawandiz in Northern Iraq prepare this dish as often as possible. Although each nation claims it as their own it is, in fact, just as popular with the Iranians, Turks and Arabs of the region as it is with them. A simple, old dish; serve it with yoghurt or as an accompaniment to meat dishes.

2 tablespoons butter or *ghee*
2 large onions, thinly sliced
225 g/8 oz fresh spinach, washed
   thoroughly, drained, stemmed
   and coarsely chopped or
   100 g/4 oz frozen spinach, thawed
1 tablespoon lime or lemon juice
About 100 ml/4 fl oz water

1 teaspoon dillweed
1/4 teaspoon nutmeg
1 teaspoon salt
1/2 teaspoon black pepper
175 g/6 oz brown lentils, washed
75 g/3 oz pre-cooked or canned
   chickpeas

Melt the butter or *ghee* in a large saucepan. Add the onion and fry until soft and golden. Add the spinach, lime or lemon juice, water, dillweed, nutmeg, salt and pepper and bring to the boil. Now add the lentils, sufficient water to cover by about 1.2 cm/1/2 in, cover the pan and simmer for 20 minutes.

Add the pre-cooked chickpeas, cover and cook for a further 10–15 minutes until the lentils are cooked. Stir occasionally and add a little more water if there is any danger of the mixture burning. Turn into a serving dish and serve hot.

shesh havij carrots with nuts

This recipe is from Iran. It is tasty and attractive and is traditionally served with a plate of saffron rice *pilav* and a bowl of fresh salad. It also goes particularly well with poultry and game. Use pomegranate juice if it is available as it gives extra zest to the dish.

3 tablespoons butter or *ghee*
1 large onion, finely chopped
350 g/12 oz carrots, peeled and
   thinly sliced crossways
5 dates, stoned and thinly sliced
1 tablespoon raisins or sultanas

1 tablespoon white wine vinegar
1 tablespoon pomegranate juice or
   2 tablespoons lemon juice
4 eggs
1 teaspoon salt
1/2 teaspoon black pepper

Garnish
1 tablespoon almonds, slivered

1 tablespoon pistachios, slivered

Melt the butter or *ghee* in a saucepan. Add the onion and fry until soft and turning golden. Add the carrots and fry for a few minutes, stirring frequently to coat the carrots with the fat. Add the dates, raisins, vinegar and pomegranate or lemon juice and mix well. Cover the pan, lower the heat and simmer for 30 minutes. Transfer this mixture to a large frying pan or shallow casserole dish.

Break the eggs into a bowl, add the salt and pepper and beat well. Pour the eggs over the carrot mixture and cook over a very low heat until set. Sprinkle with the nuts and serve immediately.

afelia mushrooms with coriander

Afelia is a Cypriot speciality. There are many such named dishes and the one item they have in common is the abundant use of coriander. It will go well with any meat, poultry or fish dish.

50 ml/2 fl oz oil
450 g/1 lb small mushrooms,
   wiped clean and thickly sliced
100 ml/4 fl oz dry red wine

1¹/2 teaspoons salt
¹/2 teaspoon black pepper
1–2 (depending on taste) teaspoons
   coriander seeds, crushed

Heat the oil in a large saucepan, add the mushrooms and fry, turning frequently, until the juices evaporate. Lower the heat, add the wine, salt and pepper, cover and cook for 10 minutes. Finally add the coriander seeds and cook for 3–4 more minutes, stirring frequently. Transfer to a serving dish.

Variations
Afelias of potatoes, carrots, cauliflower, beans, etc. can be prepared in this same way.

shakarov tutum glazed pumpkin

A Caucasian speciality, excellent with *kibbeh* and *pilav* dishes and especially with poultry and pork dishes.

225 ml/8 fl oz water
175 g/6 oz sugar
2.5 cm/1 in piece root ginger,
   peeled and halved

1.35 kg/3 lb pumpkin, peeled and
   cut into 2.5 cm/1 in cubes
pinch salt
juice 1 lemon

Garnish
2 tablespoons almonds, blanched

1 tablespoon pistachios, slivered

Bring the water to the boil in a large saucepan. Stir in the sugar and root ginger. Add the pumpkin and salt and cook until tender, occasionally stirring carefully. Remove and discard the ginger. Stir in the lemon juice and transfer the pumpkin to a serving dish.

Toast the almonds and pistachios under a hot grill for a few minutes, turning frequently to prevent burning. Sprinkle the nuts over the pumpkin and serve.

Serves 6 people.

baghala ba kadoo broad beans with lettuce

A magnificent vegetable dish from Iran that goes well with rice *pilavs*, roasts and kebabs.

If by chance you are entertaining a Yazidi (a tribe of Kurds who live in eastern Turkey and northern Iran) never, under any circumstances, offer them lettuce either as a salad or, as in this recipe, cooked. They will be extremely offended for the Yazidies believe that the Devil (Shaytan) lurks in the lettuce leaves, and since they are Devil worshippers you would have insulted them!

450 g/1 lb fresh or dried broad beans	6 tablespoons parsley, finely chopped
1 lettuce, preferably Cos	2 teaspoons salt
12 small button onions, peeled or 1/2 onion, finely chopped	1/2 teaspoon black pepper
1/2 teaspoon dried thyme	5 tablespoons water
	3 tablespoons butter, melted

If using dried broad beans then soak overnight. If using fresh beans then shell and remove the transparent skins. Wash the lettuce, shake off excess moisture and chop. Place the broad beans, lettuce, onions, thyme, parsley, salt, pepper and water into a saucepan and mix well. Cover and cook over a low heat for about 30 minutes, stirring occasionally. Remove from the heat, stir in the melted butter and serve.

levivot fried potato pancakes

Before the arrival of potatoes these pancakes were made with cream cheese, but the Jews of Russia substituted and took this, as well as many other European-inspired dishes, with them to Israel.

Levivots are still called *latkes* by the Ashkanazim Jews of America and Europe, and naturally there are many such recipes. The one below is of Russian-Jewish origin and makes an excellent change for sautéed potatoes.

Traditionally served on the Feast of Chamcah — the Feast of Lights.

3 large potatoes	1 teaspoon salt
1 small onion	1/2 teaspoon white pepper
2 small eggs, beaten	oil for frying
3 tablespoons self-raising flour	

Peel the potatoes and grate finely so that they are almost reduced to a pulp. Place in a sieve to drain for 10 minutes. Squeeze as much liquid as possible from the potato pulp and then place in a mixing bowl. Grate the onion and add it to the potatoes. Add the eggs, flour, salt and pepper and mix well until you have a smooth batter.

Heat a little oil in a frying pan and when it is hot put in tablespoons of the batter, flattening each with the back of the spoon to make the pancakes about 7.5 cm/3 in in diameter. Cook over a moderate heat until brown on one side. Turn and cook on the other side. About 5–7 minutes on each side will allow time for the pancakes to cook through. Remove and drain on kitchen paper. Serve immediately.

batata musulyeh potatoes with yoghurt

A Kurdish dish from Musul, North Iraq.

The Kurds, of course, are the greatest people in the world! I think not, but so they claim; and I quote a few lines from J. Murray's *Sketches of Persia* to give an idea of the fiercely proud character of this sadly little known race of man:

The evening before we went to Sennah I read the introductory pages of the history of the Kurds. It is written by a native and, according to this patriotic author, all the virtue and courage this world has ever known was nurtured amid the wilds and mountains of Kurdistan. Its inhabitants, he affirms, attained great glory in former ages and would have subjected the universe, but for the caution of the prophet Muhammad who, struck by the fierce look and gigantic form of a Kurd ambassador, prayed to God that this formidable race might never be united. This prayer was heard, adds my author, and the warriors of Kurdistan have ever since been at variance with each other.

Now we know, but seriously — they have produced one of the greatest leaders of history, namely Saladdin. Also many delicious dishes still comparatively unknown and this is one of them.

6 large potatoes, peeled
25 g/1 oz butter or *ghee*
3 tablespoons yoghurt
4 egg yolks
1/2 teaspoon sweet marjoram
1/2 teaspoon cayenne pepper

1 teaspoon salt
2 tablespoons sesame seeds
4 tablespoons walnuts, very finely
  chopped
3 tablespoons toasted breadcrumbs
oil for frying

Garnish lettuce leaves, tarragon leaves, spring onions and radishes

Cook the potatoes in boiling, salted water until they are tender. Drain them and mash until smooth. Put the mashed potatoes into a large bowl with the butter and yoghurt and stir until well blended. Add 2 of the egg yolks, the marjoram, cayenne pepper, salt and sesame seeds and mix well.

Take a spoonful of the potato mixture, roll between wet palms to form a walnut-sized ball. Repeat with remaining potato mixture.

Beat remaining egg yolks together in a small bowl and mix the walnuts and breadcrumbs together on a plate. Heat some oil in a large frying pan.

Dip each potato ball into the beaten egg, roll in the walnut mix and fry, a few at a time, turning until they are golden all over. This will only take a few minutes. Drain on kitchen paper, arrange on a bed of lettuce leaves and serve with garnishes.

ailazan armenian vegetable casserole

Ailazan means 'different kinds' — suggesting that any type of vegetable can be used. The recipe below is a family favourite.

Serve it hot with roasts, grills or *pilavs* and cold with cold meats and poultry.

1 aubergine, cut crossways into 1.2 cm/$1/2$ in slices
1 green pepper, seeded and cut into 8 pieces
2 carrots, peeled and cut into 0.6 cm/$1/4$ in rounds
1 onion, thinly sliced
1 courgette, cut into 1.2 cm/$1/2$ in rounds
100 g/4 oz French beans, trimmed and halved
100 g/4 oz peas

3 tomatoes, blanched, peeled and coarsely chopped
2 tablespoons parsley, finely chopped
2 tablespoons mint, finely chopped
1 clove garlic, crushed
1 tablespoon sumac powder
2 teaspoons salt
1 teaspoon black pepper
70 ml/$21/2$ fl oz olive oil — if to be eaten cold or 50 g/2 oz butter
150 ml/$1/4$ pint water

Place all the vegetables in a large ovenproof casserole, placing the tomatoes on top of the rest. Sprinkle the parsley, mint, garlic, sumac, salt and pepper over the top. Dot with the butter or pour in the oil. Add the water, bring to the boil, cover and place in an oven preheated to 180°C, 350°F, gas mark 4. Cook for about 1 hour or until the vegetables are tender, stirring gently occasionally. Taste and adjust seasoning if necessary.

chatzilim mevushalim israeli aubergine casserole

This is the Israeli 'ratatouille'. Serve with meat dishes.

2 aubergines, cut into 1.2 cm/$1/2$ in slices
3 tablespoons dry mustard
1 teaspoon salt
$1/2$ teaspoon black pepper
$1/2$ teaspoon cayenne pepper
50 g/2 oz butter, melted

1 large onion, thinly sliced
2 large tomatoes, sliced
1 stalk fennel, diced
2 green peppers, seeded and cut into 0.6 cm/$1/4$ in slices
$1/2$ teaspoon allspice

Coat each aubergine lightly with the mustard, sprinkle with the salt, black and cayenne pepper and arrange on a large plate. Grease a large casserole with a little of the butter and arrange half the aubergine slices over the bottom. Now arrange the onion, tomatoes, fennel and green peppers over the aubergines. Top with the remaining aubergine slices and sprinkle with the allspice. Dribble the rest of the butter over the top then cover the casserole and bake in an oven preheated to 190°C, 375°F, gas mark 5 for about $11/4$ hours or until the vegetables are tender. Serve warm.

sabahna doual arab vegetable casserole

The literal meaning of this dish is 'Seven States'. A typical vegetable casserole which is popular throughout the Middle East. Serve with any meat, poultry or fish dish.

175 ml/6 fl oz oil
1 large onion, thinly sliced
225 g/8 oz haricot beans,
    soaked overnight in cold water
1.2 litres/2 pints water
2 large potatoes, peeled and
    thinly sliced
3 carrots, peeled and cut crossways
    into 0.6 cm/$1/4$ in slices

1 celeriac, peeled and sliced
6 spring onions, chopped
2 cloves garlic, thinly sliced
$1^1/2$ teaspoons salt
$1/2$ teaspoon black pepper
$1/2$ teaspoon allspice
2 bay leaves

Garnish **2–3 tablespoons parsley, finely chopped**

Heat the oil in a large saucepan, add the onion and fry until soft.

Drain the beans and add to the pan with the water. Bring to the boil, then lower the heat and simmer for 1–$1^1/2$ hours or until the beans are tender. Add the potatoes, carrots, celeriac, onions, garlic, salt, pepper, allspice and bay leaves. If necessary add a little more water to just cover the vegetables and then simmer until they are all cooked and most of the liquid has evaporated. Pour into a large serving dish and sprinkle with the parsley.

ayvali sabzisi kurdish vegetable casserole

A dish popular throughout Kurdistan, Northern Iran and the Caucasus, where the use of fruit in casseroles and stews is an old one. A colourful dish which has an interesting combination of flavours and textures. It is traditionally served with a burghul or rice *pilav* and grilled meats.

900 g/2 lb red cabbage,
   damaged leaves removed and cut
   into 4 quarters
100 g/4 oz butter or *ghee*, melted
1¹/₂ teaspoons salt
¹/₂ teaspoon black pepper

¹/₂ teaspoon ground cinnamon
2 tablespoons lime or lemon juice
2 large quinces or cooking apples
1 tablespoon sugar
2 tablespoons walnuts, coarsely
   chopped

Garnish
2 tablespoons fresh tarragon, finely chopped or 1 tablespoon dried tarragon

Remove the stalks and thick ribs of cabbage then wash under cold water, drain and chop coarsely. Grease a large casserole dish with a little of the melted fat and arrange the cabbage in the bottom. Sprinkle with the salt, pepper, cinnamon and lemon or lime juice and pour the melted butter or *ghee* evenly over the top. Cover the dish and place in an oven preheated to 180°C, 350°F, gas mark 4 for 1¹/₄ hours.

Meanwhile, peel the quinces or cooking apples, core and cut into 0.6 cm/¹/₄ in thick slices. Remove the casserole from the oven, arrange the slices over the cabbage and sprinkle with the sugar and walnuts. Cover, return to the oven and cook for a further 30–40 minutes or until the cabbage is well done. Serve sprinkled with the tarragon.

dolmas — stuffed vegetables

Dolma is a Turkish word meaning to fill, to stuff. The idea is very old and very simple; vegetables, rice, burghul (cracked wheat), meats, fruit, nuts and spices are mixed and then stuffed into or used to fill vegetables or fruits. Vegetable and fruit corers have been found in sites as far apart as Knossos, Crete and Medzamor, Armenia (5–6000 years ago). Mentions are made too of wrapped vine leaves both in Greek and early Persian historical accounts, but it was probably during the late Middle Ages in Constantinople that the true *dolmas* of today were first perfected.

With the conquest of that city by the Ottomans in 1453, and with the subsequent enlargement of their empire, many aspects of the arts, science and domestic culture not only changed names but also spread through the newly acquired territories. This is why *dolma*-type dishes appear in North Africa, the Balkans, Saudi Arabia, Iran and as far away as the borders of India.

Dolma dishes were first the prerogative of the 'Porte' — Emperor or Sultan — they were created for the gratification of the rich and the mighty. The Ottomans, whose own cuisine had been extremely poor, avidly took up everything that came their way. It is interesting to note that even today there are no *dolma* or *dolma*-type dishes in the lands from where the original Turkic-Mongolian tribes came, i.e. Turkmenistan, Uzbekistan and Khazakstan.

To prepare *dolma* is an acquired art. It is time consuming, a little elaborate, but the final result is — as it was meant to be — regal. The basic requirements are time, a corer and a generous amount of imagination.

There are several standard fillings which are used throughout the Middle East. There are also some little known regional variations, some of which I have included in this section. It is important to note that stuffed vegetables can be served hot or cold. Usually the cold versions do not include meat and are offered as part of the *mezzeh* table or as savouries with *sughtorov-madzoon* — yoghurt-garlic dressing.

Hot *dolma* are always served as a main meal. In the past — and still today with the peasants and mountain folk — certain vegetables were cored and dried under the sun for winter use, a primitive form of preserving. Today fresh vegetables are available throughout the year and this process has been abandoned by the urbanized housewife who has also abandoned the habit of frying the stuffed vegetables in *ghee* or oil before cooking. This process enriches the flavour of the meal, but makes it rather heavy.

Both vegetables and fruits can be stuffed. The following are by far the most common ones — artichokes, aubergines, courgettes, peppers, onions, potatoes and tomatoes. The following items are also wrapped around fillings — vine leaves, cabbage leaves and silverbeet leaves. Although these are often called *dolmas* this is an erroneous description. They should be named *sarma* (Turkish) or *patoug* (Armenian) as I have done.

cold dolma fillings

The following fillings are general favourites, although they are often flavoured with different spices and herbs.

The quantities given are enough for 1–1.2 kg/2–2¹/₂ lbs of vegetables, but this does of course vary according to the size and particular vegetable used and the amount of pulp scooped out of it.

It is approximately equivalent to 6 medium aubergines, 8 medium-large tomatoes or 8 medium green peppers or courgettes.

You can also use 350 g/12 oz vine leaves — see *derevi blor* page 168.

filling 1

Rice, raisins and onion — Istanbul style.

225 g/8 oz long grain rice, washed thoroughly under cold water and drained
1 large onion, finely chopped

3 tablespoons parsley, finely chopped
2 tablespoons raisins
2 teaspoons salt
¹/₂ teaspoon black pepper

filling 2

Typical Middle Eastern type.

175 g/6 oz long grain rice, washed thoroughly under cold water and drained
3 tomatoes, blanched, peeled and chopped
1 large onion, finely chopped
3 tablespoons parsley, finely chopped

2 tablespoons pine kernels
1 tablespoon raisins
1¹/₂ teaspoons salt
1 teaspoon dillweed
¹/₂ teaspoon black pepper
¹/₂ teaspoon ground cinnamon

filling 3

An Iranian favourite.

50 g/2 oz chickpeas, soaked overnight in cold water, then cooked in simmering water and drained
100 g/4 oz long grain rice, washed thoroughly under cold water and drained
3 tomatoes, blanched, peeled and chopped

1 large onion, finely chopped
1 teaspoon dried mint
1 teaspoon dried tarragon
1 teaspoon dillweed
1 teaspoon salt
¹/₂ teaspoon black pepper
¹/₂ teaspoon cinnamon

To prepare the fillings put all the ingredients into a large bowl and knead until well blended. Then use to stuff the vegetables of your choice.

Fill each one until 3/4 full — this will leave room for the rice to swell while cooking.

filling 4

Rice and mushroom — a Caucasian favourite.

4 tablespoons *ghee*
1 large onion, finely chopped
450 g/1 lb mushrooms, wiped clean
 and coarsely chopped

1¹/₂ teaspoons salt
1/2 teaspoon black pepper
1/2 teaspoon allspice
1 tablespoon chopped fresh dill or
 1 teaspoon dried dillweed

Heat the *ghee* in a large frying pan, add the onion and fry until soft. Add the mushrooms and sauté for 2–3 minutes, stirring frequently. Add remaining ingredients, stir and proceed to stuff vegetables as directed.

filling 5

An all vegetable filling.

3-4 tablespoons oil
2 large onions, finely chopped
2 sticks celery, finely chopped
6 medium carrots, peeled and grated
2 large tomatoes, blanched,
 peeled and chopped

3 tablespoons parsley, finely chopped
1 teaspoon salt
1/2 teaspoon black pepper
2 tablespoons tarragon or dill,
 finely chopped,
 or 2 teaspoons dried tarragon or dill

Heat the oil in a frying pan, add the onions and fry until soft. Add the celery, carrots and tomatoes and fry for a further 3–4 minutes, stirring frequently. Stir in the remaining ingredients and remove from the heat.

Fill the vegetables of your choice with any of the above fillings. Those using filling 5 can be baked in the oven (190°C, 375°F, gas mark 5) with a sauce of 1.2–1.8 litres/2–3 pints water, juice 1/2 lemon and 1/2 teaspoon salt.

Any vegetable with a rice or burghul filling should be placed in a saucepan, held down with a plate and weight, covered with a sauce and cooked over a medium heat. For a typical sauce see *derevi blor* on page 168.

derevi blor vine leaves filled with rice and nuts

350 g/12 oz vine leaves — fresh ones are perfect, but if they are not available you can buy packets from Continental or Middle Eastern stores.

Filling

150 ml/^{1}/$_4$ pint oil

2 onions, thinly sliced

1 green pepper, seeded and thinly sliced

175 g/6 oz long grain rice, washed thoroughly under cold water and drained

^{1}/$_2$ teaspoon chilli pepper

1 teaspoon allspice

1 teaspoon salt

1^1/$_2$ tablespoons tomato purée

25 g/1 oz chopped almonds

1 tablespoon parsley, chopped

Sauce

1 tablespoon tomato purée

600–900 ml/2–3 pints water

3–4 cloves garlic, crushed

1 teaspoon salt

^{1}/$_2$ teaspoon chilli pepper

3 tablespoons lemon juice

Wash the leaves in cold water, place in a saucepan and add enough water to cover the leaves. Bring to the boil and simmer for about 15 minutes and then drain into a colander.

Heat the oil in a large saucepan, add the onions and green pepper and cook for 5–10 minutes, stirring occasionally, until the onions are soft, but not brown. Stir in the rice, chilli pepper, allspice, salt and tomato purée and cook gently for a further 10 minutes, stirring occasionally to prevent the mixture sticking. Remove from the heat, stir in the chopped almonds and parsley, turn into a large bowl and leave to cool.

To make each *blor*, spread a leaf out flat, veins uppermost. Cut off the stem. With the cut end towards you place I tablespoon of filling near the cut end. Fold the cut end over the filling and then fold the two sides over the filling towards the centre. Roll the leaf up towards the tip and you will be left with a small cigar-shaped parcel. When you have used up all the filling use any remaining leaves to cover the bottom of a medium saucepan — this helps to prevent burning. Pack the parcels carefully and closely into the saucepan in layers and then place a plate on top to cover as many as possible and hold it down with a small weight — this prevents them from moving while cooking and becoming undone.

Mix the ingredients for the sauce together in a bowl and pour into the saucepan. The sauce should completely cover the *blor*. If it doesn't then add a little more water. Bring to the boil, lower the heat and simmer for 1^1/$_2$–2 hours. Add more water if necessary. Remove from the heat, take off the weight and plate and remove one *blor* to test if the leaf is tender. Allow to cool, remove from the saucepan and arrange on a serving dish. Garnish with some lemon wedges.

lahana dolmasi

cabbage leaves filled with rice and nuts

A popular recipe from Turkey. You can also use any of the other fillings suggested. Serve cold or warm with lemon wedges.

1–1.35 kg/2–3 lb head of white cabbage, thick core removed

Filling

3 tablespoons oil

2 onions, finely chopped

100 g/4 oz long grain rice, washed
thoroughly under cold water
and drained

1 tablespoon pine kernels

1 tablespoon blanched almonds,
coarsely chopped

1 tablespoon raisins

1/2 teaspoon allspice

pinch paprika

1 1/2 teaspoons salt

1/2 teaspoon black pepper

225 ml/8 fl oz water

juice 1 lemon

Garnish **2 tablespoons parsley, chopped and lemon wedges**

Bring a large saucepan two-thirds full of lightly salted water to the boil. Place the cabbage in the water and boil for 7–8 minutes. Remove the cabbage and, when cool enough to handle, carefully peel away the outer leaves taking care not to tear them. Place the leaves in a colander to cool.

When it becomes difficult to remove the leaves return the cabbage to the water and boil for a few more minutes. Continue removing the leaves until you have all that you need. Reserve the small inner leaves. Meanwhile, heat the oil in a saucepan, add the onions and fry until soft. Add the rice, pine kernels and almonds and fry, stirring frequently, until the nuts begin to turn golden. Add the raisins, spices and water and bring to the boil. Reduce the heat, cover and simmer until the liquid is absorbed. Remove from the heat, stir in half the lemon juice and set aside.

To fill a leaf place one on a board, veins uppermost, and cut out the hard stem. With the cut end towards you place 1 tablespoon — exact amount depends on the size of the leaf — near the cut end. Fold the cut end over the filling and then fold the two sides over the filling towards the centre. Roll the leaf up towards the tip and the result will be a cigar-shaped parcel. Continue in this way until you have used up all the leaves and filling. Use any remaining leaves to cover the base of a medium saucepan. Pack the parcels carefully and closely into the saucepan in layers and sprinkle with the remaining lemon juice. Place a plate over the leaves to cover as many as possible and hold down with a small weight — this prevents leaves from unwrapping while cooking. Pour in enough water to cover and bring to the boil. Lower the heat and simmer for about 1 hour or until the leaves are tender. Add a little more water if necessary. Remove from the heat and take off weight and plate. When cool enough to handle arrange on a serving plate. Serve garnished with the parsley and lemon wedges.

vospov litsk

vine leaves filled with lentils, burghul and prunes

A regional dish from the Caucasus. It is usually served during the forty days of Lent. In the Caucasus they usually use fresh plums and plum syrup. Unless you can find these I suggest you use prunes and pomegranate juice or lemon juice.

225 g/8 oz vine leaves

Filling

75 g/3 oz brown lentils, rinsed
50 g/2 oz coarse burghul
4 tablespoons oil
1 small onion, finely chopped
6 stoned prunes, soaked overnight
 and then sliced
1 tablespoon raisins

1 teaspoon salt
1/2 teaspoon black pepper
1/2 teaspoon dried mint
1/2 teaspoon nutmeg
1 tablespoon pomegranate juice or
 lemon juice
225 ml/8 fl oz water

Sauce

1 tablespoon oil
1 teaspoon salt

water

Wash the vine leaves in cold water, place in a saucepan half filled with water and bring to the boil. Simmer for 15 minutes and then drain in a colander.

Meanwhile, boil the lentils in lightly salted water for 15 minutes and then strain and set aside.

Wash the burghul in a bowl until the water you pour off is clear.

Heat the oil in a saucepan, add the onion and fry until soft. Add the lentils, burghul, prunes, raisins, salt, pepper, mint and nutmeg and stir. Add the pomegranate or lemon juice and the water and simmer over a low heat until the liquid has been absorbed. Remove from the heat and leave to cool. To fill the leaves see *derevi blor* on page 168. Use any remaining leaves to line the base of a saucepan. Pack the filled vine leaves carefully into the pan in layers.

Place an inverted plate over the top to cover as many as possible and place a weight on the plate. This will prevent the vine leaves moving about and becoming undone during the cooking. Add the oil, salt and sufficient water to cover. Bring to the boil, then lower the heat and simmer for 1–1 1/2 hours. Add more water if necessary. Remove from the heat and take off the weight and plate. When cool arrange on a serving plate.

hot dolmas

Below are a few of the more popular fillings.

filling 1

A rice filling popular with Armenians and Turks.

450 g/1 lb lamb, minced twice
175 g/6 oz long grain rice, washed
  thoroughly under cold water
  and drained
1 small onion, finely chopped

1 large tomato, blanched, peeled
  and chopped
2 tablespoons parsley, finely chopped
1 teaspoon salt
1/2 teaspoon black pepper
1/2 teaspoon ground cinnamon

filling 2

A rice filling Iranian-style.

450 g/1 lb minced lamb
100 g/4 oz long grain rice,
  washed thoroughly under
  cold water and drained
50 g/2 oz yellow split peas,
  soaked overnight and then
  cooked until just tender

1 small onion, finely chopped and
  sautéed in 2 tablespoons butter
2 tablespoons parsley, finely chopped
1 teaspoon salt
1/2 teaspoon black pepper
1/4 teaspoon nutmeg
1/2 teaspoon ground cinnamon

filling 3

Another Iranian favourite used in *dolmeh-ye bademjan* — aubergine dolma.

1 large onion, finely chopped
  and sautéed in 50 g/2 oz butter
450 g/1 lb minced lamb or beef
2 tablespoons tomato purée
6 tablespoons lemon juice
1 teaspoon salt
1/2 teaspoon black pepper
3 spring onions, finely chopped
4 tablespoons parsley, finely chopped

1 tablespoon fresh mint, chopped
  or 1 1/2 teaspoons dried mint
1 tablespoon fresh tarragon, chopped
  or 1 1/2 teaspoons dried tarragon
100 g/4 oz long grain rice, washed
  thoroughly under cold water
  and drained
3 hard-boiled eggs, shelled and
  chopped (optional)
1 tablespoon sugar

filling 4

An Assyrian favourite used in *batinjan mishi* — aubergine dolma.

450 g/1 lb lamb, minced twice
1 small onion, finely chopped and
    sautéed in 2 tablespoons butter
100 g/4 oz long grain rice, washed
    thoroughly under cold water
2 tablespoons raisins
2 tablespoons pine kernels

1½ teaspoons salt
½ teaspoon black pepper
3 large tomatoes, blanched, peeled
    and chopped
½ teaspoon dried marjoram or basil
½ teaspoon ground cinnamon

filling 5

A burghul and meat filling which is an Armenian recipe — *sumpoogi litsk* — aubergine dolma. Burghul is used in much the same way as rice and can be used instead of rice in any of the above recipes.

450 g/1 lb minced lamb
1 small onion, finely chopped
175 g/6 oz coarse grain burghul, washed
    under cold water and drained
1 green pepper, seeded and chopped
1 tablespoon parsley, finely chopped

1–2 cloves garlic, crushed
1 tablespoon tomato purée
1 tablespoon allspice
1½ teaspoons salt
½ teaspoon chilli pepper
½ teaspoon black pepper

Below is described a method for preparing a typical *dolma* meal. It applies to any of the above fillings.

    The vegetable prepared here is the aubergine, but you can prepare in a similar fashion courgettes, tomatoes or green peppers – the latter two do not need to be soaked in salted water. Vine leaves can also be filled with any of the above fillings.

patlıçan dolması aubergine dolma served warm

Preparation of the aubergines — Cut the stalks off each aubergine. With an apple corer remove as much of the flesh as possible from each vegetable taking care not to split or make a hole in the shells. Leave to soak in cold salted water for 30 minutes. Rinse under cold running water. They are now ready to be stuffed.

Preparation of the filling — Place all the ingredients for the filling of your choice in a large bowl and knead until well blended. Place some of the filling in each vegetable until it is ³/₄ full. This ensures that there is room for the rice or burghul to swell during cooking. Arrange the vegetables in a large saucepan, cover with an inverted plate and hold it in place with a weight. This prevents the vegetables from moving while cooking and keeps the fillings in place.

Preparation of the sauce — The simplest sauce consists of 1.8–2.4 litres/3–4 pints of water seasoned with 1 teaspoon salt, 1/2 teaspoon black pepper and the juice of 1 lemon. To this basic sauce you can, if you wish, add one or more of the following ingredients — 1 tablespoon tomato purée, 2–3 bay leaves, 1 teaspoon of either mint, thyme, dillweed, basil or marjoram.

One of the tastiest sauces is the one usually used to cook *sumpoogi litsk*. Mix together the following:

1.8–2.4 litres/3–4 pints water	1/2 teaspoon chilli pepper
3 tablespoons tomato purée	1 tablespoon dried mint
2 teaspoons salt	4 cloves garlic, halved
	juice 1 lemon

Another interesting sauce is the sweet and sour one used for *dolmeh-ye bademjan*.

1.8–2.4 litres/3–4 pints water	100 g/4 oz sugar
100 ml/4 fl oz vinegar preferably	1–2 teaspoons saffron
tarragon vinegar	

Mix whatever ingredients you are going to use for the sauce in a large bowl and pour into the saucepan. The sauce must cover the vegetables by at least 2.5 cm/1 in and so add more water if necessary. Bring to the boil and then lower the heat and simmer for 1 hour. The cooking time will vary a little depending on the thickness of the vegetable shells. To taste if they are tender use a fork. If the prongs enter easily then the *dolma* is cooked. Add a little more water if necessary while cooking. Serve the *dolma* with a little of their sauce and with yoghurt and/or salads.

sheik-el-mahshi

courgettes filled with meat and nuts

Literally translated this famed Arab dish means 'King of stuffed vegetables', for it contains just meat and nuts and does away with rice — hence a regal meal. Although sometimes aubergines are substituted for courgettes, I think the latter are much more successful. This recipe is from Northern Syria. Serve with a plain rice *pilav* and fresh salad.

12 small or 8 medium courgettes	oil

Filling

450 g/1 lb minced lamb or beef	2 tablespoons parsley, finely chopped
1 teaspoon salt	1 small onion, finely chopped
1/2 teaspoon black pepper	1 tablespoon tomato purée
1 teaspoon allspice	100 g/4 oz pine kernels
	or 100 g/4 oz chopped walnuts

Sauce

25 g/1 oz butter	600 ml/1 pint water
1 clove garlic, crushed	1 teaspoon salt
1 tablespoon tomato purée	1/2 teaspoon black pepper

Cover the base of a large frying pan with about 1.2 cm/1/2 in oil.

Slice the stalk ends off the courgettes. Remove as much flesh as possible from each courgette using an apple corer. Ideally the shell should be about 0.6 cm/1/4 in thick. Take care not to split or make holes in the shells. Wash the courgettes under cold running water and dry with kitchen paper. Heat the oil in the frying pan, add the courgettes a few at a time and fry gently for about 10 minutes, turning from time to time. When cooked set aside on kitchen paper to drain and cool.

To make the filling put the meat and onion in a saucepan and cook over a moderate heat for 20–30 minutes, stirring frequently to prevent sticking. Stir in the remaining filling ingredients and cook for about a further 10 minutes. Spoon the meat mixture into the courgettes. Lay the vegetables side by side in an ovenproof dish.

Prepare the sauce by heating butter in a saucepan, adding the garlic and tomato purée and cooking for 3–4 minutes, stirring occasionally.

Add the water, salt and pepper, bring to the boil and pour over the courgettes. Place the dish in an oven preheated to 190°C, 375°F, gas mark 5 and bake for about 30 minutes or until the courgettes are tender. Test with a fork.

badenjan mahshi min tamar

aubergines stuffed with dates and nuts

A fascinating recipe from Babylon — a small town in Iraq near the ancient capital with its hanging gardens.

Dates and hazelnuts are the two outstanding products of the land (not counting the black oil) and this recipe makes a clever use of both.

Serve with a rice *pilav* of your choice or as an accompaniment to poultry dishes.

4 medium aubergines, about 175 g/6 oz each, hulls removed	2 large tomatoes, blanched, peeled and coarsely chopped
5-6 tablespoons butter or *ghee*	8 stoneless dates, thinly sliced
1 onion, finely chopped	3 tablespoons hazelnuts, coarsely chopped or slivered almonds
1 clove garlic, crushed	
1 large green pepper, seeded and thinly sliced	1/2 teaspoon salt
	pinch turmeric
3-4 mushrooms, thinly sliced	3-4 tablespoons orange or apple juice

Cut each aubergine in half lengthways, arrange the halves in a baking dish and bake in an oven preheated to 200°C, 400°F, gas mark 6 until the flesh is soft. Remove and leave until cool enough to handle. Scoop the flesh out with a spoon leaving a shell about 0.6 cm/¹/₄ in thick. Reserve the flesh.

Melt the fat in a saucepan, add the onion and fry until soft. Add the garlic, green pepper, mushrooms and tomatoes, stir well and fry for about 5 minutes. Chop the aubergine flesh and add to the pan. Add the remaining ingredients, mix thoroughly and cook for a further 3–4 minutes, stirring frequently. Remove from the heat.

Grease a large, shallow baking dish and arrange the halved aubergines in it, side by side. Spoon the date and nut mixture into the aubergines and bake in an oven preheated to 190°C, 375°F, gas mark 5 for 12–15 minutes. Remove from the oven and serve.

batatat mahshi

potatoes stuffed with meat and nuts

Popular with all, particularly in Saudi Arabia.

12 medium-large potatoes, peeled

3 tablespoons *ghee* or butter

Filling

450 g/1 lb minced lamb or beef
1 small onion, finely chopped
1 tablespoon tomato purée
100 g/4 oz pine kernels or
    chopped walnuts

2 tablespoons seedless raisins
1 teaspoon salt
¹/₂ teaspoon black pepper
1 teaspoon allspice

Sauce

3 tablespoons tomato purée
450 ml/³/₄ pint water

1¹/₂ teaspoons salt
¹/₂ teaspoon black pepper
6–7 tablespoons oil

Hollow out the potatoes with an apple corer or small teaspoon. Melt the *ghee* or butter in a pan, add the potatoes and fry for 2–3 minutes, turning frequently.

To make the filling put the meat and onion in a saucepan and cook over a moderate heat for 20–30 minutes, stirring frequently to prevent sticking. Stir in the remaining filling ingredients and cook for a further 10 minutes. Spoon this filling into the potatoes.

Lightly oil the inside of a large casserole dish and pack the potatoes in tightly in a single layer with the openings uppermost.

Dilute the tomato purée in the water and add the remaining sauce ingredients. Pour the sauce over the potatoes. If the potatoes are not half covered then add a little more water. Bring to the boil then place in an oven preheated to 190°C, 375°F, gas mark 5 and cook uncovered for 10 minutes. Cover and continue to cook for 45–50 minutes or until the potatoes are tender, but not soft enough to fall apart. Serve with *pilav* and salads.

tapoukhai adama im tered

potatoes stuffed with spinach

This is an attractive Israeli dish which is served as a starter or with roasts and kebabs and is often topped with *sughtorov-madzoon* — yoghurt-garlic dressing.

4 large potatoes, peeled

Filling

25 g/1 oz butter

1 onion, finely chopped

225 g/8 oz spinach, washed
  very thoroughly

4 tablespoons stock

1/4 teaspoon allspice

1 hard-boiled egg, shelled and chopped

1 teaspoon salt

1/2 teaspoon black pepper

2 tablespoons matzo meal (optional)

oil for frying

Garnish lettuce, finely chopped

pinch paprika

To serve 150 ml/3/4 pint *sughtorov-madzoon*, see recipe page 280

Place the potatoes in a pan of water, bring to the boil and simmer for about 10 minutes. Drain and set aside until cool enough to handle.

Meanwhile, heat the butter in a saucepan and sauté the onion until soft.

Squeeze excess water from the spinach, chop it and add to the onion together with the stock. Cook for 5–7 minutes or until the spinach is limp. Stir in the allspice and drain off any liquid that has not evaporated. Put this mixture into a bowl and add the chopped egg, salt, pepper and matzo meal and mix well.

Cut the potatoes in half lengthways and carefully scoop out the centres leaving a shell about 1.2 cm/1/2 in thick. Fill the centres with the spinach mixture. Heat some oil in a large frying pan, add the halved potatoes and cook until the potatoes are golden and crusty. This is easiest if you add enough oil to just come to the rim of each halved potato. Garnish a serving dish with the chopped lettuce, arrange the potatoes on top and spoon a little of the yoghurt sauce over each. Sprinkle with the paprika and serve.

foudja-al-jaddah

apples stuffed with chicken and nuts

From Jeddah, Arabia this is a most sophisticated dish of undoubted Persian origin. Serve with a rice *pilav* and pickles.

8 medium cooking apples

Filling

225 g/ oz/2 lb cooked chicken flesh,
   minced or finely chopped
1 teaspoon salt
1/2 teaspoon black pepper
50 g/2 oz breadcrumbs
6 cloves
50 g/2 oz chopped nuts

1/4 teaspoon turmeric
75 g/3 oz raisins
1/2 teaspoon cinnamon
1/4 teaspoon ginger
water
sugar
50 g/2 oz butter

Wash the apples, core them and scoop out enough flesh to make a hole about 2.5–4 cm/1–1¹/2 in in diameter.

In a small bowl mix the chicken with the salt, pepper and breadcrumbs. Add the cloves, nuts, turmeric, raisins, cinnamon and ginger and mix thoroughly. Now stuff the apples with the mixture, but do not press too hard. Arrange the apples in a large ovenproof dish and add sufficient hot water to come about half-way up the apples. Sprinkle some sugar on to each apple. Cut the butter into 8 pieces and put a knob on top of each apple. Bake the apples in an oven preheated to 180°C, 350°F, gas mark 4 for 30–40 minutes. Take care not to overcook or the apples will split. Serve immediately.

sehki itzoog stuffed melon

Only an Armenian would stuff a melon, cry over a large chunk of rock [meaning Mount Ararat — the symbol of Armenia] and claim all defeats are really victories.
(Turkish saying.)

As the Turks say, this is a classic of the Armenian cuisine — an unusually fragrant, delightful and original dish. A speciality of the region of Van (Western Armenia), this dish is also prepared using pumpkins.

Serve with a rice or burghul *pilav* of your choice.

1 large melon, cantaloupe or honeydew

Filling

2 tablespoons oil
1 small onion, finely chopped
225 g/8 oz minced lamb or beef
75 g/3 oz long grain rice, washed
   thoroughly under cold water
   and drained

50 g/2 oz pine kernels
50 g/2 oz raisins
1/2 teaspoon cinnamon
1 tablespoon sugar
300 ml/¹/2 pint water or
   stock
salt and pepper to taste

Wash the melon. Slice about 2.5 cm/1 in off the top and reserve if for later use as a lid.

Clean out and discard the seeds. Scoop out about a cupful of the flesh and chop it up.

To prepare the filling heat the oil in a saucepan, add the meat and onions and fry, stirring frequently, for a few minutes. Add all the remaining ingredients and the chopped flesh, stir well and simmer until the liquid has been absorbed. Leave to cool and then spoon into the melon. Replace the reserved top and secure it with wooden toothpicks.

Set the melon in a greased baking dish just large enough to hold it comfortably. Bake in an oven preheated to 180°C, 350°F, gas mark 4 for about 1 hour or until tender. Cut and serve in wedges.

ashdaragi dolma

apples and quinces stuffed with nuts

Ashdarag is a city in Armenia famed for its delicious fruits. If quinces are unavailable use more apples or unripe pears. Serve as an appetizer with bread or as a main dish with a *pilav*.

Filling

450 g/1 lb minced lamb or beef	1¹/₂ teaspoons salt
1 small onion, finely chopped	¹/₂ teaspoon black pepper
1 teaspoon basil	75 g/3 oz cooked long grain rice
1 teaspoon allspice	75 g/3 oz chopped walnuts
4 cooking apples	50 g/2 oz prunes, stoned and
4 quinces	coarsely chopped
50 g/2 oz dried apricots, coarsely	300 ml/¹/₂ pint stock
chopped	salt and pepper to taste

Garnish 1 tablespoon parsley, finely chopped

First prepare the filling by placing the meat in a saucepan and cooking over a low heat for 15–20 minutes, stirring frequently to prevent sticking. Add the chopped onion, basil, allspice, the salt and pepper, stir and cook for a further 10–15 minutes or until the meat is cooked. Stir in the cooked rice and chopped walnuts, mix well and set aside.

Core the fruit and then scoop out much of the flesh leaving a shell about 1.2 cm/¹/₂ in thick. Discard the flesh. Fill the fruit with the meat mixture. Arrange the fruit upright in an ovenproof dish and sprinkle the dried fruits around them.

Bring the stock to the boil, season and carefully pour into the dish. Place in an oven preheated to 180°C, 350°F, gas mark 4 and bake for 20–30 minutes. Keep an eye on the fruit and as soon as they show any sign of splitting remove immediately as they are cooked. Serve with its own sauce and sprinkled with the parsley.

Variation

The Iranians also stuff apples *dolmeh sib* and quinces *dolmeh beh*. The usual filling is 450 g/1 lb minced meat with 2-3 tablespoons cooked rice, 1/2 teaspoon cinnamon, 1 teaspoon salt and 1/4 teaspoon black pepper.

The sauce is usually 300 ml/1/2 pint water with juice of 1 lemon, 2 tablespoons brown sugar or 1 tablespoon honey. Cook as above.

karni yarik anatolian baked, stuffed aubergines

This dish literally means 'the stomach cut up'! It is a favourite aubergine *dolma* of Turks, Armenians and Kurds — in fact of every Anatolian, present and past! — including, I am sure, St George, St Nicholas (Santa Claus) and St Paul of Tarsus.

This is a family recipe. Serve with rice *pilav*, salads and pickles.

4 medium aubergines	6 tablespoons oil

Filling

2 tablespoons butter	3 tablespoons parsley, finely chopped
1 small onion, finely chopped	1 teaspoon salt
350 g/12 oz minced lamb or beef	1/2 teaspoon black pepper
2 tomatoes, blanched, peeled and chopped	2 cloves garlic, finely chopped

Sauce

150 ml/1/4 pint stock or water	1 teaspoon dillweed
1 teaspoon salt	1-2 tablespoons lemon juice

Cut the stems and hulls off the aubergines and discard.

Peel each aubergine lengthways in 1.2 cm/1/2 in strips to create an attractive stripey appearance. Heat the oil in a large saucepan or frying pan, add the aubergines and fry gently, turning frequently, until they are soft on all sides. Remove with a slotted spoon and drain on kitchen paper. Arrange the aubergines side by side in a shallow ovenproof dish.

Melt the butter in the pan with any remaining oil, add the onion and fry until soft, stirring frequently. Add the meat and fry, turning frequently until it is lightly browned. Add half the chopped tomatoes and cook for a further 5 minutes, stirring from time to time to prevent sticking. Add the parsley, salt, pepper and garlic, mix well, cook for 10 minutes and remove from the heat. One at a time slit the aubergines lengthways to within 1.8-2.5 cm/3/4-1 in of either end and only down into the middle of each vegetable.

Gently ease each slit open a little to form a pocket. Fill each pocket with some of the minced meat and place the remaining tomato over the top. Add the stock or water, sprinkle with the salt and dillweed and cover. Bake in an oven preheated to 180°C, 350°F, gas mark 4 for 30 minutes. Uncover, add the lemon juice, recover and cook for a further 10-15 minutes. Remove and serve.

pilavs

For a handful of pilav he sold his soul. — Armenian saying.

Rice and rice-based dishes are the basic diet of most Middle Easterners. Rice first appeared in the region some 3000 years ago via the Far East, probably with the advent of the Indo-Iranian tribes (modern Persians, Kurds, Armenians and countless others whose names have now disappeared).

With the Arab conquest of Persia rice appeared in the bazaars of Baghdad, Damascus and Alexandria, whence it travelled to Moorish Spain and, in time, to most of Europe.

However, while in the West rice is still often regarded as a side accompaniment to main dishes, in the East it has acquired a vast cuisine of its own, rich and imaginative. The masters of this cuisine are undoubtedly the Iranians whose poets have called it 'the staff of life' and the 'soul of Allah', and whose housewives have, over the ages, created some of the most delightful and exquisite dishes known to us.

This chapter deals only with *pilavs*, i.e. meatless rice dishes, which are served as accompaniments to meat, poultry and fish dishes. Other rice dishes appear under sections on meat, poultry and fish.

Rice is never served plain boiled. It is cooked with salt, water and some fat — *ghee* or butter or, as in centuries past, *imag* or *alya* — sheep's tail fat. There are several methods of cooking rice and the following three are probably the most popular.

It is easier to cook rice by volume, i.e. for the first cup of rice (175 g/6 oz) use two cups (450 ml/3/4 pint) water and for the next cup of rice use 1 1/2 cups (350 ml/12 fl oz) water. Always use long grain rice, e.g. Basmati. Italian or Spanish short grain rice is normally used in risottos and puddings. If you can find Basmati use it as it is the nearest to that used in the Middle East.

method 1

Roz — plain rice *pilav*. General favourite throughout the region, except Iran, Iraq and the Gulf States.

50 g/2 oz butter or *ghee*
250 g/9 oz long grain rice, washed
    thoroughly under cold water
    and drained

1 teaspoon salt
600 ml/1 pint water, boiling

Melt the butter or *ghee* in a saucepan. Add the rice and fry, stirring frequently, for 2–3 minutes. Add the salt and boiling water and boil vigorously for 3 minutes. Cover the pan, lower the heat and simmer for about 20 minutes or until all the liquid has been absorbed. The grains should be tender and separate and there should be small holes in the surface of the rice. Turn off the heat, remove the lid, cover with a teatowel, replace the lid and leave to 'rest' for 10–15 minutes. Fluff up the rice with a fork and serve.

method 2

Popular throughout Syria, Lebanon and Turkey.

600 ml/1 pint water
1/2 teaspoon salt

250 g/9 oz long grain rice, washed
    thoroughly under cold water and
    drained
50 g/2 oz butter or *ghee*

Bring the water to the boil. Add the salt and rice and boil vigorously for 3 minutes. Cover the pan, lower the heat and simmer for 20 minutes or until the water has been absorbed. Remove from the heat, remove lid, cover with a teatowel, replace lid and leave to 'rest' for 10–15 minutes. Meanwhile melt the butter or ghee in a small pan and pour evenly over the rice after it has rested. Cover the pan again and leave for a further 5 minutes before serving.

Method 3

Chelo — Iranian plain rice.

Another Westerner — W. H. Forbis in his book *Fall of the Peacock Throne* — following in the footsteps of earlier travellers, e.g. J. Fryer, Sir J. Chardin, Lord Curzon, etc., is filled with profound admiration and describes the step by step preparation of this 'jewel' of the Iranian cuisine. I have quoted his words more out of interest than as a recommended method.

The Iranian housewife goes through 14 steps to make a bowl of *chelo*, crusty steamed rice. Starting with two and a half cups of good long-grain rice, she washes it and rinses it three times in lukewarm water. She soaks it overnight, covered, in heavily salted water. The next day she sets two quarts of water to boiling with two tablespoons of salt, and adds the drained, soaked rice in a stream. She boils the rice for 10–15 minutes, stirring it once or twice, than puts it in a strainer and rinses it with lukewarm water. Next she melts half a cup of butter, and puts a third of it in a cooking pot, to which she adds two tablespoons water. She spoons the boiled rice into the pot so as to make a cone, and pours the rest of the butter evenly over it. She covers the pot with a folded teatowel, to make the rice cook evenly, and then puts on the lid. She cooks it for 10–15 minutes over a medium heat, and for 45 more minutes over a low heat. She places the pot in cold water, to make the rice come free from the bottom of the pan. She turns it out so that the golden crust on the bottom, which is the specific asset that makes Iranian rice the world's best, flecks and accents the whole fluffy mound of distinctly separate grains. She puts 2 or 3 tablespoons of rice into a dish and mixes in a tablespoon of saffron. She pours the coloured rice over the rest, and she is done.

Here is my much simplified version of *chelo* — and the final result, I assure you, will be equally successful.

250 g/9 oz long grain rice, washed thoroughly under cold water and drained
2 tablespoons salt

about 1.2 litres/2 pints water
50 g/2 oz butter, melted

Place the rice in a deep bowl, add 1 tablespoon of the salt and enough cold water to cover by 2.5 cm/1 in. Leave to soak for 2 hours.

Bring about 2 litres/1³/4 pints of water, and the remaining salt, to the boil in a heavy saucepan with a close fitting lid. Drain the rice thoroughly then pour it slowly into the water so that it doesn't go off the boil. Boil for 5 minutes and then drain into a sieve. Pour 150 ml/1/4 pint water and half the melted butter into the saucepan, add the rice and pour the remaining butter over the top. Cover the pan with a teatowel, fit on the lid and lift the ends of the cloth on to the lid so that there is no danger of fire. Steam over a very low heat for about 25–30 minutes or until the liquid has been absorbed and the grains are tender and fluffy. Leave to rest for 10 minutes before serving.

chelo ta dig steamed crusty rice

Ta dig, meaning literally 'bottom of the pan', is a crusty, crunchy layer at the bottom of the saucepan and is golden brown in appearance. To achieve this result either (a) mix 75 g/3 oz of the par-boiled rice with 1 egg yolk and spread it over the bottom of the pan before adding the rest of the rice, or (b) mix 75 ml/3 fl oz of yoghurt with 1/2 teaspoon of saffron and 75 g/3 oz par-boiled rice and spread this mixture over the bottom of the pan before adding the rest of the rice.

Cook as the *chelo* on page 182, but steam for 15–20 minutes longer than stated. The result is a golden layer of crunchy *ta dig* which is then broken up and cut into small pieces and arranged around the rest of the rice, golden side up.

kazmag pilav rice and dough pilav

This is an Azerbaijanian variation from the Caucasus.

Make a dough by mixing together 1 egg and 75 g/3 oz flour, knead well and roll out to fit the base of the pan.

Brush the base of the pan with a little melted butter, add the dough, brush its surface with a little more butter and then pile in the par-boiled rice and top with remaining melted butter.

Steam as with *chelo*, but for 15–20 minutes longer.

To serve pile the rice on to a large plate and garnish with wedges of the golden brown *kazmag* crust. It is sometimes sprinkled with pomegrante seeds for extra colour.

saffron pilav

Saffron is used to give colour to *pilavs* and it has an intrinsic delicate flavour. Its appearance on a dinner table gives that extra glow (the Middle Easterners are very fond of the colours gold and crimson) to the already colourful table. The simplest saffron *pilav* would be to follow method 1 for plain *pilav* and to add 1/2 teaspoon saffron to the rice when it is frying.

However, a much more exotic variation, popular in the Gulf States and particularly with the Afghans and Baluchis of south east Iran, usually includes cloves, cinnamon and cardamom.

Often, particularly in Iraq and the Gulf States 3/4–1 teaspoon of turmeric — 'poor man's saffron' — is substituted for the real thing since saffron is an extremely expensive spice — even in the lands where it is cultivated.

sehriyeli pilavi *pilav with vermicelli*

In the old days, before commercial versions inundated the shops, women at home prepared their own versions of vermicelli, noodles and pastas. They made many different kinds, e.g. 'elephant's ears', 'shells', 'balls', 'angel's hair', etc. Using their forefingers and thumbs the women shaped the dough into thin threads about 2.5–4 cm/1–1¹/₂ in long which were then dried and stored in jars for later use in *pilavs* and stews. The Muslims prepare this dish on the second day of the New Year 'so that one may have as many children as the *sehriyelis* in the *pilav*'. Armenians eat this *pilav* on Easter Sunday and Christmas Day and call this dish 'Angel's hair *pilav*' because of some moot superstition about being worthy of an 'Angel's hair'!

50 g/2 oz butter or *ghee*
25 g/1 oz vermicelli, broken into
   2.5 cm/1 in pieces
250 g/9 oz long grain rice, washed
   thoroughly under cold water
   and drained

2 tablespoons raisins (optional)
1 teaspoon salt
600 ml/1 pint water, boiling

Melt the butter or *ghee* in a medium saucepan. Add the vermicelli and sauté until light golden. Add the rice and raisins and proceed as with *roz* — plain rice *pilav*, from method 3, page 182.

plov azzari *ginger and sesame pilav*

This recipe is from the Caspian coastline and is a speciality of the Turkish speaking Azerbaijanian people of the former Soviet Republic and Iran.

50 g/2 oz butter or *ghee*
250 g/9 oz long grain rice, washed
   thoroughly under cold water and
   drained
¹/₂ teaspoon ground ginger

2 teaspoons sesame seeds
600 ml/1 pint water, boiling
1 teaspoon salt
¹/₂ teaspoon black pepper

Garnish 50 g/2 oz slivered, toasted almonds

Melt the butter in an ovenproof casserole, add the rice and fry gently, stirring frequently, for about 10 minutes. Add the ginger and sesame seeds and fry for a further 2–3 minutes. Add the water, salt and pepper, stir and bring to the boil.

Place the casserole, uncovered, in an oven preheated to 180°C, 350°F, gas mark 4 for about 35 minutes, or until the water is absorbed and the rice tender. Turn the oven off and, after 10 minutes, toss the rice with a fork. Leave for a further 15–20 minutes and then toss again. Remove from the oven, sprinkle the almonds over the top and serve.

domatesli pilavi *tomato pilav*

Popular everywhere, with many variations, tomato *pilav* is a must with all kebabs. Has a light pink colour and a delicious flavour.

50 g/2 oz butter or *ghee*
3 large tomatoes, blanched,
   peeled and chopped
1 small onion, finely chopped
1 clove garlic, finely chopped
1/2 teaspoon dried basil
2 tablespoons parsley, finely chopped

1/2 teaspoon black pepper
1 teaspoon salt
250 g/9 oz long grain rice, washed
   thoroughly under cold running
   water and drained
600 ml/1 pint water, boiling

Melt the butter or *ghee* in a medium saucepan. Add the tomatoes, onion, garlic, basil, parsley, pepper and salt and sauté stirring frequently, for a few minutes until the onion is soft. Stir in the rice and fry for 2–3 minutes. Proceed as for *roz* — plain rice *pilav* method 3, page 182.

sultan resat pilavi *aubergine pilav*

A Turkish dish named after a Sultan who swore by this *pilav* — Sultans, of course, swore a great deal in their time! Variations of this *pilav* appear throughout Iran, Armenia and northern Syria and Iraq.

   Often eaten as a savoury, with yoghurt and pickles, by the Anatolian villagers, this *pilav* is nevertheless excellent with all roasts and kebabs.

2 large aubergines, peeled
50 g/2 oz butter or *ghee*
1 onion, roughly chopped
2 large tomatoes, blanched,
   peeled and chopped
50 g/2 oz vermicelli, broken into
   2.5 cm/1 in pieces

1 teaspoon salt
1/2 teaspoon black pepper
175 g/6 oz long grain rice, washed
   thoroughly under cold water and
   drained
900 ml/1 1/2 pints water
a few leaves fresh mint

Cut the aubergines into roughly 1.2 cm/1/2 in cubes. Place the cubes on a plate, sprinkle with salt, place another plate over the top and leave for 30 minutes.

   Meanwhile, melt the butter or *ghee* in a large saucepan, add the onion and fry until soft, but not brown. Stir in the tomatoes, vermicelli, salt and pepper and fry for about 3 minutes.

   Rinse the aubergine cubes thoroughly and dry on kitchen paper. Add the aubergines to the saucepan and fry, stirring frequently, for a further 2–3 minutes. Stir in the rice, water and mint leaves and bring to the boil. Lower the heat and simmer for 15–20 minutes until the liquid is absorbed and the rice tender. Leave to 'rest' for 10–15 minutes and serve.

tutumi pilav *pumpkin pilav*

Marrows and pumpkins are much used in the Armenian cuisines. This is a *pilav* of pumpkin with sultanas, apricots and rice and it is typical of the Caucasian-Iranian sweet and sour dishes.

Dried apricots are sometimes substituted by thinly sliced apricot paste.

175 g/6 oz long grain rice, washed
   thoroughly under cold water
   and drained
225 ml/8 fl oz water
1 teaspoon salt
1 teaspoon dillweed

50 g/2 oz sultanas
3–4 dried apricots, thinly sliced
450 g/1 lb pumpkin, peeled and sliced
   lengthways into 1.2 cm/$1/2$ in slices
50 g/2 oz sugar
75 g/3 oz melted butter

Place the rice in a saucepan with the water, bring to the boil and then simmer for 10 minutes. Stir in the salt, dillweed, sultanas and apricots and simmer for a further 5 minutes. Strain into a sieve and run cold water through the rice.

Lightly butter a baking or casserole dish. Arrange half the pumpkin slices over the bottom and sprinkle with a third of the sugar and a third of the melted butter.

Put the rice into a bowl, add half the remaining sugar and butter and mix thoroughly. Spread the rice over the pumpkin slices.

Pour the remaining butter into a frying pan and sauté the remaining pumpkin slices for a few minutes, turning once.

Arrange the pumpkin slices decoratively over the rice and sprinkle with the remaining sugar and any butter left in the pan. Cover and place in the centre of an oven preheated to 180°C, 350°F, gas mark 4 and bake for 40–45 minutes. Remove from the oven and serve.

ciftlik pilavi farmer's pilav

An Anatolian *pilav* that makes good use of all the vegetables available. A vegetable risotto, often eaten with bread and a bowl of yoghurt as a main dish.

Allah hu
Pilav su
Allah hay
Kahve chay!

This is a skit on the Arabic sounds which the villagers recite thinking of them as prayers, but in reality which simply mean:

God ho
Pilav water
God hi
Coffee tea!

An allusion to the deep ignorance of the Anatolian peasants. (Quoted from *A Village in Anatolia*, Mahmut Makal.)

1 carrot, peeled and cut
   into 0.6 cm/¼ in rings
4 mushrooms, wiped clean and sliced
1 small green pepper, thinly sliced
3 tablespoons garden peas
50 g/2 oz butter for frying
½ teaspoon black pepper

50 g/2 oz butter
250 g/9 oz long grain rice, washed
   thoroughly and drained
1 teaspoon salt
600 ml/1 pint water, boiling
1 tablespoon sultanas
2 tablespoons parsley, finely chopped

Bring a saucepan half-filled with lightly salted water to the boil, add the carrot rings and simmer until just tender. Remove with a slotted spoon and reserve. Add the mushrooms, green pepper and peas and simmer for 5 minutes. Remove and reserve with the carrots.

Melt 50 g/2 oz of the butter in a pan, add the vegetables and the black pepper and fry for 2–3 minutes, stirring frequently. Set the vegetable mixture aside.

Melt the remaining 50 g/2 oz of butter in a large saucepan, add the rice and fry, stirring frequently, for 2–3 minutes. Add the salt and water. Cover the pan and simmer for 10 minutes then remove the lid, add the fried vegetables, sultanas and parsley and mix thoroughly. Recover and continue cooking until all the liquid had been absorbed. Uncover, turn off the heat and leave to rest for 10–15 minutes. Fluff up with a fork and serve.

turkestan pilavi *carrot pilav*

In Turkey this dish is often cooked in a mould with stunning effect. It is an attractive golden yellow speckled with black, brown and green. However, it is equally tasty and almost as attractive if cooked and presented in the normal way.

This recipe was given to me by a Turkish friend from Kaysari, Central Anatolia, who assured me that it was authentic since his 'ancestors brought it over from beyond the mountains'. Nevertheless there is more than a little touch of Iran about it, particularly in the use of cinnamon, rosewater and pistachios. Serve with kebabs and roasts.

75 g/3 oz *ghee* or butter
at least 225 g/8 oz grated carrots
1/2 teaspoon whole black peppercorns
1 tablespoon seedless raisins
1 teaspoon sugar
1/2 teaspoon ground cinnamon

350 g/12 oz long grain rice, washed thoroughly under cold water and drained
750 ml/1 1/4 pints water, boiling
1 1/2 teaspoons salt
1 tablespoon rosewater

Garnish

2 tablespoons parsley or tarragon, finely chopped

1 tablespoon pistachios, chopped

Melt the *ghee* or butter in a medium saucepan, add the grated carrots and peppercorns and fry for 3 minutes, stirring frequently. Sprinkle in the raisins, sugar and cinnamon, stir and fry for another minute. Add the rice and fry for 2–3 minutes, stirring constantly. Add the water and salt, stir and boil vigorously for 3 minutes. Cover pan, reduce heat to very low and simmer for about 15 minutes or until the liquid has been almost absorbed.

Now **either** lightly oil a round mould and spoon the rice mixture into it. Sprinkle with the rosewater, cover and place in an oven preheated to 180°C, 350°F, gas mark 4 for a further 5–7 minutes; **or** continue cooking in the saucepan for about another 5 minutes or until all the water has been absorbed.

Remove mould or pan from the heat and leave to rest for 10–15 minutes. Invert a plate over the mould and turn it out or spoon the mixture from the pan into a serving dish. Sprinkle with the parsley or tarragon and the pistachios and serve.

muhamar *sweet pilav*

A speciality of the Gulf States, this recipe from Bahrain makes clever use of saffron, cardamom, honey and rosewater.

This *pilav* is said to be the favourite of the pearl divers — a vocation now almost extinct due mainly to newly acquired oil wealth, but which was once the only industry of the islands.

Serve it with kebabs of all kinds particularly those of fish and prawns — another favourite of the region.

3 tablespoons rosewater

1/2 teaspoon saffron threads

4 cardamom pods, cracked

600 ml/1 pint water, boiling

250 g/9 oz long grain rice, washed
thoroughly under cold water

2 teaspoons salt

3 tablespoons honey or
2 tablespoons sugar

50 g/2 oz *ghee* or butter

Pour the rosewater into a cup, add the saffron and cardamom pods and leave to rest.

Place the boiling water in a saucepan, add the rice and salt and boil for 10 minutes. Drain into a colander. Place the rice in a bowl, add the honey or sugar and mix thoroughly.

Melt the *ghee* or butter in a saucepan, add the rice, cover the pan and cook over a very low heat for 15 minutes. Uncover, add the saffron mixture, mix well, recover and simmer for another 10–15 minutes or until the rice is tender. Leave to rest for 10 minutes before serving.

roz-bil-tamar pilav with almonds and dates

A Bedouin dish. The love of the desert to the Bedouin seems to have been even stronger than that of the sea to the sailor. Even in their days of glory the Califs were more at home in their desert tents than in the ornate palaces of Damascus or Baghdad. My favourite Arab poet Abulla-el-Mahari (973–1058) expresses this Bedouin passion most succinctly with these words:

A-weary am I of living in town and village —
And oh, to be camped alone in a desert region,
Revived by the scent of lavender when I hunger
And scooping into my palm, if I thirst, well-water!

50 g/2 oz butter or *ghee*

250 g/9 oz long grain rice, washed
thoroughly under cold water
and drained

1 teaspoon salt

600 ml/1 pint water, boiling

Garnish

50 g/2 oz butter

50 g/2 oz blanched almonds

75 g/3 oz stoned dates

50 g/2 oz seedless raisins or sultanas

1 teaspoon rosewater

Cook the rice following the instructions for *roz*, method 1, page 181 — plain rice *pilav*.

While the rice is 'resting' melt 25 g/1 oz butter or *ghee* in a large frying pan. Now add the almonds and fry, stirring frequently, until they begin to turn a light golden colour. Add the remaining butter, the dates and the raisins or sultanas. Fry for a few more minutes, stirring frequently. Remove from the heat and stir in the rosewater. To serve spoon the rice on to a serving dish and arrange the fruit and nut mixture over the top.

harsaniki pilavi wedding pilav

One evening Nasrudin quarrelled with his wife and shouted at her so fiercely that she fled for refuge to a neighbouring house, where he followed her. As it happened, a wedding feast was in progress, and the host and guests did all they could to calm him down, and vied with each other to make the couple reconciled, to eat and enjoy themselves. The Mulla said to his wife:

'My dear, remind me to lose my temper more often — then life really would be worth living!' (The Pleasantries of the Incredible Mulla Nasrudin)

An Armenian favourite from Yerevan, this dish is exotic and colourful like Armenian illuminated manuscripts and richly patterned carpets. A must — as the name suggests — at weddings and festive occasions. Serve with all roasts, kebabs and stews.

50 g/2 oz butter or *ghee*	1 teaspoon salt
250 g/9 oz long grain rice, washed thoroughly under cold water and drained	600 ml/1 pint water, boiling

Sauce

50 g/2 oz butter	50 g/2 oz seedless raisins or sultanas
50 g/2 oz apricots, soaked overnight in cold water	50 g/2 oz blanched almonds, split
50 g/2 oz prunes, soaked overnight in cold water and stoned	2 tablespoons honey
	1 tablespoon hot water

Melt the butter or *ghee* in a saucepan. Add the rice and fry for 2–3 minutes, stirring frequently. Add the salt and water, stir and boil vigorously for a few minutes. Lower the heat, cover and simmer for a further 20 minutes or until all the water has been absorbed. Turn off the heat, remove the lid, cover the pan with a clean teatowel, replace the lid and leave to 'rest' for 10–15 minutes. Loosen the grains with a fork.

Meanwhile, prepare the sauce which will garnish the *pilav*. Melt the butter in a saucepan. Add the fruit and nuts and fry, stirring frequently, until the nuts are lightly browned. Mix the honey and water together and pour it into the saucepan. Lower the heat and cook for about 10 minutes, stirring frequently, until the mixture has thickened.

To serve, pile the *pilav* on to a serving dish and pour the sauce over the top.

tzavarov pilav cracked wheat pilav

Burghul, *tzavar*, is the staple food of Armenians, most Anatolians and Kurds. Although it is used by Syrians, Lebanese and Cypriots in their *kibbeh* dishes, burghul is only 'second fiddle' to rice outside the Anatolian Plateau — where, most probably, it originated several millenia ago. A very touching reference is made to it in a thirteenth century Armenian colophone (Jerusalem Museum) where the scribe had added on the margins of a page the following words:

For generations my people [Armenians] hidden in mountain ravines and caves lived on *tzavar* [burghul] and a little rice, when available, while the barbarian hordes [Seljuks and Mongols] ravaged our biblical land, destroying churches, castles, burning villages, everything, everything! that lay in their way. But we survived thanks to the God given goodness of those tiny grains that possessed the waters of the seas, the rays of the sun and all the goodness of life.

Blessed is the Lord, blessed be the life giving grains of *tzavar* and of rice.

Burghul-based *pilavs* are often substituted for those of rice, adding variety and interest and indeed some, including me, regard burghul *pilavs* as superior to their rice counterparts. Use large-grained burghul which is found in all Middle Eastern, Indian and health food stores.

250 g/9 oz large grained burghul
50 g/2 oz butter or *ghee*
1 small onion, finely chopped

450 ml/³/₄ pint water, boiling
1 teaspoon salt
¹/₂ teaspoon black pepper

Put the burghul into a bowl or fine sieve and wash several times until the water runs clear. Leave to drain.

Melt the butter or *ghee* in a saucepan. Add the onion and fry gently until soft and golden. Add the burghul and fry for 2–3 minutes, stirring frequently. Add the boiling water, salt and pepper and stir well. Bring to the boil and boil vigorously for 5 minutes. Lower the heat and simmer for 8–10 minutes or until the water has been absorbed. Turn off the heat, cover the pan with a clean teatowel, clamp on the lid and leave to rest for 10–15 minutes.

Variations

telahaysov tzavari pilav burghul pilav with vermicelli

Follow the recipe for *sehriyeli pilavi* (see page 184), but use burghul instead of rice.

Similarly you can prepare most of the rice *pilavs* with burghul, e.g. tomato *pilav*, mushroom *pilav*, spinach *pilav*, aubergine *pilav*, etc.

mujaddarah cracked wheat and lentil pilav

A medieval dish sometimes called 'Esau's favourite' or 'the food of the poor'. *Mujaddarah* appears in several countries under differing names. It is known as *kitry* in Iraq, *adas pollo* in Iran, *muaddas* in the Gulf States and, in far away India as *kitcheri*.

In the Middle Ages (still today in India) *mujaddarah* included several vegetables, e.g. carrots, peas, aubergines, etc. as well as meat or fish, but today the basic ingredients are simply rice or burghul, lentils and onion.

It is often eaten as a main dish with fresh salads, yoghurt and pickles. The recipe below uses burghul, but you can substitute an equal amount of rice.

175 g/6 oz brown lentils, washed
   and drained
900 ml/1½ pints cold water
300 ml/½ pint olive or vegetable oil
2 large onions, thinly sliced
2 teaspoons salt

½ teaspoon black pepper
300 ml/½ pint boiling water
175 g/6 oz large burghul, washed in
   a bowl with cold water until the
   water runs clear

Put the lentils into a saucepan, add the 900 ml/1½ pints of water and bring to the boil. Lower the heat, cover and cook for 25-30 minutes or until the lentils are almost cooked and the water mostly absorbed.

Meanwhile, in a frying pan heat the oil, add the sliced onions and fry, stirring frequently, until they are dark golden, but take care not to burn them. Reserve half the onions and the oil.

Stir the other half of the onions into the lentils. Add the salt, pepper and the boiling water and bring to the boil. Stir in the burghul, cover and simmer for a further 15-20 minutes or until the lentils and burghul are tender and the water absorbed. Remove from the heat and leave to rest for 10-15 minutes. Pile the *mujaddarah* on to a plate and garnish with the remaining onions and oil.

Variations

adas pollo

This is a simpler version without the onion and with 25 g/1 oz each of toasted slivered almonds, and raisins sprinkled over the top of the cooked *pilav*.

kitry

This uses 2 cloves crushed garlic fried in a little oil instead of the onions and also includes 1 tablespoon tomato purée and ½ teaspoon turmeric.

kebabs

With the discovery of fire came cooked meat, then barbecues, and kebabs. Ancient civilizations knew all about grilling meats of all kinds on fire. That was nothing new. What was new, however, was, and this came much later, the art of marination, basting and smothering the meats in herbs and spices.

Homer, in his *Iliad*, describes how Achilles played host to Odysseus outside the walls of Ilium.

Petroclus put down a big bench in the firelight, and laid on it the backs of a sheep and a fat goat and the chine of a great hog rich in lard. Automedon held these for him, while Achilles jointed them, and carved up the joints and spitted the slices. Meanwhile, Petroclus. . . made the fire blaze up. When it had burned down again and the flames disappeared, he scattered the embers and laid the spits above them, resting them on logs. . . When he had roasted it and heaped it up on the platters. . . Achilles divided the meat into portions.

In the Middle East, scenes like this are still an everyday occurrence. To celebrate a birth, wedding, anniversary or religious festival large groups of people drive to the fields or hills, prepare impromptu grills — usually in small depressions in the ground — light dry branches, slaughter lambs and skin them. The innards are removed — the heart and livers are set aside as they make excellent kebabs in their own right — and the lambs are rinsed in a nearby brook. Long wooden or metal rods are pushed right through the lamb from the breast to the hindquarters and the legs are trussed. The fire is blazed and then 'when it had burned down again and the flames disappeared', the spits are laid above them.

Next time you have a large party try this whole lamb kebab — it will be the talk of the year!

A fascinating method — still popular in Anatolia, Caucasus, Iran and, I understand, with the Aborigines of Australasia — is to make a shallow (60–90 cm/2–3 ft) pit approximately 90 x 180 cm/3 x 6 ft in the ground and a bed of charcoal laid in the pit. The lamb is laid on the glowing charcoal and the whole is covered with earth. Five to six hours later the lamb will be cooked. It is then removed, brushed to remove the soil clinging to the skin and placed on a large tray. Two hefty people shake the tray until the meat drops from the bones. The meat is sprinkled with salt, black pepper and herbs and eaten.

In the Middle East lamb has always been the most popular meat. Indeed, to an Arab 'meat' simply means lamb or mutton, although in the past kid and gazelle were also eaten as well as camel's meat which is hung from high ceilings in the semi-dark meat markets.

Cattle are seldom bred, except for buffalo — particularly in Egypt and Southern Iraq, but 'Buffaloes are never killed for food; never, indeed, unless they are dying anyway of some disease . . . their lives are passed in a rich and placid leisure immune alike from fear and frustration. They are maintained in privileged luxury for the sake of their milk and their dung.' (*Food in History*)

Today beef and veal are gradually becoming more popular. Pork, of course, is only eaten by Christian populations (Greeks, Armenians, Georgians and the Maronites of Lebanon and Syria).

Finally a word of warning. There are too many dishes falsely labelled *kebab*. The word simply means 'cooked meat'; in the oven or on fire; and is derived from one of the early Indian languages, not Turkish as is often claimed.

In this section I have grouped together kebabs of meat, chicken, game and fish — all either basted or marinated and most skewered and cooked over charcoal. All kebabs are traditionally served on a bed of rice or burghul with fresh salads, pickles, yoghurt and yoghurt drinks.

The choice is wide and I suggest you experiment.

şiş kebab

This is by far the most famous Middle Eastern dish and has countless local variations. This kebab was most probably created by shepherds who spent months alone on the hills and, deprived of home cooking and the availability of domestic utensils, produced this simple dish of chunks of meat — lamb or goat — threaded on to wooden sticks and grilled over dried wood.

However, grilled meat does not necessarily make kebabs. For the secret of a good kebab lies in the art of marination, and any kebab that is not marinated or basted is not a kebab, but merely grilled meat or barbecued meat.

Şiş kebab is traditionally prepared with lamb (leg) and the following points should be noted when preparing the meat:

(a) Remove tough membranes and ligaments.
(b) Cut the meat across the grain.
(c) Marinate the meat for at least 8 hours.

Below is a standard recipe with several suggestions for marinades.

900 g/2 lb lamb (or beef) cut into 2.5 cm/1 in cubes

A favourite Armenian marinade
150 ml/¼ pint oil
1 teaspoon allspice

150 ml/¼ pint red wine
salt and black pepper to taste

A Greek favourite
150 ml/¼ pint oil
juice 1 lemon
2 onions, chopped and crushed to
    extract the juice — use garlic
    press or extractor

2 bay leaves
2 teaspoons oregano
pulp of 2 tomatoes
salt and black pepper

A Turkish favourite
150 ml/¼ pint oil
2 onions, chopped and crushed to
   extract juice — use garlic press
   or extractor

1 teaspoon cinnamon
salt and black pepper to taste

A yoghurt marinade
300 ml/½ pint yoghurt
juice 1 onion, chopped and crushed
   to extract juice — use garlic press
   or extractor

salt and black pepper to taste

Wine marinade
150 ml/¼ pint red wine
5 tablespoons vinegar
1 clove garlic, crushed

¼ teaspoon black pepper
½ teaspoon crushed dried mint
3 sprigs parsley

Mix all the ingredients for the marinade of your choice in a large bowl. Add the pieces of meat and turn until they are all well coated with the marinade. Cover and leave in the refrigerator for at least 6–8 hours or preferably overnight.

When ready to cook thread the pieces of meat on to skewers and cook over charcoal or under a grill — the latter will not, of course, produce the same end results but it is more convenient. Turn the skewers occasionally so that the meat is cooked evenly. Cook for 12–15 minutes or until the meat is brown and cooked on the outside, but still a little juicy in the centre.

Serve on a bed of *pilav* with salads of your choice.

Variation
Often the pieces of meat are alternated with pieces of onion, halved tomatoes, bay leaves, pieces of green pepper, mushrooms, etc.

kebab-e-barg fillet of lamb kebab

This is the national dish of Iran when served with *chelo* rice. It is usually made from lamb fillet. The fillet is cut from the bone, laid in a strip and sliced open lengthways, flattened out and cut crossways to the grain into 5 cm/2 in pieces.

Fillet of lamb is rather expensive since in the West butchers cut the fillet (with the bone) into lamb chops. I suggest you use a 1–1.5 kg/2–3 lb shoulder of lamb instead. Ask your butcher to cut it into 0.6 mm/¼ in thick and 12.5 cm/5 in long slices. Then pound each piece and place in a shallow dish with the marinade.

1–1.5 kg/2–3 lb shoulder of lamb

Garnishes
chelo rice — see recipe page 182
4 egg yolks

sumac
4 raw onion rings (optional)

Marinade 1
3 tablespoons oil
1 large onion, finely chopped or grated

3 tablespoons lemon juice
salt and black pepper to taste

Marinade 2
300 ml/½ pint yoghurt
salt and black pepper to taste

1 large onion, finely chopped or grated

Prepare the meat as described above and lay the strips in a shallow dish.

Mix the ingredients of the marinade of your choice together and pour over the meat. Turn the strips of meat until they are well-coated and then cover and refrigerate for at least 24 hours.

Lay the strips of meat on a kebab grill, and cook fairly quickly, turning frequently so that the meat cooks without drying.

Lay each individual portion on a plate and cover with *chelo* rice. Sprinkle sumac over the rice and place a pat of butter and an egg yolk on top of each portion of rice. To eat mix the rice, sumac, butter and egg yolk up and garnish with an onion ring if you wish.

Serve with yoghurt, fresh salads and a drink of *tan ayran* (page 356).

mtswadi caucasian kebab

A recipe from Tiblisi, Georgia — the mythical land of Colchis where Jason and the Argonauts journeyed in quest of the Golden Fleece. Tiblisi (Tiflis) has been the capital for 1500 years. It is a great modern city spread on both sides of the river Kura and is one of the great centres of art and science of the former Soviet Union.

Marinade

3 cloves garlic, crushed
300 ml/1/2 pint vinegar
2 tablespoons parsley, chopped

1 onion, chopped
1/2 teaspoon black pepper
1 teaspoon salt

900 g/2 lb lean lamb, cut into
    2.5 cm/1 in cubes
75–100 g/3–4 oz streaky bacon,
    rind and bone removed

25 g/1 oz butter, melted
1 onion
100 g/4 oz mushrooms, wiped clean
50 g/2 oz spring onion, chopped

Garnish

2 tomatoes, sliced

1 lemon, cut into wedges

To serve **pomegranate juice — optional** (It is possible to buy bottles of pomegranate juice in some delicatessens. Alternatively squeeze the juice from 2 pomegranates, add 1 teaspoon of sugar, bring to the boil, simmer for 2 minutes and leave to cool.)

Mix the marinade ingredients together in a large bowl. Add the cubed meat and stir. Cover and leave in the refrigerator overnight.

Cut the bacon into 2.5 cm/1 in pieces.

Quarter the onion and separate the various layers.

Thread the lamb on to skewers alternating with pieces of bacon and onion and the occasional mushroom. Cook for 10–15 minutes, turning frequently. Slide the kebabs from the skewers on to a serving dish and sprinkle with the melted butter and spring onions. Garnish with the sliced tomatoes and lemon wedges.

If using pomegranate juice either sprinkle some over the meat or serve in very small individual dishes and dip the chunks of meat in it before eating.

karski shashlig lamb and kidney kebab

Eastern Anatolia — land of mountains, sheep and ruined Christian churches and castles — was once a hive of industry and commerce with centres such as Erzerum, Trabzond, Kars, and Van. All are still there, but depleted of their wealth and populace.

During the first Russo-Turkish wars of the last century, (Alexander Pushkin gives a vivid account of the times in his *Journey to Erzerum*), Tzarist soldiers were first introduced to this and similar dishes which they took back with them to 'Mother Russia'.

This kebab is usually served on small flaming swords which look very attractive.

900 g/2 lb leg of lamb,
   cut into 8 large pieces

6 lamb's kidneys, halved

Marinade
1 onion, chopped
2 tablespoons parsley, chopped

2 tablespoons vinegar or the juice of
   1/2 lemon
salt and pepper to taste

Garnish lemon wedges

Mix the marinade ingredients in a large bowl. Add the lamb cubes and halved kidneys, turn to coat with the mixture and leave for 6–8 hours or overnight if possible. Thread 2 pieces of meat on each skewer, each piece sandwiched between kidney halves, i.e. 2 pieces of meat and 3 kidney halves on each skewer. Cook slowly, turning and basting frequently. Serve with lemon wedges and a plain rice *pilav*.

Variation
Another kebab from Kars makes use of lamb chops and is also usually served on small flaming swords.

Marinade
150 ml/1/4 pint oil
150 ml/1/4 pint red wine
1 clove garlic, crushed

1 teaspoon salt
1/2 teaspoon black pepper
1 teaspoon allspice

8 lamb chops
4 tomatoes
8 mushrooms, wiped clean

2 green peppers, each cut into
   8 pieces
16 pieces onion

Mix the marinade ingredients together in a large bowl. Add the chops and turn until they are well coated. Cover and leave in the refrigerator overnight. If you have long skewers thread 2 chops on to each skewer alternating them with 1 tomato, 2 mushrooms, 4 pieces of green pepper and 4 pieces of onion. You can also cook the chops on a rack and just thread the vegetables on to skewers and then apportion them after they are cooked.

hirino souvlaki pork kebab

The Middle Eastern pork repertoire is very limited. The Muslim religion forbids its use and only Christians officially eat it; although I know many a good Arab and Jew who secretly relish it — may Allah forgive them!

The Greeks make a lovely kebab of pork served with salads, olives and cheese. You will find this kebab, with many local variations, served in most Cypriot and Greek restaurants.

900 g/2 lb belly pork

Marinade
juice 1 lemon
1 onion, finely chopped
1 clove garlic, finely chopped
3-4 bay leaves

150 ml/1/4 pint white wine
4-6 tablespoons oil
2 teaspoons curry powder (optional)
1/2 teaspoon turmeric (optional)

Garnish **2 lemons, cut into wedges**

Cut the meat into 1.8 cm/3/4 in cubes without removing the fat. Mix the marinade ingredients in a large bowl, add the meat, mix well, cover and leave for 5-6 hours or, preferably, overnight in the refrigerator. Thread the meat on to skewers and cook over charcoal for 15-20 minutes, turning frequently so that the fat doesn't burn. Serve with the lemon wedges which you squeeze over the meat.

kharapak khorovadze

pork kebab with pomegranate juice

A recipe from the mountains of Kharapak high up in the Caucasus. The meat is marinated in pomegranate juice giving it a most unusual flavour and sharpness. If you wish to prepare your own see the Glossary, page 370. Serve with *pilav* of your choice and salads.

900 g/2 lb boned leg of pork cut into 4 cm/11/2 in cubes

Marinade
150 ml/1/4 pint oil
1 large onion, finely chopped
11/2 teaspoons fresh tarragon, chopped
   or 1 tablespoon dried tarragon

11/2 teaspoons salt
1 teaspoon black pepper

To serve **pomegranate juice**

Mix the marinade ingredients together in a large bowl. Stir in 3 tablespoons pomegranate juice, add the meat, mix well, cover and leave in the refrigerator overnight. Thread the pieces of meat on to skewers and grill for 20–30 minutes, turning frequently until the meat is cooked through. Serve the kebabs accompanied by a small bowl of pomegranate juice into which you dip each piece of meat before eating.

kasbi mishwi liver kebab with garlic

Liver, either lamb's or calf's makes excellent and succulent kebabs. The recipe below is from Jordan.

900 g/2 lb liver, lamb or calf, soaked in cold water for 20 minutes then drained

Marinade
5–6 cloves garlic, crushed	**1¹/₂ teaspoons salt**
1¹/₂ teaspoons dried mint	**1/₂ teaspoon black pepper**
100 ml/4 fl oz oil	Garnish **lemon wedges**

Remove any skin and sinew from the liver and then cut into 5 cm/2 in cubes. Mix the marinade ingredients together in a large bowl then add the pieces of liver and turn until well coated. Cover and set aside at room temperature for about 30 minutes. Thread on to skewers and cook over charcoal, turning frequently, for 8–10 minutes. Do not overcook or the liver will dry out. Serve with a little of the remaining marinade spooned over the top and garnished with lemon wedges.

Variation

liver with tomato

This is an Armenian favourite.

900 g/2 lb liver

Marinade
2 tablespoons tomato purée	**1 teaspoon chilli powder**
1 clove garlic, crushed	**1 teaspoon salt**
juice 2 lemons	**1 teaspoon cumin**

Mix all the marinade ingredients together in a large bowl, add the pieces of liver and turn until well coated. Leave at room temperature for 30 minutes. Thread on to skewers and cook as above.

kafta kebab minced meat kebab

Kafta kebab (*kafah* or *kofteh* in old Aramaic and Persian) is the general name given to all kinds of minced meat kebabs — lamb, beef or a mixture of the two. It is by far the most popular form of kebab. There are many variations throughout the region and some are regional specialities. I have noted a few to show the possibilities, but you can also experiment at your leisure.

The meat should be minced twice, although in Iran it is often minced three or four times. The secret of a good *kafta* kebab lies in its seasoning. Apart from salt and pepper, chopped onion and/or parsley, cumin, coriander, mint, chilli pepper and cinnamon are often used in differing combinations.

basic recipe

900 g/2 lb lamb (or beef or a
    mixture of the two), minced twice
2 onions, very finely chopped

1–2 eggs
salt and pepper to taste

Put all the ingredients into a large bowl and knead until very smooth. Take a lump of meat about the size of an egg and, with damp hands, pass a skewer through it and then squeeze the meat out gently until the kebab is thin and sausage-shaped. Continue until you have used up all the meat. Cook on a well oiled grid, turning frequently, for about 10 minutes.

soong kebab mushroom kebab

Ingredients as for the basic recipe

32 button mushrooms

Prepare the meat as described above. Divide the mixture into 24 small balls. Thread the balls and mushrooms alternately on to skewers, starting and ending with a mushroom. Allow 3 meatballs and 4 mushrooms per skewer. If the mushrooms show a tendency to split soak them for a little while in warm water. Cook as with the basic recipe.

urfa kebab

A favourite from Urfa, a city in Turkey.

Ingredients as for the basic recipe

3–4 aubergines

Prepare the meat as described in the basic recipe. Divide the mixture into 24 small balls.

Cut the hulls off the aubergines and then slice crossways into 1.2 cm/1/2 in thick rings.

Thread the meatballs and aubergine slices alternately on to skewers. Allow 3 or 4 of each on each skewer depending on length of skewers and size of fire. Cook as in the basic recipe, turning frequently. The aubergines usually take a little longer to cook than the meat and so continue cooking, turning frequently to prevent the meat burning, until the aubergines are tender. Serve with hot bread and a garnish of onion rings and tomato slices.

lulu kebab

This is an Armenian favourite.

900 g/2 lb minced lamb
2 tablespoons parsley, finely chopped

2 onions, very finely chopped
salt and black pepper to taste

Garnish
8 medium tomatoes
3–4 tablespoons parsley, finely chopped

1 medium onion, finely chopped

Put the meat, parsley, onions, salt and pepper into a large bowl and, with damp hands, knead for several minutes until well blended, smooth and malleable. Take a lump of meat about the size of an egg, pass a skewer through it and, with damp hands, gently squeeze the meat out along the skewer until it is thin and sausage-shaped. Continue until you have used up all the meat. Cook on a well-oiled grid, turning frequently, for about 10 minutes.

At the same time thread the tomatoes on to skewers and cook them over the fire. When the kebabs are cooked and ready to serve remove the tomatoes to a plate and skin them. Chop the tomato flesh, put in a bowl and mix in the chopped parsley and onion. Use the tomato mixture as a base and serve the kebabs on top.

kebab-e-koubideh

An Iranian favourite.

700 g/1¹/₂ lb lamb or beef, minced
   twice

1 large onion, finely chopped
¹/₂ teaspoon salt

Garnish sumac, 4 egg yolks and butter

Mix the meat, onion and salt together with damp hands until smooth. Take a lump of meat about the size of an egg and pass a skewer (preferably a flat one) through it. Squeeze the meat out firmly until it is thin and more rectangular than round in shape. Continue until you have used up all the meat. Cook over charcoal, turning frequently, for 8–10 minutes.

To serve slide 2 kebabs from the skewers on to a plate and then cover with a mound of *chelo* rice and sprinkle with some sumac. Top with an egg yolk and pat of butter. Stir the rice so that the egg, melted butter and sumac are all mixed together.

This dish is usually eaten with a spoon rather than a knife. Some Iranians also like to eat this dish with a slice of raw onion and a grilled tomato.

sheftalia cypriot sausage kebab

A classic kebab of Greek origin, but equally popular with Armenians. Caul fat (*panna*) from the pig, which is the outer covering of the paunch, can be purchased from most butchers. In the Middle East it is sold by street vendors who follow their mules from street to street offering — amongst other things — sausage casings, lamb's heads, sweetbreads, livers, kidneys, hearts, etc. When *panna* is opened flat it has a patterned appearance of fat on very fine tissue. Usually served as a main dish with a rice *pilav*, salads and pickles these kebabs also make marvellous appetizers.

450 g/1 lb lamb or beef, minced 3 times
450 g/1 lb fatty pork, minced twice
1 large onion, peeled and minced
4 tablespoons parsley, finely chopped

2 teaspoons salt
1/2–3/4 teaspoon black pepper
225 g/8 oz *panna* (caul fat from pig)
warm water

In a large bowl mix the meats, onion, parsley, salt and pepper together and knead for about 3 minutes or until smooth.

Dip the *panna* into a bowl of water for about 2 minutes. Remove and carefully open, one at a time, on a clean working top. Cut the *panna* into 10 cm/4 in squares using scissors or a very sharp knife.

Scoop out a spoonful of the meat mixture and shape it into a sausage about 5 cm/2 in long. Place this sausage near one edge of a piece of *panna*. Fold the edge and sides over and roll up firmly. When all the sausages are made thread them on to flat skewers, 2–3 per skewer and grill over charcoal, turning frequently. The *panna* will slowly melt away keeping the sausages moist. Serve immediately.

poultry and game

Chickens are excellent for grilling over a charcoal fire. Use only young ones — 900–1350 g/2–3 lb in weight or poussins (baby chicken — 4–6 weeks old) — which have proportionately more meat on their bodies in relation to their weight.

All kinds of poultry and game make excellent kebabs, e.g. duck, goose, turkey, guinea fowl, capon, quail, woodcock, partridge, pheasant and pigeon. Many of these are, unfortunately, not so easily available or are seasonal and therefore expensive. Rabbit also makes an excellent kebab and is available all the year round.

The basic preparation for grilling whole chicken is as follows:

Tie the wing tips over the breasts and fasten the neck skin to the back with a skewer. Push the spit through the bird from the tail end towards the front — the spit should emerge between the branches of the wishbone. Tie drumsticks and tail together.

Alternatively you can cut each chicken in half lengthways. If using a long spit thread the chicken halves crossways on to the spit piercing each one through the thigh meat. If using individual skewers then push 2 lengthways through each half. This makes it easier to turn without it slipping around the skewer.

At this stage you can either place the chicken in a marinade for a few hours or brush the bird with oil or a baste and cook it immediately. Cook over charcoal turning and brushing with any remaining marinade or with the oil or baste frequently. To test if the chicken is cooked pierce a thigh where the meat is thickest. If the juice runs clear and not pink then the chicken is ready.

Below are a few marinades which are ideal for whole, halved or jointed chicken:

A typical marinade from Turkey

300 ml/½ pint oil

3 cloves garlic, finely chopped

juice 1 lemon

salt and black pepper to taste

Blend the ingredients in a large bowl, add the whole or jointed chicken and mix well. Leave at room temperature for at least 2 hours. Use any remaining marinade as a baste while cooking.

A Kurdish baste

75 g/3 oz butter, melted

½ teaspoon whole savory

½ teaspoon rosemary

½ teaspoon thyme

½ teaspoon marjoram

½ teaspoon sweet basil

Mix all the herbs together in a small bowl and stir in the melted butter. Thread the chicken on to skewers and brush all over with the baste. Cook brushing frequently with the baste.

An Arab favourite from Libya and Egypt

1 tablespoon paprika

1 teaspoon cumin

1/2 teaspoon chilli pepper

salt to taste

75 g/3 oz melted butter

Mix all the ingredients together and use to baste the chicken frequently while cooking.

judi kebab chicken kebab

A classic from Armenia where chicken is marinated in oil, spices and garlic. This recipe uses poussins, but you can use one larger chicken and cut it into serving pieces. Serve with *pilavs* or bread and salads of your choice.

4 poussins

Marinade

150 ml/1/4 pint oil

2 cloves garlic, crushed

1 lemon, thinly sliced

1 tablespoon sumac (optional)

2 teaspoons salt

1 teaspoon black pepper

Sauce

1 clove garlic, crushed

juice 1/2 lemon

2 tablespoons olive oil

1/4 teaspoon cumin

Wash and dry the poussins. Cut each one into 8 pieces, i.e. 2 breasts, 2 wings, 2 drumsticks and 2 thighs.

Mix the marinade ingredients together in a large bowl. Add the chicken pieces, stir to coat, cover and refrigerate for at least 8 hours or overnight. Remove the pieces from the marinade and pat with kitchen paper, but do not dry.

Thread the pieces on to wide, flat skewers so that each skewer holds the 8 pieces of one poussin. Cook over charcoal, turning and basting regularly with the remaining marinade. Cook for 15–20 minutes then remove from the fire and slide the kebabs off the skewers on to a large serving dish. Mix the sauce ingredients together and sprinkle it over the chicken immediately before eating.

Variation

An equally famed Iranian chicken kebab *kabab-e-joojeh* which is always accompanied by *chelo pilav*, a pat of butter and sumac.

4 x 450–700 g/1–11/2 lb poussins, cut as above or 2 x 900–1200 g/
2–21/2 lb chicken, each cut into 8 pieces

Marinade

225 g/8 oz finely chopped onion
6 tablespoons fresh lemon juice
1¹/₂ teaspoons salt

¹/₄ teaspoon nutmeg
¹/₄ teaspoon cinnamon

Baste

50 g/2 oz butter

pinch ground saffron dissolved in
2¹/₂ teaspoons warm water

Mix the marinade ingredients in a large bowl. Add the chicken pieces and turn until well coated. Cover and leave in the refrigerator overnight.

If using poussins thread all the pieces of one poussin on to each skewer, but if using 2 larger birds thread one wing, breast, thigh and drumstick on to each skewer. Melt the butter in a small pan and then stir it and the saffron into any remaining marinade. Brush the kebabs with this mixture and grill for 15–20 minutes, turning and basting occasionally. Serve the kebabs with *chelo* rice. Place a pat of butter on top of the rice and sprinkle liberally with sumac. As the butter melts mix the rice up so that the butter and sumac are distributed evenly throughout the rice.

kebab me auff israeli chicken kebab

Mrs Stein entered a kosher poultry store and asked the price of stewing chickens.
'Forty cents a pound,' said the butcher.
'Forty cents!' cried Mrs Stein. 'Why, just around the corner
Ellenberger sells for thirty-six cents a pound.'
'If Ellenberger sells stewing chickens for thirty-six cents a pound, why don't you buy there?' asked the butcher impatiently.
'Because he happens to be out of them today.'
'Look, lady,' said the butcher, 'as soon as I run out of stewers I'll sell them to you for only twelve cents a pound — and you can't beat that price anywhere!'
(Encyclopedia of Jewish Humour)

A colourful and tasty recipe from Israel. The meat is marinated in wine, oil and garlic and garnished with fresh vegetables.

4 large chicken breasts

Marinade

juice 4 lemons
150 ml/¹/₄ pint oil
150 ml/¹/₄ pint dry red wine
2 cloves garlic, finely chopped

2 bay leaves
1 teaspoon ground coriander
1 teaspoon salt
¹/₂ teaspoon black pepper

Garnish

2 green peppers, seeded and quartered
2 onions, quartered
2 sticks celery, each cut into 4
4 large mushrooms, wiped
    clean and trimmed

2 avocados
50 g/2 oz sugar
1 tablespoon lemon juice
150 ml/¼ pint red wine
fresh mint leaves

Skin and bone the chicken breasts and cut into 2.5–4 cm/1–1¹/₂ in pieces.

Mix the marinade ingredients together in a large bowl. Add the pieces of chicken, toss to coat well then cover and refrigerate overnight.

Thread the chicken pieces on to skewers alternating with pieces of green pepper, onion, celery and a mushroom. Brush the meat and vegetables with any remaining marinade and grill for 10–15 minutes, turning and basting frequently.

While the kebabs are cooking cut the avocados in half and remove the stones. Mix the sugar, lemon juice and wine together and pour into the halved avocados. Garnish with the mint leaves and serve with the kebabs.

pasianni khorovadze pheasant kebab

This 'classic' from the Caucasus is usually served with *tkemali* sauce made of prunes, garlic and coriander.

2 pheasants
50 g/2 oz melted butter

salt and pepper to taste

Tkemali sauce — see recipe page 283

Split each pheasant in half and wash thoroughly and dry. Brush each piece on both sides with some of the butter and sprinkle them with salt and pepper. Thread on to skewers and cook for about 30 minutes, turning and basting occasionally with the remaining butter. Take care not to overcook as pheasant flesh tends to dry out quickly. Serve on a bed of rice *pilav* with the *tkemali* sauce spooned over the top.

Variation

Iraqis and Iranians often use a marinade of:

¹/₂ teaspoon ground saffron diluted
    in 3–4 tablespoons hot water
6 tablespoons olive oil

juice 1 large lime or lemon
1 teaspoon salt
¹/₂ teaspoon paprika

The halved pheasants are marinated in this mixture for 2–3 hours before cooking. Serve on a bed of saffron *pilav* with yoghurt and salads.

fish kebab

Fish is healthful for the eyes. — Nedashin 54b.

Of the hundreds of different fish available to the Middle Eastern housewife about thirty are commonly used and easily available at the numerous fish shops scattered the length of the Mediterranean coastline. They are; auberjack, anchovy, bass, bonito, block, carp, comber, crab, eel, grey mullet, gurnard, lobster, mackerel, mussels, octopus, prawns, perch, red mullet, salmon, sardines, sea-bream, prawns, sole, squid, sturgeon, swordfish, trout, turbot and whiting. Of these the most popular are red and grey mullet, sea-bream, bass, swordfish, carp and trout. Certain recipes suggest a particular fish, but wherever possible I have also recommended fish that are locally available in the West.

There are two main methods of cooking fish in the Middle East: (a) frying in oil; (b) grilling over charcoal. Both methods are used in the numerous seaside restaurants of Egypt, Lebanon, Turkey and Cyprus.

Before grilling, the fish slices are marinated in herbs, spices and wine mixtures and then they are either threaded on to skewers or contained in a lightly oiled double grill. Sometimes aromatic herbs are thrown on to the coals to give extra aroma to the fish. Always make sure the grilled fish is soft and juicy inside with a crisp brown skin. To achieve this baste regularly with the marinade or with melted butter flavoured with a little lemon juice.

Large as well as small fish are suitable for charcoal cooking, but I suggest you make several diagonal slits on the sides and then tie with string to retain the shape. Some people like to fill these slits with garlic, bay leaves, cloves, thyme, etc.

A favourite Armenian marinade
150 ml/¼ pint oil
1 clove garlic, crushed
1 teaspoon salt

3 bay leaves
grated rind 2 oranges

A Caucasian favourite
4 tablespoons pomegranate juice
1 teaspoon lemon juice
1 teaspoon salt

½ teaspoon black pepper
150 ml/¼ pint yoghurt or soured cream

A Syrian favourite
4 tablespoons oil
4 tablespoons lemon juice
1 clove garlic, crushed
1 teaspoon salt

½ teaspoon black pepper
½ teaspoon ground coriander
3 bay leaves

A Turkish favourite

300 ml/¹/₂ pint beer
1 tablespoon chives, chopped
2 tablespoons parsley, finely chopped
1 tablespoon dry mustard

2 cloves garlic, crushed
1 teaspoon salt
¹/₂ teaspoon black pepper
¹/₂ teaspoon oregano

A Gulf speciality

In the Gulf region the Arabs like to spread puréed dates over the fish and set aside for 30 minutes.

To make the purée put some dried and stoned dates into cold water and leave to soak for 45 minutes. Rub the dates through a sieve or blend in a liquidizer with a little water to make a soft paste. With your hands spread the mixture over both sides of each fish and leave for about 30 minutes. Grill in the usual way.

kiliç şişte swordfish kebab

The fish of the Turks, swordfish is found in abundance along the Mediterranean coastline as well as the Black Sea. It is marinated and then grilled over charcoal. If swordfish is not available I suggest you use cod or halibut.

Serve with a *pilav* of your choice and *tarator* — see recipe on page 284.

900 g/2 lb swordfish

Marinade

1 onion, cut into 0.6 cm/¹/₄ in slices
   and then separated into rings
3 tablespoons lemon juice
2 tablespoons oil

1¹/₂ teaspoons salt
1 teaspoon paprika
¹/₂ teaspoon black pepper
about 20 large bay leaves

Garnish 1–2 tablespoons parsley, finely chopped

Skin and bone the fish and cut into 2.5 cm/1 in cubes.

In a large bowl put the onion rings, 1¹/₂ tablespoons lemon juice, 1 tablespoon oil and the salt and paprika and black pepper. Add the pieces of fish and toss to coat well with the marinade. Marinate for 2–3 hours at room temperature.

Meanwhile, soak the bay leaves in boiling water for ¹/₂–1 hour and then drain.

Remove the fish from the marinade and thread on to skewers, alternating the pieces with bay leaves. Press firmly together so that the flavour passes from the leaves to the fish. Mix the remaining lemon juice and oil together and brush the kebabs with this baste. Cook over charcoal for about 10 minutes or until golden, turning and basting frequently. Serve with rice and *tarator* sauce.

NB If you do not wish to use the *tarator* sauce I suggest you make a simple dressing by mixing together 2 tablespoons lemon juice, 3 tablespoons olive oil, 2 tablespoons finely chopped parsley and ¹/₂ teaspoon paprika. Spoon this over the kebabs.

trabzon yilan baligi turkish eel kebab

From Trabzon on the Black Sea coast this recipe is a favourite of the Laz people — Georgian Muslims who emigrated from the Caucasus in the seventeenth century to the Ottoman Empire. Lazes are famed for their beautiful women, wild dances (*lezginka*) and great acumen for business.

There are several types of eel, any of which will do well.

900 g/2 lb conger eel, skinned and
    filleted, washed, dried and cut
    into 2.5 cm/1 in pieces
1 teaspoon salt
1 teaspoon black pepper

4 slices white bread, crusts removed
    and cut into 2.5 cm/1 in pieces
8 small tomatoes, halved
4 bay leaves
3 tablespoons oil

Garnish lemon wedges, tarragon leaves, shallots or spring onions

Rub the eel cubes all over with the salt and pepper. Thread the pieces of eel, bread cubes and tomato halves alternately on to 4 skewers, placing one bay leaf in the centre of each skewer. Brush the kebabs all over with the oil. Cook for 8–10 minutes, turning frequently until the bread is toasted and the eel cubes are tender when pierced with a sharp knife. Serve immediately on a bed of rice *pilav* with lemon wedges and a side plate of tarragon leaves, shallots or spring onions.

taparagan mackerel in a spicy tomato sauce

A family favourite. My mother always used mackerel, but trout, red or grey mullet or any fish steaks will do equally well. The fish is marinated, grilled and served with a salad – *taparagan* (literally meaning 'the wanderer') of onions, tomato purée and spices.

Serve with fried vegetables and a *pilav* of your choice and/or fresh salads.

4 medium-sized mackerel

Marinade

1 tablespoon tomato purée	1 teaspoon salt
4 tablespoons oil	1 teaspoon allspice
4 tablespoons lemon juice	1/2 teaspoon chilli pepper

Salad

2 large onions, thinly sliced	2 tablespoons lemon juice
1 tablespoon parsley, chopped	1 level teaspoon salt
1 level tablespoon tomato purée	1 level teaspoon allspice
2 tablespoons olive oil	1/4 teaspoon chilli pepper

Cut the heads and tails off the fish. Slit down the whole length of the stomach and remove the insides, backbone and as many of the other bones as possible. Wash thoroughly.

Mix the marinade ingredients together in a shallow bowl and rub the marinade over both sides of each fish. Fold each fish over to take its original shape, cover and leave in the refrigerator overnight.

When ready to cook lay the fish flat out on an oiled double grill and cook for 10–15 minutes, turning once or twice. Take care not to overcook or they will become dry. If the fish are large and your grill not very big then you may find it necessary to cook 2 at a time, keeping the first 2 warm.

While the fish are cooking prepare the salad by mixing together in a bowl the tomato purée, olive oil, lemon juice, salt, allspice and pepper. Stir in the sliced onions and chopped parsley.

When the fish are cooked place them on a large platter, arrange the salad around the edges and garnish with lemon wedges.

fish dishes

fried fish

Next to cooking fish over charcoal or under the grill the most popular method is frying in sizzling hot oil. Arabs squeeze a little lemon juice over the fish and eat it with fresh vegetables.

Below is a simple method for frying fish in oil.

Wash, clean and scale the fish if necessary. Leave small fish whole, but cut larger ones into steaks or fillets. Pat dry with kitchen paper. For each 500 g/1 lb of fish use 150 ml/¼ pint oil. Heat the oil to sizzling in a large pan, add the fish and fry for 5–10 minutes. Turn at least once and shake the pan once or twice to prevent the fish sticking. Remove the fish, drain and transfer to a large serving dish. Sprinkle with a little salt and chopped parsley and squeeze a little lemon juice over the top.

Sometimes the fish is dredged in flour or flour seasoned with salt, pepper and spices, e.g. cumin, paprika, ground coriander, etc. before deep frying.

Arabs often fry bread in the fish oil and serve it as a garnish.

a typical flour batter

100 g/4 oz flour
200 ml/7 fl oz warm water or milk
1 tablespoon olive oil

1 teaspoon salt
1 teaspoon black pepper
1 egg, beaten

Sift the flour into a bowl and make a well in the centre. Gradually stir in the water or milk until you have a smooth batter. Fold in the remaining ingredients and mix thoroughly. Dip the fish into the batter and deep fry until cooked through and golden.

an istanbul-style batter

100 g/4 oz flour
1 teaspoon baking soda
1 teaspoon salt
¼ teaspoon black pepper
¼ teaspoon cayenne pepper

1 bay leaf, finely chopped
½ teaspoon oregano
1 egg, beaten
2 tablespoons *raki* (ouzo)
150 ml/¼ pint water

Sift the flour and soda into a large bowl and mix in the salt, black pepper, cayenne pepper, bay leaf and oregano. Add the beaten egg and mix in with a wooden spoon. Mix in the *raki*. Gradually stir in the water and beat until the mixture is smooth. Dip the fish into the batter until completely coated and then deep fry in hot oil until cooked through and golden.

NB The batter in the 2 recipes above is sufficient for 900 g/2 lb of small fish, e.g. sardines, sprats, anchovies, etc. which have been cleaned and washed, but which have their heads and tails left on.

fish with sauces

Another attractive and tasty way of presenting fish is to first fry it and then to serve with a sauce. There are many sauces, a few are given below.

samak magli kousbariyeh

fried fish egyptian-style

900 g/2 lb small whole fish or
   large one, thickly sliced

300 ml/$^1/_2$ pint oil

Sauce

2 tablespoons oil
1 large onion, thinly sliced
3 large tomatoes, blanched, peeled
   and coarsely chopped
100 g/4 oz hazelnuts or walnuts,
   chopped

50 g/2 oz pine kernels
a little water or dry white wine
3 tablespoons parsley, finely chopped
1$^1/_2$ teaspoons salt
$^1/_2$ teaspoon black pepper
$^1/_2$ teaspoon allspice

Fry the fish or fish slices as described at the beginning of this section, page 213.

   Heat the oil in a large saucepan, add the sliced onion and fry until soft. Add the tomatoes and continue to simmer until soft. Add the nuts and fry for 2 minutes. Add enough water or wine to cover and season with the parsley, salt, pepper and allspice. Simmer for a few minutes then add the fried fish, turn to coat with the sauce and simmer for 12–15 minutes. Serve with a rice *pilav*, salads and bread.

samak-bi-tahina   sesame cream sauce

An Arab favourite, particularly in Lebanon, Syria and Palestine. Traditionally this dish is colourfully and artistically decorated with olives, pomegranate seeds, parsley, radishes, etc.

You can either fry or bake the fish before adding the sauce. If you are frying then follow the directions on page 213. This recipe, however, is for baked fish.

Serve cold either as part of a buffet spread or a main dish with a *pilav* and salads.

900–1350 g/2–3 lb whole fish, e.g.
   snapper, sea-bass, John Dorey, etc.
2 tablespoons lemon juice

1¹/₂ teaspoons salt
¹/₂ teaspoon black pepper
2–3 tablespoons olive oil

Sauce

2 cloves garlic, crushed
1 teaspoon salt
10 tablespoons tahina cream

juice 1 lemon
6 tablespoons water
3 tablespoons parsley, finely chopped

Garnishes An attractive combination of the following: pomegranate seeds, olives, chopped parsley or tarragon, roasted pine kernels, thinly sliced radishes, cucumbers, etc.

Clean and scale the fish if necessary. Leave the head on, but remove the eyes. Rinse and dry and make 2–3 slits on each side of the body.

Mix the lemon juice, salt, pepper and oil together, rub all over the fish, place in a shallow dish, cover and refrigerate for 1 hour.

Oil a shallow baking dish, put the fish in it and pour any remaining oil and lemon juice mixture over the top. Bake in the centre of an oven preheated to 180°C, 350°F, gas mark 4 for 30–40 minutes or until the fish is cooked. Test with a fork — if the fish flakes easily then it is done. Baste with the pan juices occasionally and do not overcook. Lift the fish carefully on to a large serving dish, cover and chill.

Meanwhile, prepare the sauce by placing the crushed garlic and salt in a bowl and mixing in the tahina. Stir in the lemon juice and water and mix until smooth and creamy. Add the parsley. Spread half the sauce smoothly over the fish leaving the head and tail uncovered, and decorate attractively with the garnishes. Chill and serve with the remaining sauce.

Variation

Often, especially in Lebanon, the fish is boned after baking. Then the flesh is seasoned with 1 teaspoon salt, ¹/₂ teaspoon black pepper and then re-shaped to its original form.

The head and tail are replaced and the body is covered with the sauce and then garnished.

barbouni red mullet in wine

Red mullet is, perhaps, the most popular fish throughout the Mediterranean coastline. It is the famed *Sultan Ibrahim* of the Arabs, *barbounya* of Turkey, and *barbouni* to the Greeks. It is a fish that fries and bakes well and has a peculiarly 'Mediterranean' taste to it. This recipe from Cyprus — hence the inclusion of wine — is particularly good.

Serve with *pilav*, salads and pickles.

900 g/2 lb red mullet, entrails removed   olive oil

Wine sauce

300 ml/¹/₂ pint dry white wine
3 cloves garlic, crushed
1 tablespoon tomato purée
2 tablespoons parsley, finely chopped
1 teaspoon dried tarragon

25 g/1 oz dry breadcrumbs
1 teaspoon salt
¹/₂ teaspoon black pepper
¹/₂ teaspoon fennel

Cut the fins off the fish. Wash thoroughly inside and out.

Line a large baking dish with silver foil, leaving enough to fold over and cover the fish. Brush the foil with olive oil and place the fish in the dish.

In a bowl mix together the wine, garlic and tomato purée and then add the parsley, tarragon and breadcrumbs. Sprinkle the fish with the salt, pepper and fennel and then pour in the wine sauce. Fold the foil over to seal in the fish. Bake in an oven preheated to 190°C, 375°F, gas mark 5 for 25–30 minutes or until the fish is tender and flakes easily. Remove the dish from the oven and carefully lift the fish on to a serving dish. Pour the sauce over the top and garnish with a little parsley.

Tomato is extensively used with fish and there are several fine tomato-based sauces. Here are two which are ideal with fried, baked or grilled fish. The quantities given are adequate for 900 g/2 lb of fish.

loligi salsa

An Armenian favourite.

50 g/2 oz butter
1 small onion, finely chopped
5–6 medium tomatoes, blanched,
    peeled and finely chopped
2 cloves garlic, crushed

2 tablespoons parsley, finely chopped
1 bay leaf
1 teaspoon salt
¹/₂ teaspoon black pepper

Melt the butter in a saucepan, add the onion and fry until soft. Add the remaining ingredients and cook over a low heat for 15 minutes or until the sauce thickens. Stir frequently. Pass through a sieve and serve warm.

tomates salsasi

A recipe from Izmir, Turkey which is popular with the Greeks as well as the Turks.

700 g/1¹/2 lb ripe tomatoes,
   coarsely chopped
2 teaspoons salt
1 tablespoon sugar
¹/4 teaspoon black pepper

25 g/1 oz butter, melted
1 tablespoon flour
¹/4 teaspoon basil
¹/2 teaspoon oregano

Place the tomatoes in a saucepan and cook over a low heat for about 10 minutes, stirring frequently. Add the salt, sugar and pepper and cook for a further 10 minutes. Pass the tomatoes through a sieve into another pan and discard the skin, seeds, etc. Cook the strained tomatoes over a low heat for a further 15 minutes.

   In a small bowl mix the melted butter and flour together and then stir in 3–4 tablespoons water until you have a smooth paste. Add this mixture to the tomatoes and stir until blended. Add the basil and oregano and cook over a lower heat for a few more minutes and then serve.

hamsi tavasi anchovy with rice

From the Black Sea coastline of Turkey, this is a speciality of Trabzon's Laz people. Serve with fresh salads and pickles.

700 g/1¹/2 lb fresh anchovies,
   cleaned and deboned
4 tablespoons salt
75 g/3 oz butter
1 onion, finely chopped
250 g/9 oz long grain rice, washed
   thoroughly under cold water
   and drained
600 ml/1 pint boiling water

2 tablespoons hazelnuts, halved or pine
   kernels or blanched slivered almonds
1¹/2 teaspoons sugar
1 tablespoon sultanas
¹/2 teaspoon allspice
1 teaspoon salt
¹/2 teaspoon cinnamon
¹/2 teaspoon black pepper

Garnish

¹/4 teaspoon dillweed
¹/2 teaspoon paprika

1 tablespoon sumac powder, optional

Place the anchovies in a large pan, sprinkle with the salt and set aside.

   Melt 50 g/2 oz of the butter in a large saucepan. Add the onion and fry for a few minutes until soft. Add the rice and fry for 5 minutes, stirring frequently. Add the water, nuts, sugar, sultanas, allspice, salt, cinnamon and black pepper and stir well. Bring to the boil and cook vigorously for 3 minutes. Reduce the heat, cover the pan and continue cooking for 15–20 minutes until all the liquid has been absorbed.

Grease a large casserole dish. Rinse the anchovies under cold water and arrange half of them in a single layer in the dish. Tip the rice mixture into the casserole and level it out then arrange the remaining anchovies over the top. Melt the remaining butter and pour it over the top. Cover the dish and cook in an oven preheated to 190°C, 375°F, gas mark 5 for about 15–20 minutes or until the fish are cooked. Remove from the oven and sprinkle with the dillweed, paprika and sumac. Serve hot with salad.

sayyadiyah fish with rice

A popular Arab speciality with numerous variations.

Sometimes the fish and rice are prepared and served separately, but in the recipe below they are cooked together. Serve with a bowl of fresh salad.

50 g/2 oz butter
900 g/2 lb halibut steaks, each
    cut in half
2 tablespoons lemon juice

1/2 teaspoon salt
1/4 teaspoon black pepper
2 tablespoons parsley, finely chopped

Stew

6 tablespoons oil
1 onion, finely chopped
2 tablespoons pine kernels
1 tablespoon sultanas or raisins
1/2 teaspoon allspice

saffron rice — prepare plain rice *pilav*
    with 250 g/9 oz rice, etc., but stir
    1/2 teaspoon powdered saffron
    into the rice while it is frying
2 tablespoons lemon juice
2 tablespoons parsley, finely chopped
1 teaspoon salt
1/2 teaspoon black pepper

Sauce

4 tablespoons oil
1 tablespoon pine kernels
1 tablespoon dried mint

1 tablespoon lemon juice
1/2 teaspoon cumin

Melt half the butter in a large shallow baking dish and add the pieces of fish. Sprinkle with the lemon juice, salt, pepper and chopped parsley. Dot the remaining butter over the fish. Bake in an oven preheated to 160°C, 325°F, gas mark 3 and cook until the fish flakes easily. Remove from the oven, leave to cool and then flake the fish and remove and discard the bones. Set the flaked fish aside.

To prepare the stew heat the oil in a large saucepan, add the onion and sauté until soft. Add the nuts, raisins, allspice and saffron rice as well as the lemon juice, parsley, salt and pepper. Mix all the ingredients together carefully. Spread half this mixture over the base of a large shallow baking dish. Spread half of the reserved fish over the top. Cover with the remaining rice and top with the rest of the fish.

Now prepare the sauce by heating the oil in a small frying pan. Add the nuts, mint, lemon juice and cumin and sauté for a few minutes, until the nuts are golden, stirring frequently. Pour the sauce evenly over the surface of the casserole. Bake in an oven preheated to 190°C, 375°F, gas mark 5 for about 15 minutes or until the ingredients are heated through. Remove and serve with a salad.

Variation

A favourite Egyptian method is to stew the *sayyadiyah*.

Cut one onion in half lengthways and then cut into thin half-moon shaped slices. Fry in 6 tablespoons oil until golden. Add the fish steaks and season with 1½ teaspoons salt, ½ teaspoon black pepper and ½ teaspoon powdered saffron. Add sufficient water to cover and simmer over a low heat for about 10 minutes.

Break up the fish into smaller pieces, discarding the bones, add 350 g/12 oz washed, long grain rice plus enough water to cover the mixture. Cover and simmer for 15–20 minutes or until the rice is tender and fluffy.

barghoon-el-bahar bil roz

prawn fried rice

One of the numerous prawn recipes from the eastern coastline of Saudi Arabia. Use saffron rice as it gives both extra fragrance and a charming appearance to the dish.

saffron rice (prepare as with plain rice
  pilav [page 181] using 250 g/9 oz
  long grain rice, etc. but stir
  ½ teaspoon powdered saffron
  into the rice while it is frying)
3 tablespoons oil
1 stick celery, cut into 1.2 cm/
  ½ in pieces

100 g/4 oz French beans cut into
  5 cm/2 in pieces
4 spring onions, thinly sliced
2 tablespoons soy sauce
450 g/1 lb prawns, frozen will do as
  well as fresh
2 eggs
2 tablespoons blanched almonds

Prepare the rice according to the recipe and keep warm.

Heat the oil in a large saucepan and fry the celery, French beans and half the spring onions for 3–4 minutes, stirring all the time. Add the soy sauce and the prawns and continue to cook, stirring gently, for a few minutes. Break the eggs into a small bowl, lightly beat and add to the pan. Lower the heat and continue stirring the mixture until the eggs are cooked.

Meanwhile, under a grill, cook the almonds for a few minutes until golden brown.

Transfer the rice to a large serving plate and top with the prawns and vegetables. Garnish with the remaining spring onions and sprinkle with the toasted almonds.

Variations

A Kuwaiti favourite — *nachbous* — makes use of turmeric and curry powder and has a garnish of prawns, tomatoes and bananas.

plain rice pilav, see recipe page
   181, and use 250 g/9 oz rice, etc.
40 g/1^{1}/$_{2}$ oz butter
2 eggs, beaten
450 g/1 lb prawns, shelled and
   deveined or frozen prawns thawed
1 teaspoon salt

^{1}/$_{2}$ teaspoon black pepper
^{1}/$_{2}$ teaspoon turmeric
1 teaspoon curry powder, optional
^{1}/$_{2}$ teaspoon paprika
1 tablespoon soy sauce
2 pineapple rings, thinly sliced

Garnish

1 tablespoon parsley, finely chopped
8 whole prawns, cooked
2 tomatoes, thinly sliced

thinly sliced cucumber
8–10 radishes halved
1 banana, peeled and sliced into thin rings

Prepare the rice.

   Melt the butter in a large pan, add the cooked rice and fry for 2 minutes, stirring constantly. Add the beaten eggs and cook until well mixed, stirring constantly. Chop the prawns finely and add to the pan together with the salt, black pepper, turmeric, curry powder, paprika, soy sauce and sliced pineapple. Mix well and cook for 8–10 minutes, stirring occasionally. Spoon the mixture into a glass bowl and press down hard to form a mould. Turn out on to a serving plate and garnish the top of the mould with the parsley and prawns. Decorate around the mould with the tomatoes, cucumber, radishes and banana slices. Serve with fresh salad.

stuffed fish

Most fish taste excellent when stuffed with fruit, vegetables, nuts, grains, etc. In the Middle Eastern cuisine it is the Greeks, North Africans, Armenians and Israelis who have perfected this method of cooking fish.

Any large fish is suitable, e.g. trout, sea-bass, mackerel, red mullet, sturgeon or carp. The fish should be thoroughly cleaned, washed and dried. If there are any roes leave them in as they are considered a great delicacy.

letzvadz tzook

A popular Armenian stuffed fish recipe.

Serve with a rice or burghul *pilav* or roast potatoes and salads.

4 medium-sized whole fish, thoroughly washed, cleaned and dried

Stuffing

6 tablespoons oil	2 cloves garlic, crushed
450 g/1 lb carrots, peeled and coarsely grated	1 teaspoon salt
	1/2 teaspoon black pepper
2 tablespoons parsley, finely chopped	2 medium onions, cut into rings

Sauce

1 tablespoon tomato purée	1/2 teaspoon salt
2 tablespoons oil	1/4 teaspoon black pepper
150 ml/1/4 pint boiling water	

Garnish **2 tablespoons olive oil mixed with juice of 1 lemon**

To prepare the stuffing heat the oil in a saucepan, add the carrots and fry over a low heat for about 10 minutes, stirring occasionally. Stir in the parsley, garlic, salt and pepper. Divide the mixture into 4 and fill each fish. Oil a large baking dish and arrange the fish in it, but separated from each other by the onion rings.

Mix the tomato purée, oil and water together in a small bowl and season with the salt and pepper. Pour the sauce over the fish and bake in an oven preheated to 190°C, 375°F, gas mark 5 for 30–40 minutes or until the fish are tender and turning brown. Place on a serving dish and arrange the onion rings around them. Pour the tomato sauce over the top. Serve the oil and lemon juice in a small jug to pour over the fish.

Variation

A Lebanese version uses water chestnuts, pine kernels and rice in the filling.

The quantities given below are for a 1.8–2.24 kg/4–5 lb whole fish and would therefore be ideal for a buffet or dinner party.

1 x 1.8–2.5 kg/4–5 lb whole fish, cleaned, washed and dried

Stuffing

250 g/9 oz cooked plain rice *pilav*,
  see recipe page 181
150 ml/¼ pint dressing made of oil,
  lemon juice, garlic, salt and pepper
1 tin (approx 150 g/5 oz) water
  chestnuts (or use fresh if available),
  halved

50 g/2 oz chopped spring onions
1 green pepper, thinly sliced
25 g/1 oz pine kernels
1 teaspoon salt
½ teaspoon black pepper
½ teaspoon oregano
50 g/2 oz butter, melted

Garnish **lemon wedges, thinly sliced radishes**

Mix all the stuffing ingredients, except the melted butter, together in a large bowl. Stuff the fish with this rice mixture. Reserve any filling left over. Sew up the opening with a fine thread. Place the fish in a large greased baking dish and pour the melted butter over the top. Cover and bake in an oven preheated to 180°C, 350°F, gas mark 4 for 30–40 minutes, basting frequently with the butter, or until the fish is tender but not overcooked. Remove from the oven and carefully transfer the fish to a serving plate. Remove the thread.

If there was any stuffing left over, heat it through in a small pan and arrange around the fish.

Garnish with the lemon wedges and thinly sliced radishes.

dag memula im chatzilim

An Israeli version.

The usual fish is carp, but trout, cod or red mullet will do well. Serve with salad, roast or fried potatoes and pickles. The stuffing is made of aubergines, eggs and cheese.

4 medium-sized whole fish, cleaned, washed and dried

Marinade

2 teaspoons salt
½ teaspoon black pepper
juice 1 lemon

100 ml/4 fl oz oil
2 bay leaves
1 onion, thinly sliced

Filling

2 medium aubergines
3 eggs, hard-boiled, shelled and
  mashed
50 g/2 oz feta cheese, grated
2 cloves garlic, crushed
¼ teaspoon mustard

1 teaspoon salt
½ teaspoon black pepper
½ teaspoon cumin
1 tablespoon mayonnaise
1 teaspoon lemon juice
1 teaspoon olive oil

Vegetables

2 tablespoons oil

2 spring onions, sliced

2 cloves garlic, crushed

2 tomatoes, sliced

2 green peppers, thinly sliced

Mix all the marinade ingredients together in a large shallow dish, add the fish, turn to coat with the marinade and leave for at least 4–5 hours.

Meanwhile, prepare the filling by cooking the aubergines, either in an oven or under the grill, until the skins are black and the flesh soft when poked. When cool enough to handle peel off the skin, scraping off and reserving any flesh which may come away with it. Chop the flesh and put into a bowl. Add the remaining filling ingredients to the aubergine pulp and mix thoroughly. Remove the fish from the marinade, reserving the marinade, and fill each fish with some of the filling.

To prepare the vegetables heat the oil in a pan and sauté the onions until golden. Add the garlic, tomatoes and green peppers and cook for about 5 minutes. Place this mixture in the bottom of a large, greased casserole dish. Arrange the fish on top of the vegetable mixture. Cover with the reserved marinade, place in an oven preheated to 180°C, 350°F, gas mark 4, and bake for about 30–45 minutes or until well cooked. Serve immediately.

sourbour trout stuffed with herbs

A speciality of Khuzestan, Iran popular with the Arabic speaking people of the region. Serve with a *pilav* or bread and salad and cooked vegetables.

4 medium-sized trout or mackerel, cleaned, washed and dried

2 tablespoons oil

Stuffing

40 g/1¹/₂ oz butter

2 tablespoons parsley, finely chopped

2 tablespoons tarragon, finely chopped

4 spring onions, finely chopped, including heads

1 tablespoon sweet basil

1 tablespoon coriander leaves, finely chopped

2 tablespoons mint, chopped

2 tablespoons radish leaves, finely chopped

2 tablespoons tamarind juice — see Glossary, page 374

¹/₂ teaspoon salt

¹/₂ teaspoon turmeric

Garnish lemon wedges, radishes

First prepare the stuffing by melting the butter in a pan. Add all the prepared herbs and onion and fry for 2–3 minutes, stirring constantly. Add the tamarind juice, salt and turmeric and fry for 2 more minutes before removing from the heat. Divide the stuffing into 4 and fill each fish. Secure the openings with toothpicks or thin thread. Heat the oil in a large baking dish, add the fish and turn in the oil. Bake in an oven preheated to 200°C, 400°F, gas mark 6 for 20–25 minutes or until the flesh flakes easily. Baste occasionally. Remove from the oven and carefully transfer the fish to a large serving plate. Garnish with the lemon wedges and radishes.

ishkan noushov stuffed fish with almond sauce

A classic, *ishkan* is the salmon trout found only in Lake Sevan, over 1370 m/4500 ft above sea level in the Caucasus.

The stuffing is made of almonds and spices and the sauce of almonds, wine and cream. This is a brilliant dish of rare sophistication. Use trout and serve with a burghul *pilav* or potatoes and salad.

4 medium-sized trout, cleaned, washed and dried. Do not cut off heads

2 tablespoons oil or 25 g/1 oz butter

Stuffing
100 g/4 oz ground almonds
juice 2 lemons
1 teaspoon salt

1 teaspoon black pepper
1 teaspoon cumin
a little water

Sauce
100 g/4 oz ground almonds
1 glass white wine
150 ml/¹/₄ pint single cream

salt and black pepper to taste
a little water or milk to mix

Garnish a few thin strips green pepper, lemon wedges

Mix the ingredients for the stuffing together in a bowl and add just enough water to produce a thick paste. Divide the mixture into 4 and fill each trout. Heat the oil or butter in a large baking dish, add the fish and turn to coat in the oil or butter. Bake in an oven preheated to 200°C, 400°F, gas mark 6 for 20–30 minutes or until tender.

Meanwhile, in a small saucepan mix the almonds for the sauce with the wine and cream and season to taste with the salt and pepper. Add sufficient water to produce the consistency of single cream. Bring to the boil and simmer very gently for about 10 minutes. Stir frequently or the mixture will stick to the pan. If the sauce becomes too thick for your liking then add a little water or milk.

Arrange the fish on a large dish and garnish with the lemon wedges. Stir the slices of green pepper into the sauce, pour a little over each trout and serve the rest separately.

levrek sultan murat

sea-bass with potatoes and artichokes

A recipe from Izmir, Turkey, a culinary centre of great repute famed for its *kufta*, sweets and fish dishes — of which this is one. Named after an Ottoman Sultan who — so we are told — was rather fond of this particular fish.

Serve with *pilav* and salads.

700 g/1¹/₂ lb sea-bass fillets — or you can use cod or halibut, etc.
2 large potatoes, peeled and cut into 1.2 cm/¹/₂ in cubes
5 tablespoons vegetable oil
¹/₂ teaspoon salt
2 artichokes
¹/₂ teaspoon salt

1 tablespoon lemon juice
juice 1 large lemon
3 tablespoons flour seasoned with ¹/₂ teaspoon salt
10 tablespoons melted butter or oil
6–8 mushrooms, quartered
2 tablespoons parsley, chopped

Garnish **lemon wedges**

Cut each fish fillet into 6–8 pieces.

Put the potato cubes in a pan, cover with water, bring to the boil and simmer for 2 minutes then drain. Heat the oil in a saucepan, add the potato cubes, sprinkle with ¹/₂ teaspoon salt, and fry gently for about 15 minutes, turning occasionally until golden all over.

Meanwhile, prepare the artichokes by first peeling the tough outer skin from the stem and cut 0.3 cm/¹/₈ in off the stem end. Remove any discoloured outer leaves and cut about 1.2 cm/¹/₂ in off the top of the remaining leaves. Quarter the artichokes lengthways, remove the pinkish leaves from the centre and scrape out and discard the hairy choke. Drop the artichoke quarters into a saucepan of water with the salt and tablespoon of lemon juice. Bring to the boil and simmer for 15 minutes.

Place the juice of 1 lemon in a small bowl, toss the pieces of fish in it and then roll them in the seasoned flour. Heat the butter or oil in a large saucepan, add the fish pieces and sauté for 4–5 minutes, turning occasionally. Transfer to a serving dish and keep warm.

Add the drained artichokes, potatoes and mushrooms to the pan and sauté for 3–4 minutes, stirring frequently. Stir in the parsley. Pile the vegetables over the fish and garnish with the lemon wedges. Serve immediately.

gormeh sabzi ba mahi iranian fish stew

An Iranian speciality which is colourful and spicy with spinach, fenugreek, limes and turmeric. There are very few interesting fish dishes of Iranian origin as most fish is either fried or grilled. This, however, is a rich stew and the traditional fish would be sturgeon or perch, but any white fish will do.

If you cannot obtain dried or fresh limes use lemon juice instead. Serve with a *pilav* of your choice.

3 tablespoons red kidney beans, washed under cold water
60 g/2¹/2 oz butter
3 tablespoons parsley, finely chopped
2 leeks, thinly sliced and thoroughly washed to remove all sand
450 g/1 lb spinach thoroughly washed, shaken dry and coarsely chopped
2 sticks celery, thinly sliced

1 tablespoon powdered fenugreek or 2 tablespoons chopped fresh fenugreek
300 ml/1/2 pint fish stock or water
5 dried limes or 2 fresh limes or juice 2 lemons
900 g/2 lb fish fillets, e.g. perch, sturgeon, haddock, halibut, etc.
1 teaspoon salt
1/2 teaspoon black pepper
1 teaspoon turmeric

Place the kidney beans in a saucepan, cover with lightly salted water and bring to the boil. Simmer for about 1 hour or until the beans are tender.

Melt the butter in a large saucepan, add the parsley, leeks, spinach, celery and fenugreek and sauté for a few minutes, stirring all the time. Add the stock, stir well, cover and cook over a low heat for 10 minutes. Cut each dried lime at one end and drop into the vegetable mixture or halve the fresh limes and add, or add the lemon juice. Add the fish, cover the pan and continue cooking for 30 minutes or until the fillets are flaky and tender.

Drain the kidney beans and add to the stew together with the salt, pepper and turmeric. Cook for 5 more minutes and then serve immediately with a *pilav*.

kagitta barbunya red mullet in foil

A most attractive way of cooking fish. In the past it was wrapped in parchment, but foil is usually used today. The flavour of the fish is retained and a succulent, tender flesh produced. Fish smells are also minimized.

The fish is wrapped whole with a few sprigs of parsley or mint and lemon wedges, or with tomato slices and herbs.

Although I have used a recipe popular in Istanbul, this fish — *Sultan Ibrahim* to the Arabs — is equally popular with Lebanese and Syrians.

Serve with cooked vegetables and/or *pilavs*.

4 medium red mullet
3 tablespoons olive oil
4 tablespoons parsley, finely chopped
juice 1 lemon

1/2 teaspoon salt
1/4 teaspoon black pepper
1/4 teaspoon paprika
1/2 teaspoon thyme

Leave the heads and tails on the fish but make a small slit in one side of each and clean out the insides thoroughly. Wash under cold running water and pat dry. Rub the fish with the olive oil. Now place each fish on a piece of foil and wrap each one up so that it is completely enclosed. Place on a baking sheet and cook in the centre of an oven preheated to 190°C, 375°F, gas mark 5 for 30–45 minutes.

Meanwhile, in a small bowl mix together the remaining ingredients. When the fish are cooked remove from the oven, unwrap and transfer the fish to a serving platter. Sprinkle with the parsley mixture and serve.

meat dishes

lamb

Tell me, love of my soul, where you graze your sheep
and where you rest them at noon?
Why should I sit here, like a nomad
among your companion's flocks,
*   and the men saying*
If you don't know where, my beauty, try
the sheep tracks — take your goats off to graze
by the shepherd's tent.
(The Song of Songs)

In the Middle East lamb is the most widely used meat — indeed one can say it is *the* meat, since beef, pork, etc. are unavailable to most due to geographical and religious limits.

I have, therefore, arranged the section on meat dishes in the following manner: it begins with whole lamb, followed by leg of lamb, chops, and ends with offal. In short, every part of the animal is shown as being used — barring the sheep's eyes, but including the head, feet and sweetbreads!

This is followed by a few recipes of beef and pork of merit and the section is completed with minced meat kebabs — an art form in which the Middle Eastern housewife is supreme.

In the chapter on kebabs (page 193) whole lamb kebab has been described, suffice therefore to say that the same treatment applies to the preparation for lamb roasted in the oven.

Whole roast lamb, sheep or goat is a festive dish and it is absolutely magnificent when stuffed with rice, meat, nuts and fruits.

Baby lamb or kid is the ideal choice; the meat is tender and tastes excellent. Use a 9–11 kg/20–25 lb lamb and order in advance from your butcher. They are not difficult to obtain, but do make sure that your oven is large and deep enough to take the whole lamb before you contemplate tackling this fabulous dish of 'kings and nomads'. I have included two recipes for stuffed whole lamb since I suggest that if you are going to go to the trouble of cooking a whole lamb then you might as well stuff it as well — this way it will feed more people!

Stuffings vary from region to region, but on pages 230-1 are two traditional ones.

butzun kuzu dolmasi stuffed whole lamb

This is a favourite throughout the region.

First prepare the lamb, ask the butcher to remove and discard the entrails, but to keep the kidney, liver and heart and the lumps of fat at the back of the kidneys — these can all be chopped and used in the stuffing.

If the lamb is frozen allow to thaw for about 24 hours. Wash thoroughly in a large sink and then dry.

Rub inside and out with salt and pepper and sprinkle with the juice of 1 large onion. You can also rub in a mixture of spices, e.g. 1 teaspoon each of ground coriander, cumin, ginger and turmeric.

Stuffing

About 1.35 kg/3 lb long grain rice, washed thoroughly under cold water and drained

1 teaspoon powdered saffron (optional)

6 tablespoons oil

3 large onions, finely chopped

225 g/8 oz almonds, coarsely chopped

225 g/8 oz walnuts, coarsely chopped

100 g/4 oz raisins

3 tablespoons salt

3 teaspoons black pepper

1 tablespoon allspice

Garnish sprigs parsley

Bring a very large saucepan, half filled with lightly salted water, to the boil. Add the rice, and saffron if using, and simmer until just tender — 15–20 minutes — and then drain.

Heat the oil in a large pan, add the onions and fry until soft. Remove the onions with a slotted spoon and add to the rice. Add the almonds, walnuts and raisins to the pan and fry until the almonds are lightly golden, stirring frequently. Add to the rice together with the salt, pepper and allspice and mix well with a large fork. Stuff the lamb tightly with the mixture and sew up the opening with a long, strong needle and thread.

Put the lamb in a large baking dish, brush with oil and cook in an oven preheated to 160°C, 325°F, gas mark 3 for about 4–5 hours, turning at least once. The exact cooking time will depend on the size of the lamb, but it should be very tender — so that the meat is almost falling away from the bones. Baste regularly with the pan juices. Transfer to a large serving tray, open the stomach and allow some of the stuffing to spill out and then garnish with sprigs of parsley.

Serve with fresh salads of your choice.

kharoof mahshi

lamb stuffed with chicken stuffed with eggs

One of the great dishes of the world, the 'Babushka' of all stuffed recipes — unless, of course, one were to stuff a camel with the lamb!

9–11 kg/20–25 lb lamb, prepared
    as described in the previous recipe
900 g/2 lb chicken, cleaned
1 teaspoon salt

$1/2$ teaspoon turmeric
$1/4$ teaspoon black pepper
3 hard-boiled eggs, shelled

Stuffing

900 g/2 lb long grain rice, washed
    thoroughly under cold water
    and drained
1 teaspoon powdered saffron (optional)
4–5 tablespoons rosewater
100 g/4 oz fat from the kidneys,
    minced or 6–8 tablespoons oil
3 large onions, finely chopped
the lamb's liver, washed and finely
    chopped

the 2 kidneys, washed and finely
    chopped
100 g/4 oz blanched almonds, chopped
100 g/4 oz pine kernels
100 g/4 oz pistachio nuts
100 g/4 oz raisins
3 tablespoons salt
3 teaspoons black pepper
1 teaspoon cinnamon
1 teaspoon cumin

Wash and dry the chicken, rub the cavity with a mixture of the salt, turmeric and pepper and set aside.

Bring a very large saucepan half filled with lightly salted water to the boil. Add the rice, saffron and 3 tablespoons rosewater and simmer for 15–20 minutes or until just tender, then drain.

Heat the fat or oil in a pan, add the onions and fry until soft. Add the chopped liver and kidneys and fry, stirring frequently for 5–7 minutes. Remove with a slotted spoon and add to the rice.

Add to the frying pan the nuts, raisins, salt, pepper, cinnamon and cumin and fry for 2–3 minutes, stirring frequently. Add to the rice and mix well together with a large fork.

Insert the hard-boiled eggs into the chicken and then spoon in a little of the rice mixture. Secure the opening with thread or a small skewer. Partly stuff the lamb with the rice, then put the stuffed chicken in and continue to fill the cavity with the rice. Secure the opening with a long, strong needle and thread.

Brush with oil and bake in an oven preheated to 160°C, 325°F, gas mark 3 for 4–5 hours or until the meat is very tender. Exact time will depend on the size of the lamb. Turn the lamb at least once and baste occasionally with the pan juices. Place on a large serving tray, open the stomach and allow some of the stuffing and the chicken to spill out. Garnish with parsley and sliced fresh vegetables such as cucumber, tomatoes, radishes, spring onions, lemons, etc.

roast leg of lamb

A popular way of cooking is to bone the meat, season it with herbs and spices and then bake in the oven with vegetables. Below are a few examples, all for a 1.8-2.25 kg/4-5 lb leg of lamb which should be sufficient to feed 8-10 people.

kari vodk

An Armenian favourite.

1.8-2.25 kg/4-5 lb leg of lamb,
   boned and trimmed of excess fat
2 cloves garlic, crushed
1/2 teaspoon thyme
1/2 teaspoon rosemary

1 tablespoon fresh mint, finely chopped
1 teaspoon salt
1/2 teaspoon black pepper
4 cloves garlic, halved lengthways
50 g/2 oz melted *ghee* or butter

Mix the crushed garlic, thyme, rosemary, mint, salt and pepper together. Spread this mixture over the inside of the leg of lamb and then tie the leg up with string to resemble its former shape. Make small, 2.5 cm/1 in deep incisions with the point of a sharp knife over the outside of the leg and put a half clove of garlic into each slit.

Put the leg into a large baking dish, fat side up, pour the melted fat over the top and bake in an oven preheated to 180°C, 350°F, gas mark 4 for 2½-3 hours or until cooked to your liking. Baste regularly with the pan juices.

Variations

A Yemeni favourite *fakhed kharouf Yemani* has the bone removed in such a way that a pocket is left which is then filled with dates.

First the inside and outside of the meat is rubbed with a mixture of 2 tablespoons oil, 1 tablespoon salt, 1 teaspoon black pepper, 1/2 teaspoon each of thyme and rosemary and 2 tablespoons chopped fresh mint or 2 teaspoons dried mint. Put 2 bay leaves and 100 g/4 oz chopped dates into the pocket and secure the opening with a small skewer or strong thread. Bake as with the recipe above.

The Syrians and Lebanese stuff the leg pocket with 50 g/2 oz chopped, dried figs, 50 g/2 oz stoned, chopped prunes and 50 g/2 oz raisins mixed with 1/2 teaspoon thyme, 1/2 teaspoon sage and 25 g/1 oz melted butter. Cook as above.

The Greek *arni lemonato* is similar to *kari vodk* except that the meat is generously rubbed with lemon juice.

Use 2 large lemons, halved and after rubbing pour the excess juice into the baking dish and baste often.

Note More often than not vegetables are cooked with the meat. Any of the following will do well:

8-10 small globe artichoke hearts — add to the meat for the last hour of cooking and sprinkle with additional herbs, salt, pepper and lemon juice, baste occasionally

450 g/1 lb or more potatoes, peeled, quartered or thickly sliced

2 or 3 large onions, quartered

450 g/1 lb tomatoes, thickly sliced

450 g/1 lb celery sticks, cut into 7.5-10 cm/3-4 in pieces and blanched in boiling water for 5 minutes before adding to the meat pan

sarapli kuzu pirzolasi lamb chops in wine

This recipe is from Istanbul.

about 8 lamb chops, trimmed of excess fat

40 g/1½ oz butter

225 g/8 oz mushrooms, thinly sliced

1 clove garlic, crushed

1 teaspoon salt

1/4 teaspoon black pepper

2 large tomatoes, blanched, peeled and chopped

1/4 teaspoon basil

1/4 teaspoon oregano

100 ml/4 fl oz dry white wine

In a large saucepan cook the lamb chops in their own fat juices for 5 minutes, turning several times, until browned on both sides. Remove and keep warm. Add the butter to the pan, then add the mushrooms and garlic and fry for 5 minutes, stirring frequently. Return the chops to the pan, add the remaining ingredients and mix well. Cover the pan and simmer for about 30-45 minutes or until the chops are tender. Serve with a rice *pilav* and salads of choice.

budugov miss lamb chops in a fruit sauce

An Armenian version from the Caucasus. Use the same amount of chops as for *sarapli kuzu pirzolasi*.

about 8 chops

50 g/2 oz butter

300 ml/½ pint water

1 teaspoon salt

1/2 teaspoon black pepper

1/2 teaspoon cinnamon

1/2 teaspoon garam masala

75 g/3 oz raisins or sultanas

175 g/6 oz dried apricots, soaked overnight in cold water and then drained

Melt the butter in a large saucepan, add the chops and fry for a few minutes until browned on both sides. Pour off most of the fat and then add all the remaining ingredients. Bring to the boil, reduce heat to low, cover and simmer for 30-45 minutes, or until the chops are tender. Stir occasionally to prevent sticking. Arrange a *pilav* of your choice around a dish and spoon the chops and fruit sauce into the centre and serve immediately.

maghleh-bil-khel fried liver with vinegar

This particular recipe is a speciality of Tripoli, Lebanon. Although it recommends lamb's liver there is no reason why calf's liver cannot be used with this and the following recipe.

Liver with vinegar is very tasty. Use wine vinegar and serve with a *pilav* of your choice.

25 g/1 oz *ghee*
700 g/1¹/₂ lb lamb's liver, gristle
    removed, sliced
1¹/₂ teaspoons salt
¹/₂ teaspoon black pepper
1 large onion, finely chopped

2 cloves garlic, crushed
1¹/₂ tablespoons dried mint
1 teaspoon flour
150 ml/¹/₄ pint wine vinegar
about 3 tablespoons water
¹/₂ teaspoon paprika

Melt the fat in a large frying pan, add the liver, sprinkle with the salt and pepper and fry until browned on both sides. Remove the liver with a slotted spoon, drain and reserve. Add the onion and fry until soft, stirring frequently. Add the garlic, mint and flour and mix well. Stir in the vinegar, a little water and the paprika and cook for 5–6 minutes, stirring constantly. Add the liver, a little bit more water to cover if necessary, lower the heat and simmer for 10–15 minutes. Serve with a rice *pilav* and fresh salads.

khorak-e jegar va gholveh

liver and kidney stew

'Khorban! Jegar!' — My love! My darling! (Persian love expression.)
A recipe from Iran. Serve with *pilavs* and roast or fried vegetables.

40 g/1¹/₂ oz butter
1 large onion, finely chopped
1 lamb's liver (or calf's), gristle
    removed, chopped
2 hearts, tough valves, etc. removed,
    chopped
4 kidneys, skin and cores removed,
    chopped

450 g/1 lb tomatoes, blanched, peeled
    and chopped
225 ml/8 fl oz water
juice 1 lemon
1 teaspoon salt
¹/₄ teaspoon black pepper

Melt the butter in a large saucepan, add the onion and fry until soft. Add the liver, hearts and kidneys and fry for a further 5 minutes, stirring frequently. Add the remaining ingredients and bring to the boil. Lower the heat and simmer for about 30 minutes or until the meat is cooked.

Variation

Kirshuh is a dish from Yemen similar to the one on page 234, except that it has a lot more spices — which give extra zest.

To the ingredients above add 1 teaspoon turmeric, 1 teaspoon coriander, 1/2 teaspoon cumin and 2 crushed cardamom pods.

Reduce the quantity of tomatoes from 450 g/1 lb to 225 g/8 oz.

Garnish with chopped parsley or coriander leaves.

larshon im rotef

lamb's tongue with a wine and raisin sauce

An Israeli recipe with a tasty sauce.

10–12 lamb tongues, washed, scraped
    and soaked in water for 3 hours
2 bay leaves

2 cloves
1/2 teaspoon allspice
1 tablespoon salt

Sauce

40 g/1 1/2 oz butter
1 small onion, finely chopped
25 g/1 oz flour
350 ml/12 fl oz stock from the tongue
25 g/1 oz sugar

50 ml/2 fl oz dry white wine
1 tablespoon lemon juice
3 tablespoons seedless raisins
1/2 teaspoon ginger

Drain the soaked tongues, place in a large saucepan, cover with water, add the bay leaves, cloves, allspice and salt and bring to the boil. Remove any scum that appears on the surface then lower the heat, cover the pan and simmer for 2 hours.

Fifteen minutes before the end of the cooking time prepare the sauce by melting the fat in a saucepan, adding the onion and frying until soft. Stir in the flour and cook for another minute. Strain about 350 g/12 oz of stock from the tongue pan and stir into the onion mixture. Cook over a low heat, stirring constantly until the sauce thickens and begins to bubble. Stir in the remaining ingredients and cook for about 5–7 minutes before removing from the heat.

When the tongues are cooked drain and leave until cool enough to handle. Skin them and remove the gristle and the bone from the root ends. Slice each tongue lengthways in half. Add the halved tongues to the sauce and then return the pan to the heat and simmer for a further 10 minutes. Serve warm with bread, roast vegetables and salads.

Variation

An Iranian version *khorak-e-zaban* prepares the tongues as with the recipe above, but makes use of a milk and lemon sauce.

Sauce

Melt 40 g/1½ oz butter in a saucepan and stir in 50 g/2 oz flour. Stir in 300 ml/½ pint tongue stock and 300 ml/½ pint water and cook until sauce thickens, stirring constantly. Season with 1 teaspoon salt, ½ teaspoon black pepper, 1 tablespoon lemon juice and simmer for 10 minutes, stirring regularly.

Prepare the tongues as in previous recipe and add to the sauce. Spoon the mixture into a serving dish and sprinkle with chopped parsley or tarragon.

khash or paça hooves, tongue and tripe stew

One of the oldest and most beloved of all Middle Eastern dishes is *paça*, often called *kele paça* which, translated from Turkish means 'head and feet'. There are several variations of this dish and most are regional specialities: e.g. in Cyprus the lamb's head is sometimes substituted with boned meat; in Iraq chickpeas, chopped tomatoes and sliced, toasted bread are added to the stew; in Turkey another version includes 350 g/12 oz soaked haricot beans cooked with the hooves; while in Egypt a very ancient dish *kawareh-bi-hummus* is still prepared where lamb's or calf's feet are cooked with chickpeas, turmeric, salt and pepper for at least 3 hours or until the meat is falling off the bones. It is really a rich soup and is served with hard-boiled eggs (traditionally cooked in their shells in the stew), bread and salad.

The most famed version, however, is the one below from Turkey and Armenia.

4 calf's hooves (lamb or goat is also suitable). Buy ready-cleaned if possible
6 lamb's tongues
900 g/2 lb calf's tripe
3 cloves garlic, crushed
salt and pepper to taste

25 g/1 oz butter
½ teaspoon paprika
1 tablespoon chopped fresh mint or 1 teaspoon dried mint
1 tablespoon parsley, chopped
juice 1 lemon

Soak the feet in a large, deep saucepan of boiling water to loosen the shoes. Remove the shoe from each foot. Singe off the hair and then soak the feet and tripe in water overnight. Place the feet in a large saucepan, three-quarters full with water, add half the garlic and bring to the boil. Remove any scum that appears on the surface and then lower the heat and simmer.

Meanwhile, cut the tripe into 2.5 cm/1 in squares, place in another saucepan, half fill with water then bring to the boil and simmer for 15 minutes. Drain off the water, then add fresh water and cook for a further 15 minutes. Drain the tripe into a sieve and then add to the feet and cook together for about 2 hours. During cooking scum will constantly appear and so remove with a slotted spoon. When the meat separates easily from the foot bones, remove all the bones.

While the feet and tripe are cooking place the tongues in water in another pan and soak until the skin peels off easily. Remove the tongues, skin and then cut into smaller pieces.

When the feet and tripe have been cooking together for about 1 hour add the pieces of tongue to the pan. While the meat is cooking you will find it necessary to top up with water from time to time. Season to taste with salt and pepper.

When all the meat is tender, melt the butter in a small pan, add the remaining garlic and the paprika and sauté for a few minutes, stirring frequently. Stir in the mint and parsley and pour the mixture into the *khash*. Serve the meat with its own broth in individual soup bowls. Squeeze a little lemon juice over the *khash* when eating.

pork

Pork, prohibited by both the Jewish and Muslim religions, is only found in Christian lands where its use is still limited due mainly to centuries of Muslim domination. After all, Greece and Cyprus only threw off the Ottoman yoke some one hundred and twenty years ago; while the Caucasians only received their freedom less than a hundred years ago. For generations therefore, the Christians of the Ottoman Empire could not eat pork — or at least could not be seen to be doing so!

Nevertheless, there are some interesting pork dishes to be found in the Middle East. The finest, perhaps, is roast suckling pig — *gourounaki pito* in Greek, *khozi khorovou* in Armenian. The recipe below, which is typical, is from Georgia.

roast suckling pig

1 suckling pig, 4.5–5.5 kg/10–12 lb — order in advance from your butcher and ask him to clean and prepare it for you
2 lemons, halved

2 tablespoons salt mixed with 1 teaspoon white pepper
about 150 ml/1/4 pint oil

Wash the pig inside and out and then dry. Rub the abdominal cavity and the skin with the cut lemons and then with the mixture of salt and pepper. Place a piece of wood or a ball of aluminium foil in the mouth — this will help keep the mouth open during cooking. Cover the ears and tail with foil to prevent them burning.

Place the pig in a kneeling position on a rack in a large roasting pan. Brush all over with the oil and pour over any juice remaining in the halved lemons.

Roast in an oven preheated to 160°C, 325°F, gas mark 3 for about 4 hours (allow 25 minutes per 500 g/lb). Baste frequently with the pan juices. When the pig is done and is golden and crisp on the outside and tender inside remove from the oven and transfer to a large serving dish. Decorate with parsley or coriander leaves, peaches, apricots, apples, tomatoes, etc. Remove the wood or foil from the mouth and replace it with an apple. Insert a cherry in each eye socket and serve with salads and *pilav*.

stuffed suckling pig

The pig is often stuffed before cooking. This is particularly popular with the Greeks and the Balkan people.

This makes a very special meal for that very special occasion.

Stuffing — popular with Cypriots and Greeks

25 g/1 oz butter
1 onion, finely chopped
4 sticks celery, finely chopped
225 g/8 oz minced pork or veal or beef
225 g/8 oz lamb's liver or chicken
    liver, finely chopped
2 cooking apples or quinces,
    peeled, cored and cubed
275 g/10 oz long grain rice, washed
    thoroughly under cold water
    and drained

750 ml/1¼ pints water
100 g/4 oz raisins
2 tablespoons pine kernels or sliced
    pistachios or slivered almonds
3 tablespoons parsley, chopped
½ teaspoon dried thyme
1 teaspoon salt
½ teaspoon black pepper
½ teaspoon cinnamon

Melt the butter in a large saucepan, add the onion and celery and fry for a few minutes, stirring frequently, until the onion is soft. Stir in the minced meat and liver and fry for about 10 minutes, stirring frequently. Add the remaining ingredients, mix well and bring to the boil. Cover the pan, lower the heat and simmer until the liquid is absorbed.

Spoon this mixture into the pig's cavity after preparing the pig as in the first paragraph in the recipe on page 237. Secure the opening with strong thread or skewers. Continue cooking as described. When cooked place on a large serving dish, open the cavity so that some of the stuffing spills out and garnish.

hirino me kithoria pork with quinces

This is a Greek favourite. Pork and quinces go well together and so try this combination if the quinces are available — otherwise substitute cooking apples.

Serve with *pilavs*, roast vegetables and fresh salads.

25 g/1 oz butter or *ghee*
900 g/2 lb pork tenderloin, cubed
    and then lightly pounded
1 large onion, finely chopped
300 ml/½ pint dry red wine
150 ml/¼ pint water
peel of a lemon or small orange

5 cm/2 in cinnamon stick
1½ teaspoons salt
½ teaspoon black pepper
900 g/2 lb quinces, peeled, cored and
    thickly sliced
1 tablespoon brown sugar

Garnish 2 tablespoons tarragon or mint or parsley, finely chopped

Melt the butter or *ghee* in a large saucepan, add the pieces of pork and fry for a few minutes, tossing and turning, until evenly browned. Remove with a slotted spoon and keep warm.

Add the onion and fry for a few minutes, stirring frequently, until soft.

Now return the pork to the pan, add the wine, water, peel, cinnamon, salt and pepper and bring to the boil. Cover the pan, lower the heat and simmer for about 1 hour. Uncover the pan, arrange the quince slices over the meat, sprinkle with sugar and recover. Cook for a further 30–45 minutes or until the pork and quinces are tender. Transfer to a large serving dish and garnish.

Variation

sergevilov khoz

An Armenian favourite from Karabakh.

Use the same quantities of pork and quinces as above.

Fry the pork cubes in 3 tablespoons of butter in a casserole, until evenly browned, then remove with a slotted spoon and reserve.

Add the sliced quinces to the pan and fry for a few minutes. Now add 4 cloves, 1/2 teaspoon cinnamon, 1 tablespoon honey or brown sugar and the fried pork. Cover and bake in an oven preheated to 180°C, 350°F, gas mark 4 for about 45–60 minutes or until the meat and fruit are tender.

Serve garnished as above.

beef

basagha im bananave tmarin

beef stuffed with bananas and dates

How beautiful, what a joy, my love!
Like a palm-tree you stand,
Your breasts, its bunches of dates.
I said,
'I will climb up this palm-tree
clasping its branches.'
                    (*The Song of Songs*)

One of the most delicious recipes from Israel making use of two of the main local fruits — dates and bananas. The idea is old. There are many such recipes in medieval Arabic, Armenian and Turkish manuscripts, but the use of beef with dates, bananas and figs is new.

Serve with roast vegetables and salads.

900 g/2 lb piece of beef — round or
  flank steak
1 tablespoon made mustard
1½ teaspoons salt
½ teaspoon nutmeg
½ teaspoon basil
½ teaspoon black pepper

2 tablespoons ground almonds
2 bananas, peeled and cut into
  0.5 cm/¼ in slices
2 pickled cucumbers, diced
8 dates, stoned and chopped
8 dried figs, stemmed and chopped
oil

With a wooden mallet pound the meat until about 1.2 cm/½ in thick. Do not over pound or the meat will tear. Coat the surface with the mustard. Mix together the salt, nutmeg, basil, pepper and ground almonds and sprinkle over the meat. Cover evenly with the sliced bananas, pickled cucumbers, dates and figs. Roll the meat up very carefully and fasten with string in about 3 places.

Lightly brush the meat all over with oil. Wrap the meat roll in foil and place in a baking dish. Bake in an oven preheated to 190°C, 375°F, gas mark 5 for about 1½ hours or until the meat is tender. Remove from the oven, discard foil and string, place on a dish and serve.

ĸala josh beef with bread and yoghurt

What besides beef can you expect from an ox?

A traditional dish from the region of Van and Erzurum in Eastern Turkey (Western Armenia). In one form or another this dish is found in Turkey, Iran and Khuzestan as well as the Caucasus where the cooks of Karabakh substitute yoghurt with soured cream. Serve with a rice or burghul *pilav* or roast potatoes and home-made pickled apples and pears.

900 g/2 lb fillet of beef, trimmed
  of fat and gristle
50 g/2 oz butter
1 small onion, finely chopped
1 clove garlic, crushed
salt and pepper to taste

½ teaspoon ground cloves
6 thick slices bread, cut into
  2.5 cm/1 in cubes
300 ml/½ pint yoghurt or soured
  cream

Pound the fillet until thin and slice the meat into 1.2 cm/½ in pieces. Melt the butter in a large saucepan, add the meat and onion and fry, stirring frequently, until the onion is soft and the meat evenly browned — 5–7 minutes. Add the garlic, salt and pepper and cook for a further 2–3 minutes, stirring frequently. Add the bread cubes and cook, turning frequently, until evenly golden. Remove from the heat and sprinkle with the ground cloves.

Pour the yoghurt or soured cream into a small pan and warm through, but do not boil. Pile the meat and bread mixture into a serving dish, spoon the yoghurt or soured cream over the top and serve immediately.

chakhokhbili fillet of beef with wine

Meat and red wine are beneficial after blood-letting. — Shabbatt 129a.

A favourite, so it is said, of the Soviet dictator Stalin, whose personal chef from Georgia often prepared this dish for his gratification.

A simple and tasty meal served with a *pilav* of your choice. This can also be made with lamb or chicken, but I prefer the beef version.

900 g/2 lb fillet of beef
1 teaspoon salt
1/4 teaspoon black pepper
100 g/4 oz butter
1 large onion, finely chopped
2 large tomatoes, blanched,
    peeled, seeded and chopped

150 ml/1/4 pint stock
1 large pickled cucumber, sliced
2 tablespoons capers
1 clove garlic, crushed
300 ml/1/2 pint red wine

Garnish 2 tablespoons coriander, tarragon or parsley, finely chopped

Trim the beef fillet of any fat or gristle, cut into 2.5 cm/1 in pieces and sprinkle with the salt and pepper.

Melt the butter in a large saucepan, add the onion and fry until soft. Push the onion to one side of the pan, add the seasoned meat and fry, turning regularly, until evenly browned. Add the tomatoes and stock and bring quickly to the boil. Add the cucumber, capers and garlic, cover the pan then simmer for about 45 minutes. Stir in the wine and simmer for a further 15–20 minutes or until the meat is tender. Transfer to a serving dish, garnish and serve with a *pilav* of your choice.

Variation

Prepare the dish as above but eliminate the wine and, 5–10 minutes before the end of the cooking time, stir in 300 ml/1/2 pint soured cream or yoghurt mixed with 2 tablespoons plain flour.

kofta and gololig minced meat dishes

Meatballs — the range is inexhaustible; starting with the simple *kofteler* and extending to the regal *ashtaraki gololig* — a large meatball enclosing a small boiled chicken or poussin which, in turn, is stuffed with a hard-boiled egg. The whole is wrapped in a cheesecloth and cooked in a wine sauce. In between these two dishes are found countless others. I have tried, in this chapter, to include as many of these as possible for they are worthy of greater recognition. Most are known throughout the region, but others are specialities of a particular city or even a village. One thing they all have in common is a smooth texture — the meat is usually minced twice and then kneaded until it becomes extremely soft. The meat, normally lamb but it can also be beef, veal or pork, is then mixed with some combination of rice, burghul, onion, garlic, aubergine, cinnamon, allspice, cumin, coriander, etc., shaped into small marble-shaped balls, or larger walnut-sized ones, flattened to a 'hamburger'-shape, rolled into finger or sausage-shapes; sometimes stuffed with fruit, nuts, eggs, etc. and then either fried, grilled, stewed or braised.

fried kofta meatballs

3 slices white bread, crusts removed
900 g/2 lb lean lamb (or lamb and
    beef), minced twice
2 eggs
1 clove garlic, crushed (optional)

1 teaspoon cinnamon or allspice
1/2 teaspoon oregano (optional)
11/2–2 teaspoons salt
1/2–1 teaspoon black pepper
oil for frying

Soak the bread in water and then squeeze dry and crumble into a large mixing bowl. Add the remaining ingredients and knead until the mixture becomes a smooth paste. Keeping your hands damp roll the mixture into small, marble-sized balls.

Heat some oil in a large pan and fry the balls, a few at a time, until they are cooked through and golden. Remove with a slotted spoon and drain. Serve hot or cold with salads and pickles.

Variation

altya kufta An Azerbaijanian speciality from the Caucasus.

Follow the recipe above, but substitute 1 finely chopped onion for the bread. Keeping your hands damp form the mixture into round patties. Dust with flour, dip into 2 beaten eggs and then coat with breadcrumbs.

Fry in oil or butter until cooked through and golden on all sides. Remove with a slotted spoon, drain, sprinkle with chopped parsley or tarragon and serve with roast potatoes, bread and pickles.

patliçan koftesi aubergine meatballs

A speciality from Izmir, Turkey. Other vegetables, e.g. courgettes, leeks, artichoke hearts and pumpkin can also be chopped, minced and then mixed with meat and fried.

450 g/1 lb aubergines, peeled
2 tablespoons salt
4–5 teaspoons oil
1 large onion, finely chopped
225 g/8 oz minced lamb or beef
25 g/1 oz grated cheese, e.g.
    haloumi, kashkaval or Cheddar

2 tablespoons parsley, finely chopped
1/2 teaspoon oregano
1/2 teaspoon sweet basil
1/2 teaspoon black pepper
1/2 teaspoon salt
flour
oil for frying

Cut the aubergines crossways into 0.5 cm/$1/4$ in slices, place in a colander, sprinkle with the salt and set aside for 30 minutes. Wash under cold running water and then pat dry.

Heat the oil in a large frying pan, add the aubergine slices, a few at a time, and fry until soft turning once. Add a little more oil if necessary. Drain the slices on kitchen paper and reserve. Add the onion to the pan and fry for a few minutes until soft and golden.

Chop the aubergine slices finely and place in a large bowl with the fried onion. Add the meat, cheese, parsley, oregano, basil, pepper and salt and knead for a few minutes until the mixture is well blended and smooth. Keeping your hands damp shape the mixture into walnut-sized balls. Roll the balls in flour, place on a large plate and refrigerate for 30 minutes.

Heat some oil in a large frying pan and fry the aubergine balls, a few at a time, for about 20 minutes, turning occasionally until cooked through and evenly browned. Remove with a slotted spoon and serve hot or cold.

armlov potatoes and minced meat baked in the oven

An Armenian speciality.

450 g/1 lb potatoes, boiled and mashed
700 g/1$1/2$ lb lamb or beef, minced
25 g/1 oz pine kernels
50 g/2 oz seedless raisins
1$1/2$ teaspoons salt
$1/2$ teaspoon black pepper

4 teaspoons parsley, chopped
$1/2$ teaspoon sumac
$1/2$ teaspoon cumin
$1/2$ teaspoon paprika
$1/2$ teaspoon basil

Topping
1 egg, beaten
breadcrumbs

6–8 tablespoons melted butter

Place the mashed potatoes and minced meat in a large bowl and knead until well blended. Add all the remaining ingredients and continue to knead until the mixture is smooth. Lightly grease a baking dish and press the mixture into it, spreading it out evenly. Brush the top with the beaten egg. Sprinkle breadcrumbs generously over the top. Cut into squares or diamond shapes with an oiled knife.

Pour the melted butter evenly over the surface and bake in an oven preheated to 180°C, 350°F, gas mark 4, for about 45 minutes or until cooked through and golden. The length of time will depend on the thickness of the mixture. Serve hot with a bowl of yoghurt and some salads.

kofta-bil-saniya minced meat loaf in a tray

An Arab dish which is also very popular in Israel. The Israelis, who have a penchant for tahina, have created a new dish from the old, and I think it is an improvement on the Arab one. I have included both versions below.

900 g/2 lb lamb or beef, minced twice
1 large onion, finely chopped
1 teaspoon salt
1/2 teaspoon black pepper
1 teaspoon cumin
1 teaspoon allspice

4 tomatoes, halved
2 tablespoons tomato purée diluted
   in 150 ml/1/4 pint water
25 g/1 oz butter
2 tablespoons parsley, finely chopped

Place the meat, onion, salt, pepper, cumin and allspice in a large bowl and knead thoroughly. Grease a baking dish about 30 cm/12 in square. Spread the meat mixture evenly over the tray so that it is about 2.5 cm/1 in thick. Arrange the halved tomatoes over the meat. Pour the diluted tomato purée over the meat and top with a few pats of butter and the chopped parsley.

Cook in an oven preheated to 190°C/375°F, gas mark 5 for about 1 hour. The meat will shrink away from the sides of the pan and the meat will be dark brown. Remove to a large serving dish and cut into squares. Serve with fresh salad and/or roast potatoes.

Variation

kufta keftidei cem tahina minced meat with tahina

900 g/2 lb lamb or beef, minced twice
1 teaspoon salt
1/2 teaspoon black pepper

1 tablespoon Worcestershire sauce
1 tablespoon chives, chopped

Prepared tahina
100 g/4 oz dried sesame seeds
1 clove garlic
juice 1 lemon
150 ml/1/4 pint water
2 tablespoons olive oil

1/2 teaspoon salt
1/4 teaspoon paprika
pinch cayenne pepper
3–4 tablespoons parsley, finely chopped

Place all the ingredients for the tahina in a liquidizer and blend thoroughly.

Put the meat, salt, pepper, Worcestershire sauce and chives into a large bowl and knead until thoroughly blended and smooth.

Butter a baking dish about 30 cm/12 in square. Spread the meat mixture evenly over the tray so that it is about 2.5 cm/1 in thick. Spread the tahina mixture evenly over the meat. Bake in an oven preheated to 190°C, 375°F, gas mark 5 for about 1 hour or until the tahina is turning a golden brown. Place on a serving dish and cut into squares. Serve with salad and/or roast potatoes.

tzirani gololig meatballs in apricot sauce

A speciality from the Ashtarag region of Armenia making use of *prunus armenicus*, the fruit of the land — apricots.

A fascinating recipe that has come down to us virtually unchanged from the distant past. If fresh apricots are not available then dried ones are perfectly suitable.

Serve with rice or burghul *pilav*.

450 g/1 lb lamb, minced
1 medium onion
1 1/2 teaspoons salt
1/4 teaspoon black pepper
100 g/4 oz cooked rice

1 teaspoon basil
1 tablespoon parsley, chopped
3 tablespoons *arak* (or ouzo)
1.2 litres/2 pints stock

Sauce

100 g/4 oz dried apricots, soaked
   overnight in 300 ml/1/2 pint
   cold water
1 clove garlic

1 tablespoon fresh coriander,
   or 1 teaspoon ground coriander
1 onion, finely chopped
1 tablespoon flour
1 teaspoon paprika

To prepare the meatballs first pass the minced meat again through a mincer — this time with the onion. Place the mixture in a large bowl and add the salt, pepper, rice, basil, parsley and *arak*. Keeping your hands damp with cold water knead the mixture until it is smooth. Shape the mixture into walnut-sized balls.

Place the stock in a saucepan and bring to the boil. Add the meatballs and simmer gently for 15 minutes.

Meanwhile, prepare the apricot sauce. Put the apricots, garlic, coriander and 4-5 tablespoons of the apricot water into a liquidizer and blend.

Remove the meatballs from the stock, and when the stock has cooked a little skim off the fat and put it into a small pan.

Heat the fat, add the onion and fry until soft. Add the flour and paprika and fry for 2-3 minutes and remove from the heat. Add the apricot mixture and gradually thin with some of the stock. Pour the mixture back into the stock, stir well, add the meatballs and simmer gently for a further 30 minutes.

kadin badu lady's thigh kofta

Lady's thigh *kofta* — it had to be a Turk to visualize such imagery. The *kofta* should be round, soft and smooth like a lady's thighs — at least, that was the fashion when this dish was created!

Serve with salads and a rice *pilav* or spaghetti.

450 g/1 lb lamb, minced twice
1 onion, finely chopped
100 g/4 oz cooked rice
2 tablespoons white cheese, grated
1 egg
25 g/1 oz flour

1 teaspoon salt
1/2 teaspoon black pepper
1 teaspoon cumin
1 egg, beaten
oil for frying

Place the meat, onion, rice, cheese, egg, flour, salt, pepper and cumin in a large bowl and knead for 5–10 minutes until the mixture is well blended and smooth. Keeping your hands damp with cold water take a lump of the mixture about the size of a large walnut and roll it into a ball between your palms. Flatten it gently by pressing one palm against the other. Repeat this with the remaining mixture and arrange all the *koftas* on a baking tray.

Heat some oil in a large frying pan. Dip a few of the *koftas* at a time in the beaten egg and fry, turning occasionally, until cooked through and golden. Remove with a slotted spoon, arrange on a dish and keep warm while you fry the remaining *kofta* in the same way. Serve warm.

terbiyeli kofta

meatballs in an egg and lemon sauce

This is popular throughout the region, but particularly with Greeks and Turks. The sauce has several names, e.g. *terbiyeli* in Turkish, *avgolemono* in Greek and *beid-el-lemoun* in Arabic. In this book the sauce is called the latter — see page 282.

900 g/2 lb lamb, minced twice
3 tablespoons ground rice
4 tablespoons parsley, finely
    chopped
1 large onion, finely chopped
1 clove garlic, crushed

1 1/2 teaspoons salt
1/2 teaspoon black pepper
1/2 teaspoon cinnamon
1/2 teaspoon allspice

Terbiyeli sauce Follow instructions for *beid-el-lemoun* on page 282.
Place all the ingredients in a large bowl and knead for 5–10 minutes until well blended and very smooth. If you keep your hands damp it will make this easier. Form the mixture into marble-sized balls.

Bring a large saucepan half-filled with water to the boil. Season with 1¹/₂ teaspoons salt and then add the meatballs and simmer for about 20 minutes or until soft and tender.

Meanwhile, prepare the sauce. Do not let the sauce boil or it will curdle — hence the Turkish name *terbiyeli* which means 'to behave'.

When cooked lift the meatballs out of the water with a slotted spoon and add to the sauce. Heat very gently for a few minutes and then serve with a rice *pilav* of your choice.

ismir koftesi meatballs in tomato sauce

Simply delicious. Serve with a rice *pilav* or with spaghetti and a bowl of fresh salad.

3 slices white bread
450 g/1 lb lean lamb or beef,
  minced twice
1 egg, beaten
1 clove garlic, crushed
1/4 teaspoon cinnamon
1/2 teaspoon paprika
1 teaspoon salt

1/2 teaspoon black pepper
2¹/₂ tablespoons plain flour
25 g/1 oz butter
5 tomatoes, blanched, peeled, seeded
  and chopped
1 green pepper, seeded and chopped
300 ml/¹/₂ pint water

Remove the bread crusts, soak the bread in a little water then squeeze dry and crumble into a large mixing bowl. Add the minced meat, egg, garlic, cinnamon, paprika, salt and black pepper and knead thoroughly until smooth. Keeping your hands damp with cold water shape the mixture into walnut-sized balls. Sprinkle the flour over a large plate and roll the balls in it.

When all the meatballs are formed and floured melt the butter in a large saucepan. Add the *koftas*, a few at a time and sauté until evenly browned all over. Transfer to a plate and keep warm.

Add the tomatoes, green pepper and water to the saucepan and simmer for 15 minutes. Return the meatballs to the pan and simmer for a further 15–20 minutes or until cooked through. Transfer to a serving dish and serve with a rice *pilav* or spaghetti.

Variation

torshi shami

This recipe is from Rasht on the Caspian coast of Iran.

75 g/3 oz breadcrumbs
150–300 ml/¹/₄–¹/₂ pint milk
1 large onion, grated
1¹/₂ teaspoons salt
1/2 teaspoon black pepper
1 tablespoon curry powder (optional)

700 g/1¹/₂ lb minced lamb or beef
40 g/1¹/₂ oz butter
juice 1 large lemon
3 tablespoons tomato purée
600 ml/1 pint water

Place the breadcrumbs in a large bowl with 150 ml/1/4 pint of the milk and mix. Add the onion, salt, black pepper, curry powder and meat and knead until the mixture is well blended and smooth. If the mixture is a little dry knead in some more milk. Keeping your hands damp take small apple-sized lumps of the mixture and form into balls. Press each ball between your palms to flatten and then punch a hole through the middle of each with your forefinger to give the *koftas* a 'doughnut' shape.

Melt the butter in a large saucepan and sauté the *koftas*, a few at a time, until evenly browned. Keep them warm while you prepare the sauce.

Add the lemon juice, tomato purée and water to the saucepan, stir well and bring to the boil. Return the *koftas* to the pan and simmer gently for 20–30 minutes, turning once or twice until they are cooked through and most of the sauce has evaporated. Serve with a rice *pilav*.

The Iranian cuisine is particularly rich in such dishes. Rice is often mixed in with the meat. *Kofta-ye-sabzi* is such a dish where rice, split peas, onion and parsley is mixed with the meat, seasoned with cinnamon, nutmeg, salt and pepper, shaped into apple-sized balls and simmered in a tomato and lemon sauce. The finest of all Iranian *koftas* are reputed to come from the region of Tabriz (Iranian Azerbaijan) in the north-east of the country bordering Armenia and Kurdistan — two very old nations stretching back into antiquity.

In the recipe below the meatballs are stuffed with eggs, dried fruit and walnuts and then cooked in a tomato sauce.

koofteh tabrizi

1 onion, finely chopped
700 g/1½ lb lamb or beef, minced
   at least twice
2 eggs, lightly beaten
75 g/3 oz rice flour or chickpea
   flour or split pea flour

2 teaspoons salt
½ teaspoon black pepper
¼ teaspoon nutmeg
½ teaspoon cinnamon

Filling
6 hard-boiled eggs, halved
12 dried apricots or stoned prunes

4 tablespoons raisins
12 walnut halves

Sauce
50 g/2 oz *ghee* or butter
1 small onion, finely chopped
1½ teaspoons turmeric
1.2 litres/2 pints stock or water

2 tablespoons tomato purée
1½ teaspoons salt
½ teaspoon cayenne pepper

Place all the ingredients for the meatballs in a large bowl and knead for several minutes until well-blended and smooth. Keeping your hands damp divide the mixture into 12 balls. With your forefinger or thumb make a depression in one of the balls and widen the hollow and pinch the meat up to form a pot shape. Place half a boiled egg, an apricot or prune, a few raisins and half a walnut in the hollow. Carefully draw the meat together to completely enclose the filling and roll the kofta around between your dampened palms to resume a ball-shape. Repeat with the remaining meatballs and filling ingredients.

In a large saucepan melt the *ghee* or butter, add the onion and fry until soft and a light golden colour. Stir in the remaining ingredients and bring to the boil. Add the *koftas*, lower the heat and simmer for about 45 minutes, turning the balls once or twice. Serve immediately with a rice *pilav*, fresh yoghurt and salads.

mussaka meat and aubergine pie

Although today *mussaka* is regarded as a Greek dish, it was first developed in the days of the Caliphs during the glorious days of the Baghdad of Sinbad, Shehrezade and Aladdin.

The medieval dish called *muhklabah* was the original form — a simple and tasty meal of minced meat and fried aubergine topped with cheese. To show my impartiality I have included the recipes for *muhklabah* (Arab), *moussaka* (Armenian) and *melitzanes moussaka* (Greek).

muhklabah arab-style moussaka

125 g/5 oz butter or *ghee*
450 g/1 lb lamb or beef, minced
2 medium aubergines, hulls removed
225 g/8 oz brown or long grain
   rice, washed thoroughly under
   cold water and drained

900 ml/1¹/₂ pints water
¹/₂ teaspoon turmeric
1 teaspoon salt
¹/₂ teaspoon allspice
¹/₂ teaspoon black pepper
2 tablespoons melted butter

Garnish **100 g/4 oz almonds or pistachios, chopped (optional)**

Melt 40 g/1¹/₂ oz of the butter in a saucepan, add the meat and fry for 10 minutes, stirring frequently.

Halve the aubergines lengthways and then slice crossways into 0.5 cm/¹/₄ in thick slices. Melt the remaining butter in a large frying pan and fry the slices, a few at a time, turning at least once until golden on both sides. Remove with a fork, drain on kitchen paper and reserve. When all the slices are fried, place half the fried meat in the bottom of a large, greased ovenproof dish. Cover with half the aubergine slices and sprinkle with half the rice. Repeat the layering again, finishing with the rice.

Place the water, turmeric, salt, allspice and black pepper in a small saucepan, bring to the boil and simmer for 5 minutes. Pour the liquid over the casserole.

Place in the centre of an oven preheated to 160°C, 325°F, gas mark 3 and bake for 1 hour or until the rice is tender. Remove from the oven, pour the melted butter over the top of the casserole, sprinkle with the nuts and serve with salad.

moussaka *armenian-style*

This is a family recipe.

450 g/1 lb aubergines, hulls removed
2–3 tablespoons salt

about 8–10 tablespoons oil

Filling
1 large onion, finely chopped
450 g/1 lb minced lamb
1 clove garlic
1 teaspoon salt
1/2 teaspoon black pepper

2 tablespoons parsley, finely chopped
2 tablespoons chopped walnuts
1/2 teaspoon allspice
3 tablespoons tomato purée
4–5 tablespoons dry red wine

Topping
2 egg yolks

6–8 tablespoons grated cheese, e.g.
Cheddar, Parmesan or kefalotiri

Cut the aubergines lengthways into 0.5 cm/1/4 in thick slices, arrange on a plate, sprinkle with the salt and set aside for 30 minutes.

Meanwhile, heat half the oil in a saucepan, add the onion and fry for a few minutes, stirring frequently, until soft. Add the meat, garlic, salt, pepper and parsley and cook for 5 minutes, stirring frequently. Add the walnuts, allspice, tomato purée and wine, stir well and fry for a further 5–10 minutes. Remove from the heat.

Rinse the aubergine slices under cold water and dry on kitchen paper. Heat the remaining oil in a large frying pan and fry the aubergine slices, a few at a time, until golden on both sides. Add more oil if necessary. Remove and drain on kitchen paper. When all the slices are cooked arrange half of them in the bottom of a large, deep, greased baking dish. Spread the meat mixture over them and cover with the remaining slices. Mix together in a small bowl the egg yolks and cheese and spread over the top. Place in the centre of an oven preheated to 180°C, 350°F, gas mark 4 and bake for 45–60 minutes until the meat is cooked and the top is golden.

melitzanes moussaka greek-style

450 g/1 lb aubergines, hulls removed
2 tablespoons salt

75–100 ml/3–4 fl oz oil for frying

Filling

25 g/1 oz butter
4 small shallots, finely chopped
450 g/1 lb lamb, minced twice
2 tomatoes, blanched, peeled and
    chopped
1 tablespoon chives, finely chopped
50 ml/2 fl oz white wine

1 teaspoon lemon juice
1/2 teaspoon dried sage
1/4 teaspoon black pepper
2 tablespoons parsley, finely chopped
1 teaspoon sugar
1/4 teaspoon cinnamon
50 g/2 oz fresh white breadcrumbs

Sauce

175 g/6 oz mizittire, ricotta,
    kefalotiri or Parmesan cheese
3 egg yolks

350 ml/12 fl oz single cream
1/4 teaspoon salt
1/4 teaspoon nutmeg

Cut the aubergines lengthways into 0.5 cm/1/4 in slices, arrange on a plate, sprinkle with the salt and set aside for 30 minutes.

Meanwhile, melt the butter in a pan, add the shallots and fry until soft. Add the meat and fry, stirring frequently, until browned. Add all the remaining ingredients for the filling, stir well and cook gently, stirring frequently, for about 10 minutes and then remove from the heat.

Rinse the aubergine slices under cold running water and dry with kitchen paper. Heat the oil and fry the slices, a few at a time, until golden on both sides. Remove with a fork and drain on kitchen paper. Arrange a third of the slices over the bottom of a deep, greased casserole dish. Spread half of the filling over them and cover with another third of the aubergine slices. Spread the remaining filling over them and cover with the remaining slices.

To prepare the sauce place the cheese in a bowl and mash with a fork until smooth. Add the egg yolks and whisk until a smooth paste is formed. Gradually stir in the cream, salt and nutmeg and then pour this mixture over the top to cover completely the aubergines. Place in an oven preheated to 180°C, 350°F, gas mark 4 and bake for about 45 minutes or until the top is golden. Remove, cut into wedges and serve with salads. There are many *moussaka* variations and you can use many vegetables instead of aubergines, e.g. potatoes, pumpkin, tomatoes, etc.

poultry and game

In our country there are more chickens than even mice! Those two legged imbeciles are everywhere — in the Hamam (Turkish bath), in streets, in the bazaars, fields, cemeteries, churches, bedrooms, over the bed, under the bed, and all they know is cluck, cluck, cluck, cluck. All they're good for is a strong wring of the neck! But they are delicious and so we tolerate them.

Remember, my son, all things that are good and tasty must be tolerated — however much the inconvenience.

Hadji Baba of Isfahan obviously liked his chicken, as do all Middle Easterners and they have, over the centuries, created a large repertoire of chicken recipes. Chicken, as well as other poultry such as duck, turkey and goose and game such as partridge, pheasant, quail, squab, woodcock, etc. are fried, roasted, grilled over charcoal, boiled with vegetables, baked in the oven, stuffed with rice, wheat, meat, nuts and fruits. They are cooked with chickpeas, aubergines and okra as well as yoghurt, pomegranate juice, etc., the list is endless.

The recipes in this section therefore are only a fragment of that rich repertoire. Use roasting chicken for all recipes unless otherwise stated.

tabaka fried chicken with prune sauce

A Caucasian recipe. Usually the chicken is fried and served with salad or, as with this recipe, with *tkemali* sauce.

4 x 450–700 g/1–1¹/₂ lb poussins, washed and dried

2 tablespoons salt

150 ml/¹/₄ pint yoghurt

75 g/3 oz *ghee* or butter

3 tomatoes, thinly sliced

1 small aubergine, cut in half lengthways and then cut into 0.5 cm/¹/₄ in slices crossways

1 clove garlic, crushed

¹/₂ teaspoon ground cinnamon

To serve **150–300 ml/¹/₄–¹/₂ pint *tkemali* sauce — see recipe page 283**

Place 1 poussin on a chopping board, back upwards. With a sharp pointed knife start at the neck and cut along one side of the backbone. Turn the poussin around and cut along the other side of the backbone thus freeing it. Break it away from the spoon-shaped bone connecting the breasts and remove both bones and the white cartilage. Loosen the skin around the leg and thigh and push it back exposing the thigh joint. Cut it half across and pull the skin back. Repeat with the other leg. Make a slit in each breast below the ribs.

Turn the poussin flesh side down, cover with greaseproof paper and then flatten with a meat mallet. Twist the legs inwards and push them through the holes in the breasts. Repeat with each poussin. Rub them with the salt and spread the flesh sides evenly with half the yoghurt.

Melt 50 g/2 oz of the butter in a large frying pan, add 2 poussins, skin sides down, place a heavy weight on top and cook over a moderate heat for 8–10 minutes. Turn the poussins over, spread with half the remaining yoghurt, weigh down and fry for a further 10 minutes until golden brown, but do not burn. Repeat with the 2 remaining poussin.

Meanwhile, melt the remaining 25 g/1 oz of butter in a saucepan and sauté the tomatoes, aubergine, garlic and cinnamon until soft.

Serve 1 poussin per person accompanied by some of the cooked vegetables and the *tkemali* sauce.

Variation

auff sum-sum sesame fried chicken

An Israeli recipe where the chicken pieces are coated in sesame seeds to give an attractive dark golden appearance and interesting texture. Serve with roast potatoes and fried or, as in Israel, boiled vegetables.

1.35 kg/3 lb chicken, cut into	freshly ground pepper
8 serving pieces	1 teaspoon paprika
75 g/3 oz sesame seeds	1 large egg, beaten
50 g/2 oz plain flour	75 ml/3 fl oz water or chicken stock
1¹/₂ teaspoons salt	oil

Dry the chicken pieces.

Mix the sesame seeds, flour, salt, pepper and paprika on a large plate.

Mix the egg and water or stock together in a shallow dish. Coat the chicken pieces lightly in the sesame seed mixture. Dip each piece into the egg mixture to coat and then coat with the sesame seed mixture again.

Heat the oil in a large frying pan, add the chicken pieces and fry until golden, turning occasionally. Take care not to burn. Transfer to a casserole or baking dish and bake in an oven preheated to 180°C, 350°F, gas mark 4, for about 30–45 minutes or until tender. Serve immediately.

tashreeb dijaj whole chicken in spicy sauce

A simple dish from Iraq. Serve it with a *pilav* of your choice or with *chelo* — as the Iraqi housewives would. Incidentally, they do not call the rice *chelo*, but *timman*; however the method and result are the same.

Limes are usually used instead of lemons, but if they are not available substitute the latter.

1.35–1.8 kg/3–4 lb chicken,	4 tablespoons *ghee*
washed and dried inside and out	2 cloves garlic, halved
1 lemon or lime, quartered	300 ml/¹/₂ pint water
2 teaspoons salt	1 teaspoon salt
¹/₂ teaspoon black pepper	2 bay leaves
¹/₂ teaspoon turmeric	2–3 cardamom pods, split

Rub the chicken inside and out with the lemon or lime quarters. Save the quarters. Mix the salt, black pepper and turmeric together and rub into the chicken.

Melt the *ghee* in a large deep saucepan, add the chicken and brown all over, basting and turning regularly. Squeeze the remaining lemon or lime juice over the chicken. Add the garlic, water, salt, bay leaves and cardamom. Bring to the boil, cover the pan and cook over a low heat for 1¹/₂–2 hours, turning and basting occasionally.

Remove the chicken from the pan and keep warm. Reduce the pan juices to half its former quantity over a high heat. Discard bay leaves and cardamom pods.

Carve the chicken and serve on a bed of rice with the pan juices poured over the top.

hav ganachov chicken with vegetables

An Armenian recipe, but typical of Turkey, Kurdistan and Iran.
Serve with a *pilav* of your choice.

2 aubergines, peeled
150 ml/¼ pint oil
1.35–1.8 kg/3–4 lb chicken,
  cut into 8 serving pieces
50 g/2 oz flour seasoned with
  1 teaspoon salt
  1 teaspoon black pepper
  ½ teaspoon chilli pepper
2 medium onions, sliced
2 courgettes, topped, tailed and
  cut into 1.2 cm/½ in rings
2 green peppers, seeded and cut into
  2.5 cm/2 in squares

450 g/1 lb green beans, trimmed and
  sliced
225 g/8 oz okra, trimmed and sliced
  (optional)
4 tomatoes, blanched, peeled
  and sliced or small tin tomatoes,
  coarsely chopped
300 ml/½ pint water
2 teaspoons salt
1 teaspoon black pepper
½ teaspoon chilli pepper
3–4 bay leaves

Garnish 1 tablespoon parsley, finely chopped

Cut aubergines crossways into 1.2 cm/½ in rings, arrange on a dish, sprinkle with salt and set aside for 30 minutes. Then rinse under cold water and pat dry.

Meanwhile, heat half the oil in a large pan. Coat the chicken pieces in the seasoned flour and fry until golden on all sides. Remove with a slotted spoon and reserve then heat the remaining oil in the pan. Add the aubergines and remaining vegetables, except tomatoes, and fry for a few minutes, turning carefully. Place all the vegetables in the bottom of a casserole, arrange the chicken joints over the top and place the tomatoes over them.

Bring the water, salt and black and chilli peppers to the boil in a small pan and pour into the casserole. Cover and cook in an oven preheated to 190°C, 375°F, gas mark 5 for about 1 hour or until chicken is tender. Sprinkle with the parsley and serve.

One day . . . things were going wrong for Boloz Mugush. His wife was threatening to leave him (that was not so bad), his sons had gone to war and business was poor; did I say poor? I meant non-existent. Must do something, he thought, while passing by the large estate of the Melikovs.

Had he been more observant he would have noticed a Russian militia standing nearby when he rushed through the gates, over the low timber fence and grabbed two fat chickens — but before the chicken could cluck, cluck, Boloz Mugush found himself in the clutches of the law.

Next day in court he stood before the chief justice, surrounded by Russian soldiers.
'Are you Bo- Bo- Boloz Mu-Mu- Mugush, the defendant?'
'Yes he is,' interjected the officers in harmony.

The prisoner, who was most inexperienced in matters legal hesitated, then whispered, 'No, your worshipful honour, your magnificent, your majesty. I am not the other one. I am Mugush who stole the chicken.'

dajaj-bil-mishmishiyeh

chicken with pasta and apricot sauce

A very old dish from Iraq described in Al-Baghdadi's medieval cookery manual. I understand home-made pasta — *rishta* — is still used with this dish and a recipe for it is included in this book. However, you can also use either spaghetti or vermicelli.

Either apricot or prune sauce is used with this dish. The latter is more popular with the Arabs of Khuzestan, Iran (see recipe, page 283).

A similar Caucasian version makes use of *tkemali* sauce and is known as chicken *mussaka*.

Serve with fresh salads.

2.25 kg/5 lb chicken cut into joints
40 g/1½ oz *ghee* or butter
juice 1 small lemon
about 150 ml/¼ pint water
1 teaspoon turmeric
1 teaspoon salt
½ teaspoon black pepper
¼ teaspoon chilli pepper

2 cardamom pods, cracked
450 g/1 lb *rishta*, spaghetti or vermicelli
3 tablespoons oil
1 teaspoon cinnamon
1 large tomato, blanched, peeled and
   sliced
1 green pepper, seeded and cut into rings

Sauce
225/g/8 oz dried apricots or
   225 g/8 oz *amarind bastegh*,
   soaked overnight

1 teaspoon sugar or honey
1 tablespoon lemon juice
1 tablespoon rosewater

Remove the skin from the chicken joints.

Melt the *ghee* or butter in a large saucepan, add the lemon juice, water, turmeric, salt and pepper and stir well. Bring to the boil, add the chicken pieces and cardamom pods. Cover the pan, lower the heat and simmer for 45–60 minutes or until the meat is tender. Remove from the heat and leave to cool a little. Remove the chicken pieces and cut the flesh from the bones. Reserve the stock. Either cut the meat into smaller pieces or chop coarsely.

Meanwhile, bring a large pan half filled with lightly salted water to the boil, add the pasta and boil for 7–8 minutes or until almost tender. Strain into a colander.

Heat the oil in a large casserole dish, add the pasta and fry for 2–3 minutes, stirring and turning with a fork. Remove and reserve half the pasta. Spread the remaining pasta over the bottom and arrange the chicken pieces over the top. Sprinkle with the cinnamon and cover with the remaining pasta. Top with the tomato and green pepper slices and pour in the reserved chicken stock. Bake in an oven preheated to 180°C, 350°F, gas mark 4 for 30–40 minutes.

Meanwhile, prepare the apricot sauce. Place the soaked apricots or thinly sliced *amarind* in a saucepan, add a scant 150 ml/¼ pint water and simmer until tender. Add the sugar or honey and the lemon juice. Reduce the mixture to a purée in a blender and just before serving stir in the rosewater. Pour a little of the sauce over each serving of the chicken and pasta.

Serves 4–6 people.

budughov judig chicken with fruits

A regal dish from the Caucasus, the chicken is cooked with apricots, prunes, sultanas and wine.

There are many chicken and fruit dishes from the Caucasus and Iran and I have also noted below a simple Turkish-Kurdish version.

50 ml/2 fl oz oil
1 large chicken, cut into 8 serving
   pieces
50 g/2 oz seasoned flour
1½ tablespoons tomato purée
300 ml/½ pint water or stock
50 g/2 oz prunes, stoned

50 g/2 oz apricots, quartered
2 tablespoons sultanas
1 teaspoon salt
½ teaspoon black pepper
1 teaspoon sumac
300 ml/½ pint red wine

Garnish a little extra sumac

Heat the oil in a large frying pan. Coat the chicken pieces in the seasoned flour and fry in the oil, a few at a time, until golden on all sides. Transfer the pieces to a casserole.

Add the tomato purée to the frying pan and stir in the water or stock. Stir in the dried fruits, salt, black pepper, sumac and wine and bring to the boil. Pour the sauce into the casserole and place in an oven preheated to 180°C, 350°F, gas mark 4. Bake for about 1 hour or until the chicken is tender. Transfer to a serving dish and sprinkle with a little sumac. Serve with a burghul or rice *pilav*.

Variation

ayvali tavugi chicken with quinces or apples

Fry 1 chopped onion in a little oil, add the chicken pieces and fry, turning frequently, for about 45 minutes, or until tender. Peel, core and thickly slice 4 quinces or apples and add to the pan with 1 teaspoon salt, ½ teaspoon allspice and 300 ml/½ pint stock or water.

Cook for a further 20–30 minutes or until the fruit is soft.

quwarmah ala dajaj curried chicken

A spicy exotic chicken dish from the Gulf region of Arabia, related to the many similar Indian dishes and undoubtedly of Indian origin. Although the Gulf States are part of the Arab world it must be remembered that not only are a great number of people of Indian extraction, but centuries of trade with the Indian sub-continent have had a very strong social and cultural influence on the ethnic Arabs. This is particularly so with the island of Bahrain where, after Arabic, Hindu is the most widely used language.

Serve with *muhamar* (see recipe, page 188) or any *pilav* dish.

1.35 kg/3 lb chicken, cut into
   8 serving pieces
2 teaspoons salt
1/2 teaspoon nutmeg
1 teaspoon cumin
1/2 teaspoon paprika
1/2 teaspoon ground cardamom
1/2 teaspoon black pepper
1 teaspoon turmeric
40 g/1¹/2 oz *ghee*
2 large onions, finely chopped

2 cloves garlic, crushed
1 teaspoon grated fresh ginger
1 teaspoon chilli powder
5 cm/2 in cinnamon stick
2 large tomatoes, blanched, peeled
   and chopped
2 *loomi* (dried limes) pierced with a fork
   or the thinly peeled rind of 1 lemon
1 teaspoon salt
300 ml/¹/2 pint water

In a small bowl mix together the salt, nutmeg, cumin, paprika, cardamom, black pepper and turmeric. Rub the chicken pieces all over with half this mixture and reserve the rest. Melt the *ghee* in a large pan, add the chicken pieces and fry, turning regularly, until they are browned all over. Remove with a slotted spoon and reserve.

Add the onions to the pan and fry for a few minutes until soft. Add the garlic, ginger, reserved spices, chilli and cinnamon stick and continue to fry for a further 5 minutes, stirring frequently. Add the tomatoes, *loomi* or lemon rind, salt and water and bring to the boil.

Return the chicken pieces to the pan, lower the heat, cover the pan and cook for about 1 hour or until the chicken is tender.

taiyika auff chicken with kumquats and honey

Honey in the mouth won't help bitterness in the heart.

An Israeli recipe.

If you cannot find kumquats — easily available in the USA and Australia, but not in Europe — then use mandarin oranges or ordinary oranges — Jaffa of course!

Serve with salad and potatoes or a *pilav* of your choice.

1.35–1.8 kg/3–4 lb chicken, halved and with backbone removed

1/2 teaspoon salt
1/2 teaspoon black pepper
150 ml/1/4 pint fresh orange juice
75 ml/3 fl oz clear honey
1 green chilli, seeded and finely chopped

8 kumquats or mandarins or
  4 oranges, peeled, white pith
  removed and segmented
2 teaspoons arrowroot mixed to a
  paste with 2 tablespoons water

Garnish
1 lemon, thinly sliced

1 tablespoon parsley, finely chopped

Sprinkle the chicken halves with the salt and pepper. Place in a casserole and pour the orange juice and honey over them. Add the chilli and kumquats or oranges. Place over a moderate heat and bring the liquid to the boil.

Cover the casserole and place in an oven preheated to 180°C, 350°F, gas mark 4. Cook for about 1 hour or until the chicken is tender. Remove from the oven, transfer the chicken halves to a board and cut each one in half. Place the chicken pieces in a serving dish and keep warm.

Stir the arrowroot mixture into the cooking juices and bring to the boil, stirring constantly. Cook the sauce over a low heat for about 3 minutes. Pour the sauce into a sauceboat.

Garnish the chicken with the lemon slices and sprinkle with the parsley. Serve immediately with the sauce.

bursa tavuğu chicken with cream and herbs

Bursa is a large prosperous city in north-west Turkey and was once the capital of the Ottomans — before their conquest of Constantinople. The finest cooks of Turkey are reputed to come from there.

This is a very tasty dish usually served with *pilavs* and salads.

1.35–1.8 kg/3–4 lb chicken, cut
  into 8 serving pieces
75 ml/3 fl oz oil
2 onions, thinly sliced
450 ml/3/4 pint chicken stock
1/2 teaspoon marjoram

1/2 teaspoon basil
1/2 teaspoon salt
1/2 teaspoon white pepper
1 tablespoon plain flour
3 tablespoons single cream
about 15 stuffed green olives

Garnish 1 tablespoon parsley, finely chopped

Heat the oil in a large casserole, add the chicken pieces and brown, turning occasionally. Remove the chicken and reserve.

Add the onions and fry, stirring frequently, until golden. Return the chicken to the pan and add the stock, marjoram, basil, salt and pepper. Bring to the boil lower the heat, cover and simmer until the chicken is tender. Remove the chicken pieces to a serving dish and keep warm.

In a small bowl blend the flour and cream until smooth. Add the flour and cream mixture and the olives to the sauce and simmer for a few minutes, stirring constantly. Pour the sauce over the chicken, sprinkle with the parsley and serve immediately.

stuffed chicken

'Soud khent elat, vankin haver oudel' — to act the fool and eat the monastery's chicken, in other words to try and get away by acting the fool.

On festive occasions or in honour of a guest, chicken is often served stuffed with rice, nuts, fruits, spices and vegetables. The bird is served on large silver or gilt trays and garnished with fresh vegetables, fruits and mounds of rice *pilavs*. The stomach is opened and the filling partly spooned out. Then the chicken is carved.

Of the many possible stuffing recipes I have chosen a few typical ones to give just an idea of the wealth and scope of the Middle Eastern repertoire.

dijaj al timman

This dish is from Iraq. The stuffing of rice, almonds, walnuts and raisins is typical of the whole region.

1.35–1.8 kg/3–4 lb chicken, washed and dried inside and out

Filling
50 g/2 oz *ghee*
1 small onion, finely choped
75 g/3 oz short grain rice, washed thoroughly under cold water and drained
1/2 teaspoon allspice
225 ml/8 fl oz water

2 tablespoons almonds, blanched, slivered
2 tablespoons walnuts or hazelnuts, chopped
2 tablespoons seedless raisins
1 1/2 teaspoons salt
1/2 teaspoon black pepper

Basting
50 g/2 oz *ghee*, melted
1 teaspoon salt mixed with
1/2 teaspoon black pepper

100 ml/4 fl oz water

Melt the *ghee* in a saucepan, add the onion and fry until soft. Add the rice and nuts and fry for 3–4 minutes, stirring frequently. Add the raisins, allspice, water, salt and pepper and bring to the boil. Cover and cook over a low heat until the liquid is absorbed. Remove from the heat and leave to cool.

Fill the chicken with this stuffing and close the opening with a small skewer or needle and thread. Put the chicken in a roasting tin, brush with the melted *ghee* and sprinkle with the salt and pepper. Pour the water and the rest of the melted fat into the tin and bake in an oven preheated to 180°C, 350°F, gas mark 4 for about 2 hours or until the chicken is tender. Baste frequently.

Variation

Syrians substitute 2 tablespoons pine kernels for the almonds and also include in the stuffing 1 tomato, blanched, peeled and chopped, 1 tablespoon finely chopped parsley and 1/2 teaspoon cinnamon.

Dajaj mahshi — a Lebanese favourite — as well as the ingredients above also includes about 350 g/12 oz fried minced meat.

tzavarov letzvadz variag

An Armenian speciality — the chicken is stuffed with burghul, liver and chickpeas.

1.35–1.8 kg/3–4 lb chicken, washed and dried inside and out

Filling

75-90 g/3-3 1/2 oz butter
the liver and heart of the chicken, coarsely chopped
1 1/2 teaspoons salt
1/2 teaspoon black pepper
1 small onion, finely chopped
1 large tomato, blanched, peeled and chopped
1 small green pepper, seeded and thinly sliced

175 g/6 oz large grain burghul
2 tablespoons parsley, finely chopped
3 tablespoons chickpeas that have been soaked overnight and cooked until tender
1/2 teaspoon cinnamon
300–350 ml/10–12 fl oz water

Melt the butter in a saucepan, add the liver, heart, salt and pepper and fry for about 3 minutes, stirring frequently. Remove the liver and heart with a slotted spoon and reserve.

Add the onion to the pan and fry until soft. Stir in the tomato and green pepper and cook for a further 2–3 minutes, stirring frequently. Add the burghul and parsley and cook for another 2–3 minutes, stirring constantly. Now add the chickpeas, cinnamon, water and reserved liver and heart. Bring to the boil, lower the heat, cover and simmer for 15–20 minutes or until the liquid has been absorbed. Leave to cool and then fill the chicken cavity. Reserve any leftover stuffing to serve later with the cooked chicken. Close the opening, place in a roasting tin, brush with a little oil and cook in an oven preheated to 180°C, 350°F, gas mark 4 for about 2 hours or until tender. Transfer to a large serving dish, fluff out the filling and serve.

morgh shekumpour

chicken stuffed with prunes, apples, raisins and apricots

This is a favourite of Iranians. It is beautiful to look at and extremely tasty. Serve with *chelo* rice or *chelo zaffran* (saffron *pilav*).

1.35–1.8 kg/3–4 lb chicken, washed and dried inside and out

Filling

40 g/1¹/₂ oz *ghee* or butter
1 small onion, finely chopped
150 g/5 oz prunes, soaked
   overnight, stoned and chopped
150 g/5 oz dried apricots, soaked
   and chopped

50 g/2 oz seedless raisins
2 apples, peeled, cored and chopped
1 teaspoon ground cinnamon
2 teaspoons salt
1/2 teaspoon black pepper
1 teaspoon brown sugar

Basting

1 teaspoon salt
1/2 teaspoon black pepper

melted butter

Melt the *ghee* or butter in a saucepan, add the onion and fry until soft. Add the chopped prunes, apricots, raisins and apples and fry for about 2 minutes, stirring constantly. Season with the cinnamon, salt, pepper and sugar and cook for 2–3 more minutes. Spoon the mixture into the chicken cavity and secure the opening. Rub the chicken with the salt and pepper and then place in a roasting tin. Brush generously with melted butter and then cook in an oven preheated to 180°C, 350°F, gas mark 4 for about 2 hours or until tender. Baste regularly with the pan juices. Serve on a bed of rice.

turkey

Although not as popular as chicken, turkey has recently acquired a degree of importance due to western influence and is fast becoming the 'guest' meal in such countries as Cyprus, Lebanon and Israel.

The locally grown bird tends to be small and tough, but those reared on the Israeli kibbutzes are big, fat and magnificent.

stuffed turkey

The fillings below are for an approximately 3.5 kg/8 lb turkey.

filling 1 — a typical Arab stuffing also popular in Israel and Turkey

2 tablespoons *ghee* or oil
450 g/1 lb minced lamb
3 tablespoons almonds, chopped, blanched
3 tablespoons walnuts, chopped
3 tablespoons pistachio nuts, chopped
3 tablespoons pine kernels, chopped

225 g/8 oz long grain rice, washed thoroughly under cold water and drained
50 g/2 oz raisins
1 tablespoon salt
1 teaspoon black pepper
1 1/2 teaspoons cinnamon
1/2 teaspoon allspice
600 ml/1 pint water or stock

Heat the *ghee* or oil in a pan, add the meat and fry for 10–15 minutes, turning and breaking up with a fork. Add the nuts and fry for a further 5–10 minutes, stirring frequently. Add all the remaining ingredients, stir well and bring to the boil. Lower the heat and simmer until all the liquid has been absorbed. Remove from the heat, allow to cool then spoon into the cavity and secure the opening.

filling 2 — from Libya and Egypt and also Lebanon

225 g/8 oz cous-cous
175 g/6 oz seedless raisins, soaked in water for 15 minutes
3 tablespoons almonds, chopped, blanched
6–7 stoned, dried dates, thinly sliced

1 teaspoon cinnamon
1 teaspoon nutmeg
1 teaspoon salt
2 tablespoons sugar
25 g/1 oz melted butter

Steam the cous-cous in a steamer or colander over boiling water for 20 minutes until the grains are soft, but still firm. Transfer to a bowl, add all the remaining ingredients and mix well. Pack into the cavity and secure the opening.

filling 3 — a Cypriot favourite

25 g/1 oz butter
1 onion, finely chopped
1 celery stick, thinly sliced
225 g/8 oz minced lamb or veal
225 g/8 oz long grain rice, washed thoroughly under cold water
turkey liver, chopped

600 ml/1 pint dry white wine or stock or a mixture of the two
75 g/3 oz raisins
75 g/3 oz almonds, slivered, blanched
1 teaspoon cinnamon
2 teaspoons salt
1/2 teaspoon black pepper

Melt the butter in a saucepan, add the onion and fry until soft. Add the celery and fry for 2 minutes, then add the meat and fry for a further 5-10 minutes, turning and mashing with a fork. Add the rice and wine or stock, bring to the boil, cover and cook for 10 minutes. Stir in the remaining ingredients and continue to cook until all the liquid has been absorbed. Spoon into the cavity and secure the opening.

To cook the turkey
Rub the skin with half a lemon and a mixture of 1½ tablespoons salt and half a teaspoon black pepper. Place in a roasting tin and pour in either 75-100 g/3-4 oz melted butter or oil and 100 ml/4 fl oz water. Cook in an oven preheated to 180°C, 350°F, gas mark 4 allowing approximately 30 minutes to every 500 g/lb. Baste regularly.

When cooked remove to a serving dish, skim the pan juices and serve in a sauceboat. Serve with salads and *pilavs*.

fesenjan-e-ordek

duck in a pomegranate and walnut sauce

One of the great dishes of Iran. In an Iranian home, if a guest is to be honoured, he is often served this meal of duck coated in a thick sauce of ground walnuts flavoured with pomegranate syrup.

You can use a large chicken instead of duck. Serve on a bed of *chelo* or other *pilav* of your choice.

1 large duck, cut into quarters
   or 1 large chicken, cut into 8
8 tablespoons oil
1 onion, thickly sliced
½ teaspoon turmeric
450 g/1 lb shelled walnuts, ground —
   reserve a few whole ones for garnish

900 ml/1½ pints chicken stock
1 teaspoon salt
½ teaspoon black pepper
150 ml/¼ pint fresh pomegranate juice
   or 3 tablespoons concentrated juice
juice 2 lemons
50 g/2 oz sugar

Heat half the oil in a frying pan, add the onion and turmeric and fry until the onion is soft and golden. Remove the onion with a slotted spoon and transfer to a large casserole. Stir in the ground walnuts and chicken stock and season with the salt and pepper. Bring to the boil and simmer, stirring occasionally, for 20 minutes.

Heat the remaining oil in the frying pan, add the duck or chicken pieces and fry, turning occasionally, until browned all over. Transfer to the casserole, mix to coat with the sauce and then cover and cook over a very low heat for about 1 hour or until the meat is tender. Stir occasionally to prevent the sauce sticking. Skim excess fat off the surface of the casserole

In a bowl mix together the fresh or concentrated pomegranate juice with the lemon juice and sugar. Stir this sweetened juice into the casserole and simmer for a further 15-20 minutes, stirring occasionally. Taste and adjust seasoning if necessary.

Arrange the duck or chicken pieces on a bed of rice, spoon some of the sauce over the top and garnish with the reserved walnuts — either whole or coarsely chopped. Serve the remaining sauce separately.

кhorovadze sag roast goose with apricots

A magnificent dish from Armenia.

Serve with a rice or burghul *pilav* accompanied by apricot sauce and freshly sliced vegetables and pickles.

3.6 kg/8 lb goose	1 tablespoon salt

Filling

2 large cooking apples, peeled, cored and thickly sliced	goose liver, chopped
	50 g/2 oz walnuts, coarsely chopped
1 large onion, thinly sliced	1 teaspoon cinnamon
juice 1 large lemon for basting	100 ml/4 fl oz dry sherry or brandy

Tzirani salsa — apricot sauce

225 g/8 oz dried apricots, thinly sliced	1/2 teaspoon nutmeg
25 g/1 oz brown sugar	50 g/2 oz pistachio nuts, halved or
2 tablespoons brandy	almonds, slivered, blanched,
1 teaspoon rosewater	or pine kernels

Wash and dry the goose inside and out. Rub inside and out with the salt.

In a large bowl mix the apples, onion, goose liver, walnuts and cinnamon. Fill the cavity with this mixture and secure the opening.

Place in a large roasting dish and cook in an oven preheated to 180°C, 350°F, gas mark 4 for about 3 hours or until the juices run clear when a thigh is pierced. Do not overcook and baste regularly with the lemon juice.

While the goose is cooking prepare the sauce. Place the apricots in a pan with enough water to cover and bring to the boil. Reduce the heat and simmer for 10–12 minutes. Add the sugar and cook for a further 5 minutes, stirring regularly. Remove from the heat and stir in the brandy, rosewater and nutmeg.

Meanwhile, roast the nuts under a hot grill, turning at least once, until golden. When cooked remove the goose to a serving dish and remove the scum from the juices in the pan. Add the dry sherry or brandy to the pan juices and cook, stirring constantly until the mixture is reduced to a smooth gravy.

Serve the goose on a bed of *pilav* garnished with sliced tomatoes, cucumbers, radishes, etc. Pour the sherry/brandy pan juices over the goose. Stir the nuts into the apricot sauce and serve in a separate sauceboat. Serves 4–6 people.

hina yemistii me kastana

A Greek-Turkish favourite with a chestnut stuffing. Follow the recipe on page 265, but prepare the stuffing with:

225 g/8 oz chestnuts, peeled and
  halved
50 g/2 oz butter

1 small onion, finely chopped
2 large cooking apples, peeled and
  chopped

Melt the butter in a pan, add the onion and fry until soft. Add the halved chestnuts and fry for a further 3 minutes. Remove from the heat and stir in the apples. Fill the cavity with this stuffing.

avaz memula im matzot

goose stuffed with matzo meal and nuts

Geese are extensively reared in Israel and large quantities are exported to France. The next time you taste the famed *pâté de foie gras* the meat will most probably have come from Israel.

This is a rich and tasty meal. Garnish it with orange and grapefruit slices. Matzo meal can be bought from most large stores and continental shops.

3.5 kg/8 lb goose
25 g/1 oz lard, melted
1 tablespoon grated orange rind

juice 1 lemon
$1/2$ teaspoon white pepper
1 tablespoon salt

Stuffing
40 g/$1^1/2$ oz lard
2 onions, finely chopped
1 stick celery, finely chopped
goose liver, chopped
3 tablespoons parsley, finely chopped
1 apple, grated
2 teaspoons paprika

50 g/2 oz walnuts, coarsely chopped
2 tablespoons pine kernels
100 g/4 oz dried prunes, soaked
  overnight
175 g/6 oz medium matzo meal
225 ml/8 fl oz chicken stock
3 tablespoons fresh orange juice
2 eggs, beaten

Baste
3 tablespoons brandy
1 tablespoon honey

1 tablespoon orange rind, grated

Remove the giblets and set aside. Wash and dry the goose inside and out.

Mix the melted fat with the orange rind, lemon juice, pepper and salt and brush this mixture all over the inside and outside of the goose.

To make the stuffing melt the lard in a large saucepan and sauté the chopped onion until soft. Add the celery, liver, parsley, apple, paprika, walnuts, pine kernels and chopped prunes and fry for 4–5 minutes. Add the remaining stuffing ingredients and mix thoroughly. Stuff this mixture into the goose cavity and close the cavity with a small skewer or needle and thread.

Place the goose in the centre of a large baking dish and cook in an oven preheated to 180°C, 350°F, gas mark 4 for about 3 hours or until the juices run clear when a thigh is pierced.

In a small cup mix the baste ingredients together and use to baste the goose regularly, especially during the last 30 minutes.

Remove the goose to a serving dish. Pour the pan juices and any remaining baste into a saucepan, spooning off as much of the fat as possible. Remove the skewer or thread from the goose cavity and scoop out the stuffing which you can serve in a separate dish. Arrange the orange and grapefruit slices decoratively around the goose and serve. Heat the pan juices and serve in a sauceboat. Serves 6 people.

kereghani paisan baked pheasant

This dish is traditionally cooked and served in a *kereghan*, large clay pot, and is particularly popular in the mountain villages of Armenia where pheasants, partridges and other wild game are found in abundance. Other particularly famed local dishes included 'stuffed bear paws' and 'boars head', but unfortunately I have had to exclude these recipes as some of the raw materials are not easy to find!

Serve with *pilavs* or roast potatoes and salads.

900–1125 g/2–2^1/$_2$ lb pheasant,
   washed and dried inside and out
2 tablespoons salt
40 g/1^1/$_2$ oz *ghee*
100 g/4 oz mushrooms, thinly sliced

1 small onion, thinly sliced
1 tablespoon walnuts, coarsely chopped
100 ml/4 fl oz dry white wine
100 ml/4 fl oz stock

Garnish
1 tablespoon parsley, finely chopped

1 tablespoon sumac

Rub the pheasant inside and out with the salt. Melt the *ghee* in a large casserole, add the pheasant and fry, turning occasionally, until evenly browned all over. Remove the pheasant and reserve.

Add the mushrooms and onion and fry for 3 minutes, stirring regularly. Add the walnuts and fry for 1 minute.

Return the pheasant to the casserole, add the wine and stock and bring to the boil. Cover and cook in an oven preheated to 160°C, 325°F, gas mark 3 for about 1 hour or until tender. Add a little more wine or stock if necessary. Transfer the pheasant to a serving dish, cut into serving pieces and spoon the pan juices over them. Garnish with the parsley and sumac and serve.

yogurtlu tavşan rabbit with yoghurt

This Anatolian recipe works equally well with hare. In Turkey yoghurt is preferred to soured cream which is more popular in the Caucasus.

Wine is used by non-Muslims, while Muslims substitute water — at least in theory. The fact is that wine is both made and drunk in Turkey without much religious polemic. It must be well understood that Turks adopted the Muslim faith more out of political expedience than religious fervour.

Serve with a *pilav* of your choice; burghul *pilav* is particularly good with this dish.

1 rabbit or hare, cut into serving pieces
300 ml/1/2 pint wine vinegar
300 ml/1/2 pint water
2 tablespoons plain flour
2 tablespoons salt
1/2 teaspoon black pepper
1/2 teaspoon oregano

1/2 teaspoon dillweed
3 tablespoons oil
100 ml/4 fl oz dry white wine or water
2 tablespoons fresh tarragon or mint
   or parsley, finely chopped
about 150 ml/1/4 pint stabilized
   yoghurt — see Glossary, page 375

Garnish
1 teaspoon paprika

1 teaspoon cumin

Place the pieces of rabbit in a bowl, cover with the wine vinegar and water and leave to soak for 1 hour. Drain and dry with kitchen paper.

In a small bowl mix together the flour, salt, pepper, oregano and dillweed. Coat the rabbit joints in the seasoned flour.

Heat the oil in a large frying pan and fry the joints for about 5 minutes or until nicely browned all over. Remove and transfer to a large casserole dish or saucepan. Add the wine or water and the chopped tarragon or mint or parsley, cover and simmer for about 1 hour. Add the stabilized yoghurt, stir well and simmer for a further 30 minutes. Spoon into a serving dish and garnish with the paprika and cumin.

firin kebabs and khoreshts

Stews and casseroles — the mainstay of any cuisine — are richly represented in the Middle East.

Lamb, beef, poultry, game, fish and sometimes pork (in the Christian regions) are combined with vegetables, pulses, fruits, nuts and herbs to be cooked slowly in the oven (*firin* in Turkish) or on top of the stove.

Firin kebabs — the title is misleading since none of these dishes are true kebabs, meat on skewers cooked over charcoal — are particularly popular in Anatolia where the peasantry have, over the centuries, developed a method of cooking which stretched the meal as far as possible. Since meat has always been the prerogative of the rich, a cut of meat was combined with other ingredients to make a substantial meal to satisfy many.

Khoreshts — stewed meat in a sauce — are always served with rice and are the mainstay of the Iranian cuisine. Most housewives will prepare a *khoresht* and rice as the main meal no matter how many other delicious side dishes are prepared. There may often be 3-4 different *khoreshts* served at one meal.

The repertoire is vast, elegant, tasty and colourful. Variations abound and it has been extremely difficult for me to decide which particular recipes to include. Do not hesitate to vary the choice of meat or fruits or nuts suggested, for once you have mastered the basic principle of making a *khoresht* you should be able to experiment at leisure.

gatzai kebab *pot kebab*

A decorative dish from Anatolia and beloved of both Armenians and Turks. Serve it with rice *pilav*, fresh salad and yoghurt.

450 g/1 lb minced lamb
1/2 green pepper, chopped
1 small onion, chopped
4 tomatoes, blanched, peeled
   and chopped
2 tablespoons parsley, chopped
1 tablespoon tomato purée

2 teaspoons salt
1 teaspoon black pepper
1 teaspoon chilli pepper
4 aubergines
4 large potatoes
4 large tomatoes

In a large bowl, mix together the meat, chopped green pepper, onion, tomatoes, parsley, tomato purée, salt, black and chilli pepper. When well blended set aside and prepare the vegetables.

Peel strips of skin lengthwise from the aubergines to give them a striped effect.

Peel the potatoes and wash the tomatoes.

Slice all the vegetables, at 1 cm/1/2 in intervals, crosswise about 3/4 of the way down so that they remain attached at the bottom.

Take each vegetable and fill the gaps with a little of the meat mixture. Arrange the stuffed vegetables tightly in an ovenproof dish so that they keep their shape and hold the meat in place. Half cover them with water seasoned with a little salt. Bake in an oven preheated to 200°C, 400°F, gas mark 6 for 1–1¹/2 hours or until the vegetables are tender.

malatya kebabi

stuffed aubergines baked in the oven

Another aubergine-based *firin* kebab is this one from Malatya (ancient Melitane) for a while part of the Crusading Kingdom of Eddessa and for centuries under Armenian sovereignty.

This dish of aubergines stuffed with meat and onions and topped with tomatoes and green peppers is a classic of the Ottoman period and equally popular with Armenians, Kurds and Turks. Serve it with rice or burghul *pilav*.

6 medium aubergines
2 teaspoons salt

8 tablespoons oil

Filling

1 large onion, finely chopped
450 g/1 lb minced lamb or beef
1¹/2 teaspoons salt
1/2 teaspoon black pepper

1/2 teaspoon paprika
2 tomatoes, blanched, peeled and
  chopped
300 ml/1/2 pint water

Topping

3 tomatoes, quartered

3 green peppers, seeded and quartered

Cut the heads off the aubergines and then cut each one in half lengthways. Remove some of the pulp from each half leaving shells about 0.5 cm/1/4 in thick. Arrange the aubergines on a plate, sprinkle with 2 teaspoons of salt and set aside for 30 minutes. Rinse the aubergines under cold running water and pat dry with kitchen paper.

Heat 6 tablespoons of the oil in a frying pan, add the aubergine halves, a few at a time, and sauté for about 3 minutes, turning regularly. Using a slotted spoon transfer the halves to a large, shallow casserole dish and arrange side by side.

Heat the remaining oil in a saucepan, add the onion and sauté until soft, stirring occasionally. Add the meat, salt, pepper, paprika and chopped tomatoes, stir well and sauté for 5 more minutes. Add the water and cook for 30 minutes, stirring regularly. Remove the pan from the heat and, with a tablespoon, fill each halved aubergine with the meat mixture. Place a quartered tomato and green pepper on each half and pour any pan juices into the dish. Bake in an oven preheated to 190°C, 375°F, gas mark 5 for about 30 minutes. Remove from the oven and serve immediately with a *pilav*.

One day Boloz Mugush asked his nephew 'What is an aubergine?'

Without a moment's hesitation the nephew replied 'A newly born ox whose eyes have still not opened.'

Boloz Mugush, amazed at this brilliant explanation, beams and announces aloud to one and all in the room 'See how bright our nephew is — this neither I nor his father taught him. This he found out for himself!'

papaz kebabi *priest's kebab*

A very ancient dish mentioned both by Apicius and the Arab historians of the Middle Ages.

Meat is cooked with milk — an aberration in Semitic and hence Islamic customs where milk and meat are not permitted to be eaten together.

As the name suggests this is a dish of Christian origins (Armenian or Greek). Serve with rice *pilav* or roast potatoes and salads.

50 g/2 oz butter	1 teaspoon salt
2 onions, thinly sliced	1 tablespoon plain flour
700 g/1½ lb lean lamb or beef,	450 ml/¾ pint milk
cut into 6 pieces	1 teaspoon salt
600 ml/1 pint water	

Melt half of the butter in a large saucepan. Add the onions and fry, stirring frequently, until soft. Add the pieces of meat, cover the pan and cook for 10 minutes. After 5 minutes uncover the pan, stir the meat mixture and cover again. After 10 minutes uncover the pan, add the water and salt, stir and continue simmering until the water has evaporated. Remove from the heat and keep warm.

Heat the remaining butter in a small saucepan, remove from the heat and stir in the flour. Gradually add the milk, stirring constantly, until the mixture is smooth. Season with the salt, return to a low heat and cook, stirring constantly, until the mixture thickens. Transfer the meat and onion mixture to an ovenproof casserole and pour the white sauce over the top. Place in an oven preheated to 180°C, 350°F, gas mark 4 and cook for 20 minutes. Remove from the oven and serve immediately.

kuzu ankara tavasi

ankara-style lamb casserole

A rich, creamy casserole from Turkey which is topped with a crust of lightly cooked eggs. Serve with salads and pickles.

25 g/1 oz butter	1 large carrot, peeled and cut crossways
900 g/2 lb lean lamb, cut into	into 0.5 cm/¼ in rounds
6 equal portions	75 g/3 oz green beans
1.35 litres/2 pints water	450 ml/¾ pint yoghurt
1 teaspoon salt	50 g/2 oz plain flour
2 onions, thinly sliced	2 eggs, lightly beaten

Garnish
1 tablespoon paprika

1 tablespoon dried dill

Melt the butter in a large saucepan. Add the pieces of meat and fry for a few minutes, turning occasionally, until they are browned all over. Add the water and salt and bring quickly to the boil. Cover the pan, lower the heat and simmer for 45 minutes. Add the onions and carrot and cook, uncovered, for 30 minutes. Add the green beans and cook for a further 10–15 minutes or until the beans are just tender.

With a slotted spoon transfer the pieces of meat to a large ovenproof casserole. Arrange the cooked vegetables over the meat.

Pour the yoghurt into a bowl and stir in the flour until it is well blended and smooth. Now stir in about 450 ml/1 pint of the warm meat liquid from the saucepan and pour the sauce into the casserole. Bring gently to the boil and simmer over a low heat for 10 minutes.

Pour the beaten eggs over the surface of the casserole and bake in an oven preheated to 190°C, 375°F, gas mark 5 for 10–15 minutes or until the egg is set and golden. Remove from the oven, sprinkle with the paprika and dill and serve with rice and/or potatoes and a salad.

arnaki se filo lamb in filo

A dish of light, crisp pastry filled with a mixture of meat, onion and tomato. Originally the filling was wrapped in parchment, but nowadays aluminium foil is usually used. However, this Greek-Cypriot recipe is for *baklava* filo. The same dish appears in Turkey as *ali pafla kebabi* and is usually made with *borek hamuru — borek* dough. You can use puff pastry instead.

The story goes that in the bad old days the Palikari (originally bandits — later the name was given to partisans fighting for the independence of Greece and Crete) wrapped the meat in parchment so that the aroma would be tightly sealed in and their hideouts not discovered.

I suggest you use *baklava* filo.

Serve with fresh salad.

25 g/1 oz *ghee* or butter	1 teaspoon salt
2 onions, thinly sliced	1 teaspoon black pepper
700 g/1¹/₂ lb lean lamb	225 ml/8 fl oz water
1 large tomato, thinly sliced	2 tablespoons parsley, finely chopped

Dough

8 sheets *baklava* filo	60 g/2¹/₂ oz unsalted butter, melted

Melt the *ghee* or butter in a large saucepan, add the onion and fry until soft and turning golden. Cut the meat into 1.2 cm/¹/₂ in cubes and add to the saucepan. Cover the pan and simmer for 5 minutes, stirring occasionally. Add the tomato, salt, pepper and water and bring to the boil. Lower the heat and simmer for about 1 hour or until the meat is tender and most of the water has evaporated. Remove from the heat, stir in the parsley and set aside to cool.

Meanwhile, open up one sheet of the filo and brush with the melted butter. Place another sheet of filo over the top. Brush one half of this second sheet with butter and fold the 2 sheets over so that they are half their original size. Place 1/4 of the meat mixture in the centre of the filo. Fold the filo over in envelope-style to enclose the meat and brush the edges with butter to hold them down. Continue with remaining meat and pastry until you have 4 'parcels' and brush the surface of each with any remaining butter.

Lightly grease 2 baking trays and place 2 'parcels' on each. Place in an oven preheated to 180°C, 350°F, gas mark 4 and bake for 20–30 minutes or until the pastry is golden. Remove from the oven and serve with a salad of your choice.

kazan kaypapi aubergine with lamb and fruits

An Azerbaijanian dish from the Caucasus that is, in reality, a *khoresht* rather than a *firin* kebab.

Makes an excellent use of fruits and spices.

Serve it with a bowl of yoghurt and a rice *pilav*.

1 large aubergine, peeled and cut crossways into 0.5 cm/1/4 in slices
1 tablespoon salt
3 tomatoes, blanched, peeled and thinly sliced
1 onion, thinly sliced
1 green pepper, seeded and thinly sliced
5–6 apricot halves, each halved
5–6 stoned prunes, halved
40 g/ 11/2 oz *ghee* or butter
450 g/1 lb lean lamb cut into 2.5 cm/1 in cubes

1/4 teaspoon cinnamon
1/4 teaspoon ground cloves
1/2 teaspoon allspice
1 teaspoon salt
1/2 teaspoon black pepper
3–5 tablespoons oil
4 tablespoons lemon juice or, preferably, pomegranate juice
6 tablespoons melted *ghee* or butter
1 medium quince or cooking apple, peeled, cored and cut into 1.2 cm/1/2 in pieces

Put the aubergine slices in a colander, sprinkle with the salt and set aside for 30 minutes.

Meanwhile, lightly grease a large casserole dish and spread half the tomato slices in the bottom. Now lay the onion and green pepper slices and half the apricots and prunes over the tomatoes.

Melt the *ghee* or butter in a saucepan, add the meat cubes and sauté until browned all over, turning frequently. Add the cinnamon, cloves, allspice, salt and pepper and cook for a further 2 minutes, stirring constantly. Transfer the spiced meat to the casserole and spread evenly over the vegetables. Lay the remaining tomato slices, apricots and prunes over the meat.

Heat the oil in a large frying pan. Rinse the aubergine slices under cold water and pat dry with kitchen paper. Fry the aubergine slices, a few at a time, until golden on both sides and then remove and drain on kitchen paper. Add more oil if necessary. Arrange the slices over the top of the casserole. Pour the lemon juice and half the melted *ghee* over the meat and vegetables.

Heat the remaining melted *ghee* in a small saucepan, add the pieces of quince or apple and fry for a few minutes, stirring and turning frequently. Arrange them over the aubergines and pour any remaining fat into the casserole. Cover and bake in an oven preheated to 180°C, 350F°, gas mark 4 for about 45 minutes or until the meat and vegetables are tender. Remove from the oven and serve.

hamuth helou lamb stew with dates

This is a rich Iraqi stew of lamb with dried fruits. Traditionally it is prepared with a thick date syrup and, to contrast, dried limes. I have suggested puréed dates (see recipe) instead of date syrup and lemon juice and peel if, as is possible, *loomi* (dried limes) cannot be obtained. Serve with a *pilav* of your choice.

50 g/2 oz *ghee*
900 g/2 lb lean lamb, cut into
   2.5 cm/1 in pieces
1 onion, chopped
600 ml/1 pint water
1¹/₂ teaspoons salt
5 cm/2 in piece of cinnamon

1 *loomi* (dried lime) or peel of
   1 lemon and its juice
6 stoned dried dates, chopped
8 dried apricots, halved
8–10 prunes, stoned and halved
3 tablespoons raisins
1 tablespoon brown sugar or honey

Melt the *ghee* in a large saucepan. Add the meat and sauté for 5–7 minutes, stirring frequently. Remove the meat with a slotted spoon and reserve.

Add the chopped onion to the pan and fry until soft. Return the meat to the pan, add half the water, the salt, cinnamon and *loomi* or lemon juice and peel. Cover the pan, lower the heat and simmer for 45 minutes.

Meanwhile, place the remaining water in a small pan, add the chopped dates and simmer over a moderate heat for 12–15 minutes until the dates soften. Transfer the mixture to a liquidizer and blend to a purée. Add this date purée to the meat mixture together with the apricots, prunes, raisins and sugar or honey. Stir well, recover the pan and cook for a further hour. When the meat is tender transfer the stew to a serving dish and remove the cinnamon stick and *loomi* or lemon rind.

cholent israeli meat and vegetable casserole

A classic of the Jewish cuisine, developed in the Middle Ages in Central Europe, as a response to religious requirements.

Cholent (also called *shalet* and *shalent*) has numerous variations — depending basically on where the particular Jewish family originate. The traditional one, still popular in Israel amongst Russian and Polish Jews, always includes potatoes (the staple food of Eastern Europe), *kasha* (buck-wheat) and turnips, carrots and meat.

The recipe below is a typical one prepared on a Friday evening and cooked very slowly to be ready for the Sabbath.

A rich and nourishing meal. Serve with a *pilav* of your choice and bread.

The Oriental Jews, of course, have their own versions, e.g. *dfeenah*.

50 g/2 oz butter or *ghee*
1.1–1.3 kg/2½–3 lb brisket
    of beef
1 onion, chopped
1 clove garlic, finely chopped
1 teaspoon salt
1/2 teaspoon black pepper
1/2 teaspoon paprika
1/4 teaspoon ginger
1/4 teaspoon cinnamon
350 g/12 oz butter beans (lima beans),
    soaked overnight in cold water

100 g/4 oz pearl barley
10 small potatoes, peeled
2 carrots, peeled and thickly sliced
1 turnip, peeled and cut into
    2.5 cm/1 in pieces
2 bay leaves
1 onion, chopped
1 tablespoon flour
1/2 teaspoon paprika
water for boiling

Garnish **2 tablespoons parsley, finely chopped**

Melt the butter or *ghee* in a large casserole, add the meat, onion and garlic and sauté until brown, turning the meat occasionally. Mix the salt, pepper, paprika, ginger and cinnamon together, sprinkle over the contents of the casserole and cook, stirring frequently, for 3–4 minutes. Add the beans, pearl barley, vegetables and bay leaves. Sprinkle with the flour and paprika and stir well. Add sufficient boiling water to cover the ingredients by about 2.5 cm/1 in. Cover the casserole and place in an oven preheated to 180°C, 350°F, gas mark 4. Cook for 2–3 hours or until the meat is tender. Remove from the oven, slice the meat and arrange in the centre of a large serving dish.

With a slotted spoon remove the beans, barley and vegetables and arrange them around the meat. Sprinkle with the chopped parsley. Pour the pan juices into a sauceboat and serve as an accompaniment.

Serves 6–8 people.

khoresht-e-albaloo meat and cherry stew

Sour black cherries should be used for this dish, but Morello cherries will do. This is a typical Iranian *khoresht* of meat, fruit and spices.

Always served with *chelo* rice *pilav*, but you can serve any *pilav* of your choice.

The Arab dish *lahma-bil-karaz* is similar to this dish except that the meat is minced and rolled into marble-sized balls and the dish is served with bread instead of rice.

Other fruits are also used, e.g. green plums — *khoresht-e-go jeh*, sour grapes — *khoresht-e-gooreh* and almonds — *khoresht-e-ghaghaleh-badmoon*, etc.

The cooking method is the same, as are the remaining ingredients and so you can experiment if you like.

50 g/2 oz *ghee*
1 large onion, finely chopped
700 g/1¹/₂ lb stewing lamb or
   beef, trimmed of excess fat
   and cut into 2.5 cm/1 in cubes
¹/₂ teaspoon cinnamon
¹/₂ teaspoon turmeric

100 ml/4 fl oz water
2 teaspoons salt
¹/₂ teaspoon black pepper
4 tablespoons lemon juice or
   4 tablespoons powdered dried lime
225 g/8 oz sour black cherries, stoned
2 tablespoons sugar — or more to taste

Melt the *ghee* in a large saucepan, add the onion and fry until soft. Add the meat cubes and fry, turning frequently, until evenly browned. Stir in the cinnamon and turmeric and cook for 2 minutes, stirring frequently. Add the water, salt, pepper and 2 tablespoons of the lemon juice or powdered lime. Mix well, cover the pan, lower the heat and simmer for about 40–45 minutes. Stir in the cherries and sugar, cover and simmer for 10 minutes.

Taste the sauce. The ideal flavour should be sweet-sour. If the sauce is too sweet then add the remaining lemon juice or lime powder, but if it is too sour then add enough sugar to suit your taste. Cover and continue to simmer for a further 20–30 minutes or until the meat is tender. Transfer to a large dish and serve with *chelo* or other rice *pilav* of your choice.

Variation

khoresht-e-ghooreh meat and sour grape stew

If you happen to have a vine then try this recipe. Follow the directions above but substitute 450 g/1 lb unripe sour grapes for the cherries and add 1 tablespoon tomato purée to the pan.

Either eliminate the lemon juice or lime powder or add only 1 tablespoon — this will really depend on the sourness of the grapes!

khoresht-e-narengi

chicken and tangerine stew

A tasty stew that typifies everything that is uniquely Iranian. A brilliant arrangement of yellows and golds.

75 g/3 oz *ghee* or butter
1.3–1.8 kg/3–4 lb oven ready
   chicken, cut into 8 serving pieces
1 large onion, thinly sliced
1/2 teaspoon saffron
600 ml/1 pint water
11/2 teaspoons salt

1/2 teaspoon black pepper
juice 1 large lemon
4 tangerines, peeled and with peel
   reserved
225 g/8 oz carrots, peeled and cut
   into 1.2 cm/1/2 in slivers
1–2 tablespoons brown sugar

Garnish
2 tablespoons toasted almonds, slivered   2 tablespoons pistachios, halved

Melt 40 g/11/2 oz of the *ghee* or butter in a large saucepan. Add the chicken pieces and sauté until almost tender, turning until evenly browned. Remove from the pan and reserve.

To prepare the sauce add the remaining *ghee* or butter to the pan, add the onion and fry until soft. Stir in the saffron and return the chicken pieces to the pan. Add the water, salt, pepper and lemon juice, lower the heat, cover and simmer for 30 minutes.

Meanwhile, with a sharp knife scrape and discard the white pith from the tangerine peel and then cut the peel into thin strips. Add to the stew together with the carrots and brown sugar. Continue to simmer until the peel and carrots are tender.

Separate the tangerines into segments and peel each segment. Add segments to the pan and cook for a further 10–15 minutes. Transfer to a large serving dish, sprinkle with the nuts and serve with *chelo* or other rice *pilav* of your choice.

sauces

There are three main types of sauces — those made with yoghurt, tomatoes or nuts. Wine and cream are little used — except sometimes in Greece, Israel and Northern Caucasia.

Most Middle Eastern dishes are eaten dry, e.g. kebabs, roasts, *pilavs*, etc. or, as is often the case, are inclusive of their own sauces, e.g. *khoreshts*, *dolmas*, stews, etc.

There are, however, a few well known sauces which often accompany vegetable, meat and rice dishes.

Yoghurt is the basis of some of these sauces. The most popular one is *sughtorov-madzoon* — a garlic-yoghurt sauce. It is versatile, easy to make and is used extensively with stews and vegetables — especially *dolmas*, *pilavs* and meat. The recipe on page 280 is a standard one.

sughtorov-madzoon garlic-yoghurt sauce

300 ml/1/2 pint yoghurt
1 clove garlic, crushed

1/2 teaspoon salt

Garnish
1/2 teaspoon dried mint

1 spring onion, finely chopped (optional)

Pour the yoghurt into a bowl. Add the garlic and salt and mix well. Sprinkle the dried mint, and onion if using it, over the top and serve.

darçinli yoghurt cinnamon yoghurt sauce

This yoghurt sauce includes cinnamon and sugar and is traditionally served as an accompaniment to roast meats as well as salads and vegetables.

300 ml/1/2 pint yoghurt

2 teaspoons sugar

Garnish 1 teaspoon ground cinnamon

Pour the yoghurt into a serving bowl. Add the sugar and mix well. Sprinkle with the cinnamon and serve.

peynirli yoghurt salsasi

yoghurt-cheese sauce

This is a regional speciality from Turkey which is ideal with cooked eggs, pastas, vegetables, salads and Anatolian pancakes.

50 g/2 oz butter
2 tablespoons flour
450 ml/3/4 pint yoghurt
100 g/4 oz grated cheese, e.g.
   Gouda, Edam or Cheddar

1/2 teaspoon paprika
1/2 teaspoon salt
pinch black pepper

Melt the butter in a saucepan. Remove from the heat and stir in the flour. Cook for 1 minute. Beat the yoghurt vigorously and slowly stir it into the flour mixture. Cook slowly over a low heat, stirring constantly, until the mixture thickens. Stir in the cheese, paprika, salt and pepper. Cook slowly until the cheese melts and then serve.

tomato sauces

Although tomatoes are a relatively new arrival to the Middle East they have been incorporated very successfully in countless dishes. They make delicious sauces such as the famed Armenian kebab sauce, the Greek-Turkish *saltsa tomata* and the spicy *dukkous al-tamata* from the island of Bahrain. More often than not nowadays tomato purée is used instead of tomatoes.

kebabi salsa kebab sauce

This is our family recipe — one that we also use in our restaurants. There are a few others, e.g. one Lebanese version includes okra, but the basic ingredients are the same.

4 tablespoons cooking oil
1 small onion, finely chopped
1 clove garlic, crushed
1 green pepper, seeded and chopped
2 tomatoes, blanched, seeded
   and chopped
2 tablespoons tomato purée

600 ml/1 pint water
1/2 glass red wine (optional)
2 bay leaves
100 g/4 oz peas
1 teaspoon ground coriander
salt and black pepper to taste

Heat the oil in a large saucepan, add the onion, garlic and green pepper and fry until the onion is golden. Add the remaining ingredients, except the peas, and stir well. Now add the peas and bring to the boil. Cook for 15–20 minutes, stirring occasionally. Taste and adjust the seasoning if necessary.

saltsa tomata tomato sauce

This is a versatile sauce used over *pilavs*, roasts and kebabs.

40 g/1¹/₂ oz butter
3 tablespoons onion, chopped
5 large tomatoes, blanched,
   peeled and finely chopped
1 clove garlic, crushed

2 tablespoons parsley, finely chopped
2 bay leaves
1/2 teaspoon salt
1/4 teaspoon allspice
1/4 teaspoon black pepper

Melt the butter in a saucepan, add the onion and fry until soft and transparent. Add the remaining ingredients and cook over a low heat for about 15 minutes, stirring frequently. Serve hot.

dukkous al-tamata spicy tomato sauce

A strong, spicy, garlic-flavoured sauce which is usually served with rice *pilavs* and roasts.

2 tablespoons oil
8 cloves garlic, crushed
900 g/2 lb ripe tomatoes, blanched
    peeled and coarsely chopped
1 tablespoon salt
1/4 teaspoon paprika

1/4 teaspoon cumin
1/4 teaspoon ground coriander
1/4 teaspoon black pepper
1/4 teaspoon ground nutmeg
1/4 teaspoon turmeric
1/4 teaspoon chilli pepper

Heat the oil in a saucepan, add the garlic and fry for 2 minutes, stirring constantly. Add the tomatoes and salt, lower the heat, cover the pan and simmer for 20–30 minutes. Add all the remaining ingredients, stir thoroughly and cook for a further 5 minutes. Serve with *pilavs*, vegetables and meat.

beid-el-lemoun egg and lemon sauce

One of the oldest known sauces this was prepared by the ancient Egyptians, Romans and Byzantines. It is extremely popular in Greece as *saltsa avgolemono*. The Greeks passed it on to the Turks — *terbiye* and to the Arabs — whose name I have used for this sauce. It is used in soups, with salads and vegetables and particularly with hot and cold fish dishes.

The recipe below is to accompany chicken dishes, but if you wish to use it with fish then use fish stock instead of chicken stock.

450–600 ml/3/4–1 pint chicken stock
1/2 teaspoon salt
1/4 teaspoon black pepper

3 egg yolks
juice 2 small lemons
1 tablespoon cornflour

Pour the stock into a saucepan and season to taste with the salt and pepper.

Beat the egg yolks in a small bowl and then add the lemon juice, stirring constantly. Pour the egg mixture slowly into the stock and stir well.

Mix the cornflour with a little water and add to the pan. Heat the sauce gently, stirring constantly using a wooden spoon, for about 10 minutes. Do not bring to the boil or it will curdle. The sauce should by now have a smooth, cream-like consistency. Serve hot or cold.

tahiniyeh garlic and tahina sauce

Used extensively in the Syrian and Lebanese cuisines. It's often eaten as a dip and is excellent with fish dishes and as a salad dressing.

Will keep for several days in a refrigerator.

150 ml/$1/4$ pint tahina paste
juice 2 lemons
300 ml/$1/2$ pint milk or water
2 cloves garlic, crushed

1 tablespoon parsley, finely chopped
1 teaspoon salt
$1/2$ teaspoon chilli pepper

Pour the tahina into a bowl and stir in the lemon juice. Slowly add the milk, stirring until you have a mixture of a thick, creamy consistency. Add the remaining ingredients and stir well. Serve as required.

tkemali sauce prune sauce

A classic Georgian sauce extensively used in the Caucasus. It is used with chicken and kebabs of meat and fish.

It is easy to prepare and will keep for a long time.

450 ml/$3/4$ pint water
225 g/8 oz prunes
1 clove garlic
1 teaspoon ground coriander

$1/2$ teaspoon salt
$1/2$ teaspoon paprika
$11/2$ tablespoons lemon juice

Bring the water to the boil in a saucepan, add the prunes, remove from the heat and set aside for 10 minutes. Bring back to the boil and cook briskly for about 15 minutes or until the prunes are tender. Pour the contents of the pan into a sieve placed over a bowl. Reserve the liquid.

Stone the prunes and put the flesh into a liquidizer with the garlic and coriander. Add a little of the reserved liquid and blend well. The sauce needs to have the consistency of thick cream and so adjust the amount of liquid you add accordingly. Transfer this sauce to a saucepan, stir in the salt and paprika and bring to the boil. Remove from the heat and stir in the lemon juice. This is usually served at room temperature.

schoog yemeni sauce

Originally from Yemen this sauce is now, perhaps, more popular in Israel — brought over by the Jews who settled in the Holy Land in the early fifties. Hot and pungent, it is often eaten on its own with bread or as an hors d'oeuvre. Also served with hot vegetable dishes, roasts and kebabs.

3 cloves garlic	2 tomatoes, blanched, peeled and
1 teaspoon cumin	chopped
1/2 teaspoon salt	juice 1/2 lemon
3 teaspoons ground coriander	1/2 teaspoon sugar
6 fresh chillies	3 tablespoons water

Put all the ingredients in a liquidizer and blend. Spoon into a saucepan and bring to the boil. Allow to cool and then serve.

tarator garlic and walnut sauce

The origin of this sauce is lost in the mists of time. I would like to think it has something to do with the Tartars and their famed sauce — better known to you and me as *sauce tartare*. Serve with poultry and fish.

100 g/4 oz walnuts	2 slices bread, crusts removed
3 cloves garlic	2 tablespoons lemon juice
1/2 teaspoon salt	olive oil

Garnish 1 tablespoon parsley, chopped

Pound the walnuts with the garlic and salt in a mortar or grind in a blender. Soak the bread in a little water and then squeeze out. Spoon the nut mixture into a bowl and add the bread. Mix thoroughly. Little by little add the lemon juice and enough oil for the sauce to become thick and smooth. Serve in small dishes, sprinkled with parsley, beside each plate.

Variations

tarator çamfishtikli pine kernel sauce

Prepare as with the recipe above, but omit the bread and use 100 g/4 oz pine kernels, 2 cloves garlic, 1 teaspoon salt, 2 tablespoons lemon juice and oil.

tarator sade garlic sauce

A Turkish sauce traditionally served with fish dishes, particularly mussels, it also goes well with cold meats and salads.

2 cloves garlic	4 tablespoons olive oil
1 teaspoon salt	2 tablespoons lemon juice

In a small bowl crush the garlic with the salt. Add 2 tablespoons of the oil and set aside for 10 minutes. Stir in the remaining oil and the lemon juice and spoon over fish, meat or vegetables.

khubz — bread

The staff of life, bread has been the major ingredient in all the Middle Eastern cuisines. In the desert regions the nomads still prepare their bread on a *saj* — a large, circular, dome-shaped piece of cast iron heated from underneath by dry sticks and camel dung. In the highlands of Lebanon the heat for cooking the bread is generated by burning pine needles, while further north in the mountains of the Caucasus and Iran the bread is traditionally cooked in a *tonir* — large clay oven — heated by wood or charcoal.

In the Middle Ages, we are informed1 that there were two basic types of bread in the Middle East — al khubz al huwmara (white flour) and al khubz al khashkar (coarse unhusked flour). Both these breads were glazed with borax (bowrag) which was imported from Armenia. Some of these breads were khushanaj (dry bread) similar to simit and choreg — see recipes; mutbag (envelope) related to pita bread still called khubz Shami or khubz Arabi — see recipes; akras mukallala (crowned loaves); khubz al-abazir (seasoned bread) similar to khubz-el-saluf or mannaeesh. There are literally hundreds of different breads throughout the region, eaten with every meal.

1   'Kitab-al-Tabikh wa islah al-aghdhiyat al-makulat' by Warrag — Bodleian Library, Oxford. Manuscript no. 187.

lavash crispy thin bread

The oldest form of bread found in the Middle East, *lavash* is a thin, crispy bread made from plain flour (wholemeal is also sometimes used).

It comes in many different shapes and sizes from small rounds to oval to large circles often 60 cm/2 ft in diameter. It keeps for a long time without going mouldy. Traditionally enough was often baked at one time to last for 3–4 months and it was then wrapped in linen until required. Normally prepared in a *tonir* — similar to the Indian *tandoor*, it can also be prepared, and often is in the Arab lands, on a large, circular, dome-shaped piece of cast iron known as a *saj* which is heated from underneath by burning wood chippings.

The recipe below is a simplified version ideal for dips, salads and for wrapping around kebabs.

15 g/1/2 oz fresh yeast or
  7 g/1/4 oz dried yeast
1 teaspoon sugar

lukewarm water
700 g/11/2 lb plain flour
1 teaspoon salt

Place the yeast in a small bowl with the sugar and dissolve in 300 ml/1/2 pint warm water and set aside for about 10 minutes in a warm place or until the mixture begins to froth.

Sift the flour and salt into a large bowl. Make a well in the centre and slowly work in the yeast mixture and enough warm water to make a stiff dough. Knead on a floured surface for about 10 minutes until the dough is smooth and elastic. Place the ball of dough in a clean bowl, cover with a cloth and leave in a warm place for about 2–3 hours or until it has doubled in size.

Transfer the dough to a floured surface, punch it down and knead again for a few minutes. Return to the bowl, cover and leave for a further 30 minutes. Flour the working surface again. Divide the dough into apple-sized balls. This amount of dough should make about 12–15 balls.

With a long rolling pin roll out each ball into a thin sheet about 20–25 cm/8–10 in in diameter. Sprinkle the working surface with flour now and again to prevent sticking.

Line the bottom of the oven with foil and heat the oven to 200°C, 400°F, gas mark 6. Place one sheet of dough on the foil and cook for about 3 minutes. Remove the cooked *lavash* and cover with a teatowel while you cook the remaining *lavash* in the same way. Serve immediately.

If the *lavash* are not to be used at once then, when completely cold, fold and wrap them in a teatowel and then in plastic or wrap and freeze. When ready to serve sprinkle them lightly with water, wrap in a teatowel and leave for 10 minutes to absorb the moisture and to soften.

khubz arabi *arab bread*

Eat of the bread made by a woman with a bleeding nose, but do not eat the bread of her who constantly reminds thee of having given it. — Arab wisdom.

Better known as pita bread in the west, khubz Arabi is the ideal bread for eating with most Arab food. Makes about 8 loaves.

15 g/1½ oz fresh yeast
   or 7 g/¼ oz dried yeast
1 teaspoon sugar

about 300 ml/½ pint tepid water
450 g/1 lb plain flour
½ teaspoon salt

Place the yeast and sugar in a small bowl, dissolve in a few tablespoons of the warm water and set aside in a warm place for about 10 minutes or until it begins to froth.

Sift the flour and salt into a large bowl. Make a well in the centre and pour in the yeast mixture. Add enough of the warm water to make a firm, but not hard, dough.

Knead on a floured working top for 10–15 minutes or until the dough is soft and elastic. If you knead in a tablespoon of oil it will make a softer dough.

Wash and dry the mixing bowl and lightly oil it. Roll the dough around the bowl until its surface is greased all over — this will prevent the dough going crusty and cracking while rising. Cover the bowl with a damp cloth and set aside in a warm place for at least 2 hours until the dough has doubled in size. Transfer the dough to the work top, punch down and knead for a few minutes. Divide the mixture into 8 pieces. Roll them between your palms until they are round and smooth.

Lightly flour the working top and flatten each ball with the palm of your hand, or with a rolling pin, until it is about 0.5 cm/¼ in thick and is as even and circular as possible. Dust the tops with flour and cover with a floured cloth. Leave to rise in a warm place for a further 20–30 minutes.

Preheat the oven to 230–240°C, 450–475°F, gas mark 8-9 putting in 2 large oiled baking sheets half-way through the heating period. When the oven is ready slide the rounds of dough on to hot baking sheets, dampening the tops of the rounds to prevent them browning, and bake for 10 minutes. Do not open the oven door during this time, but after that it is safe to open it to see if the pitas have puffed up. Slide on to wire racks as soon as you remove from the oven. They should be soft and white with a pouch inside.

Variation

pideh

The Armenians like to sprinkle sesame seeds over this bread. The bread is prepared as above, except that wholemeal flour is often used, and before being placed in the oven the tops of the rounds are scored with a knife to form a diamond design and then brushed with milk and sprinkled evenly with sesame seeds.

khubz-el-saluf fenugreek and coriander bread

In the Yemen, as well as the adjacent regions of Muscat and Oman, a spicy bread is prepared which is topped with a paste of fenugreek called *hulba* which gives the loaves a beautiful aroma.

You can prepare the loaves with plain flour or with half plain and half wholemeal flour — I prefer the latter.

Serve with meat, fish and kebab dishes.

15 g/1/2 oz fresh yeast or
   7 g/1/4 oz dried yeast
about 350 ml/12 fl oz warm water

450 g/1 lb plain flour or 225 g/8 oz
   plain and 225 g/8 oz wholemeal flour
1/2 teaspoon salt
a little melted *ghee*

Topping

2 teaspoons fenugreek seeds —
   soaked in 100 ml/4 fl oz water
   in a small bowl overnight
1 clove garlic

50 g/2 oz chopped coriander leaves
1/2 teaspoon salt
1 tablespoon lemon juice
2 tablespoons water

Place the yeast in a small bowl and dissolve it in a few tablespoons of the warm water. Set aside in a warm place until it begins to froth.

Sift the flour and salt into a large mixing bowl and make a well in the centre. Pour the yeast mixture into the bowl and gradually add enough of the water to make a firm but not hard dough. Transfer to a lightly floured working surface and knead for about 10 minutes until the dough is smooth and elastic. Cover and put in a warm place for at least 2 hours or until the dough has doubled in size.

Meanwhile, prepare the topping by draining off the water from the bowl of fenugreek soaked overnight. Transfer the fenugreek to a liquidizer, add the garlic, coriander leaves, salt, lemon juice and water and blend to a paste. Turn into a small bowl, cover and refrigerate until needed.

Preheat the oven to 250°C, 500°F, gas mark 10 and half-way through the heating period slide 2 greased baking sheets into the oven.

Punch the dough down and knead for a few more minutes. Divide the mixture into 8–10 portions and roll between your palms until smooth. Roll or press each ball out to a circle about 18–20 cm/7–8 in in diameter and prick the surface of each in several places with a fork to prevent the dough puffing up while cooking. Brush the top of each loaf with a little melted *ghee*. Carefully spread a teaspoonful of the topping over each loaf. Slide the loaves carefully on to the hot sheets and bake for 5 minutes. Serve warm.

zeytin ekmeği olive bread

While olives produce forgetfulness of what one has learned, olive oil makes a clean head. — Midrash Tehillim.

A regional speciality from Antakya (historic Antioch, once one of the glories of Roman and later Byzantine empires, today a typical sleepy Turkish town). And although I have given it its Turkish name this bread, made of olives and onions, is a particular speciality of Greeks and Armenians belonging to the Eastern Orthodox church and was traditionally prepared during the forty days of Lent to give extra interest to their limited fare (no meat, eggs or dairy produce were permitted during that time).

Outside Cyprus, where it is well known and popular as *elioti*, and amongst Armenians, who call it *tsit-hats*, this bread is also eaten by the members of the Allaoui sect in Northern Syria who call it *khubz-el-zeytoun*.

A wonderful and extremely tasty bread.

Dough

15 g/½ oz fresh yeast or
   7 g/¼ oz dried yeast
1 teaspoon sugar

about 300 ml/½ pint tepid water
450 g/1 lb plain flour
½ teaspoon salt

Olive filling

1 tablespoon olive oil
1 medium onion, finely chopped

15–20 olives, halved and stoned
oil for glazing

Prepare the dough as described in *khubz Arabi* on page 287. Divide the dough into 2 equal parts and roll between palms to form smooth balls. Roll each ball out into a rectangle about 20 x 40 cm/8 x 16 in and 0.5 cm/¼ in thick. Cover with damp cloth while you prepare the filling.

Heat the oil in a small saucepan, add the onion and fry until soft and transparent. Stir in the halved olives and set aside to cool. Then spread half of the olive mixture over one of the rectangles, leaving the edges clear, and then roll up from one of the longer sides to form a loaf shape. Seal the edges and place on a greased baking sheet with the join underneath. Repeat with the remaining rectangle of dough and filling.

With a sharp knife make 3–4 diagonal slashes across the top of each or make the traditional pattern of the cross. Cover with a cloth and set aside in a warm place for 30 minutes. Brush tops with oil and bake in an oven preheated to 190°C, 375°F, gas mark 5 for about 40 minutes or until golden and baked through. Serve warm or cool on a wire rack.

challah sabbath bread

Three things are good in little measure and evil in large — yeast, salt and hesitation. — Jewish wisdom.

This is the Jewish bread and indeed it is more than a mere bread since it is intertwined with so much of their religion, culture and history.

However, the finest *challahs* that I have tasted have all been cooked by Arab bakers — there must be a moral there somewhere!

The recipe below makes a large plait about 30 cm/12 in long.

15 g/½ oz fresh yeast
  or 7 g/¼ oz dried yeast
1 tablespoon sugar
600 ml/1 pint lukewarm water
700 g/1½ lb plain flour

2 teaspoons salt
3 tablespoons oil
1 egg
1 beaten egg yolk

Garnish **2 tablespoons poppy seeds**

Place the yeast and sugar in a small bowl, dissolve in a few tablespoons of the warm water and set aside in a warm place for about 10 minutes or until the mixture begins to froth.

Sift the flour and salt into a large bowl and make a well in the centre. Add the oil, egg, yeast mixture and enough of the warm water to make a stiff dough. Knead the dough on a floured surface for about 10 minutes until smooth and elastic. Cover and leave in a warm place for about 2 hours until it has doubled in size. Transfer to the work top, punch down and knead for a few minutes. Divide the dough into 3 parts — 1 large, 1 medium and 1 small.

Take the large portion of dough, divide into 3 equal parts and roll each into a sausage about 36 cm/14 in long and plait the 3 together. Repeat with the medium lump of dough and then with the small one. Lay the largest plait on a greased baking sheet, press the medium plait on to it and the small plait on top of that. Brush the whole surface of the loaf with the beaten egg and sprinkle with the poppy seeds.

Bake in the centre of an oven preheated to 180°C, 350°F, gas mark 4 for about 1 hour or until it sounds hollow when knocked on the bottom. Cool on a wire rack.

khubz basali onion bread

Onion bread is a North Syrian speciality from the region of Antakya (Antioch), the Taurus mountains and the plain of Cilicia (Southern Turkey).

The bread of the poor, it was often eaten as a complete meal or, with the city-dwelling merchant classes, as part of their breakfast table with eggs, *laban* and cheese.

The recipe below is for 1 large loaf, but if you prefer you can make the dough into smaller loaves about the size of *khubz Arabi*.

450 g/1 lb self-raising flour
1 teaspoon salt
2 teaspoons baking powder
about 300 ml/$1/2$ pint water
about 20 black olives, stoned
    and coarsely chopped

1 medium onion, finely chopped
1 teaspoon cumin
1 teaspoon thyme
$1/2$ teaspoon chilli pepper
25–50 g/1–2 oz self-raising flour
8 tablespoons oil

Sift the flour, salt and baking powder into a large bowl and make a well in the centre. Gradually add enough water to make a firm but not hard dough. Add all the remaining ingredients except the oil.

Lightly flour a work surface and knead the dough for about 10 minutes until it is smooth and elastic. You will probably find that the addition of the onions and olives make the dough a little sticky and I suggest you gradually knead in a little extra flour. Knead in the oil. This will not only help to give the dough its particular flavour, but will also help to soften it.

Press the dough out into an oblong about 30 cm/12 in long and 10–13 cm/4–5 in wide and about 1.2–1.8 cm/$1/2$–$3/4$ in thick and lay on a greased baking sheet. Alternatively divide the dough into 6–8 portions and press each out into a small round about 1.2–1.8 cm/$1/2$–$3/4$ in thick and arrange on greased baking sheets.

Bake in an oven preheated to 180°C, 350°F, gas mark 4 for 45–60 minutes or until the crust is golden. Remove, cool on a wire rack and serve.

torshi — pickles

Although today there are a few *torshi* sellers with donkeys found in the streets of the Middle Eastern towns, *torshi* is still sold in abundance in small, specialist shops often tucked into a corner of the local bazaar. These are fascinating establishments full of colour and flavour where — and here I vividly recall certain instances from my childhood — customers come to taste and compare before making a purchase. Large barrels are filled with different pickled vegetables, e.g. turnips, carrots, aubergines, peppers, small or large cucumbers, etc.

One day my maternal uncle took me with him to the shop of a friend of his in the Dora district of Beirut. After the initial greetings the shop owner and my uncle entered into the second phase — that of bargaining.

'How much are the cucumbers?'
'For you, 50 piasters.'
'Why for me?'
'You are a friend.'
'Cut that out. How much?'
'Alright then 45.'
'25.'
'No way.'
'Come on man, what do you take me for?'
'A good friend.'
'That's what you charge a good friend!'
'Be reasonable. It cost me 40 piasters to produce the stuff. I only use the tenderest, smallest cucumbers which, as you well know I personally select and, as you damn well know, I go all the way up the Bakka valley. . .'
'Give me a handkerchief, I can't control myself.'
'Be reasonable. I have to make a living, what with four growing children and a fifth (blessed be the Lord) on the way, my in-laws, her brother, cousins and me the only one with honourable work, and you. . .'
'We all have our problems, that is no excuse. 35 piasters is too high.'
'I didn't say 35. I said 45, are you deaf or something?'
'45? I thought you said 35, and I was upset. So it's 45 eh!'
'You don't have to buy you know.'
'You are damn right. Your's isn't the only shop.'
My uncle grabbed my hand and we tried to leave.
'Now hold on, what's the matter, we are old friends. Now come back!'
We returned.
'Taste this, feel the flavour, look how delicious it is. Here little one, you try it.'
I did.
'You like it?' he asked me.
I nodded my head.
'You see, even a child knows how delicious my torshi is.'

'What do you expect from children.'
'Be reasonable friend. Life is getting more and more expensive each day. A man has to make a living. Here, I'll throw in a bottle of rosewater.'
'25.'
'40.'
'30.'
'35.'
'Done.'
'Good!'
'Give me 10 kilos and 5 peppers and 5 cauliflowers.'
'Fine, fine. It's always good to do business with a friend who appreciates quality and flavour.'

We left laden with jars of pickles, hailed a horse-drawn cart and went home. My uncle content with himself, his friend content with his lot and I, for my part, happy to be licking at an ice-cream. Overall it had been a successful day. The ritual of buying and selling had been performed to perfection.

I have selected a few pickle recipes that are typical of the region. Most are common throughout the area, but a few are regional favourites. Everything that can be is pickled and what was once a method of preserving perishable goods has, in time, become a way of life.

betingan makbouss aubergines in olive oil

A Syrian-Lebanese speciality, the aubergines are pickled in olive oil and served as a *mezzeh*, cut lengthways.

Lemons, limes, small cucumbers and small marrows can be pickled in the same way. Keep for 3 weeks before serving.

12 or more small aubergines
5–6 tablespoons walnuts,
   coarsely crushed
2 teaspoons salt

2 tablespoons paprika
4 lemons, thickly sliced
olive oil or corn oil

Half-fill a large saucepan with water, bring to the boil, add the aubergines and simmer for 10 minutes. Drain and dry with a kitchen towel. With a knife make an incision lengthways into the middle of each aubergine, big enough to take a slice of lemon and a teaspoon of walnuts.

Mix the walnuts, salt and paprika together. Place a slice of lemon in each slit and add a teaspoon of the walnut mixture. Arrange the aubergines in large sterilized jars and completely cover with olive oil. Seal the jars and leave for at least 3 weeks. By this time the aubergines should be soft and fragrant.

lemoun makbouss lemons in olive oil

Another Syrian-Lebanese speciality. This is for pickled lemons in oil.

Use 20 lemons, scraped and sliced

Sprinkle with 6 teaspoons salt and leave to rest in a colander overnight. Arrange the slices in sterilized jars, sprinkling each layer with a little paprika — use 2-3 teaspoons paprika altogether. Completely cover with oil, seal tightly and leave for 3-4 weeks before serving.

titvash mixed pickles

This is probably the most popular form of pickling throughout the Middle East. There are numerous regional variations, especially in the choice of vegetables, but basically the ones listed below are those most commonly used. I suggest you suit your own taste. It is advisable to make a fairly large quantity of this pickle. The recipe below makes about 4.5 litres/1 gallon, but you can increase or decrease the amounts accordingly.

2 small cauliflowers, separated
   into florets
8 carrots, peeled, quartered lengthways
   and cut into 8 cm/3 in pieces
8 small cucumbers, 5-8 cm/
   2-3 in long
225 g/8 oz green beans, trimmed

6 sweet yellow peppers, quartered
   and seeded
6 small hot red peppers
6 cloves garlic, peeled and halved
6 fresh dill sprigs
1.8 litres/3 pints water
600 ml/1 pint white wine vinegar
100 g/4 oz salt

Wash the vegetables thoroughly. Pack them into large sterilized jars portioning out the garlic and dill sprigs evenly.

Place the water, vinegar and salt in a large saucepan and bring to the boil. Pour the vinegar mixture over the vegetables until completely covered. Seal tightly and store in a cool place for 6-8 weeks. Serve as a salad with all kinds of meat and vegetable dishes.

mukhalal luft pickled turnips

These are very popular with everyone, particularly Iraqis and Iranians. In this recipe the turnips acquire a beautiful pinky-red colour. They are excellent with all types of kebabs.

1.8 kg/4 lb small white turnips
2 beetroot
leaves from the top of 4–6 celery
  sticks

2 cloves garlic, or more depending
  on the number of jars used
1.8 litres/3 pints water
600 ml/1 pint white wine vinegar
8 tablespoons salt

Peel, wash and then quarter the turnips. Peel and slice the beetroot. Pack the quartered turnips into sterilized jars, arranging beetroot slices between the layers. Add some celery leaves and a clove of garlic to each jar. Place the water, vinegar and salt in a large bowl and mix well. Pour this mixture into the jars until the vegetables are completely covered. Seal the jars tightly and store for at least 4 weeks.

torshi-ye hafte-bijar pickled herbs

A unique pickle recipe from Iran where herbs, fresh, dried or pickled, are used extensively. The following list of herbs is merely a suggestion. All kinds of herbs are suitable as long as they are fresh.

Use equal amounts of:
leeks
tarragon
spinach
mint
parsley

celery
basil
beetroot leaves
dillweed
fenugreek

Pickling mixture:
coarse salt
fresh red peppers
peppercorns
dried oregano

dried marjoram
cloves garlic, peeled
black pepper
vinegar

Wash the herbs and leaves and spread out on kitchen paper to dry. When completely dry chop finely. Mix thoroughly in a large bowl and then fill sterilized jars with the herbs. Sprinkle with some salt. To each jar add half a red pepper, a few peppercorns, some oregano and marjoram, 2 or 3 cloves garlic and a little black pepper. Fill the jars to the top with vinegar and seal tightly. Store for at least 2 weeks.

torshi-ye-miveh fruit pickles

The bear has twelve dreams — and they are all about bears. — Armenian saying.

Particularly attractive is the concept of making pickles from fruits such as peaches, cherries, grapes, orange rind, dates, etc. They are kept in wine vinegar and spices, sealed in jars for at least a fortnight and then served with meat and vegetable dishes.

The masters of this kind of pickling are the Iranians and Caucasians. The method is simple and I have included several recipes under this heading as I think that with the excellent fruits now available in the West good pickles can be prepared.

torshi-ye-barg-e holoo pickled peaches

An Iranian recipe.

900 g/2 lb dried peaches
900 ml/1¹/2 pints white wine vinegar
175 g/6 oz sugar
1 teaspoon ground ginger
1 teaspoon ground coriander

2 cloves garlic, finely chopped
1 tablespoon tamarind
1 teaspoon dry mustard
1 teaspoon paprika
¹/2 teaspoon cinnamon

Place the dried peaches in a large bowl, add the vinegar and leave to soak for 2 days. Transfer to a saucepan, add the remaining ingredients and bring to the boil. Lower the heat and simmer for about 1 hour. Pour the mixture into sterilized jars making sure you distribute the peaches evenly. Seal the jars tightly and leave for at least 10 days.

torshi-ye-gilas pickled cherries

Simple and delicious, this is another masterly recipe from Iran.

450 ml/³/4 pint white wine vinegar
4 tablespoons salt
900 g/2 lb cherries, discard the
   stems and over-ripe and
   discoloured ones

4 sprigs tarragon
10 peppercorns

Place the vinegar and salt in a large saucepan and bring to the boil. Simmer for 3 minutes and then remove from the heat and leave to cool. Wash the cherries and place in sterilized jars. Pour the vinegar mixture into the jars until the cherries are completely covered. Distribute the tarragon leaves and peppercorns between the jars, seal tightly and leave for 3–4 days. Pour the vinegar mixture out of the jars. Make up a new mixture and when it is cool pour it over the cherries. Seal tightly and leave for at least 2 weeks.

khaghoghi titvash pickled grapes

This recipe is from Armenia.

1.8 kg/4 lb firm white grapes, stemmed,
   washed and with overripe
   ones discarded

1.2 litres/2 pints white wine vinegar
1 tablespoon salt

Dry the clean grapes on kitchen paper.

   Put the vinegar and salt into a saucepan, bring to the boil and simmer for 3–4 minutes. Remove from the heat and allow to cool. Pack the grapes into sterilized jars. Pour the vinegar into the jars until the grapes are completely covered. Seal the jars tightly and leave for at least 10 days.

torshi-ye-khorma pickled dates

The greatest of all pickles, this is absolutely delightful and can be served with all meats. The pride of Iranian and Iraqi picklers.

   Both sumac and tamarind can be bought from most continental and Middle Eastern stores.

75 g/3 oz sumac
225 g/8 oz dried tamarind
900 ml/1$\frac{1}{2}$ pints water
juice 1 lemon
450 g/1 lb dates, stoned

2 cloves garlic, crushed
$\frac{1}{2}$ teaspoon salt
$\frac{1}{4}$ teaspoon black pepper
$\frac{1}{4}$ teaspoon cinnamon
$\frac{1}{4}$ teaspoon nutmeg

Soak the sumac in 450 ml/$\frac{3}{4}$ pint of water in a bowl overnight. Do the same with the tamarind in another bowl. Now strain both the sumac and the tamarind through muslin and reserve the liquid. Place the liquids in a saucepan with the lemon juice and boil for 3 minutes.

   Mince or finely chop the dates and add to the boiling liquids. Add the remaining ingredients, stir well and then pour the mixture into sterilized jars and seal tightly. Use after 1 week.

desserts

To be an Arab and not have a sweet tooth is to be a Muslim and not believe in Paradise.

Most Middle Eastern desserts are very sweet — literally soaked in honey or syrup or a combination of the two. They are made and served in abundance and any occasion (birth, christening, circumcision, wedding — a hot favourite — religious festival, pilgrimage and even a funeral) is a good enough excuse for the housewives to indulge in an orgy of sweet making.

These desserts are exciting and original and most are very different from those found in the West. Their origins are older than most of the races of the Middle East today. The Ancients — Sumerians and Assyrians in particular as well as the Hittites — are known to have had a great penchant for all things sweet.

Although most of these desserts are found — in one form or another — throughout the entire region, there are some which are still local in character. A few of these I have included besides the more famed ones — the latter are the pastry-based sweets, e.g. *baklava*, *kadayifi*, etc., which have, in recent years, made their appearance in the West.

Apart from the pastry desserts I have included several *halvas* — semolina-based sweets, several fritters — the forerunners of the doughnut, fruit-and-nut-based desserts, milk-and-rice-based puddings as well as many dry biscuits and cakes.

Many of these are easy and inexpensive to make while others take more time and require more expensive and sometimes not such readily available ingredients, but you will find that these desserts are well worth the time and trouble.

pastries

baklava flaky pastry with nuts and syrup

This is perhaps the most famous Middle Eastern 'pastry' dessert, whose ownership is claimed by all — Arabs, Turks and Greeks. However, it is not mentioned in any medieval Arab manuscript and it only arrived in the Ottoman court in the late fifteenth to early sixteenth centuries after the conquests of Cilicia and Cappadocia by the Turks.

Baklava, in fact, is an Armenian sweet (*Bahk* meaning Lent, *halva* from ancient Akkadian meaning sweet). Traditionally *baklava* (*bahlawah* in Arabic) consists of forty layers of flaky pastry — one for each day of fasting — filled with almonds and walnuts and soaked in syrup. It was eaten on Easter Sunday after mass.

There are several variations of this magnificent sweet, a few of which I have included. It is easiest to use ready-made filo, but if you wish to be really authentic you can make your own (see Glossary, page 369).

1 packet (450 g/1 lb) filo pastry	Syrup
225 g/8 oz unsalted butter,	350 g/12 oz sugar
melted and with froth removed	1 tablespoon lemon juice
225 g/8 oz walnuts, chopped or	350 ml/12 fl oz water
coarsely ground	2 tablespoons rosewater

First prepare the syrup by placing the sugar, lemon juice and water in a saucepan and bringing to the boil. Lower the heat and simmer for about 10 minutes or until the syrup leaves a slightly sticky film on a spoon. Add the rosewater and set aside to cool.

Most packets of pastry have sheets 50 x 28 cm/21 x 11 in, but it is not easy to find a tin with these dimensions. I use one 30 x 20 cm/12 x 8 in and trim the sheets to make them fit. As I am loathe to waste good food I simply slip the trimmings between the sheets in such a way as to maintain an even thickness. The one important thing is that the tin must be at least 2.5 cm/1 in deep.

Grease the baking tin with a little melted butter. Lay 2 sheets of the pastry on top of each other in the tray and then dribble a tablespoon of the melted butter over the second sheet. Repeat in this way until you have 6 or 8 sheets in the tray. While you are layering the sheets try to press on them as little as possible. This ensures that air is trapped between the layers and so enables the sweet to rise. Spread half of the crushed nuts over the last sheet of pastry.

Continue with the layers of pastry and spoonfuls of butter until you have laid down a further 6 or 8 sheets. Spread the remaining nuts over the last sheet.

Continue layering the pastry with spoonfuls of melted butter dribbled over alternate sheets until you have used up all the pastry. Spoon any remaining butter over the last sheet, discarding the milky residue at the bottom of the pan. Lightly brush this butter all over the last sheet so that every bit of pastry is covered.

Cut the *baklava* into lozenge shapes using a sharp knife and taking care to press as little as possible on the actual *baklava*. Place the tin in an oven preheated to 180°C, 350°F, gas mark 4 and cook for 30 minutes.

Lower the temperature to 150°C, 300°F, gas mark 2 and cook for a further hour or until the pastry is turning a pale golden.

Set the *baklava* aside until it is warm and then pour the cold syrup all along the gaps. Set aside until completely cold. To serve first run a sharp knife along the gaps to make sure that all the layers have been completely cut through.

The quantities given here will make 24-30 pieces.

Variations

Below are several suggestions for alternative fillings. In each case prepare the *baklava* as above and simply substitute the filling of your choice.

almond filling

225 g/8 oz almonds, chopped, blanched

4–5 tablespoons caster sugar
1 teaspoon ground cinnamon

coconut filling A Turkish favourite.

225 g/8 oz dessicated coconut
6–7 tablespoons caster sugar

2 teaspoons vanilla essence
2–3 tablespoons water

fruit filling Another popular Turkish-Armenian filling. You can use many fruits such as apples, cherries, oranges, pumpkin, etc.

350 g/12 oz apples, peeled and grated
225 g/8 oz caster sugar

1 teaspoon ground cinnamon

Mix the grated apples and sugar together, put them in a muslin bag and squeeze out as much juice as possible.

Empty the mixture into a bowl, stir in the cinnamon and proceed with the recipe.

pumpkin and walnut filling

225 g/8 oz pumpkin, peeled and grated
225 g/8 oz caster sugar

100 g/4 oz walnuts, chopped
1 tablespoon rosewater

Mix together and proceed as with the *baklava* recipe.

souarzeh 'bird's nest' pastries

A light, delicate pastry from the Aleppo region of Northern Syria — also popular in Southern Turkey where it is known as *Anteb bulbulu* — Anteb nightingale.

10 sheets filo pastry

225 g/8 oz unsalted butter, melted

Syrup
450 g/1 lb sugar
450 ml/3/4 pint water
1 tablespoon lemon juice

Garnish
6–7 tablespoons pistachio nuts,
 very finely chopped

Lay the sheets of pastry out flat, on top of each other, on a work top. Each sheet is approximately 50 x 28 cm/21 x 11 in. Mark the top one into 6 portions each about 18 x 13 cm/7 x 5^1/$_2$ in and then cut down through all 10 sheets. Stack the 60 pieces of pastry on top of each other and cover with a damp cloth to prevent them drying out.

Remove 1 piece of pastry and brush the top all over with a little melted butter. Roll up the pastry as you would a cigarette so that you have a roll 13 cm/5^1/$_2$ in long. Carefully bend the roll into a circle and squeeze the two ends of the pastry together. They will stick easily if you dampen your fingers first. Repeat with all the remaining pieces of pastry.

Arrange on lightly greased baking trays about 1.2 cm/^{1}/$_2$ in apart and brush the outer surfaces of the circles with butter. Place in an oven preheated to 160°C, 325°F, gas mark 3 and bake for 20–25 minutes or until they are just turning a light golden colour. While they are cooking prepare the syrup by placing the sugar, water and lemon juice in a saucepan and bringing to the boil. Boil quite vigorously for about 5 minutes and then remove from the heat. When the *souarzeh* are cooked place them in a shallow dish, pour the boiling syrup over them and leave for 2 hours to cool. Lift from the syrup and arrange the pastries on a large serving plate. Dust with the finely chopped pistachios.

Makes 60 pastries.

madig almond fingers

Another popular way of using filo pastry is to fill the sheets with nuts and then roll up like cigars. There are countless variations of this sweet. Arabs call it 'Zeinab's fingers' and the Turks *vezir parmagi*.

These are simple to prepare and will keep for several days. They make an ideal after dinner dessert.

100 g/4 oz unsalted butter

1 packet (450 g/1 lb) filo pastry

Filling
225 g/8 oz almonds, coarsely ground
2 teaspoons cinnamon
2 teaspoons sugar

Syrup
450 g/1 lb sugar
350 ml/12 fl oz water
juice 1 lemon
2 tablespoons rosewater

First prepare the syrup by placing the sugar, water and lemon juice in a saucepan and bringing to the boil. Lower the heat and simmer until the syrup leaves a sticky film on a spoon. Add the rosewater and set aside to cool.

Prepare the filling by mixing together the almonds, cinnamon and sugar.

Melt the butter in a small pan over a low heat. Brush a baking sheet with a little of the melted butter.

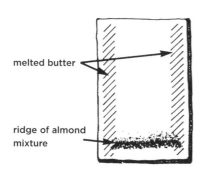

melted butter

ridge of almond mixture

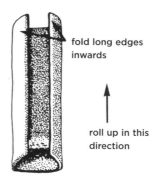

fold long edges inwards

roll up in this direction

Open out the filo pastry and cut along the fold so that each sheet is divided into 2 rectangles. While you are using each piece of pastry keep the others covered as they dry out quickly. Lay a rectangle of pastry on a work top, short side nearest you, and brush the 2 long edges with butter. Arrange a teaspoon of the almond mixture in a ridge across the short edge nearest you. Fold the 2 long edges inwards over the edges of the almond mixture and then roll up to form a cigar shape.

Place each roll on the baking sheet, opening underneath. Brush them all with any remaining melted butter. Cook in an oven preheated to 190°C, 375°F, gas mark 5 for 20–30 minutes or until golden. Dip the hot rolls into the cool syrup and then arrange them on a serving dish.

Makes about 40 pastries.

kunafeh shredded pastry with nuts

Kunafeh swimming in butter,
Bearded with right vermicelli,
God has not given my belly
Half of the words it would utter
Of kunafeh's sweetness
And syrup's sweetness.
Kunafeh lies on the table
Isled in a sweet brown oil,
Would I not wonder and toil
Seventy years to be able
To eat in Paradise
Kunafeh's subtleties?
                    (*The Book of 1001 Nights*)

This sweet is known as *kadayif* to Greeks and Turks, but this is a misnomer as *ataif* is a pancake and very Persian in origin.

I remember my grandfather preparing these shredded pastries on Christmas and New Year's Eve. He would make a batter from flour and water and pass it through a sieve on to a hot metal sheet heated by charcoal. The dough would set in seconds and we children would sweep it to one side straight into an earthenware bowl.

Kunafeh pastry looks like vermicelli or 'shredded wheat' and it is sold in 450 g/ 1 lb bags under the name of *kadayifi filo*. There are many variations of this dessert. The first one below is a family favourite — indeed it is the very same my grandfather used to prepare.

1 packet *kunafeh* or *kadayifi* pastry
— usually 450 g/1 lb

350 g/12 oz unsalted butter, melted
and with froth removed

Filling
175 g/6 oz walnuts, chopped or
coarsely ground
2 tablespoons sugar
2 tablespoons cinnamon

Syrup
350 g/12 oz sugar
350 ml/12 fl oz water
juice 1 lemon
2 tablespoons rosewater

First prepare the syrup by placing the sugar, water and lemon juice into a saucepan and bringing to the boil. Lower the heat and simmer until the syrup begins to leave a film on the back of a spoon. Add the rosewater and set aside to cool.

Lightly brush a baking tin, about 30 x 23 cm/12 x 9 in or about 25 cm/10 in in diameter and at least 2.5 cm/1 in deep, with a little of the melted butter. Put the pastry into a large bowl and gently ease apart the strands without breaking them. Remove any hard nodules of pastry which you may find in some brands. Pour three-quarters of the melted butter into the bowl and gently rub all the strands between your fingers until they are all well-coated with the butter. Divide the pastry into 2 equal parts and spread one part evenly over the base of the tin. Mix the filling ingredients together and spread evenly over the pastry, pressing down firmly. Arrange the remaining pastry evenly over the top, tuck in any strands hanging over the sides and press the pastry down firmly. Spoon the remaining melted butter evenly over the top, discarding the white residue in the bottom of the pan. Place in an oven preheated to 180°C, 350°F, gas mark 4 and cook for 30 minutes. Lower the heat to 150°C, 300°F, gas mark 2 and cook for a further 1½ hours or until golden.

Remove from the oven and pour the syrup slowly over the *kunafeh*, covering as much of the surface as possible. Cover with silver foil, place a large board over the top and add a heavy weight in order to flatten the *kunafeh*. Leave to cool and then cut into squares or lozenges 3.8–5 cm/1½–2 in in size.

Makes 24–30 pieces.

Variations

kaymakli tel-kadayif

This is a popular Turkish version where the shredded pastry has a 'cream' filling made of milk and semolina. This is a light and delicious sweet.

1 packet (450 g/1 lb) *kunafeh* pastry

225 g/8 oz unsalted butter, melted
    and with froth removed

Filling
450 ml/¾ pint milk
25 g/1 oz fine semolina or
    25 g/1 oz ground rice
1 tablespoon rosewater

Syrup
350 g/12 oz sugar
350 ml/12 fl oz water
juice 1 lemon
1 tablespoon rosewater

Prepare the syrup as for *kunafeh* above. Prepare the filling by first bringing the milk to the boil in a saucepan. Add the semolina and rosewater and simmer for 5 minutes, stirring constantly, until the mixture thickens. Remove from the heat and set aside to cool.

Put the pastry into a large bowl and gently ease apart the strands without breaking them. If you squeeze portions between the palms of your hands it will make this easier. Pour the melted butter into the bowl, discarding the milky residue at the bottom of the pan. Gently run all the strands between your fingers until they are all well coated with the butter. Lightly grease a baking tin about 30 x 23 cm/12 x 9 in or about 25 cm/10 in in diameter and at least 2.5 cm/1 in deep. Spread half the pastry over the bottom of the tin.

Pour the filling over the pastry and spread it out evenly with the back of a spoon. Arrange the remaining pastry evenly over the filling. Press down lightly and tuck in any loose strands. Place in an oven preheated to 180°C, 350°F, gas mark 4 and cook for 45 minutes or 1 hour until golden.

Remove and immediately pour the cold syrup evenly over the top. Cover with silver foil, place a board over the sweet and top with a heavy weight in order to compress the sweet. Set aside to cool and then cut into squares or lozenge shapes.

kunafeh-bi-jibn

A speciality of Damascus where the shredded pastry is filled with a soft and unsalted cheese. You can either pour the syrup over the *kunafeh* when it is removed from the oven or serve it separately.

1 packet (450 g/1 lb) *kunafeh* pastry

225 g/8 oz unsalted butter, melted and with the froth removed

Filling
350 g/12 oz soft, unsalted cheese, e.g. ricotta, akkawe or mizithra, grated
1 tablespoon sugar
grated rind 1 lemon
1 tablespoon rosewater

Syrup
350 g/12 oz sugar
350 ml/12 fl oz water
juice 1 lemon
2 tablespoons rosewater

Prepare the syrup as with *kunafeh* on page 303, and set aside to cool.

To prepare the filling place the grated cheese in a bowl with the sugar, lemon rind and rosewater and beat with a wooden spoon until it is well blended and soft.

Prepare the pastry and baking tin as described in the second paragraph of instructions in *kaymakli tel-kadayif* on page 304. Spread the cheese mixture evenly over the pastry. Top evenly with the remaining pastry, press down lightly and tuck in any loose strands. Place in an oven preheated to 180°C, 350°F, gas mark 4 and cook for 45 minutes to 1 hour or until golden.

Remove and pour the cold syrup immediately over the *kunafeh* or set aside to cool without the syrup. Cover with foil, place a board over the top of the sweet and top with a heavy weight in order to compress the sweet. When cold cut into squares or lozenge shapes and serve with the syrup if you haven't already soaked the sweet in it.

balurieh white kunafeh

Also known as the 'Queen of *Kunafehs*', *baluriehs* are a Syrian speciality, milk-white in appearance, tightly packed and stuffed with pistachios.

Keep the oven door slightly ajar to achieve the whitish appearance. Like all *baklava* or *kunafeh* pastries these *balurieh* will keep for several days.

This is my favourite pastry. Serve with cream.

450 g/1 lb *kunafeh* filo

150 g/5 oz unsalted butter, melted and skimmed
1 tablespoon clear honey

Filling
175 g/6 oz pistachio nuts, coarsely chopped
40 g/1¹/2 oz caster sugar
¹/2 tablespoon cinnamon

Syrup
450 g/1 lb sugar
450 ml/³/4 pint water
1 tablespoon lemon juice

Garnish 2 tablespoons pistachio nuts, very finely chopped

Pour the melted butter into a bowl, discarding the milky substance in the bottom of the pan, and place the bowl in the refrigerator until the butter is semi-solid. Remove from the fridge, add the honey and whisk until the mixture begins to foam. Pour the mixture into a baking tray about 30 x 20 cm/12 x 8 in and at least 2.5 cm/1 in deep.

Open up the packet of pastry and lay it out on a clean work top. In order to loosen the strands I suggest that you divide the pastry into 4 portions and squeeze each portion between the palms of your hands — as though you are making a snowball — for about 2 minutes. Take 2 sections of the pastry and, without breaking the strands, gently ease the pastry out spreading it over the bottom of the tray.

Mix the filling ingredients together in a bowl. Spread this filling evenly over the pastry in the tray. Gently ease apart the 2 remaining portions of pastry and arrange them evenly over the filling. Press the pastry down firmly and tuck in any strands of pastry hanging over the edge of the tray. Place in an oven preheated to 150°C, 300°F, gas mark 2 and bake for 20 minutes. Keep the door ajar — this will prevent the *balurieh* from changing colour.

Meanwhile, prepare the syrup by placing the sugar, water and lemon juice in a saucepan and bringing to the boil quite vigorously for 5 minutes and then remove from the heat.

After the *balurieh* has been cooking for 20 minutes take it from the oven. Very carefully lift the tray to an angle and pour the butter and honey mixture into a bowl.

Now completely cover the sweet with another flat surface such as a kitchen board or the back of another tray and turn the *balurieh* over on to this surface. Very gently and carefully slide the sweet — now bottom side up — back into the tin. Return to the oven and, still keeping the door open, cook for a further 20 minutes. Remove from the oven. Pour the boiling syrup evenly over the surface of the sweet. In order to get the tight and compact appearance of the sweet put an empty tray over it and hold it down with some kind of heavy weight while the sweet cools.

When cold cut into 5 cm/1½ in squares. Sprinkle some of the very finely chopped pistachio nuts over each square and serve.

Makes 24–30 pieces.

kunafeh mabrouma

rolled kunafeh with pistachios

These *kunafeh* (*burma* in Turkish) are shaped in whirls and then cut into 5–7 cm/2–3 in pieces. A fairly dry, but rich sweet with the green pistachios contrasting colourfully with the golden brown of the pastry.

1 packet (450 g/1 lb) *kunafeh* or
    kadayifi pastry
350 g/12 oz unsalted butter,
    melted and with froth removed

Filling
350 g/12 oz whole pistachio nuts, shelled
75 g/3 oz almonds, finely chopped
3 tablespoons sugar

Syrup
350 g/12 oz sugar
350 ml/12 fl oz water

juice 1 lemon
1 tablespoon orange blossom water

Prepare the syrup by placing the sugar, water and lemon juice in a saucepan and bringing to the boil. Lower the heat and simmer until the syrup begins to leave a sticky film on a spoon. Remove from the heat, stir in the orange blossom water and set aside.

Put the pastry into a large bowl and gently ease apart the strands without breaking them. Divide the pastry into 3 portions. Take one of the portions and lay it out flat on a clean work top. Flatten it as much as possible with your hands until it is about 0.6–1.2 cm/¼–½ in thick and then shape it into an oblong approximately 30 x 15 cm/12 x 6 in. With a pastry brush, brush the surface with some of the melted butter.

Take a flat stick about 45 cm/18 in long and approximately 2.5 cm/1 in wide and lay it diagonally across the flattened pastry. Mix the filling ingredients together and then lay a third of the mixture evenly along the stick. Roll the strands of dough around the stick as tightly as possible. Carefully slide the stick out leaving the filling inside. Brush some melted butter all over the roll of pastry. Prepare the other portions of pastry in the same way.

Lightly butter a baking tray about 30 x 20 cm/12 x 8 in. Arrange the 3 pastry rolls in the tray and pour any remaining butter evenly over the rolls, taking care to discard the milky residue. Cook in an oven preheated to 180°C, 350°F, gas mark 4 for 30 minutes, then lower the temperature to 150°C, 300°F, gas mark 2 and cook for a further 1½ hours until the *kunafeh* is golden. Remove from the oven and pour the cold syrup evenly over the rolls, turning each one so that it is covered all over with the syrup. Leave to cool and then cut, at a slant, each roll into 5–7.5 cm/2–3 in long pieces.

Makes 12–15 pieces.

halawiyat semolina sweets

This section comprises sweets made with ground rice, semolina and cous-cous — each with its own flavourings, textures and colours.

These cream puddings are popular throughout the region, but more so with the Arabic speaking people of Egypt, Syria, Iraq, Lebanon and Palestine.

One of the most popular *halawahs* is called *basbousa* in Egypt and Lebanon. It is a semolina-based sweet to which nuts, spices and essences are added. It is then baked in the oven, cut into squares or lozenge shapes and soaked in syrup.

A typical *basbousa* is the recipe below made with milk, semolina and coconut.

basbousa-bil-joz el hindi

halva with coconut

50 g/2 oz plain flour
1 teaspoon baking powder
350 g/12 oz semolina
225 g/8 oz caster sugar
50 g/2 oz dessicated coconut

100 g/4 oz unsalted butter, melted
225 ml/8 fl oz milk
1 teaspoon vanilla essence
$1^1/2$ teaspoons cinnamon

Syrup
225 g/8 oz sugar
150 ml/$^1/_4$ pint water

1 tablespoon lemon juice

First prepare the syrup by placing the sugar, water and lemon juice in a saucepan and bringing to the boil. Simmer for 6–8 minutes or until the syrup has thickened. Remove from the heat and then cool and refrigerate.

Sieve the flour and baking powder into a large bowl. Add the semolina, sugar and coconut and mix well. Pour in the melted butter, milk and vanilla essence and stir until completely mixed. Stir in 1 teaspoon of the cinnamon. Spoon this mixture into a greased tin about 28 x 18 cm/11 x 7 in so that it is about 1.2 cm/$^1/_2$ in thick. Bake in an oven preheated to 160°C, 325°F, gas mark 3 for about 30–40 minutes until the top is crisp and golden brown. Remove from the oven and sprinkle the remaining cinnamon over the top. Cut into lozenge shapes and quickly pour the cold syrup evenly over the *basbousa*. Serve hot or cold, with a little double cream if liked.

Makes 20–24 pieces.

imrig khavitz semolina halva

An Armenian *halva* which is also a personal favourite.

Syrup
200 ml/1/3 pint water
75 g/3 oz sugar

1 tablespoon rosewater

40 g/1 1/2 oz butter
75 g/3 oz fine semolina
1 tablespoon pine kernels

1 tablespoon raisins
1 tablespoon almonds, blanched
1 tablespoon cinnamon

First prepare the syrup by placing the water and sugar in a small saucepan and bringing to the boil. Lower the heat and simmer for about 10 minutes or until the syrup coats the back of a spoon. Remove from the heat, stir in the rosewater and set aside to cool.

Melt the butter in a saucepan, add the semolina and stir well. Cook over a medium heat for several minutes, stirring constantly, until the semolina has slightly browned. Add half the pine kernels, the raisins and almonds and cinnamon, and stir well. Gradually pour in the syrup, stirring constantly. Cook for about 5 more minutes until the syrup is absorbed and the mixture has thickened. Remove from the heat and allow to cool for about 5 minutes. Now scoop a tablespoon of the mixture into the palm of your hand, close your fingers around it, press tightly and then place on a serving plate. Repeat until all the *halva* is thus arranged.

Sprinkle the remaining cinnamon over the *halva* and stick one pine kernel into each piece. Serve warm with tea or coffee.

One day Boloz Mugush woke up early, 'Good morning wife,' he said. 'I have this terrible craving for imrig khavitz. Make some for lunch, there's a good wife.'

She made a large quantity filled with raisins, almonds and pine kernels. After work Boloz Mugush returned home, took his shoes off, sat on the verandah and ate — nearly all of it.

That night, when the wife had counted her last sheep, he woke her up.

'What's up?'

'I have just had a thunderously fantastic thought.'

'What is it?'

'First bring me the rest of the khavitz and I will tell you.'

She got up, went to the kitchen and returned with the imrig khavitz. He ate, splurging and licking his fingers and lips.

'Well," said the wife, 'what was your brilliant thought? Come on man, tell me, for I'll never be able to sleep otherwise.'

Boloz Mugush stroked his belly. 'The thought,' he said, 'was this — never go to sleep without having finished all the imrigi khavitz that has been made during that day.'

revani semolina cake

This is a Turkish speciality that is also popular throughout the Balkans. It is made of semolina, eggs and nuts and is soaked in syrup. The blanched almonds can be substituted with equal amounts of chopped walnuts or pistachios or hazelnuts. There are countless variations. Grated orange or lemon rind is often added to give the cake a fruity flavour.

Revani can be served warm, but it is at its best cold with *kaymak* or whipped or clotted cream.

6 large eggs, separated
225 g/8 oz sugar
225 g/8 oz semolina
1 teaspoon baking powder

2 tablespoons blanched almonds,
 finely chopped
2 tablespoons brandy
pinch salt

Syrup
350 g/12 oz sugar
600 ml/1 pint water

1 stick cinnamon 7.5–10 cm/3–4 in long

Place the egg yoks in a large bowl, add the sugar and beat until smooth and light in colour. Add the semolina, baking powder and almonds and stir thoroughly. Stir in the brandy.

In another bowl beat the egg whites until stiff. Add the salt and whisk a little longer until the egg whites stand up in peaks. Fold the egg whites gently into the semolina mixture.

Grease a cake tin approx 25 x 25 x 5 cm/10 x 10 x 2 in, add the cake mixture and smooth over. Place in an oven preheated to 180°C, 350°F, gas mark 4 and bake for 30–40 minutes or until golden.

Meanwhile, prepare the syrup by placing the sugar, water and cinnamon stick in a small saucepan and bringing to the boil. Reduce heat, simmer for 15 minutes then remove from heat and set aside. When the cake is cooked remove it from the oven and spoon the syrup over it. Use enough syrup to be easily absorbed, but do not make the cake too soggy. Leave to cool and then refrigerate. Before serving cut into 50 cm/2 in squares. This cake can be eaten by itself or with cream.

Makes 25 pieces.

haytaliah floating scented pudding

'She moves like a *balouza* and floats in the air like *haytaliah*.' — Compliment paid to belly dancers whose tummies are likened to the jelly-like movement of the sweet.

One of the most beautiful puddings in the world and a true Arab classic. *Haytaliah* are small squares of cornflour pudding floating in a scented syrup with raisins, almonds, pistachios and a few rose petals to give an attractive touch of colour.

A must during all Muslim festivals. Huge bowls of this pudding adorn all delicatessens and homes. It is particularly loved by children.

To prepare this sweet you first have to make the pudding which is called *balouza*. *Balouza* can be eaten on its own, chilled and garnished with chopped pistachios, but the sweet becomes a classic when served as a *haytaliah*.

Balouza

100 g/4 oz cornflour
1.8 litres/3 pints water
275 g/10 oz sugar

100 ml/4 fl oz orange blossom water
  or rosewater
50 g/2 oz pistachios, chopped or
  almonds, chopped, blanched

Garnish **1 teaspoon cinnamon**

Syrup

1.2 litres/2 pints water, cold
100 g/4 oz sugar
6 tablespoons rosewater (or more
  depending on taste)
100 g/4 oz raisins

2 tablespoons pistachio nuts, halved
seeds 1 small pomegranate
a few rose petals, washed and dried
ice cubes

Place the cornflour in a large saucepan and add about 300 ml/½ pint of the water. Stir in the rest of the water and the sugar and stir over a low heat until the sugar dissolves. Bring to the boil, stirring constantly, then lower the heat to a minimum and simmer for about 5 to 10 minutes or until the mixture thickens and coats the back of a spoon. Stir occasionally to prevent burning. Stir in the orange blossom water and cook for a further 2 minutes. Add the chopped nuts and stir thoroughly. Remove from the heat and leave to cool for 2 minutes. If you are going to serve it by itself then pour into glass bowls and chill for several hours. Before serving sprinkle with a little cinnamon.

If making *haytaliah* pour the *balouza* into a square or rectangular baking tray moistened with cold water and even it out with the back of a spoon. The *balouza* should not be thicker than 2.5 cm/1 in. Cool for 15 minutes and then refrigerate for several hours. Remove from the fridge and then cut into 2.5 cm/1 in squares.

Now prepare the syrup by mixing the water and sugar in a large bowl and stirring until the sugar dissolves. Add the rosewater, raisins, pistachio nuts, pomegranate seeds and stir well. Pour into a large serving dish, add a few rose petals and drop in squares of *balouza* and some ice cubes. Serves about 10 people.

mamounia aleppan halva

This *halva* — named after a famed Arab Caliph Al-Mamun (813–833) — is a speciality of Aleppo, Syria.

Mamounia is eaten daily for breakfast, is highly recommended to women in labour and is generally distributed to the poor and the weak. A Syrian old wives tale claimed 'A bowl of *mamounia* a day will keep malaria, typhoid, consumption, etc. etc. away,' — not forgetting the great bogey *Sheytan* (the Devil). Not being very superstitious I would like to say that I eat it because I like it!

This is a family recipe. Some people like to pour *kaymak* or double cream over it, but I prefer it as it comes — warm and plain.

100 g/4 oz unsalted butter
100 g/4 oz semolina
1 teaspoon ground cinnamon

Syrup
600 ml/1 pint water
175 g/6 oz sugar
1 tablespoon lemon juice

First prepare the syrup by placing the water, sugar and lemon juice in a saucepan and bringing to the boil. Lower the heat and simmer for 10 minutes, then remove from the heat and set aside.

Melt the butter in a large saucepan. Add the semolina and fry, stirring constantly, for about 5 minutes or until the mixture becomes crumbly in appearance. Pour in the syrup and mix thoroughly with a wooden spoon. Cook for a further 2–3 minutes. Remove from the heat and set aside for 12–15 minutes. Spoon into a serving bowl, sprinkle with the cinnamon and serve while still warm.

mahlebieh almond cream pudding

The most popular of all Middle Eastern rice puddings, *mahlebieh* (Arabic meaning 'with milk') should be served chilled. It is often decorated with chopped pistachio nuts, pomegranate seeds and/or a mixture of chopped almonds with honey-based syrup scented with orange blossom water.

There are many variations. A particularly tasty one, which I have included below, is flavoured with mastica (gum mastic) and pistachios. It is called *sakiz muhallebisi* and is from Turkey. This recipe for *mahlebieh* is a family one which my mother always prepared for Christmas.

100 g/4 oz ground rice
2 level tablespoons cornflour
1.2 litres/2 pints milk
8 tablespoons sugar

2 tablespoons orange blossom water
    or rosewater or a mixture of the two
1/4 teaspoon grated nutmeg
100 g/4 oz ground almonds

Garnish 1 small pomegranate, seeded

2 tablespoons pistachio nuts, chopped

In a large bowl mix together the ground rice and cornflour. Add about 10 tablespoons of the cold milk and stir until you have a smooth paste.

Bring the rest of the milk to the boil in a large saucepan. Add the sugar and stir until it is dissolved. Slowly pour the hot milk on to the rice paste, stirring constantly. Pour the mixture back into the saucepan and cook over a low heat, stirring constantly, until the mixture thickens. Stir in the orange blossom water or rosewater and the nutmeg and cook for a further 3–4 minutes, stirring constantly. Remove from the heat and stir in the almonds. Pour into a serving bowl, leave to cool and then place in the refrigerator to chill. Before serving decorate with the pomegranate seeds and pistachio nuts.

Variations

sakiz muhallebisi

Prepare as with *mahlebieh* and when it is cooked, remove from the heat and stir in 100g/4 oz unsalted, halved pistachio nuts and 1 teaspoon powdered mastica with the ground almonds. When chilled decorate with a few pistachio nuts and sprinkle all over with 1 teaspoon ground ginger.

Ground almonds can be substituted by ground walnuts or hazelnuts or desiccated coconut.

In Turkey 2 tablespoons powdered coffee or cocoa are often added to give colour and variation of flavour.

gatnabour armenian rice pudding

A personal favourite. Traditionally served to visitors and well-wishers on the birth of a son. When I asked my mother what people served on the birth of a daughter, she gesticulated with her hands, shrugged her shoulders and said, 'Oh, a glass of orangeade or something like that.'

This is a magnificent dessert, highly recommended by all who have tasted it.

75 g/3 oz round grained rice
1.2 litres/2 pints milk
peel of 1 lemon
100 g/4 oz sultanas
100 g/4 oz sugar

2 tablespoons vanilla essence
50 g/2 oz split almonds, toasted
    under a hot grill until golden
white rum or any other favourite
    flavouring, to taste

Wash the rice under cold running water. Place the rice in a large saucepan with 600 ml/1 pint of the milk and the lemon peel. Bring to the boil, lower the heat and then simmer very gently until the rice is tender and the milk absorbed. You may need to add a little more milk and stir occasionally to prevent sticking. Stir in the sultanas and simmer for a few more minutes. Remove from the heat and stir in the sugar, vanilla essence and almonds. If the mixture is very thick stir in a little more milk. Place in the refrigerator to chill.

When ready to serve remove the lemon peel, add more milk if you like to make the consistency you prefer and then flavour with the rum. Spoon into a serving dish and serve.

Serves 6–8 people.

Variations

There are inumerable rice-based puddings in the Middle East starting with the simplest *roz-bil-halib* (rice with milk) of the Arab villages. There is *kishkel fukhara* (poor man's sweet) similar to the Turkish *sakiz muhallebisi* except that the powdered mastic is tied in a small muslin bag and removed after cooking — for further use no doubt — hence the name of the sweet as mastic is expensive. The Iranian *shir berenj* (sweet rice) includes 2 teaspoons ground cardamom, 1 teaspoon cinnamon and is served with honey; while *shol-e-zard* (Saffron pudding), as the name suggests, includes 1 teaspoon powdered saffron to give that golden colour for which it is justly famed.

A very interesting variation *meghli*, from Syria-Lebanon, is also traditionally served on the birth of a son and has a unique aroma of caraway, fennel and aniseed. I do not know what is served on the birth of a daughter, but I suggest that this delicious pudding should be prepared.

aşure anatolian vegetable and rice pudding

This unusual rice pudding is prepared with great ceremony on the tenth day of the month of *Muhareem* (late October) which is also called the month of *Aşura*. By tradition vast quantities are made and distributed among neighbours, friends, relatives and the poor.

One of the oldest surviving recipes that has come down to us, according to tradition, from our mutual ancestor — Noah. It was his wife, daughters and daughters-in-law who created this pudding by accident, so we are told, on their last day in the Ark when they used up all the remaining ingredients and created — it is written on the wings of time — this classic Anatolian dish. Some people purée the rice after it has been cooked and the dish is then called *beyaz asure* (white aşure). Traditionally it is made with the wheat *bugday*, but this is not readily available outside Anatolia and I suggest you substitute it with large burghul.

50 g/2 oz haricot beans, soaked
   overnight in cold water
50 g/2 oz chickpeas, soaked
   overnight in cold water
50 g/2 oz large burghul
50 g/2 oz long grain rice
900 ml/1¹/₂ pints water or milk
150 ml/¹/₄ pint milk
225 g/8 oz sugar

50 g/2 oz sultanas
4 dried figs, chopped
4 dried apricots, chopped
2 tablespoons rosewater
40 g/1¹/₂ oz walnuts, coarsely chopped
25 g/1 oz pine kernels
25 g/1 oz pistachio nuts, halved
25 g/1 oz butter

Place the haricot beans and chickpeas in separate pans with their soaking water, bring each to the boil and then simmer until tender. Add more water if necessary and remove any scum that appears on the surface. The chickpeas will take longer than the beans.

Rinse the burghul and rice and place in a saucepan with the water or milk. Bring to the boil, lower the heat and then simmer for 20–30 minutes.

When tender strain the beans and chickpeas and add to the rice pan together with the milk and simmer for a further 10 minutes. Add the sugar, sultanas, figs, apricots and rosewater, stir thoroughly and simmer for another 10 minutes. Stir in the nuts and butter. By now the mixture should resemble thick porridge. If you think it is still a little thin then simmer for a few more minutes. Pour the *aşure* into individual bowls or a decorative serving dish and decorate, making patterns with some combination of the following: sultanas, ground cinnamon, pomegranate seeds, chopped blanched almonds, halved walnuts, etc.

Serves 6–8 people.

tavuk goğsu chicken breast pudding

A most unusual pudding made with chicken, milk and cream and served chilled. A truly magnificent sweet of the Ottoman period.

1 chicken breast	**1/4 teaspoon salt**
enough water or dry white wine to	**175 g/6 oz sugar**
cover the chicken	**3 tablespoons ground rice**
900 ml/1 1/2 pints milk	**2 tablespoons cornflour**
300 ml/1/2 pint single cream	

Garnish **1 teaspoon ground cinnamon**

Place the chicken breast in a saucepan and add enough water or dry white wine to cover by 1.2 cm/1/2 in. Bring to the boil and then simmer until almost tender. Drain the chicken and then finely shred it or pass it through a mincer. Return the meat to a saucepan, add sufficient water to cover by 2.5 cm/1 in and bring quickly to the boil. With a slotted spoon remove any fatty residue that builds up on the surface. Drain, add fresh water and bring to the boil again. Again remove any residue and then drain and set aside.

Put the milk, cream, salt and sugar in a saucepan and bring slowly to the boil, stirring constantly until the sugar has dissolved. Place the ground rice and cornflour in a small bowl and mix to a smooth paste with a little cold water. Add this mixture to the boiling milk and continue cooking, stirring constantly, until the mixture thickens. Add the chicken, stir and cook over a very low heat for a few minutes, stirring frequently. Pour into individual bowls, sprinkle with the cinnamon and serve.

doughnuts and pancakes

awamyat epiphany doughnuts

These doughnut balls are popular throughout the Middle East and were known in the region long before they were introduced into Europe.

They are called *lokma* in Turkey, *zalabyeh* in Egypt, *lokumades* in Greece and *jalabi* in Iran. There are many variations. Some of the better known ones are *luqumatal quadi* — sweet tongue of the judge; *dilberdudagi* — sweet lips doughnuts and *gobegi* — lady's navel fritters. All very descriptive!

Awamyat are prepared traditionally on the morning of Epiphany by the Christians of Syria and Lebanon and the recipe below is a simple family one.

'The *zalabyeh* is forbidden to the dogs,' say the Egyptians since these doughnuts were so highly regarded that non-muslims 'dogs' and the poorer classes were unworthy of them.

Syrup

450 g/1 lb sugar	1 tablespoon rosewater
450 ml/3/4 pint water	1 tablespoon orange blossom water
1 tablespoon lemon juice	

Dough

1/2 teaspoon fresh yeast or	oil for frying
1 teaspoon dried yeast	450 g/1 lb plain flour
1 teaspoon sugar	1/2 teaspoon salt
300 ml/1/2 pint water	300 ml/1/2 pint milk

Garnish 1 tablespoon cinnamon

First make the syrup by placing the sugar, water and lemon juice in a saucepan and bringing to the boil. Lower the heat and simmer for about 10 minutes or until it is slightly sticky and just coats the back of a spoon. Remove from the heat, stir in the rosewater and orange blossom water and set aside.

Meanwhile, place the yeast and sugar in a small bowl and dissolve in a little of the water, warmed, taken from the 150 ml/1/2 pint. Set aside for about 10 minutes or until the mixture begins to froth.

Sift the flour and salt into a large bowl and make a well in the centre. Pour the rest of the water and the milk into the yeast mixture and beat thoroughly. Gradually add this liquid mixture to the flour and gradually beat the flour in until the dough is soft and smooth, but not quite a liquid. Cover and leave to rise in a warm place for 1 hour. Beat the dough at least once more and leave to rest again. The final dough should be a well fermented, sponge-like mixture.

Pour about 5 cm/2 in oil into a large, deep saucepan and heat through until hot.

When the dough is ready wet a teaspoon, take a teaspoonful of the mixture and drop it into the oil. Another method is to take up some of the dough in one hand and gently squeeze it up between thumb and forefinger to form small walnut-sized balls. Fry a few at a time. The balls will rise to the surface shaped like walnuts. Turn them over and remove when crisp, golden all over and cooked through. Drain on kitchen paper. Dip them immediately into the cold syrup and lift out with a slotted spoon. When they are all cooked arrange them in a pyramid shape on a large plate. Sprinkle with the cinnamon and serve while still warm.

Serves 6–8 people.

mushabbak patterned doughnuts

These doughnuts are sold throughout the bazaars by street vendors. They are traditionally patterned in never ending circles, and are often coloured red, golden or pink.

The dough must be soft enough to enable the doughnut to retain much of the syrup.

Syrup **see awamyat above**

Dough **see awamyat above**

Food colouring of your choice   **oil for frying**

To prepare the dough and syrup follow the instructions for *awamyat* to the last paragraph.

While the oil is heating decide what colours you are going to use and divide the dough into the requisite number of portions. Add a little different food colouring to each portion and beat well. By now the oil should be hot.

Spoon one of the coloured portions into a piping bag with a 0.6 cm/¼ in nozzle and slowly squeeze a thin stream into the oil. You can make any patterns of your choice. Traditional ones are: (a) intertwining circles; (b) a circle filled with an intertwining design; (c) names etc. Fry them until golden and then remove with a slotted spoon and drain on kitchen paper. Dip immediately into the cold syrup, remove with a slotted spoon and arrange decoratively on a serving plate.

Repeat with the remaining coloured portions of dough, taking care to rinse out the bag when changing colour. Serve when cold as a dessert or with coffee.

kaygana anatolian sweet crêpes

These thin batter pancakes, made of eggs, milk and flour, are fried on both sides and served hot. Anatolian-style crêpes have been made by the peasants for centuries and although they can be savoury as well as sweet, it is the latter which is the most popular.

I have given below the basic dough recipe, as well as the recipe for apricot *kaygana*, but there is no reason why you cannot experiment with apples, strawberries, pistachios and other fruits and nuts or mixtures of the two.

In the villages of Turkey and Armenia these crêpes are made much thicker than their wafer-thin cousins in Europe, but I suggest you try and make them as thin as possible.

Batter
225 g/8 oz plain flour, sifted
1/2 teaspoon salt
4 eggs

a little vegetable oil
4 tablespoons melted butter
500 ml/16 fl oz tepid milk

Place the flour and salt in a large bowl. Make a well in the centre and add the eggs, one at a time, stirring them in with a wooden spoon. Add the melted butter and stir in thoroughly. Now gradually add the milk, stirring continuously, until you have a smooth batter with no lumps. Cover the bowl with a cloth and leave in a cool place for 1 hour.

With a pastry brush lightly grease a 15–18 cm/6–7 in heavy-based frying pan with a little of the oil. Place the pan over a moderate heat and warm the oil until it is very hot. Remove the pan from the heat and pour 4 tablespoons of the batter into it. Tilt the pan in all directions to help the batter spread. Return the pan to the heat and cook for 30–40 seconds. Shake the pan gently to loosen the crêpe. With a palette knife gently lift the crêpe and turn it over. Brown the reverse side for 20–30 seconds and then slide the *kaygana* on to an ovenproof plate and keep it warm. Continue making the *kaygana*, greasing the pan each time, until you have used all the batter.

kayisili kaygana crêpes with an apricot filling

Batter **see recipe above**

Filling
400 g/1 lb fresh apricots
350 g/12 oz caster sugar

juice 1 lemon
100 ml/4 fl oz water

Garnish **100 g/4 oz icing sugar, sifted**

Prepare the *kaygana* following the recipe above and keep warm.

Drop the apricots into a bowl of boiling water for 1 minute, then remove and peel. Cut them in half, remove the stones and then halve the halves. Place the apricots in a saucepan, add the sugar, lemon juice and water, bring to the boil and then simmer gently for 15 minutes, stirring regularly. Remove from the heat and leave to cool. Strain off the juice and reserve.

Bring the *kaygana* to a work top, take one, spread it out and place 2 tablespoons of the apricots onto one half of the crêpe. Fold the crêpe in half and then over again into quarters. Continue until you have filled and folded the remaining *kaygana*.

Preheat the oven to 200°C, 400°F, gas mark 6.

Arrange the *kaygana* in a shallow ovenproof dish and heat for 5 minutes in the oven. Remove from the oven, sprinkle generously with icing sugar and serve warm. In a small pan reheat the apricot juice and pour a little over each *kaygana* as it is served.

Variation

(a) apples — peel, core and slice 450 g/1 lb apples. Cook with 3 tablespoons water over a low heat with 350 g/12 oz caster sugar until just soft. Stir in 1 teaspoon cinnamon and set aside to cool.

(b) strawberries — 450 g/1 lb. Hull, wash and drain and then mash with 225 g/8 oz caster sugar. Stir in 100 g/4 oz crushed cream crackers or sweet tea-time biscuits, and fill the *kaygana*.

ataif arab pancakes

Ataif are pancakes dipped in syrup and they were traditionally served on festive occasions. Nowadays they can be purchased from bakeries and delicatessens. The recipe below is a family one and will make 15–16 pancakes.

Syrup
225 g/8 oz sugar
150 ml/¼ pint water
1 tablespoon lemon juice
1 tablespoon rosewater

Batter
1 teaspoon dried yeast or
   7 g/¼ oz fresh yeast
½ teaspoon sugar
300 ml/½ pint tepid water
100 g/4 oz plain flour

Place the yeast and sugar in a small bowl, add 3 tablespoons of the tepid water, mix to dissolve and then leave to rest in a warm place for about 10 minutes or until the mixture begins to bubble.

Sift the flour into a large bowl, add the yeast mixture and work it in with your hand. Little by little add the remaining water and continue kneading and, when the mixture begins to become liquid, beat until you have a smooth batter. Cover with a tea towel and place the bowl in a warm place for 1 hour.

Prepare the syrup by placing the sugar, water and lemon juice in a saucepan and bringing to the boil. Lower the heat and simmer until the syrup begins to leave a sticky film on a spoon. Remove from the heat, stir in the rosewater and set aside.

Lightly brush the inside of a large frying pan with oil and heat the pan for a few minutes until it is really hot. Reduce the heat to medium. Pour 1 tablespoon of the batter into the pan and tilt the pan around to allow the batter to spread. After a minute or two the batter will begin to bubble and become pale golden. With a palette knife lift the pancake and turn it over to cook the other side. Remove the pancake to a large plate and continue to make pancakes, piling them on top of each other when cooked.

The traditional method of eating *ataif* is to pour some syrup over each one and spread with *kaymak* or clotted cream. Sometimes chopped pistachios or almonds are then sprinkled over the top.

You can omit the cream and just pour over some syrup, or spread with honey, and sprinkle with nuts.

You can also spread them with cream and then sprinkle with a little cinnamon and pour a spoonful of mulberry syrup or *bekmez* (grape syrup) over the top. And, of course, you can stuff them.

ataif-bil-joze pancakes filled with nuts

Batter and syrup see *ataif* above

Filling
225 g/8 oz walnuts, coarsely
   chopped, or chopped pistachios
   or almonds or any combination
4 tablespoons sugar

2 teaspoons ground cinnamon
1 teaspoon orange blossom water
1 teaspoon rosewater

Prepare the pancakes as described above, but only cook one side of each one.

Mix the filling ingredients together. Take one *ataif* and place it on a working top uncooked side upwards. Place 1 tablespoon of the filling in one half of the pancake. Fold the other half over to make a half-moon shape and pinch the edges together very firmly.

Heat some oil in a large pan until hot and then deep fry the *ataif* for 2–3 minutes or until golden. Remove with a slotted spoon, drain on kitchen paper. Dip into cold syrup and serve warm or cold.

ataif-bil-jibn pancakes filled with cheese

Batter and syrup see *ataif*, page 319

Filling 225 g/8 oz cheese, e.g. akkawa, ricotta or feta

Prepare the pancakes as described on page 319 but only cook one side of each one.

Place the cheese in cold water overnight and then drain and grate. This will remove most of the saltiness. Continue as with *ataif-bil-joze* (above) using the cheese filling instead of the nuts.

fruit and nut desserts

kompostolar fruits cooked in syrup

Wherever one eats in Turkey, and to a lesser extent in the Balkans, one is inevitably offered a *komposto* at the end of a meal, be it of quinces, apples, pears, apricots, peaches, strawberries, oranges, etc. Dried as well as fresh fruit can be prepared in this way and 2 or more kinds of fruit can be cooked together.

The *kompostolar* are sometimes flavoured with cinnamon, cloves, rosewater or orange blossom water. I have included a few recipes below, but you can experiment with any fruit, or combination of fruits, of your choice.

ayva kompostosu quinces in syrup

900 g/2 lb firm quinces, peeled,
  cored and quartered
450 g/1 lb caster sugar

900 ml/1¹/₂ pints water
1 tablespoon lemon juice
6 cloves

Wash the quinces under cold running water and drain.

Place the sugar, water and lemon juice in a large saucepan and bring to the boil, stirring until the sugar has dissolved. Add the quinces and cloves and simmer for about 30 minutes or until the fruit is tender. Do not overcook or the fruit will disintegrate. Remove from the heat and leave to cool. Transfer to a serving bowl or individual dishes and chill. Serve with *kaymak*, cream or yoghurt.

portakal kompostosu oranges in syrup

4 medium oranges, peeled
175 g/6 oz caster sugar

300 ml/¹/₂ pint water
3 tablespoons orange blossom water

To ease the removal of any white pith drop the oranges into boiling water for 30 seconds and then remove and strip off as much of the pith as possible. Separate the segments.

Place the sugar and water in a large saucepan and bring to the boil, stirring until the sugar dissolves. Add the orange segments and simmer for 15–20 minutes. Remove from the heat, stir in the orange blossom water and leave to cool. Place in a large serving dish and chill. Serve with *kaymak*, cream or yoghurt.

çilek kompostosu *strawberries in syrup*

450 g/1 lb firm, fresh strawberries,
hulled and rinsed under cold water
225 g/8 oz sugar
300 ml/1/2 pint water

juice 1/2 lemon
4 tablespoons fresh strawberry juice
— if available

Place the sugar, water and lemon juice in a saucepan and bring to the boil. Simmer for 10 minutes. Drop in the strawberries and simmer for a further 5–10 minutes. Don't let the strawberries overcook. Remove from the heat and stir in the strawberry juice if you are using it. Leave to cool then pour into a serving dish and chill. Serve with *kaymak*, cream or yoghurt.

Since nothing is new under the sun here is how Apicius advised his contemporaries to prepare a fruit compôte:

That they clean the hard-skinned early fruits, remove the seeds and keep cold in a pan. In a separate pan crush pepper (allspice or nutmeg?) with dry mint. Moisten with water, a little honey, some raisins, wine and wine vinegar. Mix well and pour over the fruit. To this a little oil was to be added and the whole cooked over a low heat until tender.

The juice was to be thickened with some roux (rice flour), and finally a little pepper (a highly prized commodity of the day) was sprinkled over the top and served.

I suggest, however, you prepare your *kompostosu* the Turkish way!

izmir kompostosu *figs in syrup*

A speciality of Izmir (Greek Smyrna), the third largest city in Turkey. Izmir is renowned for her figs and grapes. You need dried figs for this recipe.

150 g/5 oz sugar
juice 1 lemon

600 ml/1 pint water
450 g/1 lb dried figs

Garnish 75 g/3 oz hazelnuts or pistachio nuts, finely chopped

Place the sugar, lemon juice and water in a saucepan and bring to the boil. Simmer for about 5 minutes. Lower the heat and arrange the figs in the syrup. Simmer very gently until the figs begin to 'plump up' and to take on something like their original shape. Remove the figs with a slotted spoon and arrange in a serving dish. Sprinkle with the chopped nuts and serve.

khoshab dried fruit compôte

Khoshab (Persian word meaning 'sweet water') is the name of a historic region of Armenia famed for her mountains, impregnable fortresses and swift-flowing mountain streams.

It is a dried fruit compôte, improvised during the centuries as a welcome dessert in winter when fresh fruit was not available.

There are many *khoshab*-type desserts throughout the Middle East, particularly in Iran and Turkey. This recipe is from the Kirovakan region of Armenia and is also known as *Kirovakan Mirkatan*.

225 g/8 oz dried apricots, soaked overnight in cold water
225 g/8 oz prunes, stoned, soaked overnight in cold water
225 g/8 oz dried peaches or pears, soaked overnight in cold water
100 g/4 oz sultanas, soaked overnight in cold water

75 g/3 oz honey
rind of 1 lemon in one piece
1/2 teaspoon nutmeg
1 stick cinnamon about 5 cm/2 in long
2 tablespoons pine kernels
2 tablespoons brandy

Drain the dried fruit and reserve about 300 ml/1/2 pint of the soaking water. Place the fruit and soaking water in a large saucepan and add the honey, lemon rind, nutmeg and cinnamon. Bring to the boil then lower the heat and simmer for 20–30 minutes or until the fruits are soft and tender. Remove from the heat and discard the lemon rind. Add the pine kernels and stir gently. Cool to room temperature and then stir in the brandy. Transfer to a deep serving bowl or individual dessert dishes, cover and refrigerate. Serve well chilled.

maadan hasultan

almond mousse topped with apricot sauce

An Israeli sweet, attractive, delicious and typical of the cuisine of a new country that is successfully marrying oriental flavours to a European concept. Will make a most suitable dessert for a dinner party.

Custard
3 eggs, separated
2 tablespoons sugar

300 ml/$^1\!/_2$ pint milk

Mousse (Sultan's delight)
50 g/2 oz toasted almonds, ground
$^1\!/_2$ teaspoon vanilla essence
$^1\!/_2$ teaspoon almond essence
the custard, cool

3 teaspoons gelatine
3 egg whites, remaining from the custard
2 tablespoons sugar
150 ml/$^1\!/_4$ pint cream

Apricot sauce
300 g/11 oz fresh ripe apricots,
    stoned or 150 g/5 oz dried
    apricots soaked overnight in water

lemon juice
sugar

Garnish 6–8 cherries or fresh strawberries

To make the custard place the egg yolks in a small bowl, add the sugar and mix well.

Bring the milk to the boil in a small saucepan. Pour a little of the milk into the egg mixture, stir and then pour it back into the rest of the milk in the pan. Stir well and lower the heat.

Fill a large saucepan or bowl with cold water and, at the first sign of the milk boiling, remove the mixture from the heat, dip the pan into the cold water and leave to cool. When the custard is cool prepare the mousse by first putting the ground almonds, the essences and the custard into a large bowl and mixing thoroughly.

Place the gelatine in a small bowl with a few tablespoons of water, place over a pan of simmering water and stir until the gelatine has dissolved. Stir the gelatine into the almond mixture.

Whisk the egg whites until stiff and fold in the sugar. Whisk the cream until thick. Fold the egg whites and cream into the almond mixture and stir carefully with a metal spoon until well blended. Either spoon the mixture into a decorative glass dish or divide between 6–8 individual dessert glasses. Do not fill each glass more than three-quarters full. Leave in the refrigerator to set and meanwhile prepare the apricot sauce.

Blend the apricots with a little water to form a purée about the consistency of double cream. Add lemon juice and sugar to taste. When the mousse has hardened pour the sauce over the top. Decorate with cherries or strawberries and serve chilled.

zardalou toush porshodeh

stuffed apricot balls

Do you know the one word
that holds the beauty of the world,
a whole world of colour,
a kaleidoscope of summer
and inexpressible magic?

You would if you had seen
that tree blossoming.
Not any tree, but the apricot
budding like Semirami's breasts
and greener than the willows in Babylon . . .

(Harout Gostantian — Armenian poet)

An Iranian dessert of dried apricots shaped into balls and stuffed with nuts. They are simple, delicious and typical of the highly sophisticated cuisine of one of the oldest surviving civilizations in the world. Make sure the dried apricots are soft and tender.

450 g/1 lb dried apricots
3 tablespoons ground pistachio nuts
4 tablespoons icing sugar

2 tablespoons orange blossom water
1/2 teaspoon ground cardamom

Filling
2 tablespoons ground almonds
2 tablespoons sugar
1/2 teaspoon cinnamon

Garnish
sifted icing sugar

Wipe the apricots with a slightly damp cloth. Chop very finely or pass through a mincer. Transfer to a large bowl, add the pistachio nuts, icing sugar, orange blossom water and cardamom. Wet your hands and knead vigorously until you get a smooth paste. Wet your hands again and shape the mixture into marble-sized balls.

   Mix the ground almonds, sugar and cinnamon together. Take 1 ball, hollow out and fill with a little of the nut mixture. Close the hole, roll the ball between your palms and then roll generously in the icing sugar. Repeat with the remaining balls. If wrapped in waxed paper and stored in an airtight tin these balls will keep for several weeks.

narinchanoush

oranges and peel in syrup and liqueur

A family favourite and one that we found to be very popular in our restaurants. The orange peel can be prepared in large quantities and stored in sealed jars for weeks, and you can use sliced pistachio nuts or chopped hazelnuts or walnuts instead of the almonds.

900 g/2 lb oranges, peeled, reserve the flesh and the rind
900 g/2 lb sugar

900 ml/1½ pints water
1 tablespoon lemon juice
3 tablespoons orange blossom water

Garnish
3 tablespoons almonds, blanched, slivered, toasted

2 tablespoons orange liqueur, e.g. Filfar or similar

Half fill a large saucepan with water, bring to the boil and drop in the pieces of peel. Simmer for about 30 minutes or until the peel is soft. Remove from the heat and drain. When cool enough to handle take a sharp knife and carefully slice off as much of the white pith as possible. Slice the peel into strips less than 0.3 cm/⅛ in thick, if possible.

Place the sugar, water and lemon juice in a large saucepan, bring to the boil and simmer for 5 minutes. Add the sliced orange peel and simmer until the syrup thickens and coats the back of a spoon. Remove from the heat, stir in the orange blossom water and set aside to cool completely.

To prepare the sweet for serving cut the oranges crossways into 0.6 cm/¼ in thick slices. In a shallow dish arrange the slices, overlapping, around the edge leaving a gap in the centre. Spoon some of the orange peel evenly over the slices and pile a little more in the centre. Pour some of the syrup over the slices and then sprinkle with the toasted almonds and the liqueur. Chill before serving.

serov hatsi kadaif

bread cooked with honey and served with cream

This is a highly sophisticated dessert. The authentic way of serving this sweet is with *kaymak* which is the thick Middle Eastern cream. If you wish to make this then follow the instructions in the first paragraph below. Otherwise use whipped double cream or, preferably, clotted cream and start the preparation at the second paragraph below.

This sweet is the creation of a great 'known' chef — Tokatlian, of Istanbul, who lived in the nineteenth century.

1 round loaf white bread, e.g. Italian or Greek — here I should mention that when I wanted to prepare this sweet in a hurry and had no white bread I used wholemeal instead and I must admit I found it just as delicious

a little milk — about 5 tablespoons   **juice 1–2 lemons**
300 ml/¹/₂ pint clear honey

To serve *kaymak* **(see Glossary page 366 and use half the quantity of double cream suggested there) or 300 ml/¹/₂ pint double cream, whipped or 300 ml/¹/₂ pint clotted cream**

Slice the loaf in half and use only the bottom half. Remove the bottom crust leaving a thick slice of bread about 3 cm/1¹/₄ in thick. Place the slice of bread in an oven preheated to 180°C, 350°F, gas mark 4 and leave until toasted, golden and crisp. Remove the bread, sprinkle on both sides with the milk and wrap in a teatowel until the milk is absorbed.

Mix the honey and lemon juice in a small saucepan and bring to the boil. Place the bread in a round ovenproof dish just large enough to hold it and spoon the honey evenly over it.

Bake in an oven preheated to 180°C, 350°F, gas mark 4 for about 30 minutes or until most of the honey has been absorbed and the bread is golden. Cut into pieces and top with the cream.

Variation
This is a quicker and cheaper method — a 'poor man's' version, but tasty nevertheless.

6 thick slices bread   Syrup
2 tablespoons sugar   **225 g/8 oz sugar**
150 ml/¹/₄ pint milk   **450 ml/³/₄ pint water**
                                 1 tablespoon lemon juice

First prepare the syrup by placing the sugar, water and lemon juice in a small saucepan and bringing to the boil. Lower the heat and simmer for about 10 minutes or until the syrup begins to form a sticky coating on the back of a spoon. Remove from the heat and set aside to cool.

Arrange the slices of bread side by side in a large frying pan. Dissolve the sugar in the milk and pour over the bread. Place over a low heat and gradually add the syrup, pouring it evenly over all the slices. Simmer until most of the syrup has been absorbed. Cool and then serve with cream.

cakes and biscuits

karabij stuffed pastries with natife

A speciality of Aleppo in Syria. These pastries are dipped in a cream called *natife* and eaten. *Natife* is made from pieces of wood called *bois de Panama* which can be bought from good health food shops and Middle Eastern stores. It is often sold in powdered form which makes its preparation simpler.

This is a unique pastry and it is well worth going to the trouble of making it.

Cream
75 g/3 oz *bois de Panama*, also
   known as '*halva* wood'
225 g/8 oz sugar

1 tablespoon lemon juice
2 tablespoons orange blossom water
4 egg whites

Filling
225 g/8 oz walnuts, finely chopped
100 g/4 oz sugar
1 tablespoon cinnamon

Dough
450 g/1 lb plain flour
225 g/8 oz unsalted butter, melted
3–4 tablespoons water

First prepare the cream by pulverizing the pieces of wood. Place in a bowl with about 150 ml/¼ pint water and leave to soak for 4–5 hours. Transfer the contents of the bowl to a saucepan and bring to the boil. Lower the heat and simmer until the liquid has thickened. Strain the mixture through fine muslin and set the liquid aside.

Dissolve the sugar in 8 tablespoons water in a small saucepan, add the lemon juice and bring to the boil. Lower the heat and simmer until the syrup has thickened — about 10 minutes. Remove from the heat, stir in the orange blossom water and the hot *bois de Panama* liquid and beat vigorously. Set aside to cool. When the mixture is cold place the egg whites in a large bowl and whisk until very stiff. Gradually add the cold syrup mixture, beating continuously until the mixture froths and expands. Transfer to a serving dish and set aside.

Mix the filling ingredients together in a bowl.

To prepare the dough sift the flour into a large bowl, add the butter and knead. Add the water and continue kneading until the dough is soft and smooth. Divide the dough into walnut-sized lumps. Take one lump, roll between your palms to form a ball and then hollow it out with your thumb, pinching the sides up until they are thin and form a pot shape. Fill the hollow with a little of the nut mixture and then press the dough back over the filling to form a ball. Gently press between your palms to make an oval shape. Repeat until you have used up all the dough and filling. Place the *karabij* on baking sheets and cook in an oven preheated to 150°C, 300°F, gas mark 2 for 20–30 minutes. Remove before the pastry changes colour — they should still be white. Set aside to cool.

When serving arrange the *karabij* on a large plate and offer a bowl of the *natife* cream. Dip the *karabij* into the cream and eat. The pastries will keep for a long time in an airtight tin, but refrigerate the cream.

Makes 30–40 pastries.

ma-moul stuffed easter pastries

A Syrian-Lebanese speciality these pastries are traditionally prepared during Easter week. Today they are sold throughout the year.

The recipe below is a family one using dates, walnuts and almonds. The Lebanese often use semolina instead of flour which gives the pastry a coarser and more earthy taste.

Filling

225 g/8 oz dates, stoned
225 g/8 oz walnuts, roughly chopped
100 g/4 oz almonds, roughly
    chopped — you can use pistachio
    nuts instead

150 ml/¼ pint water
100 g/4 oz sugar
1 heaped teaspoon cinnamon

Dough

450 g/1 lb plain flour
225 g/8 oz unsalted butter, melted

2 tablespoons rosewater
4–5 tablespoons milk

Garnish **icing sugar**

First prepare the filling. Chop the dates and place them in a saucepan with the nuts, water, sugar and cinnamon. Cook over a low heat until the dates are soft and the water has been absorbed.

Sift the flour into a bowl, add the melted butter and mix by hand. Add the rosewater and milk and knead the dough until it is soft and easy to mould. Divide the dough into walnut-sized lumps. Take one lump, roll it into a ball and then hollow it out with your thumb, pinching the sides up until they are thin and form a pot shape. Fill the pot with some of the date mixture and then press the dough back over the filling to enclose completely. Roll into a ball and then gently press with your palm to flatten it slightly or, if you have a wooden spoon with a deep curved bowl, mould each pastry with that. Repeat until you have used up all the pastry and filling.

Arrange the pastries on baking sheets. Make interesting patterns with a fork on each pastry. The traditional one is to mark straight lines down the length of each pastry. Bake in an oven preheated to 150°C, 300°F, gas mark 2 for about 30 minutes. Do not let them change colour or the pastry will become hard. Remove from the oven and allow to cool. When cold roll in sieved icing sugar and store in an airtight tin.

Makes 30–40 pastries.

tahinov hats sesame-cream cakes

A speciality from southern Turkey — the Armenian kingdom of Cilicia that flourished in the Middle Ages.

Most delightful cakes, filled with sesame cream (tahina) and sugar, which are ideal with tea and coffee.

Traditionally eaten during the forty days of Lent. these cakes will keep for several weeks.

I like my *hats* very sweet, but you can vary the sugar content according to taste.

1/2 teaspoon dried yeast
1/2 teaspoon sugar
175 ml/6 fl oz water, warm

225 g/8 oz plain flour
1/2 teaspoon salt
100 ml/4 fl oz cooking oil

Filling
tahina
sugar

ground cinnamon

In a small bowl dissolve the yeast and the sugar in the warm water. Place in a warm place and leave for about 10 minutes or until the mixture begins to froth. Sift the flour and salt into a large bowl, make a well in the centre and pour in the yeast mixture and the cooking oil. Mix together and then knead well until the mixture is smooth. Roll the dough into a large ball, place in the bowl, cover with a tea towel and leave in a warm place until the dough has doubled in size. Pour some tahina into a bowl and stir until it is smooth. Divide the dough into 6 balls. Lightly flour a work top and roll one ball out into a circle about 0.3 cm/1/8 in thick.

Spread a tablespoon of the tahina over the circle of dough and then sprinkle 1–2 tablespoons sugar over the top. Vary sugar according to taste. Sprinkle a pinch of cinnamon over the sugar. Roll the circle up into a sausage, grasp it in your hands and squeeze gently. This closes the sausage and doubles its length. Cut the sausage in half. With each piece, fold the 2 ends over to the middle — one slightly overlapping the other. Press the cake down gently to secure the ends and flatten slightly. Repeat with the remaining balls of dough.

Place the cakes on lightly greased baking sheets. Cook in an oven preheated to 200°C, 400°F, gas mark 6 for 30 minutes or until golden. Remove and leave to cool.

Makes 12 cakes.

zadgva katah easter cake

Traditionally, during Easter, Armenians make this cake and many others. Basically they are dry, bread-like cakes, sometimes with a filling, but often without. They are delicious when sliced and eaten with tea or coffee.

Dough

15 g/^{1}/$_2$ oz fresh yeast or 7 g/
  ^{1}/$_4$ oz dried yeast
225 ml/8 fl oz tepid milk
50 g/2 oz sugar

100 g/4 oz butter, melted
400 g/14 oz plain flour, sifted
^{1}/$_2$ teaspoon salt

Khoritz (filling)

2 tablespoons raisins
2 tablespoons walnuts, chopped
1 tablespoon brown sugar
1 tablespoon white sugar

1 teaspoon cinnamon
1 tablespoon sesame seeds
1 oz butter, melted

Garnish **beaten egg**

Place the yeast in a small bowl and add half the milk.

Pour the remaining milk into a large mixing bowl, add the sugar and stir until dissolved. Add the melted butter to this mixture. When the yeast has softened pour the mixture into the mixing bowl and stir. Gradually stir in the flour and salt. When well-blended transfer the dough to a well-floured work top and knead for at least 10 minutes. Roll the dough into a ball, place in a clean bowl, cover with a cloth and set aside in a warm place until it has doubled in size. Remove the dough to a work top, punch down and knead for a few more minutes.

Now prepare the filling by mixing all the ingredients, except the butter, together in a small bowl. Divide the dough into 3 equal parts. Take one part and roll out on a floured surface until 0.3–0.6 cm/^{1}/$_8$–^{1}/$_4$ in thick. Brush the surface all over with melted butter. Fold the edges into the centre to make about a 12.5 cm/5 in square. Place a third of the filling in the centre of the square and bring the opposite corners of the square over to cover the filling completely. Then gently roll the cake out until it is about 15 cm/6 in square, taking care not to let the filling ooze out. Place on a greased baking sheet. Repeat with the remaining dough and filling. Brush the top of each with beaten egg and set aside in a warm place for a further 30 minutes.

Heat the oven to 200°C, 400°F, gas mark 6, add the cakes and bake for about 20 minutes or until risen and golden. Remove and cool on wire racks. Serve sliced with tea or coffee.

choreg festive biscuits with sesame seeds

Choreg are dry bread sticks of Armenian origin (*chor-ekmek* — dry bread), which have, over the centuries, become equally popular in Turkey and Greece — *choureks*. Traditionally prepared over Christmas — *Zenunti choreg* and Easter — *Zadgi choreg*, they are excellent with tea or coffee at any time of the day, either plain or with cheese, jam or honey.

Usually prepared in large quantities they last for a long time when stored in air-tight tins.

Mahaleb (from the kernel of the black cherry stone) gives this biscuit its very unique flavour and I strongly recommend that you try to use it although it is expensive and sometimes difficult to find. Good Middle Eastern stores should have it.

1 teaspoon dried yeast or 7 g/
  1/4 oz fresh yeast
1 teaspoon sugar
1 teacup warm water
450 g/1 lb plain flour

pinch salt
100 g/4 oz butter
1 teaspoon *mahaleb*, crushed
100–225 ml/4–8 fl oz water
1 teaspoon cooking oil

Topping
1 egg, beaten

sesame seeds

Place the yeast and sugar in a small bowl. Add the teacup of warm water, stir to dissolve and then leave in a warm place until the mixture begins to froth.

Sieve the flour and salt into a large bowl. Add the butter and rub it in until the mixture resembles fine breadcrumbs. Stir in the crushed *mahaleb*. Make a well in the centre of the flour and pour in the yeast mixture. Blend the flour and yeast mixture together until you have a stiff dough. Now add a little of the water at a time and knead until you have a soft dough. The amount of water you add will vary because of the differing qualities of the various brands of flour. When the dough comes easily away from the sides of the bowl remove to a clean work top and knead for about 10 minutes until it is easier and pliable. Add the oil and knead it in. Roll the dough into a ball, place in a clean bowl, cover with a tea towel and leave it to rest in a warm place until it has doubled in size.

When the dough is ready: (a) heat the oven to 200°C, 400°F, gas mark 6; (b) grease baking sheets with cooking oil; (c) place the beaten egg in a small bowl; (d) pour some sesame seeds on to a plate.

Punch down the dough a few times and then break off a piece about the size of a walnut. Roll it between your palms to form a ball. Place it on your working top and roll it to and fro with your palms until you have a long strip which is pencil thin and about 30 cm/12 in long. These strips are made into many different shapes which often vary from family to family. The two described here were favoured by my mother.

The twisted circle

Bring one end of the strip over to meet the other, thus halving its original length. Lightly roll your palm over the 2 loose ends 2 or 3 times to obtain a twisted strip. Bring the 2 ends of the strip together and press the uncut end over the 2 loose ends to form a circle.

The plait

Break off a third of the strip and press one end of it half way along the remaining strip. Plait the 3 strips of dough together and then press the 3 loose ends together.

Place each *choreg* on to a baking sheet leaving a little space between each one. Brush each one with the beaten egg and then sprinkle with sesame seeds. Turn the oven off, place the baking sheets inside and leave the *choreg* to rise a little. Turn the oven up to 200°C, 400°F, gas mark 6 again and cook until golden. As the *choreg* become golden remove the trays from the oven and pile all the *choreg* on to one of the trays. Turn off the oven and return the tray to the oven and leave for several hours to dry out. When cold store in an air-tight tin.

gurabiah lover's shortbread

Gurabiah is prepared in most countries of the Middle East as well as North Africa and the Balkans.

Arab by origin these almond-based sweets can be made with flour or semolina. Although fairly simple to make they do need careful handling and careful cooking. The name *gurabiah* comes from the Arabic word *gharib* meaning to miss, to yearn, etc. which suggests longing for one's loved one — hence the sweets are often heart-shaped.

By far the most tasty recipe is this one from Syria which just melts in the mouth.

450 g/1 lb unsalted butter
225 g/8 oz icing sugar, sifted

450 g/1 lb plain flour, sifted
blanched, halved almonds

Melt the butter in a small saucepan over a low heat. Spoon off any froth and pour the yellow liquid into a large mixing bowl, discarding the milky residue in the bottom of the pan. Put the bowl in the refrigerator and leave until the butter has solidified.

Beat or whisk the butter until it is white and creamy. Add the icing sugar, a little at a time, and continue beating. Add the flour, a little at a time, and continue to mix until the mixture is stiff. Collect the dough up and knead it by hand until it forms a ball and becomes smooth and pliable. Leave to rest in the bowl for about 10 minutes.

Preheat the oven to 150°C, 300°F, gas mark 2.

On a clean surface shape the mixture into walnut-sized balls. Roll one into a sausage and join the ends to form a circle. Place on a baking sheet and then place an almond over the join. Continue until you have used up all the mixture, placing the *gurabiah* about 2.5 cm/1 in apart on the baking sheets. Place in the oven and cook for 20 minutes or until the almonds are a very light golden, but the biscuits are still white.

barazeh shami damascus sesame biscuits

One of the oldest cities in the world, Damascus — of biblical fame — is little known (outside her city walls) for her excellent cuisine. But excellent it is, for some of the finest meat and vegetable dishes and desserts — particularly those made with the fruits of the Orontes valley, and the mastic-based ice cream popular throughout the Arab world — are all of Damascus origin.

These sesame biscuits are typical of that sophisticated and yet extremely simple culinary art evolved over the ages. I would like to think that St Paul, Muhammad and the infamous Genghis Khan all ate these sesame-coated biscuits with their milk or tea.

$^1/_4$ teaspoon fresh yeast or
  $^1/_2$ teaspoon dried yeast
1 teaspoon sugar
225 ml/8 fl oz tepid water
450 g/1 lb plain flour

225 g/8 oz caster sugar
175 g/6 oz butter
225 g/8 oz sesame seeds
50 g/2 oz butter, melted

Place the yeast and sugar in a small bowl, add a little of the warm water, stir to dissolve and place in a warm place for about 10 minutes until the mixture begins to froth.

Sift the flour into a large bowl and stir in the sugar. Cut the butter into small pieces, add to the flour and rub in until the mixture resembles fine breadcrumbs. Make a well in the centre, add the yeast mixture and gradually add the remaining water, mixing with your hand until a dough is formed. Knead for about 5 minutes until the dough is soft and easy to handle. If necessary add a little more water. Cover the bowl with a cloth and leave in a warm place for about 1 hour or until the dough has doubled in size. Remove the dough and place on a lightly floured working top. Punch the dough down and knead for a further 1–2 minutes. Divide it into 2 equal portions.

Sprinkle the work surface with a little more flour and roll out one portion until about 0.3 cm/$^1/_8$ in thick. Using a 10 cm/4 in cake cutter cut out as many rounds as possible. Repeat with the remaining portion of pastry.

Grease 2 or 3 baking sheets. Spread the sesame seeds out on a plate. Lightly brush both sides of each biscuit with butter and then dip into the sesame seeds so that both sides are coated.

Arrange, 2.5 cm/1 in apart, on the baking sheets and bake in an oven preheated to 160°C, 325°F, gas mark 3 for 20–25 minutes or until the biscuits are golden and dry. Remove from the oven, cool completely on wire racks and store in an airtight tin.

sweets

rahat lokum turkish delight

The most famed sweet of Turkey, known throughout the world, is *rahat lokum*. It is often better known simply as *lokum* — 'giving rest to the throat'.

Although this sweetmeat is produced in many countries no make can equal the famed produce of the House of Hadji Bekir — a family business reputed to have been established for over 250 years and still going strong in Istanbul.

Traditional *lokum* consist of the pulp of white grapes or mulberries, semolina, flour, rosewater, honey and apricot kernels. There are many variations, some of which I have indicated below.

The recipe below is one my mother often prepared which I am assured is based on one passed down to her from her grandmother.

Rahat lokum is easy to prepare and has a certain mystique surrounding it — one of romance, adventure, abandonment and leisure!

butter
450 g/1 lb sugar
300 ml/1/2 pint water
1 teaspoon lemon juice
25 g/1 oz gelatine dissolved in
   100 ml/4 fl oz hot water
1/2 teaspoon vanila essence

1 tablespoon pistachio nuts, halved
3 drops food colouring, e.g. red,
   yellow or gold
1 tablespoon rosewater
50 g/2 oz icing sugar
25 g/1 oz cornflour

Grease a 15 x 15 cm/6 x 6 in baking tin with the butter and set aside.

Put the sugar, water and lemon juice in a saucepan and bring to the boil. Continue boiling until the temperature reaches 120°C, 250°F on a sugar thermometer. If you do not have one then drop a little of the syrup into a bowl of cold water. If it has reached the required temperature it will form a hard ball. Remove the pan from the heat and leave to stand for 10 minutes. Stir in the dissolved gelatine and the vanilla essence and beat with a wooden spoon until the mixture is well blended.

Pour half the mixture into the baking tin, and sprinkle the halved nuts over it.

Stir the rosewater and colouring into the remaining mixture and mix well. Pour this mixture into the tin and set aside in a cool place overnight.

Sift the icing sugar and cornflour on to a large plate. Turn the *lokum* out on a clean board and cut into 2.5 cm/1 in cubes. Toss the cubes in the sugar mixture and make sure they are thoroughly coated. Shake off any excess sugar. Either wrap individually in waxed paper or store in an airtight container.

Variations
You can use chopped walnuts or almonds instead of the pistachios or you can prepare the *lokum* plain, i.e. without any nuts.

Mulberry or strawberry lokum

Cook 225g/8 oz of the fruit in a little water. Drain off any liquid, mash the pulp and incorporate into the mixture above, omitting the other flavourings.

Crème de menthe lokum

Replace the food colourings and the flavourings above with 2¹/₂ tablespoons crème de menthe and ¹/₂ teaspoon green food colouring.

Gikolat lokumi

Prepare the *lokum* as with the recipe for *rahat lokum* and after you have cut it into cubes dip them individually into melted hot chocolate and dry on a greased wire rack.

Covered with dessicated coconut

When the *lokum* has been cut into cubes roll them individually in dessicated coconut until completely covered.

tamrieh date sweets

Legend goes that when the prophet Muhammad meditated for forty days in the wilderness he lived on dates and goat's milk. Arab historians relate how the early Arab armies marched on date, rice and fruit. While in our time Bedouin (and there are still millions of them regardless of the pace of industrialization and urbanization) in the deserts still make great use of the fruit of the oasis — the date.

In Oman and Yemen fresh dates are dipped in *ghee* and eaten with relish. Throughout the desert regions most Arab countries cultivate this fruit in a big way. Particularly successful is Iraq whose dates are renowned worldwide.

There are three basic date types: Kahastawari, Khadrawi and Zhehdik — all of which are dried. The best known fresh dates are Baban and Berhi and they usually come from Israel and Lebanon.

The fruit is versatile. When it is being dried a thick dark syrup is exuded which is used in many dishes creating a sweet-sour flavour. This syrup is often mixed with butter *marys* and eaten with bread and *kaymak*.

I have selected a few date desserts under the general heading *Tamrieh*, but dates also appear in many other recipes in this book.

halawah temar date halva

One of the simplest and most popular date sweets found throughout Arabia, Iraq and the Gulf States. Its brilliance lies in its simplicity.

450 g/1 lb dates, stoned and chopped	2 tablespoons toasted sesame seeds
225 g/8 oz walnuts, coarsely chopped	(optional)
225 g/8 oz almonds, coarsely chopped	icing sugar

Mix the dates and nuts together in a large bowl and knead until smooth.

If using sesame seeds knead these in too.

Lightly dust a board with icing sugar. Place the ball of dates and nuts on the board and with a rolling pin dusted with icing sugar roll it out into a square about 1 cm/^{1}/$_{2}$ in thick. With a sharp knife cut into 2.5 cm/1 in squares. Dust a serving plate with icing sugar, arrange the squares over it and then dust with a little more icing sugar. Serve with *kaymak*, clotted or double cream.

This will keep if wrapped in wax paper and stored in an airtight tin.

mischlachat ha negev

date rolls stuffed with nuts

Dates are not, of course, the prerogative of the Arabs. All Middle Eastern people love and use them in their dishes.

The following Israeli sweet, the creation of a well known local chef Roger Debasque, is a good example of a variation on a traditional theme. Dedicated to the 'Negev Expedition' it can be made in large quantities and kept in an airtight tin after being wrapped in waxed paper.

4 eggs
5 tablespoons double cream
600 ml/1 pint milk
10 tablespoons sugar
green food colouring
200 g/7 oz butter

150 g/5 oz plain flour
40 dates, stoned
150 g/5 oz shelled hazelnuts, whole
250 g/9 oz roasted almonds, chopped
1 tablespoon vanilla essence
1 tablespoon almond essence

Topping **40 almond or walnut halves**

Separate the eggs and reserve the whites for another recipe. Mix the yolks and cream together in a small bowl.

Bring the milk to the boil in a saucepan, add the sugar and 1–2 drops green food colouring to obtain a light green colour.

In another saucepan melt the butter, add the flour and stir constantly over a low heat until the flour begins to fry. Add the boiled milk gradually, stirring constantly to ensure it is smooth and free from lumps. When the mixture turns smooth, hard and even stir in the egg yolk mixture. Place in the refrigerator to cool.

Meanwhile, stuff each date with 3 hazelnuts.

When the dough mixture is cool place on a work top and knead until pliable. Add the chopped almonds and the essences and knead a little more. Flatten the dough and cut 40 strips about 5.5 x 0.6 cm/2^{1}/$_{2}$ x ^{1}/$_{2}$ in. Fold a strip of dough lengthways around each date and then decorate each with half an almond or walnut. Serve as a sweetmeat after a meal and with turkish coffee and tea.

jams and preserves

The word *murababbiyah* meaning jams or preserves, is of Arab origin, but this method of fruit preservation is of much older vintage. Our ancestors developed special techniques to help enjoy the fruits of summer throughout the year. Jams and preserves are two of the more important ones.

Traditionally honey was used in the making of these preserves, but in time sugar was substituted — since honey tends to thicken and often crystallize the preserve.

For my money the greatest preserve of all is *varti-anoush* — rose petal jam. This jam is popular throughout the Middle East, the Balkans and India and I have tried several commercial brands, but nothing can beat the home-made version.

One day a great admirer of the Hodja sends him a large pot of home-made rose petal jam. The Hodja is delighted, but unfortunately had to attend the funeral of a close friend. He places the pot in a safe place and warns his pupils (at this stage Hodja was a schoolmaster) not to touch the contents of the pot for 'You can never trust anyone nowadays. I suspect an adversary of mine has sent it and it may well be poisoned.'

He left. Immediately his nephew retrieved the pot of jam and called to his fellow pupils, 'Let's eat!'

Some objected saying that they were afraid it may be poisonous.

'Stupid,' said the nephew, 'he wanted you to believe so. Look, it's nothing of the sort.' Saying this, he ate a spoonful. 'Mmm – beautiful.'

His classmates followed suit and in a matter of minutes there was no rose petal jam in the pot.

'Leave it to me,' said the nephew, 'I know how to tell my uncle.'

He took Hodja's pen sharpener and broke it.

When Hodja returned he was aghast to see his pen sharpener cracked. 'Who is the guilty party?,' he angrily demands and immediately everyone points to his nephew who bursts into tears.

'Explain,' demands the Hodja.

'Uncle,' says the nephew, 'my pen sharpener broke so I borrowed yours and, clumsy as I am, I broke it. I knew you would be angry with me. I felt so sick I wanted to kill myself. I thought of the school well, I wished to drown, but I remembered my friends drink of that well. And then, just then I remembered the pot of jam and how you thought it was poisoned. So I ate it all and, begging forgiveness from all and everyone sat down on my cushion and waited for the angels to take me to hell — but, nothing happened.' He continued to weep, so loud and with such gusto that some of his classmates began to accompany him.

'Oh God,' whispered the Hodja, 'I know you have been generous with your distribution of wisdom and guile amongst the lot of our clan, but this is too much — I am all for sapience and cunning, but this young dog is teaching me new tricks.'

varti-anoush rose petal jam

I have tried to prepare this jam with roses from my garden, but unfortunately the petals remain a little tough and there is little fragrance. Make sure, therefore, that you boil the petals until really tender and I suggest that you add rosewater to get that wonderful fragrance. Use fresh red petals, cut off their white ends and wash thoroughly — especially if they have been sprayed.

450 g/1 lb fresh rose petals, red and with as strong a fragrance as possible
juice 2 lemons

600 ml/1 pint water
450 g/1 lb sugar
3–4 tablespoons rosewater, depending on strength

Put the washed rose petals into a large glass bowl, squeeze half the lemon juice over and leave for 10 minutes.

You can cook the petals whole, but because they might be tough I suggest you pass them through a mincer. My mother used to knead them by hand, but this took her ages. Put the petals into a large saucepan with any of the lemon juice left in the bowl (this will help to set the jam). Add the water, bring to the boil and then lower the heat and simmer until the petals are tender. This may take anything from 10 minutes to 1 hour depending on the petals. Add the sugar and remaining lemon juice and bring to the boil, stirring continuously until the sugar dissolves. Simmer, stirring frequently, until the syrup thickens — about 10 minutes. Remove from the heat and stir in the rosewater. Leave to stand for a few minutes and then skim off any scum on the surface. After about 15 minutes stir and then pour into warm sterilized jars. Seal when cold.

ayva reçeli quince jam

Once very popular in Western Europe the quince nowadays is little used except for making preserves — excellent ones at that. Try this recipe from Turkey which is also a great favourite with Kurds, Armenians and Caucasians. It has an exquisite flavour emanating from the cloves, cinnamon and rosewater.

6 large quinces, peeled, cored and quartered
450 g/1 lb sugar
900 ml/1½ pints water

2 tablespoons lemon juice
5 cm/2 in stick cinnamon
3 whole cloves
3 tablespoons rosewater

Halve the quartered quinces. In a large saucepan bring the sugar and water to the boil, stirring constantly until the sugar has dissolved. Add the quince slices, lemon juice, cinnamon and cloves and boil for 3 minutes. Lower the heat and simmer for about 2 minutes, stirring frequently, until the syrup thickens and coats the back of a spoon. Remove from the heat and discard the cinnamon stick and cloves and stir in the rosewater. When completely cold seal tightly.

sumpoogi kaghtsr whole aubergine preserve

One of the great classics of the Armenian cuisine. Use small, 5–7.5 cm/2–3 in, long aubergines. Serve individually with a little syrup.

900 g/2 lb small aubergines, peeled
2.3 litres/4 pints water
2 tablespoons lime powder
  (obtainable from your chemist)
1¹/₂ teaspoons cinnamon

1 teaspoon cloves
1 tablespoon rosewater
900 g/2 lb sugar
2 litres/3¹/₂ pints water

Mix the water and lime powder together in a large saucepan, add the aubergines and leave them to soak overnight. To keep them submerged invert a large plate over them and weigh it down.

Next day rinse the aubergines in a colander under cold running water. Remove as much moisture as possible from the aubergines by squeezing each one between your palms. Place them in a large saucepan, add water, bring to the boil and simmer for 5 minutes. Drain, rinse once more under cold water and squeeze each one again between your palms to remove all traces of bitterness.

Place the sugar and water in a large saucepan and bring slowly to the boil, stirring constantly. Drop the aubergines into the syrup, add the cinnamon and cloves, lower the heat and simmer for 2 hours or until the syrup is thick. Stir carefully so as not to break up the fruit. Remove from the heat, stir in the rosewater and leave to cool. Spoon into warm sterilized jars and when completely cold seal tightly.

badrijani muraba aubergine jam

A recipe from Batumi on the Black Sea coast. Makes a beautiful jam.

1.8 kg/4 lb small, peeled aubergines
2 tablespoons salt
4 lemons
4 cloves

2.5 cm/1 in piece fresh root ginger,
  peeled and bruised
1.3 kg/3 lb sugar
100 g/4 oz crystallized ginger, chopped

Cut the aubergines into 0.6 cm/¹/₄ in cubes. Place the cubes in a large colander, sprinkle with the salt and set aside for 30 minutes.

Peel the lemons and cut the rinds into thin strips. Squeeze and reserve the juice.

Rinse the aubergine cubes under cold water and then pat dry. Put the cubes in the top part of a steamer and half fill the bottom part with water.

Or put in a colander over a saucepan and cover with the lid. Bring to the boil and then steam the aubergines until tender — about 10–15 minutes. Remove from the heat and transfer the aubergines to a large pan and add the lemon juice.

Put the lemon rind, cloves and ginger in a muslin bag, tie tightly and add to the pan.

Add the sugar, mix thoroughly, cover the pan and leave to stand undisturbed for at least 24 hours.

Next day bring slowly to the boil, stirring continuously until the sugar has dissolved and then simmer for 10 minutes, stirring frequently. Add the crystallized ginger, raise the heat and boil vigorously until the jam thickens. Remove from the heat, discard the muslin bag and leave to cool. Spoon into warm sterilized jars and seal when completely cool.

murabbiyeh-bil-amar date preserve

Delicious preserves from Iraq which are also popular throughout Syria and the Gulf region. For this preserve you need fresh dates, the large yellow or red varieties which sometimes appear in the shops, usually air-flown from Israel or Morocco.

1 kg/2$\frac{1}{2}$ lb fresh dates	6 cloves
3 litres/5 pints water	3 tablespoons orange or tangerine
toasted slivered almonds	rind, thinly sliced
450 g/1 lb sugar	2 tablespoons lemon juice

Peel the dates and place them in a large saucepan with the water. Bring to the boil and then simmer for about 1 hour or until they are tender. Remove from the heat and, with a slotted spoon, transfer the dates to a large plate. Reserve the liquid. When the dates are cool enough to handle use a small, sharp knife to remove and discard the stones. Push 2 slivers of toasted almonds into each date.

Sprinkle a third of the sugar evenly over the bottom of a medium saucepan. Lay a third of the dates and 2 cloves over the sugar. Repeat these layers twice more.

Make the reserved liquid up to 1 litre/1$\frac{3}{4}$ pints with cold water if necessary and pour into the pan. Cover the pan and leave to rest overnight. The next day bring this mixture to a quick boil and boil vigorously for 5 minutes. Lower the heat and simmer for about 30 minutes. Stir in the orange or tangerine rind and the lemon juice and simmer until the syrup is thick enough to coat the back of a spoon. Remove from the heat and cool. Spoon into warm sterilized jars and when cold seal tightly.

engouyzi-anoush green walnut preserve

A superb classic. Naturally you do need a walnut tree. If one is not available — read on, and wish you had a walnut tree!

But first a few cautionary words. The walnuts must be picked when the green fruit is not yet full size and the inner shell is still soft. To test I suggest that you use a strong needle and pierce the nut in 3–4 places. If there is no resistance then the nuts are suitable to preserve. Walnuts will stain your hands black so use rubber gloves.

This recipe is from the Caucasus where the finest walnut preserves are made. Although it is also known in adjacent lands, e.g. it is called *morabaye gerdu* in northern Iran, and as far as Cyprus where it is known as *glyko karithi*, its home is definitely the Caucasus — and in particular, Georgia. Lime powder (slake lime) helps to harden the outer skin of the nuts otherwise they will disintegrate while cooking. You should be able to purchase it from your local chemist. Do explain that it is for cooking purposes.

about 50 walnuts
8 tablespoons lime powder (slake lime)
900 g/2 lb sugar

600 ml/1 pint water
$1^1/_2$ tablespoons lemon juice
5 cloves
10 cm/4 in piece cinnamon bark

Remove the outer green walnut shells. Place the walnuts in a large pan and soak in water for 2 days, changing the water 3 times a day. On the third day drain the nuts, add fresh water, stir in the lime powder and soak the nuts for 24 hours. Next day drain the walnuts and rinse very thoroughly under cold running water. Pierce each nut in several places with a thin skewer and then soak in fresh water for a further 2 days. Drain into a colander.

Place the sugar, water and lemon juice in a saucepan and bring to the boil. Lower the heat and simmer until the syrup thickens and coats the back of a spoon. Add the nuts, cloves and cinnamon and cook for 3 minutes. Remove the pan from the heat and leave to cool. Return the pan to the heat, bring to the boil, simmer for 1 minute and remove. Repeat this process twice more.

Finally remove the pan from the heat and discard the cloves and cinnamon. When cool spoon into warm sterilized jars and when completely cold seal tightly. Serve 2 at a time with a little of its syrup as a finishing touch to a meal or with coffee.

tutumi kaghtsr pumpkin preserve

Pumpkin makes an excellent preserve. You can shred the vegetable instead of cutting it into squares, and some people like to add three tablespoons of slivered almonds or sliced pistachio nuts at the end of the cooking process.

This recipe is from Armenia.

1 small pumpkin, peeled and seeded.
   You need about 1.1 kg/2¹/₂ lbs flesh
2.3 litres/4 pints cold water
2 tablespoons lime powder (slake lime)
900 g/2 lb sugar
1.2 litres/2 pints water
2.5 cm/1 in cinnamon stick

3 cloves
2 tablespoons lemon juice
175 g/6 oz sugar
1 teaspoon vanilla essence
3 tablespoon almonds, slivered, or
   pistachios, sliced (optional)

Cut the pumpkin into 0.6 cm/¹/₄ in thick slices. Now cut these slices into 4 cm/1¹/₂ in squares or shred. In a large deep pan mix the water and lime powder together and soak the pumpkin in it overnight. Next day drain the pieces into a colander and then rinse very thoroughly under cold running water to remove all traces of the lime. Drain thoroughly.

In a large pan bring the sugar and water to the boil, stirring constantly until the sugar dissolves. Add the pieces of pumpkin, lower the heat and simmer about 1 hour. Pour some of the syrup into a smaller pan and to it add the cinnamon, cloves, lemon juice and 175 g/6 oz sugar. Bring to the boil, simmer for 2–3 minutes and pour this mixture back into the pumpkin pan. Lower the heat and simmer until the syrup thickens and coats the back of a spoon. Remove from the heat and stir in the vanilla essence and nuts if using them. When cool spoon into warm, sterilized jars and, when completely cold, seal tightly.

mourbaba-al-bousfeir *preserved orange rolls*

A popular Middle Eastern preserve where the orange peel is rolled, strung on to thread and then cooked in syrup.

You can prepare grapefruit, lemon and watermelon peel in much the same way. The finest such preserve of all is called *mouraba-al-kabbad*, a Syrian-Lebanese speciality made with the peel of bitter oranges.

Serve as a dessert or with tea or coffee.

6 large Jaffa oranges	600 ml/1 pint water
500 g/18 oz sugar	1 tablespoon lemon juice

Lightly grate the surface of the oranges to remove the shine. Cut the rind, skin deep, into 6 vertical sections and peel them away from the flesh. With a sharp knife carefully remove as much of the white pith as possible from the pieces of peel without cutting them. Tightly roll up each piece of peel and then with a needle and heavy thread string up the rolls. I suggest 18 rolls (from 3 oranges) on each string. Tie the ends of the threads together to form 2 garlands.

Put the threaded rolls into a large saucepan, cover with cold water, bring to the boil and then drain. Repeat this process at least 2 more times — this will remove the bitter taste. Place the rolls in the saucepan, cover with cold water again, bring to the boil and cook for about 30–40 minutes or until the rolls are tender. Drain them and pat dry.

Place the sugar, water and lemon juice in a large saucepan and bring to the boil. Add the strings of rolls and simmer for about 45 minutes or until the syrup is thick and the rolls are beautifully glazed. Remove from the heat and leave to cool. Carefully remove the strings and store the rolls, in their syrup, in sterilized jars. Seal tightly and store in a cool place.

Variation

mouraba-al-griffon *preserved grapefruit rolls*

Follow the recipe above but:
a) use 4 grapefruit
b) cut the rind of each into 8 vertical sections
c) boil in water 4 times instead of 3 to remove bitterness.

morabaye hendevaneh

preserved watermelon rind

This recipe is from Iran, but the basic concept is the same throughout the region. The Greeks and Arabs would add a thinly peeled strip of lemon rind, a 5 cm/2 in piece cinnamon bark and 3–4 tablespoons toasted almonds towards the end of the cooking time.

700 g/1½ lb watermelon rind, peel green skin from the rind and remove all pink flesh
900 g/2 lb sugar
1.2 litres/2 pints water
1½ tablespoons lemon juice

1 tablespoon crushed cardamom
5 cm/2 in stick cinnamon (optional)
1 thinly peeled strip lemon rind (optional)
3-4 tablespoons toasted, blanched almonds (optional)

Cut the rind into 2–2.5 cm/¾–1 in cubes. You will probably end up with about 400–450 g/14–16 oz of cubed rind. Put the rind in a large saucepan, cover with water and bring to the boil. Lower the heat and simmer for about 1 hour or until the rind is translucent and tender. Drain into a colander.

Place the sugar, water and lemon juice in a large saucepan and bring to the boil. Add the crushed cardamom seeds and the cinnamon and lemon rind if using them. Add the drained rind and simmer for 15 minutes, skimming off any froth that appears on the surface. Remove the pan from the heat, cover and set aside for 18–24 hours.

Next day return the pan to a moderate heat and bring to the boil. Lower the heat and simmer for about 20 minutes or until the syrup has thickened and coats the back of a spoon. Remove cinnamon and lemon rind and add the almonds if using them, stir well then remove from the heat and set aside to cool. Spoon into warm sterilized jars and seal when completely cold.

One day Hadji Baba of Isphahan was confronted by a young man who wished to test the reputed wisdom of the master clown.

'Tell me Hadji,' he asked, 'which is the most useful and perfect fruit?'

'Why, it's the watermelon of course,' replied Hadji Baba calmly.

'How come?'

'Because one eats the fruit, munches the seeds and makes a lovely morabaye with the skin.'

'I thought the skin was for one's donkey?'

'No way, young ass. I wouldn't give it to you, let alone to a donkey!'

Then, smiling to himself, he went his way.

orojig grape juice and walnuts

This sweet is also known as sweet *soujouk*, but in Eastern Turkey and Armenia where it originated it is better known as *orojig* or *roejig* meaning 'round balls'. Basically, it is halved walnuts dipped in a grape juice and sugar syrup. There is an equally popular sweet where a halved walnut is alternated with a blanched almond, etc. and then dipped in the syrup — this is known as *goshdig* — meaning 'crooked one' since it lacks the evenness of the former and is coarser in shape.

Sometimes other fruit juices are used instead of grape juice, but in my opinion nothing beats the original version given below.

Needless to say this sweet should be dried under the sun, but as is often the case one has to improvise and near a radiator or in an airing cupboard will do.

350 g/12 oz plain flour, sifted
450g/1 lb sugar
100 g/4 oz cornflour

3.4 litres/6 pints grape juice
   (or apple juice or orange juice)
halved walnuts
icing sugar, sifted

Mix the flour, sugar and cornflour together in a large bowl. Add a little of the grape juice and mix to a smooth paste. Little by little add the rest of the juice, stirring all the time.

Take a length of string and a strong needle and thread the first 2 walnut halves back to back into the middle of the piece of string. The nuts on either side of the 2 centre nuts should face the same way as those 2 nuts.

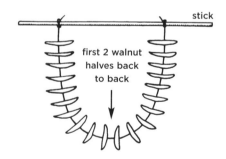

Tie the 2 ends of the string to a stick leaving a gap of at least 7.5 cm/3 in so that the nuts do not touch. The flat surface of the nuts must be facing upwards so that the thickened grape juice does not slip off.

Pour half of the grape juice mixture into a large saucepan and gradually bring to the boil, stirring constantly. Lower the heat and simmer, still stirring, until the mixture thickens. Dip the strung nuts into this juice 4–5 times, or until they have picked up most of the liquid. Hang to dry overnight above something in which to catch the drips.

Repeat the previous paragraph of instructions with the remaining juice, but this time leave to dry for several days. When completely dry cut into 15 cm/6 in lengths, roll in icing sugar and store in an airtight container.

ice cream

Dondurma or ice cream is the name given to a sweet confection usually made of cream or milk (and in recent years with yoghurt), then flavoured and frozen.

China is claimed to be the original homeland of this invention, but I really can't accept this mythical reasoning since at no time have the Chinese ever mastered or developed this wonderful sweet.

It all probably started in Northern Persia and from there passed to the Greeks and Romans. It arrived in Britain via France in the seventeenth and eighteenth centuries, but it was already well established in the Middle East over one thousand years ago. The Khalif of Baghdad (in the tenth century), while on a pilgrimage, ordered his servants to bring snow, loaded on the back of countless camels, from the mountains of Persia so that he could drink cold sherbet flavoured with orange or mulberry juice.

In my childhood ice cream was made — as it was in Britain up until the early decades of this century — in large barrel-shaped cylinders with hollow centres filled with ice and salt. The whole thing was continually rotated with a thick wooden pole enabling the ice cream to freeze.

The finest ice creams in the Middle East, in my opinion, are still made in Damascus, Syria. Particularly the brilliantly white *dondurma kaymakli* which is literally hung up like an animal carcass in the ice cream shops and parlours — and in the middle of summer. Mastic (gum arabic) acts as the glueing element and hardens the ice cream. The recipe below is for this marvellous sweet. Try it and you will, I hope, agree with me that it is truly a great work of art.

dondurma kaymakli mastic ice cream

1 teaspoon powdered *sahleb*
  or 1½ tablespoons cornflour
900 ml/1½ pints milk
300 ml/1½ pints single cream

225 g/8 oz sugar
½ teaspoon powered mastic
3 teaspoons orange blossom water

Garnish **chopped nuts of your choice**

Dissolve the *sahleb* or cornflour in a little of the cold milk.

Pour the remaining milk into a large saucepan and stir in the cream and sugar. Bring slowly to the boil, stirring constantly until the sugar has dissolved. Pour a little of the hot milk into the *sahleb* or cornflour mixture and mix well. Pour into the large saucepan, add the mastic and simmer, stirring constantly, until the mixture thickens. Remove from the heat, stir in the orange blossom water and beat thoroughly with a wooden spoon. Pour the mixture into freezing trays and freeze.

Three to four hours later remove the trays, spoon the ice cream into a large bowl and beat lightly. Return to the trays and freeze again. Repeat this once more. Serve the ice cream sprinkled with the nuts of your choice. Serves 8 people.

seftali dondurmasi peach ice cream

This is a particularly refreshing ice cream. The recipe is from Southern Turkey.

1 tablespoon powdered gelatine
350 ml/12 fl oz water
175 g/6 oz sugar

5 fresh peaches
3 tablespoons lemon juice

Garnish 1 tablespoon pistachio nuts, finely chopped

Put the gelatine to soften in a small bowl with 4–5 tablespoons of the water.

Meanwhile, boil the rest of the water in a saucepan. Add the sugar and continue to simmer for about 5 minutes. Remove from the heat, stir in the gelatine mixture until it dissolves and set aside to cool.

Blanch, peel and slice the peaches. Using a liquidizer purée the peach flesh. Add the purée to the sugar mixture, together with the lemon juice and mix thoroughly. Transfer to a freezing tray and freeze for 1 hour. Remove from the freezer and beat with a fork for 1–2 minutes. Return to the freezer until the edges have frozen, but the centre is still soft. Remove and beat again. Repeat this process once more and then leave in the freezer until hard.

Half an hour before serving transfer the ice cream to the refrigerator to soften a little. Serve sprinkled with the chopped nuts. Serves 6 people.

glidat egosim pistachio ice cream

This is an Israeli ice cream, the creation of a brilliant chef, Roger Dabasque. A simple and exceptionally attractive sweet that will delight all. Use unsalted pistachio nuts which are available from most Middle Eastern stores.

3 eggs, separated
6 dessertspoons sugar
pinch salt

100 g/4 oz pistachio nuts, unsalted and
    shelled
300 ml/1/2 pint double or whipping cream
few drops green food colouring

Place the egg yolks in a Pyrex bowl with half the sugar and beat thoroughly. Add the salt, place the bowl over a pan of simmering water and cook until the sugar dissolves and the mixture reaches a toffee consistency. Place in the refrigerator to cool.

Chop the pistachios finely. Beat the egg whites in a bowl until stiff and then fold in the remaining sugar. Whip the cream in another bowl until stiff.

Place the egg yolk mixture in a large bowl and then fold in the egg whites, cream, three-quarters of the pistachio nuts and just enough food colouring to give a pale green appearance. Sprinkle the remaining nuts over the bottom of 1 large or 2 smaller freezing trays and then pour the mixture over the top. Freeze and then turn out on to a serving dish when required.

paludeh sorbet

In the Middle Ages there was a popular sweet in Baghdad called *faludaj* which was made of ground almonds, sugar and rosewater, about which the Arab chronicler Ibn-al-Jawzi remarked that:

'Had Moses come to Pharaoh with Faludaj he would have accepted Moses' mission, but alas, he came to Pharaoh with the stick.' Quoted from *Social Life under the Abbasids*.

Unfortunately the recipe for the above sweet does not exist, but what is available is a sorbet bearing the same name which is pure white with large crystals sparkling in it which is served with a syrup of choice poured over the top.

The recipe below is one of Iran's favourite and the topping is made of mulberries, although there is no reason why other syrups, e.g. strawberry or raspberry, cannot be used.

paludeh mulberry sorbet

Sorbet

1 tablespoon powdered gelatine	2 tablespoons sultanas
2 litres/1³/₄ pints water	1 tablespoon rosewater
275 g/10 oz sugar	2 tablespoons pistachio nuts, finely chopped

Topping 75–100 ml/3–4 fl oz mulberry syrup or 225 g/8 oz mulberries mashed with sugar to taste

Put the gelatine in a small bowl with 4–5 tablespoons of the water to soften for 5 minutes.

Meanwhile, bring the remaining water to boil in a saucepan. Add the sugar and simmer for 5 minutes, stirring constantly until the sugar dissolves. Add the softened gelatine and continue to stir until it dissolves. Remove the pan from the heat and stir in the sultanas, rosewater and pistachio nuts. Pour the mixture into freezing trays and set aside to cool.

When cold place in the freezer for 2–3 hours or until almost frozen. Remove from the freezer and spoon the mixture into a bowl. Stir lightly with a fork — this should distribute the sultanas and nuts evenly. Return to the trays and freeze until solid.

When ready to serve spoon the sorbet into individual dishes and pour a little of the mulberry syrup or the mashed mulberries over the top.

Serves 8 people.

oghi sorbet *raki sorbet*

Sorbet
450 ml/³/₄ pint fresh orange juice
150 ml/¹/₄ pint fresh lemon juice
600 ml/1 pint water

350 g/12 oz sugar
2 tablespoons orange blossom water

Topping
12 strawberries (or raspberries or
   mulberries)
1 small apple, peeled, cored and
   thinly sliced
1 small pear, peeled, cored and
   thinly sliced

1 apricot, peeled, stoned and thinly
   sliced
3 tablespoons *raki*

Strain the orange and lemon juice.

Place the water and sugar in a saucepan and bring slowly to the boil, stirring constantly until the sugar dissolves. Simmer for 5 minutes. Remove from the heat and stir in the orange and lemon juice and the orange blossom water. Set aside to cool.

When cold pour into freezing trays and place in a freezer for 2–3 hours or until nearly solid. Remove from the freezer, spoon the mixture into a bowl and beat lightly with a fork. Return to the trays and place in the freezer until solid.

Meanwhile, prepare the fruit-*raki* mixture. Place all the prepared fruit in a bowl, add the *raki*, toss so that the fruit is coated and then set aside for 45 minutes to marinate. To serve scoop several tablespoons of the orange sorbet into each individual dish and spoon some of the fruit mixture over each.

An ideal after-dinner sweet.

Serves 8 people.

madzna sherbet yoghurt sorbet

The last sorbet I have chosen is a relatively new one from a restaurateur friend of mine in Yerevan, Armenia. It makes use of yoghurt. To traditionalists this may seem unthinkable, but times have changed and new innovations, when successful, are more than welcome.

I like this ice and you can, of course, substitute the strawberries with raspberries, pears, peaches, etc.

450 ml/3/4 pint natural yoghurt
350 g/3/4 lb ripe strawberries or
    raspberries or 2 ripe peaches,
    blanched, peeled and chopped
about 175 g/6 oz sugar

Beat the yoghurt with a fork and pour into a freezer tray. Freeze for 2–3 hours or until the yoghurt is 'mushy'.

Purée the strawberries (or other fruit) with the sugar in a liquidizer or mash with a fork. Remove the freezer tray and spoon the yoghurt into a bowl. Stir in the strawberry purée until well blended and then return to the freezer tray. Freeze until solid.

Serve scoops of this sorbet garnished with chocolate flakes or fresh strawberries.

Serves 6–8 people.

khumichk — drinks

One day King Djem was sitting in his tent, watching his archers practising, when there appeared in the sky a great bird hardly able to fly because of a snake which had wrapped itself around its neck. This would be an intolerable sight to an Aryan, since birds belonged to Good Creation while reptiles were the most frightful of the Bad. Djem ordered one of his archers to aim at the snake and kill it, and to take care not to harm the bird. The arrow delivered a mortal blow to the snake, which immediately released its prey and fell to the ground, while the bird flew off and disappeared over the horizon.

Not many moments passed before it reappeared and landed on the ground in front of Djem, and as if wishing to show its gratitude dropped some seeds from its beak at his feet.

These seeds, which were of a kind no one had seen before, were picked up and planted, and in a little time put forth a plant which grew and flourished in its season, producing beautiful fruit in great bunches. It was the vine.

The king noticed that the delicate skin of the lovely fruit enclosed a liquid content which would be easy to separate from the pips; so he set his servants to work to do this, and enclosed the resulting juice in a jar. After a few days the king decided to taste it, no doubt assuming it would be something like mead or similar drinks. However, he was repelled by such a strange, bitter taste that he thought it must be poisonous and kept it on one side with the thought — or so the oriental narrator candidly opines — that it might one day be useful in affairs of state.

It so happened however that Djem had a very beautiful and dearly loved girl slave. One day when he was out hunting she was taken ill with violent pains in the head so that she was unable to have a moment's rest. Nothing that others could do could bring her solace. At last, driven mad and in despair, the poor girl decided to kill herself and remembered the poison the king had put aside. She opened the jar and began to drink. She drank so much that she fell asleep, and when she awoke she found that she was perfectly well again. When Djem returned, she told him what had happened. As a result the king changed his opinion of the nature of the beverage whose recipe he had discovered; instead of using it for devious purposes of state he used it as a medicine, with such success in so many cases that wine came to be known to the old Persians as Darou-e-Shah, meaning 'the king's medicine'.

The World of the Persians, J. A. de Gobineau.

Thus according to ancient vedic tradition wine was invented, a drink that, one way or another, originated in the Middle East. Noah, we are told, after descending from the Ark became a husbandsman 'and he planted a vineyard; and he drank of the wine, and was drunken; and he was uncovered within his tent.'

The Greek God Bacchus was reputed to have been born in Asia Minor, and throughout the ages the vineyards of Armenia and Iran were famed. Yet with the arrival of Islam this rich viticulture was almost devastated, so much so that the Pahlevi Persian word for wine sharab (the king's water) came to suggest all types of drinks made of syrups, fruits etc.

There is a great paucity of alcoholic beverages in the Middle East due primarily to religio-social demands. The only areas that have continued the age-old tradition of wine making are — apart from mainland Greece — Cyprus, Lebanon and the Caucasus — all Christian lands where the influences of Islam have remained minimal. Where Islam has taken root, wine has been uprooted.

Today in Israel, Lebanon, Cyprus and the Caucasian Republics there exists a flourishing wine industry. Particularly good are the wines of Cyprus, Georgia and Israel, the araks of Lebanon, the brandies and champagnes of Armenia. When all is said and done the drinking habits of the Middle Easterner are those of a sober, sweet-tongued teatotaller and what he has lost on drinks alcoholic he has made up tenfold with drinks non-alcoholic.

The Egyptians have various kinds of sherbets or sweet drinks. The most common kind is merely sugar and water, but very sweet; lemonade is another; a third kind, the most esteemed, is prepared from a hard conserve of violets, made by pounding violet-flowers and then boiling them with sugar. This violet-sherbet is of a green colour. A fourth kind is prepared from mulberries; a fifth from sorrel. There is also a kind of sherbet sold in the streets which is made with raisins, as its name implies; another kind, is a strong infusion of liquorice-root, and called by the name of that root; a third kind, is prepared from the fruit of the locust tree, and called in like manner by the name of the fruit. Manners and customs of the Modern Egyptians, Lane.

The love of the Middle Easterner for things sweet is well known. However, little is known to date of the methods whereby he achieves this 'sweetness'. Here is a little story about Al-Hallaj who drew straight out of rivers and streams delicious water smelling of attar of roses and camphor. To achieve that effect he took a brand-new water pot or pitcher, dissolved high-quality white sugar in rosewater and reduced it to a stiff paste over a fire. He then put it in the new pot and the clay vessel selected for the purpose, spreading it in an even layer over the inside walls. The vessel absorbed it and so it became like an internal coating. He kept the water pot beside him. When anyone asked him for a drink, he used it to draw the water, waited for a moment to let some of the paste dissolve in the water and then gave it to the man. Those who drank it were unaware of all this. They thought the water had been transformed into rose syrup and they believed whatever he wanted them to. Al-Hussein ibn Mansour al-Hallaj — Muslim theologian and mystic. The Subtle Ruse.

'Sous-sous', chanted the street vendor. 'Aryan-aryan', echoed another trying to out-do the songs of the donkey and horse-drawn carts and the moans of the *hamals* who often acted as human donkeys. These vendors carry a selection of colourful drinks made of mulberry or sous, yoghurt, lemons, oranges, rosewater, tamarind, etc. The large glass flasks are held by a strap balanced on the shoulders. In recent years modernization has brought a certain amount of change to the lives of the street vendors; some are now in kiosks where, apart from the age-old favourites, they also offer their thirsty customers, with the aid of certain modern contraptions, freshly squeezed juices from almost any fruit or vegetable of their choice.

The recipes below are a personal selection from the extremely rich non-alcoholic repertoire of the Middle East. All are well worth preparing if only to remind oneself how much more delectable the products of nature are when compared with all things commercial and synthetic.

visne serbeti cherry syrup

The most successful drinks are those made of fruits and of those the most famed, especially amongst Turks and Iranians, is a syrup made from big, black cherries which was called 'the Queen of Queens' by an infatuated Persian poet. It has a unique sweet, yet tart flavour.

450 g/1 lb large dark sour cherries
  washed
900 g/2 lb sugar

600 ml/1 pint water
1/4 teaspoon vanilla essence

Place the sugar and water in a large saucepan and bring to the boil, stirring constantly until the sugar dissolves. Lower the heat and simmer for 15 minutes. Add the cherries and simmer for a further 20 minutes, stirring frequently, until the syrup thickens. Remove from the heat and cool for 10 minutes.

Strain the mixture through a muslin bag into a bowl and add the vanilla essence. If possible suspend the bag over the bowl and let the liquid drip through. When cold squeeze the bag tightly to extract all the liquid. Pour the syrup into sterilized bottles and seal. To serve dilute to taste with water and ice.

tout sherbat mulberry syrup

A fabulous drink beloved by all orientals from Morocco to Iran. Use large black, ripe mulberries — the kind that stain your hands dark red. Place them in a muslin bag and squeeze to extract all the juice. Measure the volume of juice and pour it into a saucepan.

To the juice add double the volume of sugar and 1 tablespoon of lemon juice for every 300 ml/$1/2$ pint of juice. Bring slowly to the boil, stirring constantly until the sugar has dissolved. Lower the heat and simmer, stirring occasionally, until the syrup thickens — it should coat the back of a spoon. Remove from the heat and leave until cold. Pour into sterilized bottles and seal. To serve dilute to taste with water and ice.

nouri osharag pomegranate syrup

A favourite drink of mine. I remember making my first pomegranate syrup when I was ten-years-old, with fruit which came from our own tree in the garden.

A pleasant, sharp, refreshing drink which is a brilliant red.

15 large, ripe pomegranates, peeled
juice 1 large lemon

$1/2$ teaspoon orange blossom water
175 g/6 oz sugar

Using a lemon squeezer or juice extractor squeeze out as much of the juice as possible from the pomegranate seeds. Strain the juice through muslin into a large jug. Add the lemon juice, orange blossom water and sugar and stir constantly until the sugar has dissolved. Chill the juice. Serve in tall glasses with crushed ice. It looks magnificent.

sharbate rivas rhubarb syrup

A particularly good drink beloved of the Iranians and ideal in the summer months.

45 g/1 lb fresh rhubarb
600 ml/1 pint water

550 g/$11/4$ lb sugar

Wash and trim the rhubarb and cut into 2.5 cm/1 in pieces. Place the water in a saucepan and bring to the boil. Add the rhubarb, lower the heat and simmer for 20 minutes or until soft. Remove from the heat and leave to cool for 10 minutes. Strain the mixture through a muslin bag into a bowl. Squeeze to extract all the liquid.

Measure the juice and make up to 600 ml/1 pint with water if necessary. Return the juice to the saucepan, add the sugar and bring to the boil, stirring constantly, until the sugar dissolves. Boil for 5–6 minutes and then set aside until cold. Pour into sterilized bottles and seal.

To serve pour 5–6 tablespoons of the syrup into a glass, stir in 6–7 tablespoons water and crushed ice.

sekanjabin sweet-sour mint syrup

Vinegar may relieve a toothache, but is injurious to healthy teeth.
Shabbatt 11a

'*Sekanjabin*,' said my sister who is married to an Iranian, 'is well worth including in your book. It is one of those versatile concoctions that the people here love. You can eat it by dipping Cos lettuce leaves in it — as they do for breakfast, brunch or as a dessert. You can drink it and, among the party-giving set, it is made into a punch.' And she gave me these recipes.

about 500 ml/17 fl oz water
350 g/12 oz sugar (or more to taste)
100–150 ml/4–6 fl oz (to taste) wine
   vinegar

4 large sprigs fresh mint, washed
   and drained

Bring the water to the boil in a saucepan. Add the sugar and stir constantly until it has dissolved. Add the vinegar and simmer for 20 minutes or until the syrup has thickened and coats the back of a spoon. Add the mint, stir well and set aside to cool. The syrup should now have the consistency of thin honey.

Strain the syrup when cold into a sterilized bottle and seal.

To serve
a) **For breakfast or as a dessert** — separate the leaves of a Cos lettuce, wash and pat dry. Pour some syrup into a bowl. Fold the leaves, dip into the syrup and eat — very refreshing.
b) **As a drink** — about one third fill a glass with syrup. Top it up with water, or, as in fashionable circles, with mineral water or soda water. Stir, drop in some ice cubes and serve.
c) **As a punch** — grate a small, sweet cucumber into a punch bowl. Add syrup, ice cubes and soda water. Stir well and garnish with mint sprigs and cucumber slices.

tan yoghurt drink

Yoghurt, one of the major ingredients in the Middle Eastern cuisine, also makes a fine, refreshing drink called *tan* or *aryan* or *dough*.

This is undoubtedly the most popular drink of all, served at home, in restaurants, by street vendors and, in recent years, in supermarkets in litre-sized bottles. The proportions below are for one person. Simply increase the ingredients in proportion to the number of people to be served.

2 tablespoons yoghurt
300 ml/1/2 pint water
1/4 teaspoon salt

1/4 teaspoon dried mint
some ice cubes

Spoon the yoghurt into a glass and very slowly stir in the water to make a smooth mixture. Stir in the salt and mint. Drop in a few ice cubes and serve.

If preparing this drink for more than one person then mix in a large jug first.

Variation

Iranians often substitute natural water with mineral water to give a lightly gaseous effect to this drink. Try it with one of the bottled varieties available.

Another delightful variation to the simple *tan* is this Armenian favourite:

salori-tan yoghurt and prune juice

450 ml/³/₄ pint juice
450 ml/³/₄ pint natural yoghurt

2 teaspoons lemon juice
¹/₄ teaspoon ground cinnamon

Place all the ingredients in a large jug and blend thoroughly. Pour into glasses and serve with a few cubes of ice.

Ideal on a warm summer's day this drink can also be made with other fruit juices, e.g. apricots, strawberries, etc.

chay tea

Tea has been known in the region for far longer than in the West. Indeed, when it first appeared amongst the conquering Arab armies in the ninth century it was highly disapproved of by the ruling élite, but the Iranian people and the Mongolian Turks regarded it as their national drink, and still do.

Although today in most Middle Eastern lands coffee has replaced tea as the social beverage, in Iran and the Gulf regions as well as Iraq and Kurdistan, tea still predominates. Indeed the Iranians, like the Russians, have created a whole school of tea drinking filled with mystique. Its brewing, its service and the very manner in which it is drunk have an aura of deep-rooted tradition which demands, in the first place, that the water is boiled in a *samovar* which is often an ornately decorated work of art and which creates a peculiar atmosphere of cosiness at the tea table. I am also assured that the tea itself tastes better when brewed with boiling water drawn from a *samovar*. The tea is never drunk with milk, and sugar is never added to it. A cube or, as in the past, a lump of concentrated sugar is put in one's mouth and tea is drunk through it. My father recalled, while living in Iran early last century, seeing people seated around a low table passing to each other a large block of crystallized sugar which was gently licked by one and all as they imbibed the aromatic black teas.

The finest tea comes from Iran, although in recent years both Turkey and particularly the Republic of Georgia have developed rich tea plantations. Incidentally, both these ventures were first started by pioneering English men who had received their experience in India.

In the Arab lands, where I spent most of my childhood, tea is only drunk in winter. It is served in small cups and sipped from a teaspoon and never from the cup — that would be regarded as impolite! To the Arabs tea has medicinal qualities and is often made with herbs and spices. Flavoured tea is recommended to the sick, the weak and the hypochondriacs! A popular one is *chay-bi-yanasoun* — tea mixed with aniseed. Below is the recipe for it. The proportions given are for one person. Simply increase the ingredients in proportion to the number of people to be served.

chay-bi-yanasoun aniseed tea

1 teaspoon tea
1/2 teaspoon powdered aniseed
sugar to taste

Make the tea in the ordinary way. Add the aniseed powder and sugar, if required, stir and allow to settle. Serve.

chay-bi-nana mint tea

Although this has become the national brew of North Africa it is also very popular throughout the Middle East. It is considered to be good for upset stomachs, colds and flu. Serves 4.

3 teaspoons green tea   **sugar to taste**
handful fresh, whole mint leaves or
**   1 tablespoon dried mint**

Warm the pot with a little hot water and pour out. Add the tea leaves, pour a little more hot water into the pot, swirl around again and pour out the water, but not the leaves! Add the mint and amount of sugar required. Add about 900 ml/1½ pints boiling water and steep for 5 minutes. If any mint surfaces remove it. Taste and serve. Do not add any sugar once it has been poured into the cup.

haygagan tey cinnamon and clove tea

The Armenians have their own famed tea — an aromatic infusion of cinnamon, cloves and tea leaves called *Haygagan tey*. Inevitably it is recommended for anyone feeling one degree under — whatever the ailment! Serves 4.

4 cups fresh cold water   **1 tablespoon tea leaves**
4 cm/1½ in piece cinnamon   **sugar to taste**
2 whole cloves

Place the water, cinnamon and cloves in a small pan and bring to the boil. Lower the heat and simmer for 5–7 minutes. Turn off the heat and stir in the tea leaves. Steep for 2–3 minutes and then strain into cups. Serve with sugar.

ainar tea with nuts

Infusions are extremely popular with Middle Easterners. Sweet basil, jasmine, rose petals, coriander, sage, verbana, etc. are all added to boiling water and drunk with gusto. One of the most popular ones, a Lebanese speciality, is *ainar* which is traditionally served when a child is born. Serves 5.

1 tablespoon caraway powder
1 tablespoon cinnamon powder
1 tablespoon aniseed
1/8 teaspoon ground nutmeg

5–7 tablespoons pine nuts,
    walnuts, almonds or a mixture
sugar to taste

Place all the spices in a small pan with 5 cups of water and bring to the boil. Simmer for 5 minutes. Strain through muslin into a tea pot. Place 1 tablespoon, or a little more, of nuts in the bottom of each cup. Add the required amount of sugar. Fill the cups with the hot, spiced water and serve.

Drink from a teaspoon, a sip at a time.

asal du kouzbara coriander honey tea

Another infusion is this recipe which is from Arabia and which is drunk hot or cold. It is highly recommended for colds and flu.

The recipe makes enough for one person. Increase proportions accordingly.

1 cup water
2 teaspoons honey

1/2 teaspoon ground coriander

Warm the water in a small pan. Dissolve the honey in the water, add the coriander and stir well. Serve hot or cold.

I cannot finish without telling the story of Boloz Mugush and his experience with a cup of tea.

One day the great wit and a friend, Hamo, were thirsty.

'Let's go to the Chaykhana [tea house] for a drink,' said one. They ordered a large glass of black tea.

'You drink your half first,' said Hamo, 'because I have a cube of sugar that's just enough for me.'

'Add it now,' said Boloz Mugush, 'and I shall drink only my half.'

'Impossible. One cube is not enough for both of us. The tea will never be sweet enough.'

Boloz Mugush went to see the proprietor. A few minutes later he returned, all smiles, with a tablespoon of salt.

'Problem solved, Hamojan,' he said. 'I am drinking first as agreed and I want my tea with lots of salt.'

kahwah arab coffee

'Let's have a cup of coffee and talk politics.' —Arab expression for a relaxing time.

Originally a poetic name for wine in old Arabic, the word was transfered to mean a drink made from the berry of the coffee tree (*coffea arabica*) and was first popularized about the thirteenth century in Arabia amongst dervishes and Muslim pilgrims who took the idea of brewing a strong cup of coffee back with them to all corners of Asia and Africa. Claudia Roden's fine book, *Coffee,* gives a full history.

In time coffee was introduced to Europe. Coffee houses sprang up everywhere. The pioneers were Armenians (as with yoghurt, backgammon, Turkish-type cigarettes and Turkish delight, etc.). In France there were *Pascal* and *Krikor*, in London *Pasqua Rosée* and in Italy *Manuel Armeno*.

In the Middle East the drinking of coffee still retains a strong religious-social mystique about it. Perhaps it is the early religious use of coffee that has given it a ceremonial character in the world of Islam. The dervishes of old drank coffee to keep awake during the nights given to religious devotion. The drink was kept warm in a large red earthenware vessel, each dervish receiving some in turn from his superior, who dipped their small bowls into the jar. They sipped the coffee while they chanted *'Allah w' akbar*!' (God is great). After the dervishes were served, the jar was passed round to the rest of the congregation. Never was a religious ceremony performed without coffee being drunk.

Today, centuries after it became secularized, coffee drinking is still in the Middle East an activity enmeshed in ritual, practised at all times throughout the day.

As the most important drink of the region coffee is claimed by Greeks, Turks, Armenians and Arabs as their very own. The truth however, is much simpler. It belongs to none, but to all. I am, of course, referring to coffee prepared in the oriental way — often called 'Turkish' or 'Greek' coffee which the French traveller Thevenot described as 'black mud' and said 'one must drink it hot, but in several instalments, otherwise it is no good. One takes it in little swallows for fear of burning oneself – in such fashion that in a café one hears a pleasant little musical sucking sound.'

You can have Arab coffee with sugar, without sugar and with spices. It is all a matter of taste and tradition.

There are several versions of this 'black mud' and some of the more important ones I have included below.

When buying the coffee remember to ask for 'Turkish' coffee beans and make sure they are 100 per cent pulverized and fresh.

Coffee is traditionally prepared in a *jaswah* (Arabic) or *ibrik* (Turkish) — a smallish, long-handled metal pot (copper or brass).

The recipe below is for one person so you can increase the proportions accordingly. The amount of sugar depends on personal taste, but the usual quantity is 1 teaspoon per person called *orto* in Turkish, *mazbout* in Arabic, *michag* in Armenian and *metrios* in Greek.

1 teaspoon sugar, 1 coffee cup water, 1 teaspoon coffee

Mix the sugar and water together in the *jaswah* and bring to the boil, stirring until the sugar has dissolved. Add the coffee, stir well and bring to the boil. As the coffee froths up remove the *jaswah* from the heat and allow the froth to subside.

Return the *jaswah* to the heat until the froth reaches the brim. Remove once again. Repeat this process 2 more times. Remove from the heat and pour into the coffee cup.

Do not add more sugar and do not stir or you will disturb the sediments at the bottom of the cup.

Variations

Armenian: As above, but add I crushed cardamom seed and 2 drops orange blossom water.
Anatolian: As above, but add 2 drops rosewater.
Cypriot: As above, but add a few drops of cold water to the coffee in the cup.
Ottoman: This is the version first popularised in the West — it is thick and very sweet. Allow at least 2 teaspoons sugar per person.
Bedouin: Known as *kahwah-al-hilo* this coffee is very thick and flavoured with cardamom and saffron.

1 teaspoon coffee	**1/2 cardamom seed, crushed**
1 coffee cup water	**1/2 teaspoon saffron, powdered**

Combine the above ingredients in a *jaswah*, stir to dissolve and bring to the boil. Reduce heat to very low and leave for 20 minutes until reduced and thick. Add sugar to taste — normally very little if any at all.

The coffee will have a slightly bitter flavour. Drink a few sips at a time.

After the coffee is drunk one always thanks the Lord — '*Shoukran Allah*', then the cups are turned upside down on to the saucers and one's fortune is read. Coffee cups are read (like tea leaves) by those in the know. Theirs is an hereditary gift that few mortals possess. My aunt was one such gifted person to whose abode came women from far and wide for a chat and a quick read. She had the gift of the gab and, most certainly, a deeper understanding than most of the human psyche. They sat around hanging on to every word she uttered — a letter, perhaps soon, from a distant relation bringing (most certainly) good news; and a paper (a cheque!) perhaps; one was to travel — perhaps across the seas; a small ailment in the family, but nothing to worry about, not serious (Praised be the Lord); then there was a certain young man waiting, hoping. Where? There, just near that blob of coffee grounds; a stag — a sign of prosperity and good times. Life would be much better soon (after the cup was drunk).

glossary

This is a selected glossary with emphasis on the rather unusual vegetables, herbs, spices and ingredients.

Most of the ingredients used by Middle Eastern housewives are now easily available in Western shops, although a few are still difficult to trace. There are also certain basic rules that apply to the preparation of some recipes and these have been included — although every individual recipe is fully explained.

Aubergine

Also known as eggplants, aubergines are indigenous to the Indian subcontinent, whence they spread to the Middle East and later, via Muslim Spain, into Europe.

They are popular throughout the region particularly with Turks and Armenians who boast over 200 recipes.

Aubergines are used in soups, make excellent dips and salads, and are stuffed with meat and/or rice or burghul. They also feature in many stews and casseroles and preserves. Recipes give details of preparation in most cases, however, as a general rule when sliced or cubed, sprinkle with salt, cover with a plate and set aside for about 30 minutes. This will ensure that the bitter juices, which are particularly so if the aubergines are from Spain or the Canary Isles, are released. Rinse the slices or cubes, pat dry with kitchen paper and proceed with the specific recipe.

The ideal way to cook the flesh for many of the dips and salads is over charcoal, but a hot oven or grill will do instead. They are ready when the skin has turned black and the flesh is soft. (They can also be cooked in a microwave oven.) Make 2–3 slits with a knife, place in a dish and cook for 4–5 minutes. In this case the skin will not change colour.

Peel off the skin and proceed with the required recipes as described.

Baharat

This is similar to allspice (*bahar*), but includes cumin, coriander, pepper and paprika.

Black-eyed beans

Native of Africa. Very popular in Ethiopia, Egypt and, in recent years, they have become more and more popular in the Middle East for they are sweeter and much quicker to prepare than some of the other beans.

Make fine soups and salads.

Broad beans, small

Also known as Egyptian brown beans. They are used only in their dried form.

First cultivated in Egypt, these are the national food of the Fellahin who make the classic *ful medames*.

Soak the beans for 14–18 hours and then cook very slowly.

Burghul (cracked wheat)

This is hulled wheat which is steamed until partly cooked, dried and then ground into 3 grades:
Large — used for *pilavs* and stuffings
Medium — for fillings
Fine — for *kibbehs*, *kuftas* and salads

The national cereal of Armenia, originated most probably with the first civilizations of Assyria and Urartu, but was replaced when rice was introduced via Iran and the Gulf regions.

Burghul is still very popular with Armenians and is extensively used by Syrian and Lebanese cooks in the preparation of the classic *kibbehs*. Armenians use burghul for *pilavs*, *dolma* fillings, salads and several puddings.

Burghul is sold in most good Indian and Middle Eastern shops.

Borekler

The Turkish name for pie-like pastries with meat, cheese, spinach, brain and many other fillings. These are either baked in the oven or deep fried.

Borekler are particularly popular with Armenians and Turks, though their origin can be traced to the Mongolian and Chinese.

Butter, clarified (see *ghee*)

Cardamom

Originally from the Indian subcontinent, this spice is particularly popular with Iranian, Iraqi and Gulf cooks.

It is available in pods, as seeds or ground.

Arab coffee often includes one or two crushed pods or a little ground cardamom to give it a characteristic pungent flavour. Is also used in *pilavs* and sauces.

Carob

An evergreen tree of Mediterranean origin. The dried pods are eaten as a snack for their sweet, chocolatey flavour. The juice of the carob is substituted for syrup and when mixed with tahina makes the classic *tahini-roub*.

Dry carob can be purchased from most health shops and carob syrup from Middle Eastern grocers.

Chickpeas (garbanzo beans)

First cultivated in Egypt, chickpeas are used extensively throughout the region. They appear in dips, salads, stews and *kuftas*. They are also roasted, salted and eaten like peanuts; or roasted, coated with sugar and served with tea or coffee.

Chickpeas need to soak for 24 hours before cooking. Some recipes require them to be skinned. In which case after they have been soaked take each pea between thumb and forefinger and squeeze firmly; it should pop out of its skin.

You can purchase skinless chickpeas from some Indian and Middle Eastern stores.

The most famous dishes are *hummus-bi tahini* and *nvig*.

Chilli

First introduced via the Gulf region where it is still widely used.

Chillies are either red or green. Whole, fresh pods can be used, with or without seeds, although it is usually better to remove the seeds as they are very hot.

More often whole, dried chillies or ground chilli is used as these are available all the year round.

Cress (rock cress)

A member of the pleasantly pungent herbs of the mustard family, rock cress grows wild in the Caucasus and northern Iran and is used in stews, salads and rice dishes in these regions. Ordinary watercress will make a suitable substitute.

Cumin (black)

These are small, black aromatic seeds used in pastries, sweets and also to flavour rolls, cakes and breads. They are used by Christians in their Easter breads and cakes but are not known to most of the Muslims of the region. Cypriots and Lebanese use them in their haloumi cheese and the Armenians in *tel-banir* (hair cheese).

Dates

A member of the palm family, *Phoenix dactylifera* is indigenous to Arabia and North Africa. It has been cultivated for over four thousand years. It was known to the Ancient Egyptians who cultivated it commercially, as did the Sumerians.

Dates are a staple source of food for the Bedouins, and one of the main ingredients in true 'Arab' cooking of the region.

Dibs (pekmez)

A syrup which is made from the Carob pod in Syria and Lebanon and from grape juice in Armenia and Turkey.

See *carob* and *pekmez*.

Dolma

This is the Middle Eastern method of cooking vegetables, such as aubergines, courgettes, peppers, tomatoes, onions, etc., whereby they are filled with meat and/or rice or burghul and flavoured with a variety of nuts and spices.

Most probably of Armeno-Assyrian origin, *dolma*, although widespread throughout the region, is still most popular amongst Armenians and Anatolians (Turks).

Dried limes

A must in both Iranian and Gulf cooking. These small but very sharp limes are grown extensively in southern Iran, Iraq and Oman. They are grey-brown, walnut-sized and very bitter.

Used in such dishes as *gormeh sabzi* and *dizzi*. Also, as in Iran, they are sprinkled with a little salt (to take away the bitterness) and then sucked for the juice.

Fenugreek

Native to the Mediterranean this most unusual herb with tiny reddish seeds is very popular in Iranian, Armenian and Yemeni cooking. The small oval leaves are used in vegetable stews.

The Armenian *aboukhd* uses it in its powdered form as a thick paste, while in Yemen it is used in sauces.

It has a very pungent, bitter flavour resembling that of burnt sugar.

Feta

A popular Middle Eastern cheese that has a soft, crumbly texture and is normally made from ewe's or goat's milk. Cow's milk produces a much firmer feta. Usually served with *lavash* or pita bread, either as a meal with fruit or as an hors d'oeuvre or side dish.

In Turkey and Iran a large portion of the populace live on feta, or similar cheeses, which they eat with bread, fresh tarragon, chives, mint, spring onions, etc.

If you like your cheese salty then eat the feta as it comes from the jar or packet (where it is preserved in brine), otherwise soak it for a few hours in cold water, changing the water from time to time.

Ghee, clarified butter

Ghee is pure butter fat which can be heated to high temperatures without burning. It is superior to ordinary butter and has a fragrance of its own. It is used extensively in Indian and Middle Eastern cooking, and is available in all Indian shops, but if you are unable to buy any then you can easily make your own which you then cover and refrigerate until you need it.

Melt 900 g/2 lb unsalted butter in a large saucepan over a low heat. Skim off the foam with a wooden spoon as it appears on the surface. Remove the pan from the heat and let rest for 10 minutes. Now skim off any foam that remains on the surface. Spoon the butter into a container, discarding the milky residue left in the bottom of the pan. Cover the container and refrigerate. 900 g/2 lb of butter should make about 700 g/1½ lb of clarified butter which can then be used in all kinds of pastries, cakes and in cooking in general and especially when frying fish.

Haloumi

A salty, sheep's milk cheese made throughout the region. It is matured in whey, is string-like in texture and is often flavoured with chives, mint or black cumin.

Halva

Halawah or *halaweh* is an ancient Akkadian word meaning simply — sweet. *Halva* nowadays means different things to different people, but basically it is a sweetmeat which usually has sesame seeds as one of the main ingredients. The other ingredients do vary but include sugar, *naffit*, *bois de Panama*, vanilla and nuts of choice.

There are countless variations (as noted in our introduction), but unfortunately it cannot easily be duplicated all that conveniently at home. *Halva* made at home usually consists of fine semolina, sugar, milk or cream and perhaps nuts and/or raisins. *Halva* can be purchased from most Middle Eastern stores. The best quality ones are from Egypt, Syria and Lebanon.

The Spanish *turron* slightly resembles *halva* — no doubt a legacy of the Moorish occupation of that peninsula.

Kaymak

Kaymak is the thick cream which can literally be cut with a knife. It is usually prepared with buffalo's milk, but can also be made with cow's milk or even sheep's.

Although often made at home it is also often bought from *kaymakjis* — small shops specializing in dairy produce. To make your own *kaymak* I suggest you follow one of the simple recipes below.

With double cream

Pour 1.2 litres/2 pints of double cream into a shallow enamelled saucepan. Use as wide a pan as possible to give the cream the greatest possible surface. Bring to the boil over a low heat. Using a ladle remove some cream and then pour it back into the pan. Do this from as high a point as possible so that bubbles are formed. Continue thus for 45–60 minutes. Turn off the heat and leave to rest for 3 hours. Place the pan in the refrigerator for 15 hours or more.

With milk

Pour 1.2 litres/2 pints of milk into a shallow enamelled saucepan. Add 300 ml/½ pint double cream and stir well. Bring to the boil over a low heat and simmer for 2 hours. Turn off the heat and leave the saucepan to rest for 5 hours. Place the pan in the refrigerator for 15 hours or more.

When you remove the pan from the refrigerator a thick layer of cream will have formed. Using a sharp knife free the edges of the *kaymak* and then cut into strips. Using a spatula remove the strips of *kaymak* to a large serving plate and then cut into squares or curl into rolls.

Kaymak is beautiful on its own topped with sugar, jam or honey; or served as a topping for pastries.

The nearest substitute is thick clotted cream.

Kebab

Kebab means meat cooked on or in the fire (i.e. oven). It does not really mean skewered cooking although this is often what is understood by the word 'kebab' these days.

Cooking on fire is, of course, one of the oldest methods of cooking, but 'kebab' cooking implies something more, i.e. being marinated in oil and spices and then cooked over wood or charcoal.

There are many variations on this method of cooking which is easy, quick and convenient.

However, there are several dishes, particularly in Turkey, called kebabs, e.g. *tas kebab*, *cop kebab*, which are not true (skewered) kebabs in that they are cooked in the oven in a Cassera dish.

Kibbeh

Of Assyrian origin *kibbeh* is minced meat with onion, burghul and spices. It is a speciality of Syria, Lebanon, Armenia and Kurdistan.

Kibbeh can be eaten raw, grilled on charcoal or baked in the oven. There are many variations with each region boasting its own as the 'finest, truest' *kibbeh*.

Kishk

A Syrian-Lebanese speciality of burghul fermented with milk and yoghurt. It is then salted, spread out to dry under the hot sun, then ground and stored for winter use. Then it is made into a soup or porridge with milk or water. *Kishk* can be purchased from some Middle Eastern stores. It is almost the same as the Armenian *tarkana*. (See recipe for *tarkana* on page 67.)

Mahaleb

This Cilician spice is gathered from the kernel of the black cherry stone. It has a sweet and spicy flavour, is pale brown in colour and is the size of a peppercorn.

Pound it in a mortar and use to flavour breads, cakes and *choreg*-type dry biscuits.

Unfortunately *mahaleb* is rather expensive and not very easily found — try good Armenian or Arab shops.

Melokhia

The young shoots of *melokhia* are harvested and the leaves (5–7.5 cm/2–3 in) are stripped from the stalks and used to make the classic Egyptian soup of the same name, popular since the days of the Pharoahs.

Fresh *melokhia* is difficult to find outside Egypt, but it is possible to find the dried version in good Middle Eastern stores.

Mezzeh

An Arab word, of Greek origin (*mazo*), loosely meaning hors d'oeuvre, but more precisely a selection of starters laid out on a large table, which precede a main meal of roast lamb, kebabs, etc.

The *mezzeh* table, which can include up to 200 starters, is a particular speciality of Syria, Lebanon and Palestine.

Nuts

There are five basic nuts used in Middle Eastern cooking: almonds, walnuts, pistachios, hazelnuts and pine kernels. Although coconuts and peanuts are known and used they are of much more recent origin.

Almonds

The almonds of Turkey have been famed throughout the ages. They are succulent, plentiful and exported in large quantities. They can be bought in shells or ready shelled. They are blanched by pouring boiling water over the kernels, leaving for 3–4 minutes and then draining and squeezing each one so that the kernel pops out of the skin.

To split an almond just separate the two halves with a thin, sharp knife.

To sliver (by far the most popular kind) soak for 5–6 minutes after blanching, cut each nut into 3–4 slivers and then dry out in a warm oven.

To grind either use the time-honoured mortar and pestle or else a blender.

Almonds are used in soups, sauces, *pilavs*, stuffings and in some of the most famed Middle Eastern desserts and puddings.

They are also roasted, covered in cocoa or with a candy coating.

Walnuts

The finest walnuts in the Middle East come from the Caucasus, particularly the Black Sea coast of Turkey and Georgia.

Walnuts can be purchased in shells or ready shelled. To slice or grind follow the instructions for almonds.

Walnuts appear in Turkish-Armenian and Caucasian dishes and are used in soups, sauces, vegetable salads, stuffings, desserts, pickles and jams.

Pistachio nuts

The pistachio nuts of Syria and Iran are the best. In the West pistachios are sold ready salted, but it is the unsalted version that is the one required for cooking. These are rather difficult to find, but specialist shops do often stock them. They are usually sold in their shells.

They can be sliced or ground as with almonds.

Pistachio nuts are particularly good in pastries and *pilavs*, and are prominent in Syrian and Iranian cooking.

Hazelnuts

The finest hazelnuts come from the Black Sea coast of Turkey and from Iraq. They are used extensively in Turkish (Laz) and north Iraqi (Kurdish) cuisines. Hazelnuts are used in sauces, stuffings, *pilavs*, vegetables and desserts. They can be purchased ready shelled and for cooking they should then be blanched and sliced or ground as with almonds.

Pine kernels

Pine kernels appear in Levantine (Mediterranean coastline) foods, particularly those of Syria, Lebanon and Palestine-Israel. They are also known as pignolia nuts and are the kernels from the cones of the stone or umbrella pine. The finest are from Lebanon, those from Turkey tend to be yellower, thicker and smaller. They are used in *pilavs*, stuffings, *kibbehs* and desserts.

Okra

Popularly known as 'Ladies fingers' or 'gumbo', okra is native to Africa and has been widely cultivated throughout the Middle East for millennia.

Okra is relatively unknown in the West, but in the East it is used in stews, vegetable dishes and pickles.

Fresh okra can be bought for only a few weeks of the year, while the rest of the time dried or tinned okra is fairly easily found in Middle Eastern and Indian shops.

If you wish to prepare okra then follow the simple method below:

Buy small, young okra with very little fuzz. Wash carefully and then dry with a kitchen cloth.

Trim the stems but do not cut into pods. Sometimes okra is tossed in vinegar for 30 minutes — this prevents it becoming slimy during cooking. Use 1 cup of malt vinegar to 1 kg/2.2 lb okra.

Okra freezes well and so it is advisable to buy large quantities while it is available and then freeze it until required. To do so wash and trim the okra. Then in a large saucepan heat 4 tablespoons oil to 1 kg/2.2 lb of okra, add the okra and fry for 5 minutes. Toss very gently using a wooden spoon so that the pods do not break. Remove from the heat and leave to cool. Put into containers, seal and freeze.

Orange flower water

A concentrated liquid flavouring distilled from the blossoms of the bitter orange tree. It is used to flavour ice creams, syrups and pastries, and is very popular with the Iranians, Turks and North Africans. You can buy it in Middle Eastern shops and certain 'gourmet' shops.

Pastry — Filo

Filo is paper-thin dough used in the making of pastries such as *baklava*. This pastry can be bought commercially from Middle Eastern or Greek shops and it keeps for a long time when refrigerated.

If using commercial pastry follow the instructions below for its uses:

Remove the filo from its wrapping. Each packet usually weighs 450 g/1 lb and contains about 20–25 sheets. Sprinkle a little flour over a work top then open the sheets out flat. Moisten a tea towel until it is evenly damp and spread it over the top of the filo. Remove each sheet as you need it and always remember to recover with the cloth. After shaping the pastry to the required sizes always cover with a damp cloth because filo dries out quickly, especially at the edges. Any dough not used should be wrapped carefully and returned to the refrigerator.

Home-made filo

Here is a simple recipe for home-made filo. All you need is patience, space and plenty of practice to achieve a thin filo, so until that day I suggest that when making *baklava* or similar pastries you use half the number of sheets recommended in this recipe. Work fast but carefully.

700 g/1½ lb plain flour
1 teaspoon salt
450 ml/¾ pint tepid water

3 tablespoons olive oil
cornflour

Sift the flour and salt into a large bowl. Make a well in the centre and, little by little, add the water and knead by pressing the dough down and pushing it forward several times with the heel of your hand and folding it back on itself. Knead for 7–10 minutes until the dough is soft. Make a ball of this dough, make a large well in the centre, add 1 tablespoon of the oil and knead into the dough. Repeat this with the remaining 2 tablespoons of oil. By now the dough should be very smooth and elastic. Cover the dough with a cloth and leave to rest for 4 hours.

Divide the dough into 18 equal portions and roll each one into a ball. Use the cornflour to lightly flour a working top. Roll out each ball, one at a time, with a floured rolling pin into a 15–18 cm/6–7 in diameter. Place each round on top of the other, each one separated by greaseproof paper. When completed cover all with a damp cloth and leave to rest for 45 minutes.

To shape the dough lift a round, stretch it over the backs of your hands and pull your hands apart slowly and most carefully until the filo is paper thin. You must work carefully but fast since the dough dries quickly. When you have stretched a sheet to about 30–33 cm/12–13 in by 46–51 cm/18–20 in place it on a work top dusted with cornflour. Trim off the thick edges and you will have a sheet of dough about 28–30 cm/11–12 in by 38–41 cm/15–16 in. Cover with a damp cloth and proceed with the other rounds.

Always keep them under a damp cloth and when all are made proceed with the preparation of the pastry of your choice.

Home-made kunafeh filo

Kunafeh or *kataifi* filo is the shredded pastry-type filo which is used to make many well known pastries.

Kunafeh filo can be bought from Middle Eastern shops. It comes in 450 g/1 lb packets and will keep for a long time in the refrigerator.

I suggest that when making pastries which require this pastry you buy it, but for interest I have given below a method for making home-made filo. Although it is quite simple to make it does require a very special container — a *kunaffahiah* — a large, shallow metal dish with small holes where the dough flows on to a large, hot metal griddle in rope-like form and solidifies in a matter of seconds. The *kunafeh* shreds are quickly lifted and separated in a large bowl. When all the dough has turned to shredded pastry proceed with the recipe of your choice.

700 g/1½ lb plain flour   **300 ml/½ pint milk**
300 ml/½ pint tepid water

Sift the flour into a large bowl, gradually add the water and knead. Add the milk, little by little, and continue kneading until you have a smooth dough. Now start thinning the dough by gradually adding more water, stirring all the time, until the dough has the consistency of batter. Have a large metal griddle ready on a low heat.

With a large soup ladle pour some of the batter into the *kunaffahiah*. The batter will drop on to the hot metal griddle in a rope-like form and solidify in a few seconds. Lift the cooked pastry into a large bowl and continue until all the batter is cooked.

Pekmez

This is usually carob or grape juice. Carob juice can be bought from good Middle Eastern or health food shops. However, concentrated grape juice cannot be easily found in the west, but it is possible to make your own. Below is a simple method.

2.7 kg/6 lb grapes, stems removed   **225 g/8 oz sugar**

Rinse the grapes then place in a large saucepan with 2.3 litres/4 pints of water and bring to the boil. Lower the heat and simmer for 15 minutes. Pour through a sieve into a large bowl. Rub the grapes through with the back of a wooden spoon and then discard the pips and skin remaining in the colander. Pour the juice and pulp into a muslin bag and leave suspended over a bowl overnight. What is collected in the bowl is pure grape juice. Pour this juice into a saucepan, add the sugar and bring slowly to the boil, stirring all the time. Lower the heat and simmer for about 15 minutes or until the mixture thickens and becomes a golden yellow colour. Remove from the heat and when cool pour into a sterilized jar, seal and store.

Pomegranate

A fruit indigenous to the region and particularly popular with Caucasians, Kurds, and Iranians. Pomegranates keep for a long time if picked before they reach full maturity and they are stored in the cool, dry cellars most Middle Eastern homes possess.

They are eaten raw as a dessert and the seeds are often sprinkled over *pilavs*, fish and meat dishes.

Pomegranates make an excellent *sharbat* and, when the juice is concentrated, it is used in many Iranian and Armenian stews and kebab marinades.

Pomegranate syrup

This is the concentrated juice of the pomegranate fruit and it is sold in some Middle Eastern shops. I suggest you make your own which is much better than the commercial kind which is, anyway, sometimes difficult to find.

8 large, ripe pomegranates   **175 g/6 oz sugar**

Remove the skin of the pomegranates with a sharp knife. Remove the seeds from their hives by tightly squeezing the segments of the fruit in your palms. Now, unless you have a fruit-juicing machine, place a handful of seeds at a time in a muslin bag and squeeze the juice out into a bowl. Pour the juice into a small saucepan and heat through. Add the sugar and bring slowly to the boil, stirring all the time until it dissolves. Lower the heat and simmer for 15–20 minutes or until the mixture thickens to a syrup. Remove from the heat, leave to cool then store in a glass jar, and use as required.

Pulses/legumes

Some pulses require soaking before cooking. The problem with soaking first is that water-soluble vitamins like thiamine, niacin and riboflavin will be thrown away if the pulses are rinsed after soaking. Therefore I think it is advisable to rinse the pulses very thoroughly before soaking, picking out any small stones, dried beans etc, and then to soak and to cook the pulses in the soaking water.

Pre-soaked pulses

A. Black-eyed, haricot, lima, red and cannellini beans. There are 2 ways of soaking these beans:
   • Wash the beans thoroughly under cold running water. Place in a saucepan and for each cup of beans add 3 cups (about 750 ml/1¼ pints) cold water and bring slowly to the boil. Boil for 2–3 minutes, cover, remove from the heat and leave until beans are fully plumped up.
   • Wash the beans thoroughly under cold water. Place the beans in a bowl and for each cup of beans add 3 cups (about 750 ml/1¼ pints) cold water.
      Leave to soak overnight.

B. Dried broad beans, chickpeas and split peas (some people don't soak the latter, but I find that they usually require it):
   • Wash thoroughly under cold, running water.
   • Place in a bowl and for each cup of beans or peas add 3 cups (about 750 ml/1¼ pints) cold water and leave to soak overnight. Most dried broad beans need about 48 hours soaking and if the room temperature is warm leave in the refrigerator or the beans may begin to ferment.

Non-soaked pulses

Lentils — brown, green or red — and mung beans do not need to be soaked.
   Rinse thoroughly in a strainer under cold running water and pick out any stones, discoloured seeds, etc.

Skinning pulses

Certain recipes ask for skinned pulses.
   Broad beans: soak these for 48 hours then squeeze each bean firmly and it should pop out of its skin. If this doesn't work slit the skin with a small knife or, as most Middle Eastern housewives do, with your fingernails and then squeeze.

Chickpeas and lentils: after soaking take a handful and rub between the palms so that the seeds rub against each other. Drop back into the bowl and the skins should float to the surface. Remove these and discard. Another method, and one I used when helping my mother, is to squeeze each chickpea between thumb and forefinger and let the pea jump into the water. A long and tiring process, but necessary for some recipes.

Quince

A small tree with a fragrant but tart fruit of unusual flavour. A quince has a greenish-yellow-golden colour. It is the size of an apple except that it is pear-shaped near the stem and has minute hairs over its surface. It is cooked in a variety of ways, e.g. stuffed with meat and rice, used in soups and stews.

In the West quince jam is well known, but otherwise this rather fascinating fruit is neglected.

Rice

Indigenous to the Far East (China and India) rice arrived in the Middle East sometime in the early centuries of our era, since it is not mentioned in the Bible. If the mainstay of Armenian and Anatolian cuisines is burghul, then that of Iran and the Arabians in general is rice. In the Middle East rice is grown in south-eastern Turkey, southern Iraq, Egypt and Iran.

In Iran there are 3 main qualities of rice (regardless of varieties):– (a) *Berenj domsiah* — long slender grains (b) *Berenj sadri* — grains slightly broken (c) *Berenj champa* — broken grains.

In the rest of the Middle East long grain rice, particularly the Basmati type, is the most popular choice.

The most imaginative rice dishes (*pilaf* in Turkish and Armenian, *pollo* in Persian and *timman* or *roz* in Arabic) are undoubtedly those of Iran, followed closely by the Anatolian *pilavs*. The rice dishes of Egypt, and Arabia in general, betray their simple nomadic background in their simplicity and limited choice of vegetables and herbs. However — and this is an important point — nowhere in the entire region will one be served a dish of plain boiled rice similar to those cooked in south-east Asia — the original home of rice.

Rice is used in soups, salads, as a stuffing for vegetables, for *pilavs* and in puddings and desserts. A bed of *pilav* is the ideal accompaniment to all kebabs and stews. Rice is also often served on its own with yoghurt as is the custom in Turkish-Iranian and Kurdish villages.

There are several methods for the preparation of rice which are given in the section on rice dishes. Whichever method you use the end result should be a light and fluffy *pilav* with each grain firm and separated and usually with a slight golden hue from the *ghee*/clarified butter. In short your rice dish should never have a sticky or mushy consistency. To achieve the perfect end follow the recipe to the letter for the amount of liquid used will be crucial in determining the final outcome of the *pilav*.

Rosewater

A characteristic fragrance of the Middle Eastern cuisine, it is distilled from rose petals — the finest being the pink-red damask rose. It can be used to flavour puddings, desserts and savouries and can be found in most Middle Eastern shops. Rosewater essence in a concentrated form is also available from many chemists. Use this sparingly in drops rather than spoon measures.

Saffron

A very expensive spice, for it takes something like the stamens of a quarter of a million blooms to produce 450 g/1 lb saffron. Saffron originated in Asia Minor and spread through the Middle East towards India.

To use pound the threads in a mortar then soak in a little liquid to bring out the colour and fragrance.

Used particularly by Iranians, Caucasians and Iraqis saffron gives colour to rice dishes, meat and chicken stews and to some desserts.

Salep

Salep is a ground powder from the dried tubers of various species of the *orchidaceae* family. It has a gelatinous quality similar to cornflour and is used in hot and cold drinks. It is rather difficult to find and arrowroot or cornflour is often substituted. The finest salep comes from Azerbaijan in the Caucasus. It is also used in ice cream and puddings.

Sesame seeds

Sesame is a rough, hairy, gummy annual about 60 cm/2 ft in height with egg-shaped leaves. It produces black and white seeds which are oily and highly nutritious.

Popular throughout the region since ancient times sesame grows well, indeed it thrives in poor soils, and its seeds yield half of their weight in the oil which is yellow, limpid and will keep for years.

The oil is called *tahina* (see page 374), and the seeds are used on breads, cakes, sweets and in the famous *halvas*.

Sumac

The dried, crushed berries of a species of the sumach tree. Sumac has a sour, lemony taste.

Crush and steep it in water to extract its essence which can then be used in stews instead of lemon juice. It is extensively used in the Caucasian, north Iranian and Kurdish cuisines in their soups, salads and *dolmas*.

Please note that most sumach trees are poisonous so never make your own, always buy it from a reliable Middle Eastern shop and ask for 'Armenian sumac'.

Syrups

A traditional feature of Middle Eastern pastries and sweets is the syrup used on and/or in them. It is a sugar-based syrup and it is either thin and liquid or thick and almost treacly. Sometimes the North Africans and Caucasians use honey for syrup, the recipe given below is almost a standard one throughout the region.

450 g/1 lb sugar
300 ml/½ pint water
1 tablespoon lemon juice (prevents crystallization)

1–2 tablespoons rosewater or orange blossom water, or sometimes both

Place the sugar, water and lemon juice in a saucepan and bring slowly to the boil, stirring constantly. Remove any scum which appears on the surface. Lower the heat and simmer for 5–10 minutes. When the required thickness has been achieved remove from the heat. Gently stir in the required fragrance and leave to cool for future use. If covered it will keep for a long time.

Note — A simple method to see if the syrup has the required thickness is to see if it coats a metal spoon or, if you have a candy thermometer, allow the syrup to reach 110°C, 225°F and then remove from the heat.

Gavour flurubu (Infidel's syrup)
This is a charming variation on the standard syrup above.

A piece of cinnamon stick about 5 cm/2 in long is added to the syrup at the beginning of its cooking time and is removed when the syrup has cooled. There is no need for any other flavouring.

Tahina

A nutty-flavoured paste made from toasted and crushed sesame seeds. The finest quality tahini comes from Syria and Turkey. There are many cheaper versions which tend to be lighter and more runny.

It originated in Asia Minor and is very popular with Armenians, Syrians, Lebanese, Palestinians, Israelis and the Copts of Egypt. Is used in dips, lenten *kuftahs* and cakes.

Tahina separates if it has stood for some time, so always stir before using.

Tamarind

'Date of India' is the large bean pod of the tropical tree indigenous to south-east Asia. It is very popular in Iraq and the Gulf states.

Tamarind sauce can be purchased from Asian stores as can 450 g/1 lb weights of the compressed dried pods. If you cannot find the sauce follow the simple method below for making your own.

Salsat-el-sbar
450 g/1 lb tamarind pods   450 g/1 lb sugar
1.2 litres/2 pints water

Clean and wash the pods. Break the pods into smaller pieces and put into a large saucepan with the water. Leave to soak for 24 hours.

The next day rub the pods through a sieve using the back of a wooden spoon, collecting the liquid and pulp in a saucepan. Place the seeds and fibres in a muslin bag and squeeze any remaining liquid into the pan. Add the sugar to the pan. Add more sugar if you want a sweeter sauce. Slowly bring to the boil stirring constantly until the sugar has dissolved. Lower the heat and simmer gently until the syrup thickens. Remove any scum which appears on the surface. Remove from the heat, leave to cool then pour into jars and seal tightly.

Tarator

A Turkish name given to sauces making use of nuts, tahina, garlic and bread. These tend to be rather thick and are served with fish and with vegetables.

Turmeric

Often called the 'poor man's saffron', turmeric is the root of a plant of the ginger family. It has a slightly bitter, resinous flavour and is yellow in colour. It should be used in very small quantities.

Although known throughout the region it is most used in the Iranian, Gulf and Kurdish cuisines in sauces, soups, *pilavs* and the many Iranian *khoresht*-type stews.

Vine leaves/cabbage leaves

Vine leaves

The natural abode of the wild vine was the Caucasus from whence it spread south and to east and west.

A hint of its Caucasian origin is to be found in both the Bible — Noah made wine and got drunk on the slopes of Mount Ararat in Armenia; and in the Avesta of the Aryans — King Djem's slave fell ill but was cured by drinking the juice of the wild vine which she mistook for poison.

The vine was, and still is, the national symbol of the Armenian nation.

It is found on ancient monuments, churches and it has even entered the Armenian Church rituals with the blessing of grapes on Holy Mother's Day every August.

Vines are also portrayed on early Parthian friezes, but disappear with the advent of Islam.

Vine leaves were known and used by the Ancient Greeks and Sassanians who 'wrapped' wheat, and later rice and nuts, and cooked them in broth — similar to the *sarma* and *yalançi dolma* of today.

You can buy preserved vine leaves from most continental shops, but if you do have access to a vine then you can use the fresh leaves instead.

To prepare preserved leaves: first rinse under cold water then place in a saucepan half filled with water and bring to the boil.

Simmer for 15 minutes and then drain into a colander.

Leave until cool enough to handle.

To prepare fresh vine leaves: stack the leaves on top of each other, drop into a pan of boiling water and simmer for about 5 minutes. If the leaves are older cook for a little longer. Drain into a colander and leave until cool enough to handle.

Cabbage leaves

These are also popular in the Middle East and fresh ones are always used.

To prepare: take about a 900–1400 g/2–3 lb head of white cabbage and remove as much of the thick core as possible.

Bring a large saucepan two-thirds filled with lightly salted water to the boil. Place the cabbage in the water and boil for 7–8 minutes.

Remove the leaves in a colander to cool them. When it becomes difficult to remove the leaves return the cabbage to the pan and boil for a few more minutes. Continue removing leaves until you have all you need.

Yahni

An Arabic term for a standard Middle Eastern method of cooking where the food is braised with onions in olive oil and after the addition of water, vegetables, spices, etc. is cooked over a low heat until the meat and/or vegetables are tender. Popular throughout the region from Egypt to Afghanistan.

Yoghurt

Until a few score years ago yoghurt was almost unknown in the West. It has now arrived and has already created a myth around itself. Yet in the Middle East it has been known and used for thousands for years.

Yoghurt was introduced by the Aryan tribes as they penetrated this region. It was, and still is, an Indo-Aryan speciality for it is only widely used in such areas of Aryan origins as Asia Minor, Kurdistan, Caucasia, Iran, Afghanistan and Northern India.

Yoghurt arrests intestinal putrefaction, has antiboitic properties and is excellent for people with weak digestion and for the aged.

It is an essential part of the Middle Eastern diet and its preparation is a must if one is to master the many delightful yoghurt-based dishes of the region.

Although yoghurt can be purchased commercially I strongly recommend that you make your own at home following the simple method below. There is no need to go to the expense of purchasing 'yoghurt makers' that manufacturers constantly tempt one with.

1.2 litres/2 pints milk

**1 soupspoon yoghurt — the starter
(culture of the bacteria *Bulgaris*)**

Bring the milk to the boil in a saucepan and when the froth rises turn off the heat.

Allow the milk to cool to the point where you can dip your finger in, and count up to 15 or, if you have a thermometer, where the temperature registers 45°C or 115°F.

Beat the spoon of yoghurt in a cup, add a tablespoon of the warm milk, beat vigorously and pour into the milk. Empty the milk into an earthenware or glass bowl and stir for a minute. Cover the bowl with a large plate and wrap in a towel or tea towel. Place in a warm place, e.g. near a radiator or in an airing cupboard and do not disturb for about 10 hours. Remove the wraps and place the covered bowl in the refrigerator.

The yoghurt is now ready to use. It can be kept for up to a week in the fridge. If using this yoghurt as a 'starter' for a new batch then use it within three days (after this the balance of the bacteria in the culture alters and the quality of the new yoghurt will be poorer).

To stabilize yoghurt

If you are to use yoghurt in hot dishes such as soups, sauces or stews, which require boiling it is necessary to stabilize it first otherwise it will curdle.

Either Stir a tablespoon of flour into a little water until you have a smooth paste and add to the yoghurt before you heat it.
Or Beat an egg into the yoghurt before cooking.

Note once the yoghurt has been stabilized and boiled it cannot be used as a 'starter' as the bacteria dies at a high temperature.

Drained yoghurt/labna

Certain recipes call for drained yoghurt or *labna*. To prepare this follow the simple recipe below.

Line a colander with a piece of damp muslin or sew a piece of muslin into a bag with a drawstring top. Spoon the yoghurt into the colander or bag and leave to drain. Suspend the bag over the sink. The whey will drain away leaving a light, soft, creamy cheese called, in Arabic, *labna*.

bibliography

C. F. Abbott, *Under the Turk in Constantinople*, Macmillan and Co. Ltd, 1920.

M. N. Adler, *The Itinerary of Benjamin of Tudelo*, Oxford, 1970.

M. M. Ahsan, *Social Life under the Abbasides*, Longman Group, 1979.

A. J. Arberry, *Aspects of Islamic Civilization*, G. Allen and Unwin Ltd, 1964.

E. Ashtor, *A Social and Economic History of the Near East in the Middle Ages*, Collins, 1976.

Gertrude Bell, *Persian Pictures*, Jonathan Cape Ltd, 1973

Gertrude Bell, *Syria, The Desert and the Sown*, Heinemann 1907.

Issa J. Boullata, *Modern Arab Poets*, Heinemann 1946.

Richard J. Burton, *The Book of 1001 Nights*, 1885.

Mahmoud Darwish, *The Music of Human Flesh*, Heinemann, 1980.

J. A. de Gobineau, *The World of the Persians*, Minerva, Geneva, 1971.

Firdusi, *Shah Nameh*, G. Routledge and Son, 1892.

S. N. Fisher, *The Middle East*, Routledge & Keegan Paul, 1960.

W. H. Forbis, *Fall of the Peacock Throne*, Harper & Row NY, 1980.

J. B. Glubb, *Syria, Lebanon and Jordan*, Thames and Hudson Ltd, 1967.

Helen C. Gordon, *Syria As It Is*, Methuen and Co., 1939.

Joan Hasler, *The Making of Russia*, Longmans, Green and Co., 1969.

Philip K. Hitti, *A Short History of The Near East*, D. Van Nostrand Co., 1966, Canada.

Diana D. Hovanessian, *Anthology of Armenian Poetry*, Columbia University Press, 1978.

Peter Jay, *Song of Songs*, Anvil Press, 1975.

Rene R. Khawam (trans.), *The Subtle Ruse*, East-West Publications, 1980.

O. Khayyam, *Rubaiyat*, Trans. E. Fitzgerald, Quaritch, 1859.

The Rubaiyat of Omar Khayyam, edited by A. J. Arberry, Dent, 1954.

E. W. Lane, *Manners and Customs of the Modern Egyptians*, J. Murray, 1860.

Tone Lane, *Men are like that*.

B. Lewis, *Arabs in History*, Hutchinson and Co. Ltd, 1950.

B. Lewis, *Emergence of Modern Turkey*, Oxford University, 1961.

Mahmut Makal, *A Village in Anatolia*, Vallentine, Mitchell and Co., 1954.

Gavin Maxwell, *The Reed Shaken by the Wind*, Longmans, Green and Co., 1959.

Nermin Menemiencioglu, *Turkish Verse*, Penguin Books, 1978.

J. Murray, *Sketches of Persia*, 1827.

Isaac Myer, *Oldest Book in the World*, Keegan Paul & French, 1900.

Shaykh Nefzawi, *Perfumed Garden*, Neville Spearman Ltd, 1963.

Alexander Pallis, *In the Days of the Janissaries*, Hutchinson and Co., 1951.

A. S. Pirouzian, *The Armenian Kitchen*, Haybed-Hrad, Armenia, 1963.

Plato, *The Republic*, Paul Shorey, Heinemann Ltd, 1930.

Pliny the Elder, *A Natural History*, Trans. H. Rackham, 1950.

Marco Polo, *Travels*, Trans. Ronald Latham, Penguin Books, 1958.

Paul Ricaut, *State of Greek and Armenian Churches*, 1679.

Claudia Roden, *A Book of Middle Eastern Food*, T. Nelson and Sons, 1968.

Claudia Roden, *Coffee*, Faber and Faber, 1977.

R. T. Rundel Clark, *Myth and Symbol in Ancient Egypt*, Thames and Hudson, 1995.

J. H. Schofield, *The Historical Background of the Bible*, Nelson & Sons Ltd, 1938.

Idries Shah, *The Pleasantries of the Incredible Mulla Nasrudin*, Jonathan Cape Ltd, 1968.

Henry D. Spalding, *Encyclopedia of Jewish Humour*, Jonathan David, NY 1969.

D. Stacton, *The World on the Last Day*, Faber & Faber, 1965.

Tacitus, *Annals*, Trans. A. H. Beesley 1870.

Reay Tannahill, *Food in History*, Eyre Methuen Ltd, 1973.

J. D. Vehling, *Apicius*, Dover Publications, NY, 1957.